Finance at Work

In the collective psyche, a financier is a capitalist. In managerial capitalism, the notion of the 'manager' emerged, and the role of the manager was distinct from the role of the 'owner'. Financial capitalism is similarly underpinned by financiers who are not the holders of the financial assets they buy, sell, trade or advise upon.

Finance at Work explores the world of financiers, be they finance-oriented CEOs, CFOs, financial journalists, mergers and acquisitions' advisors or wealth managers. Part I investigates the professional trajectories of members of corporate boards and financialisation as the dissemination of financial logic outside its primary 'iron cage'; Part II responds by studying financiers at work within financial occupations or financial operations involving external actors; while Part III pursues the issue of financial boundaries by seeking out the way financial logic crosses these boundaries. Part IV takes back the hypothesis of differentiations within finance presented in Part I, and analyses the internal boundaries of asset management, wealth management and leveraged buyout (LBO) acquisitions.

This book is essential reading for researchers and academics within the field of finance who aim to understand the 'spread of finance' in contemporary societies.

Valérie Boussard is Professor of Sociology and Head of the Department of Sociology at the Paris Nanterre University, France. Her works are focused on the managerialisation and financialisation of contemporary firms through the analysis of professional and occupational groups which take part in such dynamics.

Routledge International Studies in Money and Banking

For a full list of titles in this series, please visit www.routledge.com/series/SE0403

84 Money, Valuation and Growth
Conceptualizations and contradictions of the money economy
Hasse Ekstedt

85 European Banking Union
Prospects and challenges
Edited by Juan E. Castañeda, David G. Mayes and Geoffrey Wood

86 Wages, Bonuses and Appropriation of Profit in the Financial Industry
The working rich
Olivier Godechot

87 Banking and Monetary Policies in a Changing Financial Environment
A regulatory approach
Wassim Shahin and Elias El-Achkar

88 Modern Monetary Theory and European Macroeconomics
Dirk H. Ehnts

89 Capital Flows, Financial Markets and Banking Crises
Chia-Ying Chang

90 Banking and Economic Rent in Asia
Rent Effects, Financial Fragility and Economic Development
Edited by Yasushi Suzuki, Mohammad Dulal Miah, Manjula K. Wanniarachchige and S.M. Sohrab Uddin

91 Finance at Work
Edited by Valérie Boussard

Finance at Work

Edited by Valérie Boussard

LONDON AND NEW YORK

First published 2018
by Routledge
2 Park Square, Milton Park, Abingdon, Oxon OX14 4RN

and by Routledge
711 Third Avenue, New York, NY 10017

Routledge is an imprint of the Taylor & Francis Group, an informa business

© 2018 selection and editorial matter, Valérie Boussard; individual chapters, the contributors

The right of Valérie Boussard to be identified as the author of the editorial material, and of the authors for their individual chapters, has been asserted in accordance with sections 77 and 78 of the Copyright, Designs and Patents Act 1988.

All rights reserved. No part of this book may be reprinted or reproduced or utilised in any form or by any electronic, mechanical, or other means, now known or hereafter invented, including photocopying and recording, or in any information storage or retrieval system, without permission in writing from the publishers.

Trademark notice: Product or corporate names may be trademarks or registered trademarks, and are used only for identification and explanation without intent to infringe.

British Library Cataloguing in Publication Data
A catalogue record for this book is available from the British Library

Library of Congress Cataloging in Publication Data
Names: Boussard, Valâerie, editor.
Title: Finance at work / edited by Valâerie Boussard.
Description: Abingdon, Oxon; New York, NY: Routledge, 2017. | Includes bibliographical references and index.
Identifiers: LCCN 2017002811| ISBN 9781138204034 (hardback) | ISBN 9781315470290 (ebook)
Subjects: LCSH: Finance–Social aspects. | Capitalists and financiers. | Industrial sociology.
Classification: LCC HG101 .F545 2017 | DDC 306.3–dc23
LC record available at https://lccn.loc.gov/2017002811

ISBN: 978-1-138-20403-4 (hbk)
ISBN: 978-1-315-47029-0 (ebk)

Typeset in Times New Roman
by Deanta Global Publishing Services, Chennai, India

Printed and bound in Great Britain by
TJ International Ltd, Padstow, Cornwall

Contents

List of figures	*viii*
List of tables	*ix*
Notes on contributors	*x*
Foreword	*xii*
Acknowledgments	*xvi*

Introduction: Financiers at work, financialisation on the march   1
VALÉRIE BOUSSARD

PART I
The boundaries of finance: Exclusionary process, social closure and inner regulation   23

Introduction: Interrogating financialisation as an analytic   25
KAREN HO

**1 Let's make the company a bunch of figures:
Professional representations in mergers and acquisitions firms**   29
VALÉRIE BOUSSARD AND MARIE-ANNE DUJARIER

**2 Matching the market: Calibration and the working practices
of quants**   42
TAYLOR SPEARS

3 Buying it: Financialisation through socialisation   57
NATASCHA VAN DER ZWAN

**4 Financial logic and bankers' institutional entrepreneurship:
The politics of the "zombies" debate in bankruptcy
proceedings at the Commercial Court of Paris (2000–2005)**   70
EMMANUEL LAZEGA, LISE MOUNIER AND SYLVAN LEMAIRE

vi *Contents*

PART II

Passing through boundaries: Financiers as intermediaries in conversion to financial logics 87

Introduction: Financialising economic activities 89
DONALD MACKENZIE

5 **The financialisation of the private wealth of farmers: Is it the work of the banks?** 92
GILLES LAFERTÉ AND ABDOUL DIALLO

6 **Financial backlash: When local bankers face social protest** 108
QUENTIN RAVELLI

7 **The assetisation of South African farmland: The role of finance and brokers** 123
ANTOINE DUCASTEL AND WARD ANSEEUW

PART III

Crossing boundaries: Individual careers as vehicles for financialisation 137

Introduction: The financialisation of finance: The transformation of the French financial elite 139
SABINE MONTAGNE

8 **The second financialisation in France, or how executives and directors with unchanged financial careers promoted a new conception of control** 142
PIERRE FRANÇOIS AND CLAIRE LEMERCIER

9 **Financialisation through the trajectories of business school graduates in France** 156
VALÉRIE BOUSSARD AND SIMON PAYE

10 **"I didn't leave financial journalism, I left classical journalism": Careers and commitments of French financial journalists at the time of financialisation** 175
ANTOINE MACHUT

Contents　vii

PART IV
Internal boundaries: Diversity, segmentation, stratification
within financial occupations　　　　　　　　　　　　　189

 Introduction: Is sociology of finance a general sociology?　191
 OLIVIER GODECHOT

11　**Early careers in portfolio and wealth management: The roles**
 of class, race and gender in occupational segmentations　194
 STÉPHANIE MIGNOT-GÉRARD, CONSTANCE PERRIN-JOLY, FRANÇOIS SARFATI
 AND NADÈGE VEZINAT

12　**Managing fortunes and privacy: Professional rhetoric and**
 boundaries within wealth management　　　　　　　210
 CAMILLE HERLIN-GIRET

13　**The duality of the LBO field**　　　　　　　　　　223
 FABIEN FOUREAULT

 References　　　　　　　　　　　　　　　　237
 Index　　　　　　　　　　　　　　　　　259

Figures

3.1	Financial flows in the Employee Partnership Fund	62
II.1	The unit cost of financial intermediation in the United States, 1884–2012	90
5A.1	Rate of ownership of financial and non-financial assets in 1986	106
5A.2	Rate of ownership of financial and non-financial assets in 1992	106
5A.3	Rate of ownership of financial and non-financial assets in 1998	106
5A.4	Rate of ownership of financial and non-financial assets in 2004	106
5A.5	Rate of ownership of financial and non-financial assets in 2010	107
9.1	Overall proportion of financial roles in careers	162
9.2	Overall proportion of each sub-sector (and of other job roles) over the first 7 years of careers	165
9.3	Sequences synchronised according to the year of the first top executive position	168
10.1	Distribution of positions held by individuals according to the class to which they belong, month by month	181
13.1	Relationship between market volume and market value	228
13.2	Multidimensional scaling (MDS) on geodesic distances in the affiliation network	230

Tables

5.1	Household asset portfolios, 2010	97
6.1	Doubtful real estate loans vs. total credit	112
8.1	Financiers on boards	148
9.1	Three career paths in the sequence data	160
9.2	Percentage of individuals in financial roles 1, 7 and 17 years after graduating	163
9.3	Overall distribution of professional sectors over 7 and 17 years	164
9.4	Overall distribution of professional sectors over 7 and 17 years	166
9.5	Percentage of individuals in top executive positions during the first 7 years after graduating	167
9.6	Proportion of individuals in financial roles 1 year before accessing top executive positions	169
9.7	Patterns of mobility towards top executive positions	171
10.1	Odds ratio obtained by means of logistic regressions, for each cluster	185
10.2	Representation of the cohorts in each cluster	186

Contributors

Editing Committee

Marlene Benquet, Sociologist, Research Fellow, Centre National de la Recherche Scientifique (CNRS), Paris Dauphine University, France.

Valérie Boussard, Professor of Sociology, Paris Nanterre University, France.

Marie-Anne Dujarier, Professor of Sociology, Paris VII University, France.

Frédéric Lebaron, Professor of Sociology, Paris Saclay University, France.

Benjamin Lemoine, Sociologist, Research Fellow, Centre National de la Recherche Scientifique, (CNRS), - Paris Dauphine University, France.

Horacio Ortiz, Anthropologist, Research Fellow, Centre National de la Recherche Scientifique (CNRS), France.

Antoine Vion, Associate Professor of Political Science, Mediterranean University, France.

Authors

Ward Anseeuw, Development Economist and Policy Analyst, Research Fellow, Agricultural Research Centre for International Development (CIRAD), France.

Valérie Boussard, Professor of Sociology, Paris Nanterre University, France.

Abdoul Diallo, Database Manager and Statistical Processing, Higher National Institute of Agronomic Sciences of Food and Environment (AGROSUP DIJON), France.

Frank Dobbin, Professor of Sociology, Harvard University, USA.

Antoine Ducastel, Socio-Economist, Research Fellow, Agricultural Research Centre for International Development (CIRAD), France.

Marie-Anne Dujarier, Professor of Sociology, Paris VII University, France.

Fabien Foureault, PhD in Sociology, Associate Researcher, CSO, Centre National de la recherche Scientifique (CNRS), Sciences Po Paris.

Contributors xi

Pierre François, Sociologist, Research Fellow, CSO, Centre National de la Recherche Scientifique (CNRS), Sciences Po Paris, France.

Olivier Godechot, Sociologist, Research Fellow, MaxPo, Centre National de la Recherche Scientifique (CNRS), Sciences Po Paris, France.

Camille Herlin-Giret, Phd in Political Science, Postdoc, Institut de recherche interdisciplinaire sur les enjeux sociaux (IRIS), École des hautes études en sciences sociales (EHESS), France.

Karen Ho, Professor of Anthropology, University of Minnesota, USA.

Gilles Laferté, Sociologist, Research Fellow, Institut National de la Recherche Agronomique (INRA), France.

Emmanuel Lazega, Professor of Sociology, Sciences Po Paris, France.

Sylvan Lemaire, Sociologist, CMH, Centre National de la Recherche Scientifique (CNRS), France.

Claire Lemercier, Historian, Research Fellow, CSO, Centre National de la Recherche Scientifique (CNRS), Sciences Po Paris, France.

Antoine Machut, PhD Student in Sociology, Sciences Po Grenoble, France.

Donald MacKenzie, Professor of Sociology, University of Edinburgh, UK.

Stéphanie Mignot-Gérard, Associate professor of Management, Paris Est University, Institut de recherche en gestion (EA 2354), France.

Sabine Montagne, Economist, Research Fellow, IRISSO, Centre National de la Recherche Scientifique (CNRS), University Paris Dauphine, France.

Lise Mounier, Sociologist, Research Fellow, CMH, Centre National de la Recherche Scientifique (CNRS), France.

Simon Paye, Sociologist, Associate Professor, University of Lorraine, France.

Constance Perrin-Joly, Associate Professor of Sociology, University Paris 13, France.

Quentin Ravelli, Sociologist, Research Fellow, CMH, Centre National de la recherche Scientifique (CNRS), France.

François Sarfati, Associate Professor of Sociology, University Paris Est, France.

Taylor Spears, Sociologist, Research Fellow, University of Edinburgh, UK.

Natascha van der Zwan, Assistant Professor in Public Administration, University of Leiden, Netherlands.

Nadège Vezinat, Associate Professor of Sociology, University of Reims, France.

Foreword

Frank Dobbin
Professor of Sociology
Harvard University

Finance at Work will change the way people think about the most important economic transformation of the last two generations – the rise and spread of financialisation. Paradigms and precepts that originated in the world of financial economics have invaded every aspect of our social, political, and civil worlds. We now think of our infrastructure, sovereign debt, pensions, homes, and educational loans as financial instruments. We use the lens of risk and return to view everything we do. The terminology of financial economics has entered the lexicon of modern common sense.

Accounts of how this happened have mostly been top-down. Economic sociologists emphasize how pioneering financial economists – Michael Jensen and William Meckling; Eugene Fama; Fischer Black, Myron Scholes and Robert C. Merton – changed the thinking of regulators, corporate chiefs and investment banks. Jensen, Meckling, and Fama revived agency theory, specifying principles for financial management of the firm – and by extension the investment bank, mutual fund, and household economy – oriented single-mindedly to increasing wealth. Social, civic, and political goals took a backseat in the new worldview. Taking care of wealth creation would take care of everything else.

The birds-eye view of the phenomenon found among organisational and economic sociologists has left us with a partial explanation. Studies have documented the theoretical foundations in financial economics, and shown some of the consequences for corporations, investment banks, mutual funds, and household investment. But new social-science paradigms are invented all of the time. Few of them change the world. What did it take to turn these ideas into actions and a new worldview?

A handful of ethnographers, sociologists of work, and sociologists of the professions have worked to explain this revolution by exploring how new financial models and ideas were put into practice by experts, how they spread around the world and across occupations, and how they entered the common-sense thinking of everyone from financial accountants to farmers.

From this group, Valérie Boussard has assembled a crack team of longstanding experts and all-star rookies who study finance from the ground up. Bringing them together at a conference in Paris, Boussard charged them with talking to one another to hone their arguments. She helped them to articulate a strong theoretical framework through which to understand the events at hand. The resulting book is

Foreword xiii

a rich but integrated tour of the workings of financialisation, observed through the eyes of the participants in this revolution.

Boussard had the vision to see that scholars working on different aspects of the revolution, from different theoretical perspectives, were sketching parts of the same puzzle. That puzzle, which comes together in *Finance at Work*, creates a picture of how the revolution was put into practice. Boussard's own scholarship, at the intersection of the sociology of professions and the sociology of management, gives her a unique vantage point from which to analyse these changes. In the last three decades, we have seen the rise of professional and expert groups within firms that claim universal financial knowledge. That claim allows them to replace traditional industry-expert executives schooled in engineering, design, and marketing. Finance experts have taken the helm of firms, and have also taken charge of departments and divisions within firms. While the field of the sociology of professions has long focused on liberal professions licensed by governments that operated their own shops – doctors, lawyers, engineers, architects – purveyors of new forms of generalised expertise in finance were largely neglected by sociologists of the professions because they were not proper professionals. Boussard's work remedies this.

Boussard's position as an expert in both professions and management gives her unique insights into how expert groups contribute to the rise and spread of new management paradigms. In her pathbreaking book, *Sociologie de la Gestion: Les Faiseurs de Performances*, (2008, Paris, Belin) she traces the role of consultants, academics, and legendary managers in creating a modern form of corporate and public-sector governance based in professional precepts. Her historical account shows how general management became professionalized, with its own language and tools, canon and heroes. *Finance at Work* carries the project of *Sociologie de la Gestion* forward, exploring how a new logic came to shape management of everything from schools to hospitals to investment banks. Her best-selling *Sociologie des Professions* (now in its fourth edition, 2015, Paris, Colin) traces some of these very changes up to the present from the perspective not of management, but of the professions.

Boussard chose established leaders in the study of the practice of finance to introduce the four main sections of the book.

Karen Ho, professor of anthropology at the University of Minnesota, is the author of *Liquidated: An Ethnography of Wall Street* (2009, Durham, Duke), which shows how the culture of shareholder value, and high-risk/high-reward financial strategies, is inculcated in Wall Street workers, and how Wall Street justifies and normalises financial practices that contribute to boom and bust cycles. In *Liquidated* she problematises the socialisation of both old and new bankers to a new paradigm based in ideas that would have been anathema a generation earlier – no rewards come without risks, and the job of investment bankers is to find high-risk opportunities that promise outsize gains. The section she introduces, on the boundaries of finance, explores how the new finance paradigm shapes thinking about mergers and acquisitions, the modeling of market risk, and the behavior of union pension fund investors.

xiv *Foreword*

As a sociologist of science, Donald MacKenzie has explored the role of economic science in the evolution of financial markets. Professor of sociology at the University of Edinburgh, he is the author of *An Engine not a Camera: How Financial Models Shape Markets* (2006, Cambridge, MIT), which examines how elegant new theories from highly regarded economists created a foundation for modern financial markets by making market prices for instruments such as derivatives predictable. Financial market participants set prices in accordance with the theories, making the theories appear to be accurate. But the new theories contributed to the market collapse of 1987 and the devastating failure of long-term capital management in 1998. The section he introduces, on how financiers proselytise for their own religion, explores how the logic of financialisation comes to shape not only the behavior of mid-level bank managers, but decisions about remote farming in France and Africa.

Economist Sabine Montagne, from the University of Paris-Dauphine, is author of *Les Fonds de Pension: Entre Protection Sociale et Spéculation Financière* (2006, Paris, Odile Jacob). There, she traces the legal foundations of the rise of mutual fund investing on the shareholder value model. If the principles of professional investment, rooted in portfolio diversification and the capital asset pricing model, epitomise financialisation today, where did they come from? She finds the roots of financialisation not only in the shareholder value model of corporate governance, but in the Anglo-American legal tradition of trusts and its incarnation in the U.S. Employee Retirement Income Security Act of 1974, which determined the abstract fiduciary responsibility of professional investors. The section she introduces explores how careers of French executives and directors, new MBAs, and financial journalists have been shaped by the rise of the financialisation paradigm, and how they in turn have helped to spread the paradigm.

Olivier Godechot, professor of sociology at Sciences-Po Paris, is the author of *Wages, Bonuses and Appropriation of Profit in the Financial Industry: The Working Rich* (2017, London, Routledge), which explains the explosive growth in bonus pay in New York, London, and Paris. Godechot explores how we came to attribute credit for profits not to people who create goods and provide services, but to those who provide what was once considered to be just another factor input alongside land, entrepreneurship, and labor – access to capital. He documents the sharp rise in bonuses and wealth in the sector, and the spread of thinking that justifies the rise and the practices that enable it. The section he introduces covers the development of distinct professional specialties within the finance industry in recent years, and the implications for decision-making.

Finance at Work brings together the insights of experts who have been working on these issues for years, and those of others working at the micro- and meso-levels who have recently applied their skills to the study of financialisation. This book looks at how the principles of finance came to infuse every aspect of modern life by tracing the work of professionals in finance and beyond.

We now take the financialisation of the world for granted, as part of the inevitable trajectory of the modern economy. This book makes clear how much work was behind making us take it for granted. The world might have moved in

Foreword xv

an entirely different direction after the US economic crisis of the 1970s. Nations might have embraced the Japanese or Nordic economic model. State planning on the French or Korean blueprint might have taken over. Stakeholder theory, positing the importance of all of the corporations' different groups of constituents, once seemed likely to create the new blueprint for capitalism. For a time, the possibilities seemed endless. So why did the ideas of a few financial economists on the US create a paradigm that has spread around the world? The macro accounts have documented that it happened. *Finance at Work* is the first extensive effort to understand how it happened.

Acknowledgments

I am grateful for a grant from the Agence Nationale de la Recherche (ANR), which made it possible to launch a large program of research on financial work. I thank the Centre National de la Recherche Scientifique (IDHES-CNRS) and the University of Paris Nanterre for their support in the organization of an international conference on financial work in October 2014. This book couldn't have existed without all the stimulating papers presented at this conference and without the reviewing work of the scientific committee. I would specially like to thank the editing committee of this book for its work on the draft chapters, as well as Olivier Godechot, Karen Ho, Sabine Montagne and Donald MacKenzie for their introductions and Frank Dobbin for his foreword. Their enthusiasm and personal commitment to the future book gave me confidence and energy to pass through all the stages of such an editorial project.

I am also grateful to the colleagues with whom I had many scientific discussions about finance and financialisation. Their help and advice were precious, especially those of Emmanuel Lazega and Théo Bourgeron, who commented on the first draft of the general introduction.

Introduction

Financiers at work, financialisation on the march

Valérie Boussard

This book gathers researches about financial work in order to pursue the investigation of financialisation. After the twentieth century's epochal financial crises, 2008 in particular, the study of financialisation has led to researchers pitting finance against economics, speculative value against real value (Orléans, 2014), and assets against earnings (Piketty, 2014). To a certain extent, the above researches set capital and labour at odds, the former following its own abstract logic while attacking the concrete basis of labour. In this perspective, finance is opposed to work as finance endangers working conditions and workers. Furthermore, finance is abstract and disembodied when work is concrete and assignable to actual organisations, occupations or individuals.

This book intends to reverse the relationship between finance and work; not by denying the terrific consequences finance has on work and labour but by considering that finance is not abstract and disembodied. A whole *host* of intermediary organisations whose activities grow as financial markets develop have emerged: banks, insurance companies, investment funds, audit firms, rating agencies, law firms, etc. New types of work have also appeared within these organisations leading to specialised occupations which were further subdivided into financial analysts, traders, asset managers, equity managers, auditors, business lawyers, etc. For organisations' and individuals' finance equates with work: organisations consider finance as labour to divide and organise and hence finance represents an occupational pursuit for the people they employ.

In this perspective, the book unpacks the financialisation process by scrutinising what financiers do when they work. The question is not so much what finance produces but how finance does work. Opening the black box of this process leads to translating the question into: 'how do financiers work?' The book tries to avoid the temptation of seeing economic phenomena being overdetermined by 'finance', where finance is considered to be an economic mechanism used to allocate capital. In contrast, it highlights the financier's work and its own impact on finance, in the sense that capital allocation mechanisms cannot operate without the people who plan, organise, select, etc. these mechanisms. Therefore, rather than setting finance against work, it considers how finance represents the outcome

2 Valérie Boussard

of a specific type of work, and how this work specifically determines the manner in which capital is allocated.

After having described the concept of financialisation and proposed to see it as a shift in the capital allocation mechanism, this introduction argues that the investigation of the financier's work is an appropriate way to unpack the process of financialisation (I). The three dimensions of work's analysis that structure the different chapters gathered in the book are then described: conditions of employment and career design, composition of the working day and professional norms (II). Such dimensions of analysis allow unveiling financialisation as an issue of boundaries, more precisely as the boundary work of financiers. Following this finding, the four sections of the book and their results are laid out (III). The conclusion elaborates on the implication of considering financialisation as the result of the boundary dynamics of finance (IV).

I Investigating financialisation

The concept of financialisation emerged in early 2000 and has continually gained importance since then. This boom suggests that a conceptual renewal was needed to describe and explain a large amount of empirical observations following the rise of finance from the mid-1990s onward (Engelen, 2008).

In the simplest sense, financialisation reflects the "spread of finance". It still remains to characterise this spread, otherwise the concept of financialisation would fail to explain the specificity of the contemporary financialisation trend compared to prior stages of financialisation during the nineteenth and the early twentieth centuries (Ertuk *et al.*, 2007) or the concept could be too loose to add value to adjacent concepts like globalisation, liberalisation, commodification, etc. (Engelen, 2008).

Financialisation: a three-fold definition

Financialisation was first characterised as the increase in the share of financial assets in economic transactions (Krippner, 2005), or put differently, as the growing importance of financial activities as a source of profits in the economy (Krippner, 2012). This definition of the spread of finance has the huge merit of being set on aggregate measures of the phenomenon. In this perspective, many studies have proposed novel metrics (Crotty, 2005; Milberg, 2008; Baud and Durand, 2012; Flaherty, 2015) extending the range of measures of financialisation. The body of work on financialisation is prone to showing how capitalist elites have shifted their investments from production to finance (Arrighi, 1994) and to describing the institutional changes undergirding this shift (Carruthers, 2015). These works underscore the increasing role of financial channels for profits constitution. Studies underline that a specific class, the rentiers, whether individuals or institutions, are at the core of this financial regime as their incomes and political or economic power have significantly increased throughout the 1980s and the 1990s (Boyer, 2000; Duménil and Lévy, 2005; Epstein and Jayadev, 2005). Some of them

Introduction 3

consider financialisation as a political project trying to protect the USA's economic and symbolic hegemony through a massive inflow of capital into American markets (Arrighi, 2003). Moreover, financialisation is associated with the spread of neoliberal ideology, both of them being two faces of the same coin. N. van der Zwan (2014) proposes to name this definition of financialisation a "new accumulation regime", as scholarship focuses on the shifts in the means to accrue profits.

Nonetheless, financialisation can not only be seen as the growing importance of financial assets and profits and therefore as the growth of financial markets. Indeed, financialisation can also be understood as the spread of the financial logic outside its initial realm (Godechot, 2016). In a first perspective, this spread has been described as the emergence of an ideological construct, the Shareholder Value, as the main guiding principle of corporate governance (Aglietta, 2000; Froud *et al.*, 2000; Lazonick and O'Sullivan, 2000; Heilbron *et al.*, 2014). The studies show that a theory of corporate governance linked to the principal-agent economic theory (Fama and Jensen, 1983; Jensen, 1986; Rappaport, 1986) has forged a financial conception of the firm (the shareholder value creation) where corporate efficiency and managers' performance are measured by their ability to distribute free cash-flow to shareholders, rather than to retain and reinvest them (Lazonick and O'Sullivan, 2000). This leads to a growing pressure of financial markets onto non-financial corporations, increasing job insecurity and job intensity for their employees (Fligstein and Shin, 2004; Lin and Tomaskovic-Devey, 2013), through the role of a new kind of top-manager (Fligstein, 1990; Fligstein and Brantley, 1992; Zorn, 2004; Zorn *et al.*, 2005). From this point of view, financialisation is the 'ascendancy of the shareholder value conception' of corporate governance (van der Zwan, 2014), viewed both as an ideological construct and its normative dissemination.

N. van der Zwan draws a third definition from the various studies using the concept of financialisation. Indeed, the spread of the financial logic outside its initial realm can be understood in another way. A large body of work is involved with the encroachment of finance into the realms of everyday life (Martin, 2002; Langley, 2008). This 'financialisation of the everyday' (van der Zwan, 2014) underscores that financial products and services are offered to the broader population, which, in parallel, have been converted to financial rationales, like purchasing financial products in order to protect against the uncertainty of life (Ertuk *et al.*, 2007b). Households embrace financial strategies (Davis, 2009a), which are the consequence of the emergence of a "finance culture" (Fligstein and Goldstein, 2015). Therefore finance-driven behaviours affect the mere citizen, not only the rentiers class or top-level managers. Moreover, the shift in the way households manage incomes, consumption, debts, savings, etc. is imputable to the rise of intermediary elites (banks, pension and mutual funds, consultants, advisors, etc.) who connect 'financialised masses' (Ertuk *et al.*, 2007b) to financial markets and change (almost) all citizens into investors.

Financialisation: shifts in capital allocation mechanism

The three definitions of financialisation (a new regime of accumulation, the ascendancy of the shareholder value conception of corporate governance and

4 *Valérie Boussard*

the rise of the citizen as investor) are not mutually exclusive (Krippner, 2012). For example, 'in an economy in which systems of corporate governance reflect the imperatives of financial markets, we could expect profits to accrue increasingly through financial channels' (ibid. p. 28). These three characterisations of the spread of finance in the early twenty-first century are obviously intertwined. If their disentanglement is heuristic, it remains necessary to understand what is transverse to them.

Indeed, the three bodies of work offer different views of the same phenomenon, depending on their focus. Regarding the descriptions and measures of changes in economics, social and political life brought by financialisation, the three approaches are globally convergent. They draw a unique phenomenon although partially described, enlightening some faces while others remain in shadow. In fact, all studies mentioned above highlight changes in the mechanisms used to channel money into the productive economy. The accumulation regime studies show that money has become a flow directed to financial activities, via financial channels, in order to be accumulated. Shareholder ascendancy studies underpin that decisions about a corporation's use of money favour the production of value for the Shareholder and therefore capital is distributed rather than reinvested in the corporation or kept under the control of the corporation's management. As regards everyday life financialisation, studies show that the use of money is headed toward investment to protect oneself against uncertainty of life and prove command over one's life course. The main mechanism at play in these changes refers to the way money, put differently, capital, is allocated. Monetary *quantifications* and financial calculations are indeed not new in economic reasoning about capital allocation. As posited by E. Chiapello (2015), what is new in the contemporary period is the progressive diffusion of new metrics that have gradually colonised the existing form of economic quantification and the reasoning about capital allocation: the net present value probability-based estimation of value and the market price as true value. Altogether these calculation devices shape a 'financialisation of financial matters' (p. 14), where capital allocation is evaluated from the investor's point of view, in a short-term rationale, favouring the liquidity of the capital. In this vein, financialisation may be defined as a shift in capital allocation since perceptions of what ought to be done with money have dramatically changed, rooted in new valuation conventions and leading to assign new roles and uses to money.

Almost all studies on financialisation describe the consequences of this change in capital allocation. Even if they need to be further broadened beyond the USA case (Kornrich and Hicks, 2015), empirical consequences of financialisation are well documented. Mainly, scholarship shows a rise in inequalities (Godechot, 2012; Lin and Tomaskovic, 2013; Flaherty, 2015; Peralta, 2015), economic growth reduction (Tomaskevic-Devey *et al.*, 2015), declining working conditions coupled with destruction (Appelbaum and Batt, 2014; Fligstein and Shin, 2014) and a change in politics, policies and institutional practices (reduction of workers' bargaining power [Darcillon 2015], and tight monetary policy [Hager, 2015; Lemoine, 2016]).

However, the three definitions strongly diverge about the reasons why the capital allocation mechanism and the valuation devices at stake have dramatically changed over recent time. Although the three bodies of work are involved in the same issue and bring evidence of the linked consequences of financialisation, they propose different narratives for its causes and process.

Unpacking financialisation

These narratives are of great importance as the book aims to unpack financialisation by focusing on the way it occurs, rather than highlighting what it produces.

On one hand, the 'accumulation' studies see the capital allocation mechanism as completely abstract, anonymous, disembodied and endogenous to financial capitalism itself. As posited by van der Zwan (2014) through accumulation studies, 'financialisation is a logic of capitalism, either driven by a wealth-maximising rentier class or the imperial aspirations of the American state' (p. 106). This work may be of interest when analysing the impact of financialisation, but it is of limited value when analysing the dynamics of financialisation. Indeed, this line of thinking ends on a rather tautological note, as it is the success of finance construed as an abstract and disembodied force that consequently elucidates financialisation. On the other hand, by offering insights for entering financialisation through a more concrete face, the two remaining sets of studies pave the way for an in-depth investigation of its process. The irresistible ascendancy of Shareholder Value can be understood as a process whereby representations of work of investors (Useem, 1996; Montagne, 2016) and of corporate managers (Fligstein and Brantley, 1992; Lazonick and O'Sullivan, 2000), as well as the procedures used in carrying out this work and the techniques, calculation methods and valuation conventions (Chiapello, 2015) that make this work possible in the first place, are progressively influenced by financial logic. As such, the spread of finance accounts for an institutional change and much more for the emergence of new professional models.

The extension of the investor's narrative to realms of daily lives raises similar issues. In a similar vein to other markets, financial markets do not develop *sui generis* (White, 1981; Fliegstein, 2001). The dissemination of cultural representations amongst households running parallel to the extension of financial markets can be explained by the role of intermediaries who configure, valuate and sell financial products. These intermediaries connect households and financial markets (Ertuk *et al.*, 2007a) and, as other market intermediaries (Bessy and Chauvin, 2013), the frame they set for this relationship (re)-organise the market itself, rather than merely enact it. Like other markets (Fligstein, 2001), finance can be considered as an institution and its concomitant norms cannot be understood without focusing on those who embody the very dynamics of the institution, the "institutional entrepreneurs" (DiMaggio, 1998; Dacin, Goodstein and Scott, 2002; Hardy and Maguire, 2008; Lawrence and Suddaby, 2006). Therefore, accounting for financialisation goes through an investigation of the work of those "entrepreneurs", as their role is never neutral for the market within which they operate. For example, the negotiating that traders do as intermediaries can help

6   *Valérie Boussard*

to interpret the shape of financial markets (Baker, 1984; Eccles and Crane, 1988; Abolafia, 1996; Zuckerman, 1999; Orléans, 2004; Knorr, Cetina and Preda, 2005; Godechot, 2007). Studies of bankers have highlighted their roles as sales consultants keen to meet their clients' needs and at the same time influence their clients' wants (Mizruchi and Brewsters Stearns, 2001). Work on consultancy firms has shown their influence on corporate management transformations, by virtue of the rhetoric about value creation coupled with the metrics they advise and sell to their clients (Froud *et al.*, 2000; Lordon, 2000). Other scholars underline that finance is performed on a daily basis by financiers thanks to technical devices that frame their way of thinking and subsequently their actions, and moreover legitimate economic theory and mathematical models (MacKenzie and Millo, 2003; MacKenzie, 2004; Knorr and Cetina, 2005). All these studies draw attention to the work of all these actors who, at different levels, participate to transform the capital allocation mechanism.

Financialisation as an outcome of a specific work

This approach implies consideration of finance as an array of occupations. As mentioned above, as a whole array of financial organisations have developed (banks, insurance companies, investment funds, audit firms, rating agencies, law firms, etc.), new specialised occupations have emerged: brokers, traders, quants, asset managers, investors, equity managers, auditors, risk managers, business lawyers, chief financial officers, financial controllers, treasurers, etc. All these financiers are workers whose tasks are defined and divided, controlled and managed, evaluated and compensated. Financiers can then be considered as other workers.

The latter assertion sounds like a provocation. In the collective psyche, a financier is a capitalist i.e. someone who holds capital. In managerial capitalism, the notion of 'manager' emerged, and the role of the manager was distinct from the role of the "owner" (Berle and Means, 1932). Financial capitalism is similarly underpinned by financiers who are most of the time not the holders of the financial assets they buy, sell, trade or advise upon, etc. The great majority of these financiers work as employees, even if their salaries/bonuses and the nature of their activity enable them to amass earnings that are vastly superior to those earned by workers outside the financial sector and that have a strong impact on social stratification (Godechot, 2012). Most of the time, financiers are not rentiers, and do not belong to the rentier class. (Ertuk *et al.*, 2008). On the contrary, they work for rentiers and for some of them, their way to accumulate capital is to 'skim value' from the capital allocation they advise, organise or trade while the rentiers are merely 'surfing on this value' (Ertuk, 2007a).

The different chapters take seriously the assertion that financiers are workers and they examine precisely the followings of such an assertion. They envision finance as a particular work that specifically determines the manner in which capital is allocated. Subsequently, they consider financialisation as the outcome of a specific work, that of financiers.

Introduction   7

II Financiers at work

All chapters of this book present recent empirical studies about financiers, be they finance-oriented CEOs, CFOs, financial journalists, mergers and acquisitions' advisors, savings bankers, investment funds' managers, asset or wealth managers, etc. The cases take place in different national contexts (France, Spain, USA, UK, South Africa).

As for other investigations about work and workers, three dimensions are scrutinised: conditions of employment and career design, composition of the working day and finally the professional norms. Some chapters go in depth with one of these dimensions while others articulate two or three of them.

Conditions of employment and the career design

First of all, as for other workers, conditions of employment and career design matter to grasp the occupational commitment and the occupational trajectories during a life course (Dalton, 1959; Glaser, 1968; Kanter Moss, 1977; Rosenbaum, 1979). In an interactionist sociological perspective, occupational careers and their various sequences, turning points and socialization processes (Becker *et al.*, 1961; Hughes, 1971) explain how a worker endorses, transforms or even rejects a professional role during his life course.

The likelihood of elevated salaries and bonuses (Godechot, 2007; Lazonick and O'Sullivan, 2000), along with developments in technology (Mayer, 1997; Muniesa, 2005), and regulatory changes (Lagneau-Ymonet, 2008; Carruthers, 2015) have led to a dramatic change in social and career trajectories in the financial field. First, this field (banks, financial markets, investment funds, consulting firms, audit firms, etc.) has reinvented itself, resulting in new, legitimate career possibilities for those who enter the field (Blair-Loy, 1999; Stovel *et al.*, 1996). Second, the social characteristics of financial actors have also evolved: being in possession of academic qualifications and theoretical knowledge e.g. expertise in probabilistic mathematical models, has to some extent replaced social and cultural capital and traditional skills as determinants of social status and professional mobility (Godechot, 2001; Ramirez, 2003; Lagneau-Ymonet, 2008).

In this backdrop, some chapters of this book shed light on the career trajectories for financiers and how these trajectories have been reinvented over time, both from the perspective of the financial domain itself and from its interactions with other professional domains (Chapters 3, 8, 9, 10). Some chapters underline financiers' compensations, status and careers to account for gender, social or ethnic differences in financial occupations (Chapters 11, 12, 13), while other chapters show how the process of occupational assessment, linked to shifts in employment conditions and careers, determines the way financiers perform their role and the kind of 'finance' they produce (Chapters 1, 2, 6).

The composition of the working day

The second dimension of the investigation into financiers' work implies an understanding of the reality of their working day and how it is composed,

8   *Valérie Boussard*

particularly in relation to organisational structure on one hand and to technical devices on the other.

Work organisation, division of labour, cooperation and control process, hierarchical structure, office hours and time control, working patterns, definitions of competence and performance, management tools, etc. are traditional characteristics of the organisational structure used by sociologists of work to account for workers' perceptions of their tasks and the way they perform them. A recent approach focuses more on specialised and technical devices which encompass many contemporary occupational activities. Launched by the anthropology of sciences, this approach explains how these devices participate in creating the problems workers are dealing with and frame solutions they can use (Callon, 1998; Callon and Muniesa, 2010). These devices, such as equations, software, screens, ratings, accounting rules, etc. are particularly numerous and varied in the financial sector where they dictate the direction of the work. This is evidenced by the appearance of instantaneous data from all over the world on the multiscreens of the trading floors (Knorr and Cetina, 2005) or by the formulae and calculation methods used in financial arbitrage (Godechot, 2001; MacKenzie and Millo, 2003). These devices shape, both materially and in substance, the various social relations at play (Muniesa, 2005), as well as *assuming* a performative role (McKenzie and Millo, 2003; Callon and Muniesa, 2009; Muniesa, 2011) that helps turn finance theory into reality (MacKenzie, 2004).

Using these approaches as a baseline, many chapters elaborate on how organisational structure or technical devices, which create frames, routines and specific representations of what ought to be done, help define the day-to-day activity of a financier (Chapters 1, 2, 7, 11, 12).

Professional norms

Complementary to these two first dimensions of work investigation, a third one is rather focused on the institutional and normative background that undergirds occupational activity and interactions. This dimension is particularly accurate when scrutinizing the role played by new financial actors in financialisation. Indeed, by continuing the work of neo-institutionalists (Meyer and Rowan, 1977), many studies (Fligstein, 1990; Fligstein and Brantley, 1992; Zorn, 2004; Zorn *et al.*, 2005) make the connection between the dissemination of norms and practices on one side and changes in the demographic composition of elite executive groups. However, these studies don't anchor their explanations into ethnographical inquiries. Subsequently, they don't deliver an overview of the way these norms are both causes and consequences of professionalism. The concept of professionalism refers to an array of knowledge and behaviour which legitimates the claim of an occupational group to monopolise a set of activities and subsequently draws the figure of the worker acknowledged to take in charge this set of activities (Hughes, 1971; Freidson, 1986; Abbott, 1988). From this point of view, the financial norms promoted by new actors like CFO, investors, etc. could be analysed as professional norms deriving from jurisdictional disputes between occupational groups striving to establish monopolies (Abbott, 1988). They could also be understood as the desire of workers to be recognised as professionals by peers, competitors, clients or other counterparts and then to gain high status, be it economic or merely symbolic (Hughes, 1958).

Following this perspective, as prior stimulating studies (Hassoun, 2005; Roth, 2006; Ho, 2009; Ortiz, 2014a), many chapters in this book highlight the professional ethos that creates the group dynamics. They show that this ethos stems from a conception of the professional role, a role which then structures daily activities and interactions (Chapters 1, 2, 3, 4, 10, 12). As financial workers conform to the norms of their professions, and as each profession tends to extend the boundaries of its activity using an appropriate rhetoric, the spread of the financial logic could be explained by virtue of this normative dissemination.

III Financialisation: a boundary issue

This boundary issue is the red thread going through all chapters. Indeed, all chapters show that financialisation is a question of boundaries, specifically professional boundaries.

The first section underlines that financiers work in closed professional worlds with relatively tight boundaries, though not formal or legal, within which a specific logic is deployed. Financial workers are therefore subject to an exclusionary process if they do not respect this logic. The financial logic of each professional world, in the sense of the choice in the mechanism of capital allocation, is the result of the confrontation between several internal logics, dependent on the balance of power of the actors involved and of the strength of the exclusionary process.

The second section shows that the financial logic of each of these professional worlds can also pass through the boundaries. Chapters in this section emphasise how non-financial actors are transformed by financial logic or how non-financial products are converted into financial assets. This section reveals the diffusion processes of financial logic outside their original worlds, which transforms the mechanism of capital allocation.

The third section moves the focus from how financial logics cross borders to how individuals cross occupational and professional boundaries. The chapters are focused on the career paths of workers who come from or pass through the finance sector. They show that these workers are also involved in the shift of capital allocation, by their own conversion to new financial logic and/or their participation in the dissemination and implementation thereof.

Finally, the fourth section returns to the issue of internal boundaries between financial worlds as discussed in the first section. This is to bring to light the segmentation process that divides and structures financial occupations. The chapters emphasise that these segmentations produce a moral hierarchy within each professional world that also corresponds to the phenomenon of social stratification.

Finally, this book describes a process whereby financial workers participate to create, strengthen, displace and expand the boundaries of financial logics. This process of demarking and negotiating boundaries is akin to a boundary work

10   *Valérie Boussard*

(Gieryn, 1983; Lazega, 1992; Lamont and Molnar, 2002). This boundary work defines who is legitimately able to take decisions in capital allocation and which knowledge and calculation devices are appropriate for such decisions. In doing so, it has a strong impact on capital allocation mechanism.

Part I: The boundaries of finance: social closure and exclusionary process

The chapters gathered in this first part explore the way everyday financial work is accomplished. Two chapters focus on the activity of financiers within financial organisations: T. Spears (Chapter 2) details the daily work of quants, those PhD-trained mathematicians, physicists and engineers employed by international banks dealing with derivatives. Quants develop mathematical models used both to value the derivatives' trade positions for accounting purpose and to hedge (i.e. reduce or eliminate) the risks associated with this trade. V. Boussard and M.A. Dujarier (Chapter 1) concentrate on the activity of financial advisors in international investment banks or auditing firms who broker transactions in the buying and selling of companies on behalf of investors (mergers and acquisitions).

The two other chapters present the financial work on its edges. E. Lazega, L. Mounier and S. Lemaire (Chapter 3) investigate the role of judges in French Commercial Courts when dealing in bankruptcy procedures. They underline both an overrepresentation of judges with financial backgrounds in the Paris Commercial Court and a strategy of the financial sector to exert influence upon the judicial work of the court. N. van der Zwan (Chapter 4) analyses the attempt of American unions to launch an investment vehicle, using the technique of the leveraged buyout but designed to benefit American workers. She focuses on the work of union leaders, investment funds managers and investment bankers to produce successive draft proposals of this vehicle.

Although the four chapters have various focus, national contexts and organisational backgrounds, they all follow a common thread: they go in depth with the work done by different protagonists and they highlight the conditions (technical, ideological, normative, interpersonal, etc.) that make the work possible. Subsequently, they demonstrate that the outcomes of the financial work, be they models to reduce financial risks, mergers and acquisitions, solutions after a bankruptcy or investment vehicles, are in return all framed by these conditions.

The four chapters underline that technical skills are necessary to perform the work and in that way, give a cognitive frame to everyday activities. Nevertheless, they are not detached from social skills. For example, Spears emphasises that financial devices used by quants are not purely technical. The chapter shows that the models developed rely on a selection of financial instruments (the calibration), i.e. a choice over multiple technical parameters. Yet, this choice implies necessarily a subjective judgment on the part of the quant, whose actions can be dangerous for the bank as the model could fail to hedge the risks accurately or to calculate the accounting value. Boussard and Dujarier underscore that mergers and acquisitions' advisors have to be skilful at manipulating figures and financial variables,

Introduction 11

which lead them to have a quantitative and abstract picture of companies they help to trade. But moreover, fulfilling the job needs to show fervour for the transaction in itself and keep away consequences of the transactions for the company and the stakeholders. The professional ethos ranges above the demonstration of a mere technical dexterity and includes a command of the normative frame of the occupation. Lazega, Mounier and Lemaire's chapter unveils another face of the social skills at stake in the work performance. They show that consular judges in the Commercial Court of Paris seek to produce pragmatic decisions, combining the judge's knowledge of economy and management with his knowledge of law and jurisprudence. But in practice, these judgements call upon the judge's sense of 'fairness', often based on individual 'feelings' and experiences on one hand and on collective norms and conventions of the business world on the other. When judges come from the financial sector, their decisions are shaped by the political positions shared by the financial sector about the good decision to take in case of bankruptcies. Political positions behind technical choices are even more striking in the case presented by van der Zwan, in which unions and financiers collaborate to design an investment vehicle. Unions leaders, with their pro-labour political positions, catch the attention of financiers. Financiers insist that the Unions leaders alter some of their initial choices about the governance of the fund in order to make the fund more attractive to investors.

The set of social skills involved in the technical accomplishment of the work ranges from individual and subjective interpretations to political positions through collective norms and conventions. These three dimensions are close-knit; together they form the basis for the credibility of the individual performing the work. This credibility is construed within each professional network: quants are assessed by the traders for which they build the models and by the hierarchy of the bank. Mergers and acquisitions (M&A) advisors are continually gauged by their colleagues, hierarchy, peers and clients. Consular judges act on behalf of companies and employers' organisations who sponsored them at the time of their election and who keep an eye on their decisions. Unions' leaders have to keep in line with the organisation that gave them a mandate to launch the financial vehicle, while financiers are watched by investors, colleagues and banks. In each case, their credibility is at stake and they act in order to conform to the social skills expected in their professional world. Otherwise, they would lose their professional reputation or they would merely be rejected out of the professional group.

This exclusionary process is subtle as it is based on the balance of power within the professional network. For example, if the two goals of quant's models were at odds and the situation created a conflict of interests, the traders who sell the derivatives might put pressure on the quants to make "aggressive" models so that the traders could more easily win business from potential clients. Yet this aggressiveness involves an understatement of the value of derivatives. To prevent this conflict of interests involving quants working in the front office with traders, banks created controlling departments, separated from the front office and staffed with other quants. These controlling quants have to validate the models built by front-office quants. However, to do so, they need to understand the tacit

12 *Valérie Boussard*

judgments made by front-office quants. They can't keep a true external position. Moreover, they resent the power of the traders and of the front office in general, which, in the end, over-determines their own choices. They can't escape the day-to-day influence and general power of trading front office over the other departments of the bank. Therefore, quants, be they front office quants or controlling quants, are at the nexus of influence and power relationships. Gaining credibility for quants means incorporating the traders' demands and aligning their social skills to the ones expected by the traders, rather than to those expected by actors with less power and legitimacy in the bank. This exclusionary process within the professional network explains the failure of the unions' investment vehicle. Indeed, unions are not considered to be a legitimate financial actor by the financial mainstream and by the political elites. To launch their vehicle, they had to be helped by financial actors operating as intermediaries between unions and financial markets. But in this intermediation process the three actors didn't have the same power. Unions had to conform to financial professional standards much more than finance had to comply with labour demands. And the intermediaries, embedded in their financial network, tipped the scales in favour of finance.

This part gives precious insights to understand the boundary work performed by financiers. The first dimension of this work insists on the resolution of the encounter of multiple claims to define the professional reality and the way to deal with it (Lazega, 1992). These four chapters draw the financial sphere as multiple social worlds (Becker, 1982), where both technical devices and professional norms create a closed network and constitute efficient boundaries. The social skills prized within these professional networks shape the work performed by the financiers.

Some actions are possible when others are inconceivable without many risks of reputation or exclusion. Within these social worlds, financial logics proliferate and are reinforced as people conform to the prized technical and social skills. The chapters also show that financial logic is not unique. Each financial world develops a specific logic, which is most of the time the confrontational encounter of different 'sub-logics' whose outcome depends on the inner balance of power. Financialisation appears as a process whereby financial logics develop within social worlds whose boundaries are so thick and tight that they protect the financial logics from being challenged by outer logics. These boundaries are neither formal nor legal; they are the outcome of technical, relational and symbolic norms of the professional game individuals commit to (Boussard, 2017). The case of the M&A advisors and of the failure of the labour unions' investment vehicle are good examples of this process. The second dimension of the boundary work regards the blurring of the boundaries (Lazega, 1992). Financialisation can also be drawn as a process where financial logics extend above their initial boundaries and influence outer social worlds. The successful endeavour of the financial sector on controlling the judicial work on bankruptcies or the power of the front office on controlling departments in banks demonstrate that boundaries between private and public sector or regulation body and regulated actors are blurred. In their chapter, Lazega, Mounier and Lemaire suggest that financial

Introduction 13

logics pervade adjacent worlds, which raises serious issues for financial regulation. As Karen Ho posits in her introduction to this part, these chapters demonstrate that it is through this boundary work that finance attempts to promulgate its spheres of influence.

Part II: Passing through boundaries: financiers as intermediaries in conversion to financial logics

The second part pursues the issue of financial boundary work by seeking out the way financial logics cross over boundaries, spreading financial norms out of the closed financial networks presented above. Chapters 5 (Laferté and Diallo) and 6 (Ravelli) aim at understanding how non-financial actors get to be touched or converted to financial ways of thinking. Chapter 7 (Ducastel and Anseeuw) presents a kind of reverse process by investigating the way financiers try to convince institutional investors to add farms to their portfolio, which are not traditional financial assets, but for this very purpose are changed into financial ones. All three chapters present the intermediation work of some financiers as central to the dissemination process of financial logics. As Donald MacKenzie underscores in his introduction to this part, this work is key in financialising economic activities.

G. Laferté and A. Diallo question the shift in financial practices of French farmers. Indeed, since 2000 onwards, French farmers became more acculturated to financial mechanisms and a growing part of their wealth is now constituted of financial products. Laferté and Diallo explain that this financialisation of the asset portfolio of farmers rests on the creation in 2008 of a private bank, by a famous and historic savings bank that had a monopoly over agricultural customers, the Credit Agricole. Since this date, this new private bank has been in charge of increasing the intake of funds from investors, namely from wealthy farmers. The chapter recounts how the private bank, and the growing number of specialised advisors it recruited since its creation, participate to change the investment practices of farmers and the geographical allocation of capital.

Q. Ravelli is also interested in the dissemination of financial products into domestic economies. His chapter concentrates on the mortgage loans boom in Spain during the 2000s. The spread of financial products concerns low-income working-class and immigrant communities and not wealthy farmers. However, like for the latter, the process implies savings banks' use of strategies to develop new markets for their loans and consequently the work of bank managers, in competition with each other, is to capture new clients. Here again, the intermediation role of these bank managers is at the core of everyday life financialisation.

A. Ducastel and W. Anseeuw develop a rather different case. The intermediaries they study, the fund managers, seek to convince institutional investment funds to invest in farmlands in South Africa. The challenge here is not to financialise these funds, as they are already financialised actors used to invest in traditional financial assets. The challenge is to frame farmlands as financial assets, which they are not by nature. The financialisation in this case goes through the translation of a mere

14 *Valérie Boussard*

commodity into an 'emerging asset class'. The expansion of financial markets arrives here not through the conversion of new consumers but through the conversion of trade commodities into financial investments. Financialisation of everyday life means, in this case, a change in day-to-day practices within the farms, in order to fit in the financial models used to account for and valuate earnings.

Whatever the polarity of the financialisation process underscored in the three chapters, they all insist on the key work of intermediaries to make the conversion to finance possible. This work is analysed through three dimensions.

The first one is merely demographic. In order to conquer market shares, banks or funds create specialised organisations and staff them with professionals. The conversion to finance rests on the emergence of new professionals specially dedicated to an intermediation role. The birth of the Credit Agricole private bank in France ushered in the creation of new services, at the branch level, at the regional level and at the sales network level. The bank recruited asset management specialists to be appointed as financial advisors in relation to customers and trained its own financial advisors to offer a broad spectrum of financial products to customers. In Spain, as Ravelli shows, the liberalization of banking practices paved the way for Spanish savings banks to be involved in commercial practices: new savings banks' local offices opened at a high rate every year. Subsequently thousands of new bank managers were hired to be in charge of the development of new markets in their respective area. As regards to the 'assetisation' of South African farmlands, it runs parallel to the development of South African asset management companies which created specialised organisations (funds) to design farmlands as "alternative assets". For this purpose, they hired individuals with classic financial backgrounds and also agronomists and consultants.

The relationship frame in which the recruited professionals work is the second dimension that can explain the way financial logics could disseminate so easily. As mentioned above, these professionals are recruited outside the new organisation or are former employees trained to fulfil new professional positions. But in each case, they are highly embedded in social and professional networks (Granovetter, 1974; Uzzi, 1997), which both facilitates and frames their work. The Credit Agricole financial advisors can rest on the monopoly of the bank over rural populations and on its long-lasting financing relationships with farmers. Bank managers have inherited, from Spanish savings banks of the past, a historic paternalistic relationship with customers that help them to have social influence. The managers of the farmlands funds in South Africa have a deep network in the financial industry and in the South African agricultural sector. As Ducastel and Anseew say, they occupy an embedded position between 'the bush' and the 'boardroom'.

However, this relationship setting has a second face, which is certainly the most enlightening for the understanding of the financialisation process. Indeed, all these professionals are working in tight competition with each other. For example, in Spain, local banks' offices are transformed into centres of profit; they are in competition with each other regarding their capacity to increase all indicators that are monitored. The same goes for managers and employees who, while feeling they have been dropped in a "small and aggressive private firm", comply with the demands by finding new customers in the immigrant populations. In South Africa, fund managers have to convince their clients that farmlands can "unlock financial value" in the same conditions as other financial assets. To do so, they use specific metrics (discounted cash flow) that allow standardised benchmarks with other financial assets and make possible comparisons and evaluations. This competing frame based on financial metrics lead afterwards to new constraints for farms and namely to changes in their agricultural production model.

Finally, a third dimension of the professional work performed by intermediaries sheds light on their specific role in the process of conversion in itself. Regarding the conversion of farmers or immigrant workers, the process supposes mainly an ideological conversion. Spanish bank managers taught to their clients some simple messages akin to 'law of the markets' that gave the clients a kind of false financial literacy. For example, they told popular classes that "home prices never go down", which pushed them to sign for mortgage loans, a very risky decision as events proved. In France, financial advisors teach their wealthy farmer customers how to optimise financial wealth and tax-exemptions during special social events hosted in luxury hotels. The financial knowledge passed on to the farmers is in this case accompanied by socialisation to a *bourgeois* ethos intended to change farmers' economic behaviour. Regarding the conversion of farmland into financial assets and parallel, the conversion of investment funds to agricultural assets, the process rests on a more cognitive operation. Fund managers seek to translate agricultural production into financial models and language understandable by financiers. Therefore they use instruments, metrics and methods shared by the financial sector. But by doing so (Muniesa, 2012) they change the very nature of the farms.

Be they Spanish bank managers, fund managers in South Africa or French rural bankers, all these intermediaries participate, by their own professional practices, in changing their clients' financial practices and therefore in changing capital allocation. Almost paradoxically, the micro level of observation focused on the intermediaries work grants access to a wide comprehension of the financialisation.

Part III: Crossing boundaries: individual careers as vehicles for financialisation

Another way to analyse the spread of financial logic beyond its original boundaries is not to analyse the changing of logic itself through a conversion effect, but through the movement of the individuals themselves. This is what the three chapters collected in this part deal with. Indeed, what they have in common is closely watching the careers of individuals whose work is concerned with finance and analysing their movements from any other occupation towards an occupation in finance or from any other sector towards the financial sector, and vice versa. In all three cases, the chapters examine how individuals cross the borders of the social worlds of finance, in one direction or the other. They detail the consequences of such passages, which can be viewed as another type of boundary work.

P. François and C. Lemercier (Chapter 8) are interested in the evolution from the 1950s to the present of the ruling elite of the 120 largest publicly listed French

16 *Valérie Boussard*

firms with CEOs on one side and members of the boards on the other. The variables they use in order to characterise these individuals come from three separate cohorts (1956, 1979 and 2009). In particular, they study the role of finance within their careers. Then, they analyse the role of moving to the financial sector and financial functions in the successive composition of the ruling elite.

V. Boussard and S. Paye (Chapter 9) follow a similar reasoning, with a different kind of ruling elite, analysing the careers of graduates since the 1980s from one of the French elite higher education institutions, a Parisian business school named HEC. This equivalent of an international business school trains future Senior Executives and Directors of the French economy. The chapter assesses the role of finance in these careers and in particular the role played by passing through the financial sector in order to access management positions, comparing three cohorts (1985, 1995, 2005).

Finally, A. Machut (Chapter 10) focuses on the careers of financial journalists. This chapter aims to understand the links that the world of journalism has with the world of finance, from the occupational trajectories of financial journalists. These individuals in particular may work in financial journalism, after having held positions in finance, or conversely join the financial sector after having worked as journalists.

These three chapters show that a past experience in finance is a crucial step for accessing executive positions in large corporate boards or in financial journalism. However, counter-intuitively, they do not show any major changes. In other words, the financialisation of the 1990s did not render financial careers more important or necessary. In this perspective, the movements from finance to financial journalism offer an interesting case. According to Machut, they are not increasing in a linear fashion depending on the progress of financialisation. Instead, they follow the economic risks of the financial sector. During a period of crisis, the financial sector does not offer the expected amount of jobs for graduates in the financial sector, and they must therefore find alternative employment in financial journalism. Conversely, during a crisis in the journalism sector, financial journalists must find work in the communication sector or the financial sector. Regarding the economic elites, the other two chapters show that, from the perspective of their switch to the financial sector, the composition remained almost unchanged. François and Lemercier show that the financial sector was already very well represented by the careers of leaders of the *SBF* (French stock market index) 120 companies before the 1990s. The characteristics of these leaders, from an academic point of view and from the view of passing through the financial sector, are fairly stable over time. Boussard and Paye emphasise that the part of financial functions in the careers of graduates of the HEC is also stable over time. They also highlight that a passage through finance was already established as a springboard for accessing management positions for graduates of the 1980s. However, what has changed is the type of financial functions involved. On returning to them in detail, they show that the financial functions related to financial markets and the commodification of companies, that is to say those concerned with the model of shareholder value, took dominance over financial functions related to the financial management of companies (corporate finance). Similarly, François and Lemercier show that

Introduction 17

the passage of elites through financial functions affected by the model of shareholder value is rising sharply: passages through financial departments (CFO), the Ministry of Finance and precisely its Treasury Department and finally passages through merchant banks such as Lazard and Rothschild.

Finally, following seminal work Fligstein (2001) these chapters underline that finance should be specified rather than homogenised in order to understand financialisation and its historical shifts. François and Lemercier point out that the current French financialisation was preceded by a first financialisation, to the extent that financial institutions were already existing in previous years. This work focuses on the careers and then leads to a better understanding of how finance has transformed itself and made this transformation the main feature of financialisation. In her introduction to this part, Sabine Montagne highlights that financialisation does not rest on a quantitative expansion of financial staff and a separation of their activities from non-financial activities. Financialisation should rather be seen as the financialisation of financial agents themselves.

François and Lemercier thus encourage a better characterisation of what distinguishes the first financialisation and the second financialisation, particularly from the perspective of the ways of doing business shared by the top managers. The question then becomes one of understanding the process by which old-fashioned financiers are converted to the form of finance of which they are now a part.

This part aims to develop a better understanding of what financiers have in mind when they occupy an executive position. Indeed, the kind of rationale they adopt, stemming from their past financial experience, could explain financialisation as the dissemination of financial logic outside its primary 'iron cage' (DiMaggio and Powell, 1983).

Through the analysis of these movements from one professional world to the other, the chapters uncover the role of financiers as agents of financialisation. They become vehicles for dissemination of the specific logic of the financial worlds with which they became acquainted. Placed at the highest corporate level, concentrating powers, they are indeed able to act directly on the turn to new governance models. Machut's chapter on financial journalists illuminates this point a little differently. The financialisation's agents are not necessarily former financiers, transforming the financial press from inside. They can also, and this is most striking, as former financial journalists, take communications jobs in the financial sector. They fuel financialisation thanks to their skills in producing news content and story-telling. So, if financialisation is driven by financiers, who access powerful positions within corporations, it can also be strengthened by non-financial actors who bring their skills to the financial sector, increasing the dissemination of financial logic.

Part IV: Internal boundaries: diversity, segmentation, stratification within financial occupations

The final part elaborates the hypothesis of differentiations within finance presented in the first part. Subsequently, it analyses the boundary work from the internal boundaries of two financial sectors, which apparently sound homogeneous: asset

18 *Valérie Boussard*

management and leveraged buyout acquisitions. S. Mignot-Gérard, C. Perrin-Joly, F. Sarfati and N. Vezinat (Chapter 11) investigate individual characteristics and social trajectories of French master's degrees graduates trained in asset management. They focus on graduates of both programs (Portfolio Management on one hand and Wealth Management on the other) from a university between 2008 and 2011. C. Herlin-Giret (Chapter 12) also analyses asset management, but from the way the segmentation of the occupation occurred since the 1980s in France. She looks in particular at the emergence of a particular segment, that of wealth management. F. Foureault (Chapter 13) analyses the leveraged buyout sector, a special category of corporate acquisition, by reconstituting the field of organisations involved in France from 2001 to 2007: target companies, private equity firms and banks.

With very different methods and focus, these three chapters emphasise the fragmentation and segmentation of these occupations, underpinning hidden variables that play a role in producing divisions and oppositions: symbolic and status hierarchy; size and capitalisation of the employer; and gender, race and social background of employees. As Olivier Godechot reminds us in his introduction to this part, the study of finance reveals classical forms of discrimination, of intersectionalism, of embeddedness and of domination within the financial field. Thus the sociology of finance is a general sociology aiming at underlying categorisations and resources at play in the production of divisions and inequalities.

By going in depth into the internal differentiations of these financial sectors, these chapters emphasise that finance is not only a thing of elites. While these occupations employ elites produced by French educational institutions, they also engage individuals with less prestigious degrees. Moreover, while many previous chapters examined finance from the top, by looking at the top executive managers or bankers, these chapters focus on lower levels in the hierarchy of jobs. The chapters present financial advisors employed by family offices or retail banks to advise more or less wealthy clients (Mignot-Gérard *et al.*; Herlin-Giret). Alongside Parisian merchant bankers working with US private equity funds on international operations, provincial branch managers of savings banks are working with small-scale funds on the acquisitions of local small and medium-sized enterprises (Foureault). These chapters show, like Chapter 5 about financial advisors of Agricultural Credit (Laferté) and Chapter 6 about Spanish bank managers (Ravelli), that all the actors of financialisation do not belong to the elites. Finance here is presented as an activity deeply embodied in a series of workers distributed on a long chain of division of labour.

Most financiers presented in these chapters are certainly neither rentiers nor top-executives. They are not only from the higher social classes. As Mignot-Gérard *et al.* show, IAE graduates are rather from the middle and working class. They are not all white men. Mignot-Gérard *et al.* emphasise the presence of women and non-Caucasians among the graduates they analysed. They also note that the disadvantage of gender and race in the financial sector differs according to each occupation. Being a woman is less of a disadvantage in wealth management than in portfolio management, which has a male culture. Being native of North Africa restricts opportunities in customer relationship aspects of wealth management much more than in dematerialised and globalised market-side activities of portfolio management.

The intense differentiations in each occupation or sector also highlight an important process of segmentation. Foureault remarks that the LBO field is structured around two moieties, i.e. two rival but complementary groups. One moiety gathers large and international organisations representing a 'large-scale' or 'Atlantic' capitalism, while the other moiety gathers small and local organisations representing a 'small-scale' or continental capitalism. The former claims to defend the true model of LBO, those inspired by a 'serial entrepreneur' model associated with contemporary America, valuing risks and the seizing of opportunities. The latter claims, on the contrary, the value of a 'patient capital' model, prizing the corporation and relationships of proximity. Together, these two moieties cover the whole French market of LBO and, collectively, they promote their profession. Mignot-Gérard *et al.* depict other forms of segmentation within asset management: on one hand, an opposition between sales and consulting activities, the former being related to jobs in retail banks, the latter to jobs in private banks; on the other hand, an opposition between back or middle offices and front or trading offices. In both cases, the segmentation is widely perceived by graduates and employees; consulting is the noble pole of this segmentation, while other activities and positions are rather associated with the dirty work (Hughes, 1971) that needs to be avoided. Herlin-Giret even goes into detail regarding the segmentation of consulting in wealth management. She shows that a specific professional rhetoric excludes financial advisors who have too much of a technical and computational approach to the customer relationship. Technical tasks are opposed to interpersonal tasks, the latter being prized while the former become devalued. Thus the internal differentiations reveal symbolic boundaries that separate, but also organise, the different tasks into a hierarchy (Bucher and Strauss, 1961; Hughes, 1971).

But what these texts uncover is that this segmentation and moral hierarchy of work (Hughes, 1971) is coupled with stratification. Indeed, the social characteristics of workers depend of the segment in which they operate, thus revealing a stratification that follows the classic social stratification. Even if women are present, this does not prevent the top of the moral hierarchy created by the profession being held by men (Herlin-Giret; Mignot-Gérard *et al.*). Similarly, it is the possession of economic and cultural capital that ultimately grants a few candidates access to the most prestigious segments of each profession (Mignot-Gérard *et al.*). There is also a strong social homology between clients and wealth management advisors: the wealthiest clients are advised by individuals belonging to the privileged classes, endowed with the cultural capital of the highest bourgeoisie and thus able to have command on relationships of proximity/complicity with their wealthy clients. In the case of the LBO field, one can notice that the characteristics of individuals associated with the two moieties refer to a social stratification based on the ranking of degrees in the French educational system.

This stratification of financial occupations does not prevent individuals seeking to achieve a better position. Financial occupations are also the place for

20   *Valérie Boussard*

social mobility. The aspiration to achieve an ascending career in finance in this case can also be considered as one of the engines of financialisation: professional ascent being achieved by compliance with legitimate financial logic in each segment, it contributes to reinforce this financial logic within its boundaries or outside of them.

IV Conclusion: financialisation as the boundary dynamics of finance

All chapters show that the financial work is carried out within boundaries created by a specific financial logic. But they also highlight that the financial work assists in creating these boundaries, even by competition between various financial logics. The financial work also assists in strengthening these boundaries in order to avoid the influences of external logics. Another part of the financial work encompasses the moving or crossing of these boundaries, in order to influence external worlds. Financiers' work is therefore a boundary work. As analysed by T. Gieryn (1983), the boundary work is a resource for a profession or an occupation to protect its autonomy over professional activities, to monopolise professional authority and exclude rivals from the inside, and finally to expand into domains claimed by rivals. In a similar vein, A. Abbott (1988) explains that professions struggle to hold a jurisdiction, therefore establishing, maintaining and expanding boundaries of their domain. A. Abbott (1995) also stresses that an entity, like a profession, is the result of a work, that of assembling various differences 'into a set of boundaries in the topologically strict sense, boundaries that define an inside and an outside' (p. 872). This finding insists on the emerging nature of boundaries. Rather than pre-existing the creation of the entity, boundaries are entailed in the creation of the entity. Moreover, once created, an entity has to rationalise the connection of the differences so that it can endure and persist. The demarcation work is an endless process, as new previously unnoticed differences can be connected together and merged in a new boundary claim. Subsequently, boundaries, viewed as institutionalised social differences (Lamont and Molnar, 2002), are vulnerable and subject to a double work: on one hand, a work associated with the activation, maintenance and transposition of the boundaries, on the other hand, a work associated to the dispute, bridging, crossing and dissolution of boundaries. These two faces of the same coin highlight the very dynamics of social boundaries. Regarding professions or occupations, this boundary dynamics is deeply rooted in professional disputes over the monopolisation of the domain of activities.

As presented in the different chapters, financialisation can be considered as the outcome of such boundary work where internal professional disputes inside the financial sector shape boundaries within which financial logics can thrive. At the same time, these boundaries are challenged, both by inner and outer rivals. At collective or individual levels, they are then maintained, protected and much more, expanded and displaced. Doing this, financial logics spread out of their initial realm and gain new jurisdictions.

The boundary work performed by financiers results in a conversion to financial logics. It can be either a cognitive or ideological conversion of non-financial actors, the conversion of non-financial items into financial assets or a forced conversion by games of influence and power relations. The juxtaposition of these conversions into a new set of financial logics seems to produce the shift in capital allocation that has been observed in recent years. However, these conversions do not appear to be orchestrated or directed, and do not all go in the same direction since financial logics are diverse and variable. This does not prevent their accumulation to produce a coherent direction that gives its specificity to contemporary financialisation. The resulting logic that is disseminated through the boundary work of financiers is indeed more financialised than financial (Chiapello, 2015), as capital allocation is evaluated from the point of view of the investor, in a short-term rationale, favouring the liquidity of the capital. As discussed below, the result of this accumulation is certainly to be found in the balance of power within the diverse financial worlds.

The peculiarity of this boundary work is that it is achieved by an array of individuals, from the highest to the lowest levels in the financial hierarchy. It is not only achieved by elites who, from above, control the dissemination of financial logics. It is also distributed and located at all levels and on all scales of the economic world. Financiers are far from being all rentiers. Some of them have more than privileged remunerations and they occupy powerful positions that give them the opportunity to expand their sphere of action, and subsequently those of financial logics. But, it is also perhaps all the daily actions repeated by many of the workers at low and mid-level positions that help to push the boundaries of finance.

The financial logic they promote and extend through their daily work is not an overlooking phenomenon that is completely abstract, anonymous, disembodied and endogenous to financial capitalism itself. Conversely, the financial logics are generated within financial and professional worlds and they reflect the internal dynamics of these worlds. They often are multiple within the same world, and sometimes in opposition. The prevailing logic is then the result of the balance of power and influence between the different actors and segments interacting within the financial world. Rather than being the outcome of a global finance, contemporary financialisation is a process where different financial worlds meddle with each other, some of them dominating and excluding the others. Here we find the idea that the (financial) market is the product of the confrontation between different views (Godechot, 2016). In this sense, the ideological and practical domination of the logic of the shareholder value can also be analysed as the result of professional disputes over a jurisdiction (Abbott, 1988). The shareholder value can be viewed as the professional knowledge and norm shared by powerful financial actors within the professional networks they control. And conversely, it is a way for them to become powerful in a social world where shareholder value has become a legitimate way of defining and solving corporate problems.

By focusing on finance workers, this book has, in some way, put in the shade the central role of the state in financialisation (Godechot, 2016; Krippner, 2012; van der Zwan, 2014). However, that is not to consider financialisation as an endogenous logic to the business world. The chapter of E. Lazega *et al.*, that of Q. Ravelli or that of P. François and C. Lemercier insist strongly on the intervention of the state or state actors in financialisation. The book argues for investigating the role of the state from the work of its agents. This is the direction proposed by the chapter of Lazega who focuses on the work of lay judges and the interest of the state in maintaining a joint regulation of consular justice. It is also the direction offered in the chapter by François and Lemercier from cross-careers between public and private sectors. In this perspective, boundaries between state and finance are blurred, and the two worlds are more intertwined than they appear (Huault and Richard, 2012; Boussard, 2016).

If all finance workers are vehicles for spreading financial logics, it is because they meet the norms of the professional worlds they inhabit. They got accustomed to them. They give worth to the moral hierarchies produced by these professional norms and aspire to careers that will be for them a sign that they are recognised as true professionals. They also aspire to master the techniques and the devices of their profession and make this mastery a sign of their expertise. In doing so, they produce, reproduce and disseminate the financial logic contained in the norms they respect and the technical devices they use.

Looming behind the existence of these different professions is in fact a labour market. This market is structured according to specialisations, qualifications, graduates, employers, locations, remuneration, careers, etc. Alongside being a market of financial products, finance is itself a labour market. Subsequently, to understand financialisation is then to also look at the institutions (Fligstein, 2001; François, 2008) that produce this financial labour market (schools, universities, employers, recruiters, state, etc.) and how they fuel its professional dynamics. This book appeals for in-depth studies of financial work and labour as a heuristic way to better understand the boundary dynamics of finance and therefore, financialisation.

PART I

The boundaries of finance

Exclusionary process, social closure and inner regulation

Introduction

Interrogating financialisation as an analytic

Karen Ho

Just as "globalisation" and "neoliberalism" were understood to be the "defining dynamics" of late global capitalism and thus became key conceptual rubrics through which many critical scholars approached the massive shifts in the global social economy at the end of twentieth century; in the contemporary moment, the concept of "financialisation" has taken on this role of symbolising and describing the socio-economic processes of a crisis-prone, unprecedentedly unequal capitalism that privileges short-term finance (Christopher, 2015). As with any sweeping representation, some scholars rightly wonder whether or not financialisation is used too universally just as "neoliberalism" was in the previous decades. For example, in "The Uses of Neoliberalism," anthropologist James Ferguson critiques academic discourses of neoliberalism for using it as a broad umbrella term to index the totality of shifts occurring in multiple social domains due to decontextualized "market forces." By universalising and decontextualizing neoliberalism, it was utilised to refer to everything and thus nothing at all. To what extent is financialisation suffering a similar analytical problematic? If scholars point to the increasing influence of financial practices, ideologies, models, and channels of accumulation in order to call attention to rising inequality and the dismantling of the multiple institutional and social safety net, to what extent do we overly imbue financialisation with too much explanatory power? Certainly, the "black box" of finance leads to such multi-pronged attribution, and engenders the question of whether or not financialisation has become too much of a meta-narrative to be a useful analytic given all that is claimed in its name. Moreover, it is important to acknowledge the perennial question of whether or not financialisation indexes and claims something really *new* about the contours and crises of capitalism.

The deeply ethnographic, contextual, and archival work of this part directly addresses these concerns in the financialisation literature through grounded work documenting and analysing the particularities through which finance constructs and cajoles influence in other sectors of the social economy. In other words, by painstakingly tracing how specific financial actors and institutions are attempting to extend their reach, their expertise, and their ways of knowing, these chapters do not simply presume linear and increasing financial capture.

26   *Karen Ho*

Rather, they demonstrate and render specific the struggles, hard work, and translations through which particular gains are made (or not). In particular, this collection of chapters shows that it is precisely through what might be termed *boundary work* that finance attempts to promulgate its spheres of influence.

As Fredrik Barth (1969) has long argued with regard to the social construction of ethnicity, boundaries index the presence and politics of group-making that are not "natural" but rather reflect cultural decisions about who or what is included in particular social domains. Similarly, in the context of the growing power of financial actors, boundaries are often understood and interpreted as either barriers or protection, depending on one's socio-economic position and cultural values in an uneven terrain of power. Analysing, then, the production, policing, erosion, and/ or breaking down of boundaries becomes a key avenue for exploring the strategies and directionality of financial actors and institutions.

For instance, Valérie Boussard and Marie-Anne Dujarier's deeply ethnographic chapter, "Let's make the company a bunch of figures: professional representations in mergers and acquisitions firms," makes the crucial observation that in order to commodify a firm – a complex social institution with multiple claims upon it – and turn it into a "bunch of figures" and "a bundle of assets," the construction of a particular boundary is necessary. Specifically, financial actors in the mergers and acquisitions (M&A) sector, in helping to affect the representation and treatment of companies as commodities, turns the liquidation of companies for purposes of short-term shareholder value *into* a game, into an exciting and pleasurable transaction that is interpreted as personal professional success. In a significant cultural twist, financial professionals understand the costs of corporate mergers and restructurings *not* as worker dislocation or unemployment but as *costs to themselves* professionally if the deal does not get done. In other words, turning companies into commodities gets internally embodied as inter-professional reputational stakes between M&A professionals, not as a larger socio-economic decision generating massive inequality. The boundary between finance and the societal costs of corporate liquidations is not premised on actual distance (as in disconnection), but rather is deliberately produced wherein the larger social costs get transformed, reduced, and reinterpreted as professional costs *if* the liquidation does *not* occur. It is, then, a fundamental misreading of financialisation to say that finance is abstracted and disconnected from the growing precarity of most workers; the precarity is actively produced yet is viewed from financiers' standpoints as professional identity, commitment, and competition.

In a related but also divergent approach to boundaries, Emmanuel Lazega, Sylvan Lemaire, and Lise Mounier, in their chapter "Financial logic and Bankers' institutional entreprenuership: the politics of the 'zombies' debate in bankruptcy proceedings at the Commercial Court of Paris (2000–2005)," demonstrate how dominant finance seeks to actively *blur* boundaries between socio-economic and political domains. In other words, judges in commercial courts who were trained and embedded within the banking industry (in stark contradistinction to judges socialised in other sectors and industries) not only ruled in favor of financial interests, but also shared similar values, ideologies, and approaches to corporate goals and purpose, which was to liquidate and restructure institutions in favour of creditors and investors, not employees. As such, in order to "extend financial logics and pragmatism beyond the boundaries of the financial sector," it is crucial to train various financial actors (who often move beyond banking to other industries such as law) in this specific methodology so that their *epistemic and institutional capture* of other arenas is framed as common-sense and good advice. I would also argue that financial actors are imbued with a sense that boundary transgressions between different socio-economic domains are a positive socio-economic good precisely because not only are markets deemed "smart" and "in the know," but also that market ideologies and practices belong in multiple realms.

It is interesting to note the double standard: when it comes to categories of people, with specific ideas about corporate governance, their crossing "into" finance is more heavily policed, and yet when financial ideas transgress multiple social domains, that boundary crossing is presumed to be proper "regulation" of the normal order of things. For example, also addressing issues of boundary-making, Natascha van der Zwan's wonderfully historical chapter "Buying it: financialisation through socialisation" shows that *financial subjectivities* are constructed as exclusive, and as cohering specifically to elite, upper-middle class (male and white) subjects, who also uphold particular financial values and approaches to investments and corporate governance. The very case of a blue-collar, unionized site (that believes in corporations as social institutions where labor has a central voice) attempting to amass a multi-million LBO (leveraged buyout) investment fund with advice and support from Wall Street investment banks created a boundary transgression precisely because of the exclusivity – in both social positioning as well as ideology – of financial subjectivities. The fact that this exclusive boundary was actively utilised to discipline the values undergirding the labor-led LBO fund (the Employee Partnership Fund) to create "mimetic isomorphism" such that an "alignment of interest between fund organizers and fund investors" that favor finance was produced, demonstrates a strategy of dominant finance. In other words, the high-status and exclusive boundary of finance was actively mobilised not only to access and lay claim to billions of new investment dollars from union pension funds, but also to socialise and culturally train these multiply positioned investor sensibilities and monies for the purposes of Wall Street priorities and experiments in financial corporate governance.

Of course, as Taylor Spears demonstrates in "Matching the market: calibration and the working practices of quants," exclusive boundaries are not simply the preserve of cross-class transgressions. In fact, the jockeying for position across Wall Street departments, between the front and middle offices, between traders, quants, risk managers, and auditors, helps to also produce, enact, and maintain internal hierarchies within banking departments. Specifically, the construction of a structure of "puppet" regulation (not to mention "thankless jobs") where those emplaced in a lower rung of the hierarchy are charged with "regulating" and "governing" those whose subjectivities and practices are not only valued by the larger firm, but upon whose interests the firm underwrites – creates an organisation where "boundaries" that are designed are deliberately meant to be circumvented. As such, unequal subjectivities and status, when combined with differently valued knowledge practices and frames, strongly construct what counts as finance, and who can make financialisation happen.

1 Let's make the company a bunch of figures

Professional representations in mergers and acquisitions firms

Valérie Boussard and Marie-Anne Dujarier

Following N. Fligstein and other academics anchored in New Economic Sociology allows the presentation of financialisation as "the ascendancy of shareholder value as a mode of corporate governance" (Krippner, 2012, p. 25). This ascendancy means that economic actors have changed the forms of analysis they use to find solutions to the current problems of organisations. The new forms intend to defend owners' interests against managers' interests and to develop strategies to increase the value difference between stock prices and equity, rather than the high rate of return on investments (Fligstein, 1990). This shift in corporate control conceptions reveals a transformation in market institutions i.e. in the cultural and normative construction of markets (Fligstein, 2001). As many scholars underline, it also sheds light on emerging finance-oriented actors, who support, promote, and disseminate these new norms (Fligstein and Brantley, 1992; Davis, 2005; Davis and Greve, 1997; Davis and Useem, 2002; Zorn, 2004).

The latter perspective paves the road for an analysis of these financial norms through an investigation of the way these new actors envision the core of their work and role. Scholarly works on traders (Godechot, 2001; Hassoun, 2005; Knorr-Cetina, 2005; Mac Kenzie and Millo, 2003; Muniesa, 2005), hedge fund investors (Montagne, 2006), stock market analysts (Sauviat, 2003; Montagne, 2009), investment bankers (Ho, 2009) and, investors (Useem, 1996; Zorn et al., 2005) have largely contributed to describe financial norms and logics from the inside. This chapter aims to participate in this description by investigating other financial actors involved in financialisation: advisors in mergers and acquisitions (M&A) who have taken on a growing part in corporate governance. If the number and volume of M&A has dramatically risen over the past 20 years, it has been linked with the development of new specialised occupations that undertake these transactions: investment bankers, auditors, financial counsellors, investing managers, etc. These occupations largely endorse and promote the shareholder value conception of control. Indeed, contemporary M&A are grounded upon a conception of the firm as a bundle of assets which are most of the time subsidiary companies. Each firm or each company is considered "as a stream of cashflows to be shuffled and reshuffled in whatever configuration would produce the highest return" (Krippner, 2012, p. 8). Firms are then seen as a set of companies that can be independently sold or bought.

30 *Valérie Boussard and Marie-Anne Dujarier*

The major hypothesis of this chapter is that the logics and norms these financial advisors share can be understood through an observation of their very daily work and of the multiple interactions in the workplace, replaced in the organizational and occupational context where work and careers take place. The chapter is therefore based on the results of a large qualitative investigation which was conducted between 2010 and 2013 in France (observations of work and 76 interviews with French M&A advisors; see box below).

The chapter concentrates on the professional representations of companies that financial advisors subscribe to in their work of buying and selling in French M&A firms. The term *professional representations* covers the set of images, frameworks, language, and meanings about the work to achieve, which is shared by a group of workers and which delineates its professional mandate. It demonstrates that the sector is dominated by the representation of companies as commodities. First, financial advisors describe companies as things to buy and sell in a competitive arena, depicted in a quantified and abstracted way; second, they do not reflect upon the consequences of such a categorisation, save upon their own professional stakes. This representation of companies leads then to the shaping of what is considered within this sector as "professionalism": it plays a major role in the process of recruitment, selection, and promotion of workers in this sector, which tends to homogenise the sector around the same norms.

To begin with, the first section presents the sector of M&A by focusing on the division of work and on the career process. The second section emphasises that the role advisors have to hold leads them to represent the company as a commodity, which means to figure it out in a quantitative and abstract manner. Rooted in this quantification and abstraction process, the commodification of companies is encouraged by professional norms which value trading in an agonistic context between advisors and firms as the true professional game and fosters distance and coldness towards consequences of such a game for companies. The third section develops this link between professional norms and the changing nature of companies from concrete economic units to commodities within a market.

Sources

These findings were obtained from a qualitative research program focused on "Careers in Finance," carried out in France between 2010 and 2013.

A total of 76 comprehensive interviews with the middlemen (51) and customers (25) of transactions were carried out in the financial district of Paris. These enabled mapping of the actors in this professional space, understanding how their tasks and actual activities are organised and tracking their professional trajectories. Participants were obtained through contacts of established contacts (snowball method), based on three different sources. The participant sample was composed of 70% males and was evenly split into age groups (less than 30 years old, 30–40 years old and older than 40 years old), which coincided with inner hierarchies (employees, managers, directors). The 76 people who took part were distributed across 48 different French and non-French firms of different sizes.

These interviews were supplemented by observations: 10 days in an audit firm specialised in transactions, alongside advisors going about their daily activities: internal meetings, meetings with their customers and the completion of reports on the computer. The continuing training given to these financial specialists, regarding the valuation of companies was also observed as well as major meetings and professional events (forums, exhibitions, awards ceremonies) over a 2 year period.

The empirical inquiry was completed by a documentary analysis of the content of financial management manuals and commercial brochures of financial services firms.

I The M&A services firms: division of work and career process

The liberalisation of financial markets, the loosening of fiscal policy, the massive privatisation of the public sector and, the transformation of the banking sector in parallel with the carving up of industrial monopolies, has led to a phenomenal growth in the buying and selling of companies since the 1980s (Batsch, 2002; Coriat, 2008; Lorrain, 2011; Ho, 2009). This growth is characterised by a new approach to company ownership which is based on the principle of shareholder value (Fligstein, 2005). In the esoteric language of finance, the term represents the "amount of value generated by a company" for "investors." Buying and selling companies is considered by investors as a way to create shareholder value. Investors can take advantage of leverage opportunities, especially leveraged buyouts (LBOs), to gain maximum return. They can also insist that a company improve its financial ratios in the time between the purchase and the resale so that the value of the company can be reassessed. The last 20 years have seen this practice mushroom out of all proportion and financial services firms specialised in M&A have developed and expanded.

The division of work amongst M&A advisors

M&A financial advisors are the people who broker transactions in the buying and selling of companies on behalf of investors. Most of the time they are employed by M&A services firms. These advisors form two complementary groups: the first put together the transaction by acting as "matchmakers" between the buyer and the seller, and can be found in investment banks and M&A shops; the second are the *analysts* who compile reports on a company and advise their clients/provide legal support in the event of litigation, and can be found in auditing firms and financial services firms. Investors purchasing the services of these advisors also consist of two groups: *corporate investors*, i.e. CEOs/CFOs acting on behalf of their shareholders (themselves included if they hold shares), and *investing managers* who buy, run, and resell companies using a pool of capital supplied by corporations, private investors, and banks (private equity funds).

The work involved in a transaction is subdivided; each set of advisors has its own roles and responsibilities. And yet despite these clear demarcation lines, the financial data they handle and the methods they use for valuating the company and the transaction are the same. They act as market intermediaries (Cochoy and Dubuisson, 2000; Bessy and Chauvin, 2013), as they contribute to set the purchase/sales price of a company and how the price should be set. Converting a multitude of characteristics into exact quantities, as in all trading scenarios, is a standard operation decided by the major players. By applying a standardised method of quantification, characteristics that are otherwise incomparable can then be compared (Desrosières, 2000; Bidet and Vatin, 2009). Financial advisors have gradually embraced a range of standardised data which has enabled them to assess the value of a company and to compare different companies. They use the same valuation methods: the patrimonial method, the multiples method, and the discounted cash flow analysis method. However, there is not one hard and fast rule for the choice of method or the preferred combination of methods. These choices are dependent on the issues during a transaction as they result in different values. As in other financial professions, there are different and conflicting valuation methods (Godechot, 2001; Zaloom, 2006; Lépinay, 2011; Ouroussof, 2010; Ortiz, 2014a). However, although the methods are incongruent regarding the final value that they calculate, they are based on the same elements needed to make the calculation. The common denominator between all three is that they are based on the same set of three indicators, upon which all of the intermediary analyses (due diligence reports) converge: EBITDA (earnings before interest, taxes, depreciation and amortisation), debt and cashflow. Each method then takes these indicators into account differently. Furthermore, every team of financial advisors can arrive at different values for each one of these variables, according to the interpretations and calculation of the intermediary variables which they are made up of. However, if these three methods allow different values to be obtained, all three of them are integrated in more general methodology, known as financial modelling, which is oriented towards the calculation and optimisation of the value of the operation, defined as value for the shareholder. This agreement on the need to create value for the shareholder overrides any conflict regarding how to calculate and produce this value.

Moreover, these firms share the same hierarchical organisation where young employees, gathered in teams, are managed by a more experienced employee in order to fulfil the mission sold (to a client) by one of the directors of the firm. Directors are responsible for the commercial side of the activity. Their days consist of meeting clients, service providers, and business introducers, and negotiating the final trade price of the company. They hire managers to supervise the work of younger staff and service providers. They must ensure that the documents and reports produced by staff comply with the terms of the deal, including the agreed deadlines. Staff, composed of young employees and managers (most of the time under 35 years old), have to produce a financial account of the company (to be bought, sold, merged or recapitalised) as it stands and as it may stand, thanks to financial valuation models. They use "Excel" software in order to manage figures production. Then, they fulfil their role by completing PowerPoint templates following a typical scenario designed to showcase the three main financial standardised indicators used by advisors and clients to assess selling or buying opportunities. They seek out bunches of business data which is then reorganised as part of a storytelling presentation, in specific reports (displaying and/or using these indicators to calculate the "value" ["due diligence report", "business plan", "managing presentations", "financial modelling", etc.]).

Promotion and recruitment: the career process

The M&A services firms recruit their staff from a pool of graduates produced by prestigious French schools (business or engineering) and elite universities. A distinguished degree is therefore the necessary passport to enter an M&A services firm but is not a guarantee of permanency.

Indeed, the explicit system of career progression excludes those who have not been promoted.

> Out of the five who began as analysts at the same time as me in Paris (in a prestigious bank), I was the only one left after three years. I had earned my credibility, I was considered as somebody that they wanted to keep.
>
> (Man, under 35, investment bank)

This process is known as the "up or out" policy and is at least an annual affair when directors agree on the list of those promoted. But the assessment process leading to this list is an extended one, operating in day-to-day activities. Employees are continuously gauged, ranged, and labelled. Every time an employee delivers a task, those observing it appreciate his skills, and behaviour (the "credibility" as told in the previous quotation). They assess his professionalism as shown during this weekly directors' meeting:

Director 1: Jérôme, is he on a job?
Director 2: Yes, we're currently at the end of an assignment.
Director 1: Can I take him off your hands?
Director 2: Yes, he is really good. He's worked at Leonardo [an investment bank].
Director 1: (to Director 3): And Amélie?
Director 3: Yes, you can rely on her. She is on an ESCP [prestigious French Business School] intern for a year.
　　　　　The remainder of the committee meeting is focused on the future promotions of junior employees to "manager" level.
Director 4: As for the managers, they really are our Achilles heel [makes a list of "managers"]. There may be some experienced juniors up for promotion, who do we have? Julien?
Director 3: Julien, yeah, he is good but there have been some mixed reports.

Employees who don't fit the criteria of the true professional are progressively pushed to resign and then quit the M&A sector to hold administrative or financial

34 *Valérie Boussard and Marie-Anne Dujarier*

positions, in industrial or services companies. Therefore, the key to staying in an M&A services firm is to meet the standard of professionalism. But this professionalism is far from only laying on technical skills. Three young advisors, who we invited to reflect upon what distinguishes their professional specificity together, explain that, above all, it is complying with the orders silently:

> You have the choice to say no to your boss [manager or director], but if you do, you're gone.
>
> (Man, under 35, investment bank)

As one director pointed out: "If you want to survive, you have to conform." The procedures that label, marginalise, and permanently exclude staff are a constant reminder to those who want to remain in the M&A services firms and join the elite that they must fit the profile of the "true" professional. Indeed, observations of activity highlight the gravity of standards relative to daily behaviour. In the rooms where staff work, language and attitudes are watched. The "managers" comment publicly on reactions and actions of the members of their teams. Gaps and drifts then become topics of conversations during coffee breaks or lunches, certain young advisors on these occasions become objects of recurring jokes which mark their stigmatisation as bad professionals.

The two following sections unpack the kind of professionalism used to select, promote, and exclude advisors. They show that this professionalism goes beyond technical skills and embraces a range of cognitive or relational attitudes which are commonly related to the representation of companies as commodities.

II The company: figures and abstraction

The work of financial advisors encompasses the presentation of routine information and the search for responses to a set of questions related to a particular project. The youngest employees all pass through this data handling stage; they dissect the figures so that they can quickly and efficiently provide the necessary data for the templates. They are almost exclusively involved in generating figures:

> You make Powerpoint presentations on companies. You map it out, go and find sales revenue figures on the Internet, look for information, format it, quickly and in a well presented way.
>
> (Man, under 35, investment bank)

Therefore, a "good" advisor is someone who is skilful at manipulating figures. The youngest members of staff have to become experts at reading, understanding, interpreting, copying, and matching figures.

> When the boss asks you to make a report, you have a huge amount of things to do and if you don't manage to prioritise, if you start to lose focus, or if you don't manage to submit the report, you are sidelined.
>
> (Man, under 35, former advisor for an investment bank)

A quantitative representation

Nevertheless, these skills, first and foremost a grasp of arithmetic, are not enough to make someone a true professional, as pointed out by this young advisor: "You have to give the impression that the work is incredibly technical, but it's not the technical side that matters." A good advisor is, principally, someone who shows interest, if not pleasure, in generating figures. Observations of the work underline that generating figures and completing templates are associated with an intellectual game, very close to puzzle games (Sudoku or a Rubik's cube). As can be frequently heard, they have to "hunt down" the figures and "make them match up" if they want to reach the desired outcome. Having to expertly manage copious, complex sets of data and resolve numerous problems in the minimum amount of time presents a challenge which is akin to that found in puzzle games.

> The figures need to be tortured into confession.
>
> (Man, Manager, investment bank)

These figures are used to define several financial ratios which are employed on a daily basis to calculate the three main indicators. The very act of calculating these ratios transforms solid economic and technical information (value of equipment, customer loyalty, expertise of personnel, etc.) into abstract financial data which is presumed to categorize a company during any professional exchanges.

This daily activity encourages a quantitative representation of the companies that advisors help to sell and buy. Both types of advisors—the directors and the employees—may be on different rungs of the ladder, but what they have in common is to only view companies in terms of figures related to the standardised financial variables. Here is how an advisor comments on a "due diligence" report:

> Afterwards we move onto the operating costs [one of the ratios necessary to the calculation of the EBITDA and Cashflow]. The management cost is implicit. It's how much if we want to make some cuts. That, it is truly the cost structure. It is particularly within this cost structure that synergies will be made [the term "synergy" refers to a mode of value calculation used in a financial modelling].
>
> (Man, Manager, Auditing firm)

Advisors argue that this quantitative representation is the way to know the company in detail, to appreciate its value and the worth of the transaction. This quantification is therefore not just any quantification: it corresponds to categories of financial accounting which are oriented towards highlighting the value generated for the shareholder by a transaction.

An abstract representation

Young advisors thus manage to transform a repetitive task under time constraint into a playful activity, in the style of the workers described by Donald Roy and

36 *Valérie Boussard and Marie-Anne Dujarier*

Mickael Burawoy (Dujarier, 2015). In their case, the game centred on mental agility in the manipulation of figures, which is supposed to put "offside" what these figures concretely represent. A part of this distanciation is rendered thanks to the confinement of the work. Indeed, the generation of figures is done in the office or in the "data room," the room where all the relevant documents for a deal are kept:

> You are confined in a windowless room for the whole day, in a team of two or three. It's not a pleasant job. You spend the weekends and nights in the data room. You speak only Excel file format. It's inhumane. But, it's good training: you learn how to interpret the figures.
>
> (Man, Chief Financial Operator, former advisor in an investment bank)

Most of the time, advisors write quantitative reports about companies they have never seen, save their accounting and managerial data gathered in other reports. The directors may know the shareholders, the heads of finance, and the CEOs, and they may have met the management team but only under exceptional circumstances do they show an interest in "the coal face" of the company: the machinery, the workforce, the products, the clients, the suppliers, waste management, etc.

> Yes, we do the tour with the CEO. It's a bit of a drag. You have to get up early, catch a train, stand for ages in the cold in places which are maybe dirty or noisy.
>
> (Women, Director, investment bank)

From the directors' points of view, a visit is more likely to represent one of the painful required elements of the commercial relationship rather than provide a profile of the company which could be used to gauge its worth. Thus, advisors, be they young employees or directors, build a quantitative and abstract picture of companies they help to buy or sell, matching with the financial categorisation at the core of the valuation process.

III The company: a commodity to trade

As explained above, seeing the firms as a set of figures, expressed through the financial category of the shareholder value, hence without taking into account its material aspect, is one of the ways to be considered as a good professional. Those who want to stay in the M&A sector and to climb the hierarchical ladder have to internalise this representation and to show it off. They have to be able to present company data in the form of financial indicators and to convert these indicators into an exchange value through an abstract point of view. The quantitative and abstract representation advisors use to figure out the companies largely supports a commodification process. Indeed, to show fervour for the transaction in itself, i.e. to see companies as opportunities for trading in a kind of gaming activity, is viewed as an excellent quality. Moreover, the commodification is continued by the inducement of professional norms to not reflect upon the concrete consequences of such a categorisation of the company. Indeed, the stakes of the commodification are only located in the results on the advisors' careers, which subsequently encourages it.

Transaction as an end in itself

Those who have been promoted also have in common an appreciation of companies in terms of the excitement they give them during the transaction process.

> What I really enjoy is working with the big operations. It's nice…glamorous. For example, the purchase of Sigram by Pernod-Ricard or when Orange purchased France Telecom. We are going to work on some massive takeover bids. The excitement, the effervescence of the deal is one of the main motivators in this profession.
>
> (Man, investing manager, private equity fund)

Directors describe their activity as very "exciting," "funny," "playful," "brilliant," and "fun." The process of transaction itself, implying several participants and complex operations, forms the interest of the work. Indeed, every mission places advisors in a competitive situation. Each of them wants to be on the side of the winner. From the seller's point of view, it is a question of managing to sell the company for the best price. From the buyer's point of view, it is a question of managing to conclude the purchase in the most favourable conditions.

Besides, these competitive games participate in the professional reputation of advisors. Awards ceremonies are held every year. They celebrate the best advisors, in terms of size, volume or complexity of transactions. "Trophies" are given to the prize-winners. These trophies are displayed in waiting rooms or offices of each of the M&A firms, as if they were sporting or hunting achievements. Investment banks which organise the transactions for the seller distribute object-memories, called "tombstones", to the advisors involved in the purchase. "Tombstones" are also placed in the offices or on the desks of advisors as signs of their prestige. What becomes a priority purpose for advisors is the competition to be part of the most outstanding transactions, those that allow them to gain an award or to appear on a "tombstone."

Though the youngest advisors are not personally involved in these competitive and agonistic relationships between directors and the firms they represent, they share the same excitement and sense of gaming as their elders. Staff are expected to work long hours and not to complain about it. On the contrary, the norm is to express pleasure and pride in overworking, especially when linked to the specific rhythm of the transaction process. The junior staff stated that their working week was 50 hours minimum, often 70 hours, and close to 100 hours in the large investment banks. They describe being always under pressure, alternating periods of intense work at the end of a transaction and periods of latency, which is a period of easing up, before the next transaction closing up. Of the workers interviewed, all extol the ambiguous virtue of a system which oscillates between pressure and an apparently exquisite sense of exhilaration. The pinnacle is the surge of momentum at the end of the transaction process when sleep is severely rationed. Subsequently, advisors do not question the number of hours they have to work or the commitment they have to show.

> Your workload is immense, you have to be flexible, smile and have a relatively high energy level.
>
> > (Man, under 30, investment bank)

This ability to demonstrate joy while accepting to overwork is related to the payroll system. Those who succeed in doing this are more likely to be well evaluated and thus associated with year-end bonuses. Competing relationships are not a mere issue about professional reputation. They entail a more materialistic face, linked with a compensation issue. This participates in the commodification process. Indeed, as do directors, staff tend to view companies as opportunities to play and enjoy in this gaming context of competitive relationships.

Do not mention what the figures refer to

According importance to transactions supposes control over the transaction process and puts the consequences of transactions for the company and its stakeholders at a distance. The division of work between the directors and the junior staff helps them to maintain the distances with the material, social, and human side of the figures. As a matter of fact, the youngest members can do the job being ignorant of the final outcome of a transaction and remaining relatively indifferent. By applying themselves to arithmetic tasks which are abstract, pressing, and fragmented, in a similar fashion to any worker whose activity has been rationalised, they can be absorbed in their activity without showing any interest or opinion towards the final result. The calculations/completion of the operation becomes an end in itself.

Moreover, a "good" advisor is one who accepts and succeeds in handling figures in an abstracted way, without feeling emotions for what they represent. The emotional traits of aloofness and coldness during meetings are preferred over a show of feelings, especially those which could be construed as feminine. Entrants to the profession therefore learn that it is not in their interest to be kind hearted: "There is no room for any softness" (a director). Competition is an accepted masculine trait, one of aggression and emotional indifference. The working observations, characterised at once by silence, muffled exchanges, and an avoidance of emotional outbursts, confirms that the suppression of strong emotions is the norm, favouring the emotional register of distance and coldness. The explicit ability to stay calm in negotiations under a verbal onslaught and to clearly pinpoint the objectives through a mass of technical detail is held in high esteem by peers, clients, and directors alike.

> The people who do not progress are those who cave under pressure or become paralysed.
>
> > (Man, under 35, former advisor in an investment bank)

Professional representations in M&A firms   39

This professional trait pushes them to achieve the maximum possible distance away from the sensitive, human, and material reality of the companies. Distancing also supposes a particular way of feeling and of evoking the consequences of its action. So, a "manager" explains:

> When you start to thrash out a cost reduction plan with a strategy consulting firm, you make all of these spreadsheets in these offices in Paris just to find out if you're gonna have to fire 50 guys. The consultant is paid a fortune and yet does not see the problem [that arises through the reduction of costs for the company workers].
>
> (Man, manager, auditing firm)

Here, referring to unemployment, redundancies, restructuring, and social costs is just not done. Hence, a "bad" worker is one who places people and objects above the worth of figures and transactions.

The norm thus is not to be moved by the concrete consequences of seeing a company as abstract figures in a model meant to produce value for the shareholder.

Deviation to the professional norm is being surprised or shocked by consequences of the transaction on the future of the company and its people. Those who failed to have an upward career comment discreetly on this implicit norm:

> We never stopped reducing the financial and fiscal risks, but there are also human risks as well. We would never highlight these social costs to our customers.
>
> (Man, former advisor in an investment bank, looking for a job at the time of the interview)

An agonistic professional context

It was clear from the interviews that those who had attained the highest ranks of the M&A services firms are those who endorsed the expected professional figure. Moreover, they are those who succeeded in embodying this figure. Most of them are laughingly pointing out that the arithmetic skills were nothing but a façade that had to be exploited. They feel that the job was "self-sophisticated," that "it sustained itself" and that "it led to the creation of bogus needs," but they do not make any value judgements in relation to these observations. They are simply following the rules of the professional game: trying to land the best transactions, being part of the best projects. For them, competing for transactions has become an end in itself, all the more important as it is linked to their reputation and career within a very small and elitist world.

> In 2007, the deals were becoming increasingly aggressive. The watchword of the bank was to be selective, but to sell loans. You had to stay in the market (remain in the league tables) … The banks have carried out a lot of structuring campaigns, employing aggressive youngsters, where deals had to be

40 *Valérie Boussard and Marie-Anne Dujarier*

> struck … Analysts were questioning themselves, when the real question was
> more : 'that young lad next door, will he not have a more aggressive offer?'
> (Man, manager, investment bank)

Indeed, directors move into narrow social circles, containing CEOs, politicians, bankers, people they consider to be smart and powerful.

> My work rate was crazy. However, it is always important to take an interest. The projects are always pleasant, you live and breathe current events. It is our bank that was making all the acquisitions and the public offerings, the majority of which were done by us. As such it felt like we were contributing to this evolution and to these strategies. So it's enjoyable.
> (Woman, director, investment bank)

Achieving a social presence is intertwined with the pleasure of being part of negotiations about transactions, epitomised in the words of one director: "Dealing and having fun!"

When they are questioned about supposedly "nightmarish" situations, directors refer to situations where they lose control over the transaction process: the impossibility to complete the work because of erroneous or unverifiable financial data, unreliable teams, clients/shareholders who refuse to listen to advice, competitors who hijack the deal, etc. In such situations, they risk losing their place in the professional moral hierarchy:

> The nightmare is finishing second. It's the worst possible scenario. You're on the verge of getting that pretty girl. And somebody else runs off with her [laughter].
> (Man, investing manager, private equity fund,
> former director of an investment bank)

From their point of view, the stakes of a transaction are high, not for the clients or the company, but for their own status and future. The most significant impact for the deal's "winners" and "losers" is on their respective careers. When directors reflect on the consequences of their work, it is in relation to their reputation and the consequences of it on their career. Therefore they do not think about the material, social, and human repercussions of their work on the companies that have been bought, sold or merged. They think about the impact that their analysis and advice may have on their own job. It is not only the transaction they are worried about losing, but their own professional standing.

> The biggest professional risk I face is giving bad advice.
> (Man, director, auditing firm)

Conclusion

The model of professionalism recognised by the French M&A sector pushes the selection and retention of employees who are the most committed to defend the

Professional representations in M&A firms 41

representation of companies as commodities. This representation is tuned to the shareholder value conception of control: making the companies exist as mere objects to be traded helps to create a market for the transaction of companies and subsequently to make firms' assets liquid. This assets liquidity is the main way to create value if value is attained by reconfiguring firms' assets in order to optimise cashflows.

M&A advisors play a major role in financialisation in France, more so because their representation is unchallenged inside the field in which they operate. Indeed, the M&A sector encourages advisors to have daily contact with other advisors or financiers involved in transactions. Their socialisation is largely shaped by colleagues who have attended the same business schools and who live in the same "classy neighbourhoods." The social and the professional become inseparable in the representation of work, making it almost impossible for such a representation to be challenged or scrutinised, and minimising the risk of professional dilemmas occurring. This phenomenon unquestionably explains the lack of challenge from within about the different professional norms and the very strong sentiment of homogeneity that thus emerges, which even goes beyond the differences of the actors' positions within the social structure of the sector (gender, age, education, reputation of the firm, remuneration, etc.).

According to this model, M&A advisors are not different from workers in any other profession. Most of the time they work with other professionals: peers, clients, and suppliers, who gravitate towards the hub of what Becker (1982) terms the same "social world." Within this world, the representations of the companies they buy/sell prove to be homogeneous and are therefore rarely questioned. With this shared professional representation, commodification of firms can flourish and the so desirable liquidity of assets can be reached.

This representation, and the financial conception of control it supports, can extend outside the M&A sector in itself. Most of the times clients of M&A advisors are previous M&A advisors. Many M&A advisors who don't pursue a career in the M&A sector leave to hold positions as chief financial operators in various firms and companies. Even those who have not been successful in embodying the complete M&A professional figure have memorised many professional traits and internalised professional criteria. Inside the world where they are now operating, they are flag bearers of the commodification of firms. They finally join the finance oriented-actors who disseminate the shareholder conception of control. One can wonder if the M&A sector in other countries, especially the most advanced ones in financialisation—such as USA or UK—has the same role in disseminating financial logics. The few interviews that have been conducted in New York and London tend to confirm these results, but they need to be completed with observations of daily work and a more systematic description of the careers system in American and English financial services.

2 Matching the market

Calibration and the working practices of quants

Taylor Spears

In February 2011, a number of sociology bloggers noticed something peculiar in the financial statements of the American Sociological Association (ASA), the non-profit association for sociologists in the United States (Healy, 2011). The ASA had apparently entered into a type of interest rate derivative[1] known as an interest rate swap 3 years earlier in February 2008, just before the onset of the financial crisis. The 30-year swap had, according to the Association's financial statements, caused a financial loss of $1,891,706 in the first year of its life, a gain of $1,194,467 during its second year, and a loss of $288,072 in its third year. The fact that the ASA had purchased an interest-rate swap caused a minor controversy on a number of sociology blogs, with some wondering whether the derivative represented an investment attempt gone awry.

The truth turns out to be far less scandalous, but is also much more illuminating as a microcosm of contemporary financialisation. In the last several decades, the markets for interest rate derivatives have become an important but often overlooked conduit for the financialisation of the broader economy and civil society (Eaton *et al.*, 2013). Interest rate swaps, futures, and options are now purchased as a matter of course by non-financial corporations, municipalities, universities, and other non-profit organisations to hedge their exposure to changes in market interest rates. Indeed, this seems to have been the case with the ASA: according to its financial statements, the Association issued approximately $8 million in municipal general revenue bonds in order to finance the construction of a new office building. Because the interest paid on those municipal bonds is not fixed but instead fluctuates with market interest rates, the ASA made the choice – an arguably prudent one – to hedge (i.e. eliminate) those floating rate exposures by entering into a fixed/floating interest rate swap. In doing so, the ASA was able to effectively transform its variable rate debt into the equivalent of a fixed-rate mortgage.

In tandem with the growth of the derivatives markets, there has also been a gradual shift among global accounting authorities towards the greater use of fair value measurements in lieu of older 'historical-cost' accounting practices (cf. Perry and Nolke, 2006; Power, 2010). Fair value accounting standards require organisations – such as the ASA – to report the value of their assets and liabilities at the amounts the organisation would receive if it were to sell its assets, or pay to transfer its liabilities to another market participant. Calculating the fair value of a derivative such as the ASA's swap requires the use of complex mathematical models that take into account the level and volatility of interest rates, as well as the credit worthiness of the two parties to the swap. Thus by entering into its swap, the ASA must conform to a particular set of calculative practices that have practical effects on both its financial position and its relationship to the broader financial markets. Indeed, changes in these model-produced fair value estimates became the rather large losses that the ASA was required to report on its balance sheet from 2008 until 2011.

While some large corporations and banks possess their own models for making such a calculation, many organisations – including the ASA, according to its financial statements – rely on fair value estimates produced by proprietary models of a relatively small number of derivative 'dealers': banks[2] that are responsible for 'making markets' in these instruments.[3] These dealers stand ready to enter into interest rate derivatives with other market participants, and then 'hedge' (i.e. reduce or eliminate) most of the resulting risks by trading with other dealer banks. Within these dealers, the mathematical models used to make fair value calculations are built and maintained by a community of primarily PhD-trained mathematicians, physicists and engineers known as derivatives 'quants', whose day-to-day activities increasingly shape how the value of derivatives are measured within and outside of banks. Of course, the ASA is a small non-profit organisation whose finances are a concern to relatively few people. Yet this episode highlights how financialisation, coupled with the growth of fair value accounting, has caused the modelling and evaluation practices of 'high finance' to become increasingly central to the routine financial activities of even organisations that appear largely disconnected from the global financial markets.

As quants become increasingly important to the global economy, their working practices have become shaped by stakeholders external to banks, including banking regulators and accounting authorities. This chapter[4] builds upon existing work on the community of 'front office'[5] derivatives 'quants', particularly by MacKenzie and Spears (2014a, 2014b) on the development of the Gaussian Copula model and its use by this community within investment banks. These quants work closely with traders to develop models that are used both to hedge (i.e. reduce or eliminate) the risks associated with banks' derivatives trades, as well as value these positions for accounting purposes. Rather than focus on the development of any *particular* financial model, this chapter instead draws attention to how quants' models are used both within and outside of dealer banks, and how their modelling practices are shaped and constrained by stakeholders both within and outside of banks. This chapter focusses on one modelling practice in particular known as 'calibration', which concerns how the mathematical parameters of a model are assigned specific numerical values. Calibration must be performed before a model can be used to price or hedge a derivative. However, because the choice of these parameters ultimately determines the model-calculated value and risk of most interest rate derivatives, the *manner* in which quants calibrate their models is a matter of concern for a variety of internal and external

44 *Taylor Spears*

stakeholders within banks. In particular, quants must not only produce models that balance the needs of traders and risk managers, who require models that are useful for measuring and hedging the risks that accrue to dealer banks, but also satisfy the demands among regulators and the accounting standards boards for measurements of the fair value of these derivatives. To balance these demands, and to constrain the influence of the front office over questions of model design, regulators require that dealers establish separate 'model validation' departments to independently verify the models produced by front office quants. Yet calibration (and model building in general) is not a practice that is easily governable, due to both the weak political position of model validation departments within banks, as well as the fact that calibration depends upon the tacit knowledge and subjective judgment of front office quants. Calibration thus shares much in common with existing accounts of practice from sociological and anthropological work on scientific laboratories, which have emphasised the 'craft' or 'tacit' dimension of scientific practice (Collins, 1974; Ravetz, 1971).

The remainder of this chapter proceeds as follows. Section one (I) briefly describes the role of quants within dealer banks and their distinctive 'culture' of modelling. This section also examines how derivatives pricing models are used both within dealer banks by traders and risk managers, and in the calculation of the 'fair value' of derivatives positions for external financial reporting purposes. As explained, traders and the US and European accounting standards setters possess distinct criteria for what qualifies as a satisfactory model. Whereas traders depend upon models that are capable of effectively *hedging* derivatives, accounting standards setters instead mandate the use of models that minimise the use of subjective inputs and assumptions. The second section (II) examines the practice of 'calibration' in detail, which reveals that quants must often make trade-offs between these two criteria. Moreover, calibration is a practice that requires a considerable amount of tacit judgment on the part of quants, and as such is a practice that is rather difficult to govern. Section three (III) examines the role of model validation quants in the governance of the activities of front office traders, as well as the limits of banks' model validation departments in constraining the activities of the front office. The chapter concludes by examining how these findings contribute to existing accounts of models and market devices within the social studies of finance.

Sources

- 27 interviews with individuals[6] who range from mid-to-senior level derivatives quants who currently or previously have worked for at least one of the G16 derivatives dealer banks, which comprises the leading derivatives 'dealer' banks in the world.[7] The primary focus of these interviews was to understand, in general terms, how models are used by quants and traders within dealer banks, how these models and practices are situated within the organisational structure of the bank, and how they have changed over the quant's career in banking. These interviews took a loose oral-history form in order to establish how each quant's career history touched on the historical development of modelling practices used within this community. These interviews were conducted between November 2011 and September 2015 in London (17), New York City (6), San Francisco (3) and Barcelona (1).

- 10 interviews with individuals with extensive experience in the markets for 'over-the-counter' derivatives,[8] but who are not derivatives quants. These included hedge fund managers, consultants, attorneys, regulators, and members of a prominent derivatives industry group. These interviews were conducted between April 2011 and August 2015 in Washington, D.C. (2), London (7) and New York City (1).

- Ethnographic work at derivatives quant conferences that took place on the following dates: 17–20 April 2012 in Barcelona, 15–19 April 2013 in Amsterdam, 14–15 May 2013 in London, 13–16 May 2014 in Amsterdam, 11–12 June 2014 in London, 18–22 May 2015 in Amsterdam.

I Front office quants and the uses of derivatives pricing models

Front office derivatives quants represent a subset of financial 'quants' whose work is focussed on developing models that are used by traders and other banking personnel within dealer banks to price and risk-manage over-the-counter derivatives. As a model developer, a quant's job is to develop both abstract mathematical models as well as computer programs that are capable of solving these models efficiently and reliably using a bank's computer systems. Doing so requires a combination of several highly-valued skills: namely competence in advanced mathematics as well as software development. Consequently, these individuals tend to be trained at PhD-level in technical fields such as mathematics, physics, theoretical chemistry, and engineering. Although much of their work involves software development rather than deal-making, most derivatives quants come from elite educational backgrounds. The quant field is, moreover, greatly over-represented by men, particularly at the senior level. Although demographic information on the field as a whole is not available, at a major derivatives quant conference attended by the author, only 8.9 per cent of quants in attendance were women.

Top quants command salaries in the six and seven figures; yet quants are not capitalists in the traditional sense, nor are they what Piketty refers to as 'supermanagers', which have attracted so much attention in recent discussions of income inequality (Piketty, 2014). Front office quants tend not to be managers, but instead are themselves managed: they work as salaried employees of banks, and their compensation is usually determined by the traders for whom they work. As John, a front office quant at a large American dealer bank, explained to me:

46 Taylor Spears

John: What I get paid every year is much more to do with what the head of rates trading thinks than what the head quant thinks....It's very clear where the accountability is.

Spears: You're accountable to your trader?

John: Yeah, exactly. If he's happy, then I'm happy. And if he's not, then I'm not. It's as simple as that.[9]

This point is crucial: front office quants are hired to support trading activities, and their compensation is largely determined by the banks' traders. Nevertheless, the *models* that a bank's front office quants develop are used for a number of different purposes, and by a variety of different agents.

Derivatives traders and quants practice a particular 'culture' of modelling that is intellectually centred around the Black-Scholes options pricing model and its intellectual descendants (MacKenzie and Spears, 2014; Lépinay, 2011). At the heart of Black-Scholes is the key insight that in a narrow set of circumstances, the *value* of a derivative written on a security (e.g. a stock) should be equal to the cost of purchasing a certain portfolio capable of *hedging* the risks that arise from holding that derivative. This portfolio, whose composition would be changed in line with changing market conditions, would contain specific amounts of cash and shares of the underlying stock (Björk, 2009). While the hedging and valuation of derivatives are indeed closely related to each other within the modelling culture practiced by quants, distinct stakeholders within and outside of dealer banks evaluate models according to different criteria. These groups articulate somewhat competing standards of what qualifies as a satisfactory model. The capacity of models to *hedge* is primarily a concern of a bank's traders and its risk managers. In contrast, the capacity of models to accurately *value* derivatives is the primary concern of auditors, the accountants standards boards, and investors. Thus before examining how banks govern these competing demands that quants face in their day-to-day modelling practices, it will be useful to first examine the criteria of each of these groups.

Fair value accounting

First, the pricing models developed by a dealer's front office quants are typically used to determine the fair value of the derivatives contracts held by that bank, information that is used by a variety of external stakeholders. For instance, a bank's auditors and ultimately its investors use this information to keep track of the financial performance of the bank, while the bank's derivatives trading partners (e.g. the ASA) may rely on valuations produced by banks to determine the fair value of their own derivatives positions.

The two major financial accounting standards boards both define the fair value of a financial instrument in terms of its 'exit price': that is, the price that a bank would receive if it were to sell an asset, or that it would need to pay to transfer a liability, at a given date (IFRS Foundation 2013, 9; Financial Accounting Standards Board 2006, 29D). These standards also specify what is known as a 'fair value hierarchy' that banks and other organisations must follow when making fair value calculations. This hierarchy requires that where possible, banks and other organisations measure the fair value of a security first using the market prices of identical securities quoted in the market. Where this is not possible, models should be used to calculate an instrument's fair value, but the model must minimise the use of information – such as credit ratings – which is not directly extracted from market prices.[10] Organisations can, in fact, be penalised for using models that incorporate 'non-observable' information, which shapes the type of data quants use as inputs in the models they build. For example, to the extent that a model uses non-observable, or 'entity-specific' information as an input to the valuation process, IFRS accounting standards require the organisation to hold a portion of the initial profit of a trade in a 'model reserve', which will only be realised in a gradual manner over time, and will thus reduce the trader's profitability in the short term (Ernst and Young, 2011, 26).[11]

The fair value of few, if any, interest rate derivatives can be calculated without a model. This is certainly true for so-called 'exotic' derivatives: highly customised derivative contracts that are sold to the client of a dealer, but for which there exists no two-way market with which the dealer could determine the exit price of the contract. But models are nearly always required to calculate the fair value of even simpler 'vanilla'[12] interest rates derivatives, such as swaps and options on swaps, for which there exists an active two-way market between derivatives dealers. Indeed, while price quotations are usually available for 'vanilla' derivatives such as swaps from other dealers, these public price quotations do not take into account certain factors that can affect the 'exit price' of a contract with a given client, such as the credit worthiness of the two parties. Moreover, most of the derivatives that are held by the bank on its balance sheet – i.e. existing trades that the bank has made with its clients, such as the ASA – will have features that no longer match those of the relatively small set of instruments quoted in the interdealer market. In fact, Daniel, a quant who works at a software vendor that specialises in financial modelling, explained in an interview that even standardised vanilla instruments such as interest rate swaps become non-standard instruments over time whose prices are not readily observable in the market.[13] In addition to being required by financial reporting standards, the practice of 'marking-to-market' is also deeply embedded within the organisational culture of banks. Traders keep a close eye on their 'profit and loss' or 'P&L', which measures changes in the mark-to-market value of the trader's book of derivatives trades on a day-to-day basis. As MacKenzie and Spears (2014) note, because traders' bonuses are largely based on the P&L of their trading books, a bank's pricing models are crucially important in determining a trader's end-of-year compensation.

Hedging

A second major use of models is to produce information for hedging, which is primarily needed by a dealer bank's traders and risk managers. These groups use models to understand the sensitivity of the bank's derivatives trading book to

48 *Taylor Spears*

changes in interest rates and market prices, and can then use this information to hedge these risks.

Models are needed for this purpose because unlike simpler instruments such as stocks, in which market makers will only temporarily own a particular instrument until it can find a suitable buyer, interest rate derivatives are long-term contracts that entail cashflows over months, years, or in some cases even decades. Just as the ASA is exposed to financial losses from its swap, these financial commitments – coupled with fair value accounting rules discussed previously – also create risks to dealers. As a consequence of fair value accounting, changes in market interest rates, for instance, will create losses or gains to the bank's existing derivatives portfolio that must be hedged if the bank wish to avoid earnings volatility. Models are used to determine how these resulting risks can be hedged at the level of an entire trading book. As Paul, a 'desk quant' who works closely with the traders at his bank explained, 'That's the only way this business works, is if I can consolidate hundreds of deals and hedge it with one'. Without such a model, 'it'd be too expensive to hedge each individually; I'd just die'.[14] Indeed, the derivatives quants interviewed for this research explained that the need to *hedge* derivatives is, in fact, the primary purpose of derivatives pricing models from the perspective of a bank's traders. Hedging client trades is complicated by the fact that there is generally a mismatch between the supply and demand for each product (Sadr, 2009, 217). Unlike a bookmaker at a horse race, it is usually not profitable for a dealer to keep a 'flat book' in which all trades are perfectly hedged with off-setting positions in the same instrument. As one article from *Risk Magazine* – a popular trade journal among derivatives quants – wrote, a derivatives market maker's job is 'to take and manage basis risk', that is: the risk that a set of client trades will be imperfectly hedged by a set of hedging instruments, thus creating a gap between the two and risk to the trader (Madigan, 2013).

Models are used to make the risk embedded in a portfolio of trades visible to the bank's traders and risk managers by calculating the *sensitivity* of the value of a book of derivatives to small changes in the parameters or input data for the model that is used to value that book of derivatives. The calculation of these 'risk sensitivities' (which are also known as 'Greeks', because they are usually represented by various letters from the Greek alphabet) is done at the very least on a nightly basis. The output of this process are tables of numbers that are routinely used by traders to determine how much of each particular vanilla instrument the trader ought to buy or sell in order to hedge the risks that have accrued in her trading book. Repeating this process for all of the derivatives owned by a bank can take hours, even with massive farms of supercomputers. Nathan, a director of quantitative research at a major dealer bank, explained that he 'would not be surprised if banks right now run the biggest computer clusters on the planet'.[15] The stakes in this game for banks are high, as Nawalkha and Rebonato explain: '[w]henever the computational time required to extract the risk metrics for a book that may contain thousands of deals exceeds 24 h, the game is, literally, over', since a trader will not be able to hedge his book in time to mitigate any risks that arise (2011, 6). For these reasons, traders are primarily concerned with the capacity of a model to produce 'good hedges' in a reasonable amount of time, thereby allowing the trader to hedge effectively and maintain a desired 'profit and loss profile'.[16]

These risk sensitivities are not only used by traders, but also by various personnel within banks to govern and manage the risk-taking activities of traders, particularly by a bank's risk management staff. Robert, a head quant at a leading dealer bank, explained that 'the same numbers [risk sensitivities] are seen by the market risk managers and they make sure that the total positions – the total risk – is within limits that they define'.[17] Another routine reporting procedure that is essential to monitoring the risk-taking activity of traders is known as 'profit and loss attribution'.[18] A P&L attribution report, which would be produced using a model built by a quant, would attempt to decompose the causes of changes in a derivatives into a set of root causes, including the model-produced risk sensitivities associated with that book. In addition to these explanatory terms, P&L attribution reports also include a category for 'unexplained' changes in a trading book's value, which cannot be attributed to factors that have been identified by a model (Shydlo, 2007). Alan, a former swaps trader who now works at a hedge fund, explained in an interview that a trading desk whose profit and loss cannot be explained can indicate the presence of a faulty model that is failing to capture the risk of a trading book, or in some cases can indicate the presence of a rogue trader who is intentionally distorting the book's value to hide trading losses.

II Matching the market: calibration and model building

The previous section stressed that quants' models must satisfy two rather distinct criteria of model efficacy: namely those imposed by accounting rules, and those of the bank's own derivatives traders and risk managers. How are these criteria balanced in the day-to-day work of model building? To understand this, it is necessary to examine an important modelling practice used by quants known as 'calibration', which refers to the process by which the mathematical parameters of a model are set to specific values so that the model can be used to make calculations. As Paul explained during an interview, calibration is always the second step of using a model, after the model itself has been selected:

> A model right out of the box is completely useless. The reason is it has things in it called 'mathematical parameters', and until you set those parameters you aren't going to be able to price anything. So the next step is always calibration.[19]

As other interviewees explained (and the existing technical literature on derivatives pricing confirms[20]), quants calibrate models in a very particular way that is known as market-implied calibration. This practice involves 'backing out' the parameters of a derivatives pricing model from the current market prices of a set of financial instruments that are specifically chosen to hedge a given derivative,

50   *Taylor Spears*

rather than by estimating these parameters from historical data. For quants, a properly calibrated model will be able to 'reproduce' the current market prices of those hedging instruments nearly exactly. If a model cannot 'reproduce' the prices of the instruments used to hedge a derivative, then quants will have little faith in the model's ability to prescribe an accurate hedging strategy for a trader, or to accurately value the derivative itself (Rebonato, 2004).

Because the selection of these hedging instruments will necessarily determine the parameters selected for the model, choices over model calibration ultimately affect how the fair value and risk sensitivities of a derivative are measured within the bank. Indeed, a few moments later in our interview, Paul noted this point explicitly:

Paul: But if you think about that, look what's happened is - whatever instruments I used to calibrate it [the model], those are the risks I see, and so it's going to be a linear combination of those instruments that are actually going to be the hedge. So you think, oh my God! How do you choose your hedging instruments?

Spears: That becomes a very crucial decision, then?

Paul: That becomes an absolutely crucial decision.[21]

What is more, these choices *necessarily* involve an element of tacit judgment on the part of quants, and cannot be reduced to simple, easily codified rules. Consider, for example, a hypothetical rule for model calibration in which a quant simply chooses to calibrate a model to *all* potential hedging instruments in order to avoid making subjective choices about which instruments are most relevant for a given derivative. This approach to calibration is technically possible, and according to interviewees, is practiced by a small minority of dealers. But as Oscar, a desk quant, explained, such a simplistic approach to calibration can actually be 'dangerous' to a bank, as it would fail to acknowledge that the market prices for certain hedging instruments tend to be out-of-date, which can cause a model, calibrated to that out-of-date information, to break down. In his words:

Oscar: When you actually sit on the desk you realise that a lot of this market data doesn't actually make sense. It represents swaptions that have not been traded for days or weeks. Whereas other points were traded ten minutes ago. So clearly you want to prioritise the swaptions that are liquid.

Spears: So if you take the whole volatility cube, that's going to have a lot of data on that is just out-of-date?

Oscar: Out of date, yeah. And in fact it's actually very, very dangerous to use it. And people have done so – they start implying very funny things about the future state of the market by trying to make the model fit data that's inconsistent, as observed of today. But that's basically because some of it should be thrown away.[22]

Stephen, a head quant at another major derivatives dealer, highlighted another problem with this simplistic approach to calibration. By calibrating to every possible hedging instrument, the resulting hedging information produced by the model 'won't be crisp, it won't tell you, "you have to hedge with *that* option, *that* maturity". Instead, it's going to give you sort-of like a fuzzy hedge profile'.[23] For these reasons, a number of quants explained to me that model building and calibration should always begin with a quant making a 'qualitative assessment' of the risks associated with a particular book of derivatives. As Paul explained:

> When you take a book of deals, you first sort of qualitatively examine the risks. What are the risks? Am I at risk for interest rates going up and down? Am I at risk for tilts in the yield curve? Am I at risk for volatilities going up and down? So, sort of qualitatively – what are the risks?[24]

Model building and calibration are thus activities that necessarily involve a considerable amount of judgment and tacit knowledge on the part of front office quants. Yet the tacit nature of this work also creates conflicts of interest for quants, who, at times, face pressure from the bank's traders and sales team to develop models that not only provide reliable hedging information to traders, but also understate the value of derivatives so that the bank can offer more competitive pricing to its clients. Aaron, a previous head of quantitative research at a major dealer, also mentioned in an interview that quants at his bank would sometimes be pressured by the sales team to make their models 'more aggressive' so that the bank could more easily win business from potential clients.[25] Aaron explained that front office quants would occasionally be told, 'Your model is rubbish. We lost to Goldman Sachs, to UBS, to RBS (Royal Bank of Scotland), to Barclays, etc. Make your model more aggressive'. As Aaron further explained, a 'more aggressive' model was often produced by intentionally calibrating to specific market prices that produce a more favourable valuation for the trader or salesperson. Roger, a retired quant who previously worked at a major dealer bank, made a similar point during an interview: he explained that the push to develop higher dimensional models at his bank (which allow for calibration to a wider range of market prices) was done, in part, to constrain traders' ability to misrepresent the mark-to-market value of their trades through selective calibration.[26]

III Governing the front office quants: the role of model validators

How do banks manage the conflicts that front office quants face over the design and calibration of models given the tacit nature of their work? Rather than entrust front office quants to balance these demands themselves, large dealer banks' dealers have created independent 'model validation' departments. These departments are staffed with their own quants, who separately test and verify that the

52 *Taylor Spears*

models developed by the front office both accurately measure the fair value of the bank's trading positions, as well as the risk associated with those positions. While banks were given considerable leeway with respect to how they governed the conflicts that front office quants face prior to the 2008 financial crisis, since the crisis both the Basel Committee on Banking Supervision (BCBS) as well as national-level banking regulators have issued explicit guidance with respect to how model validation ought to be performed by banks operating in their jurisdictions (cf. Morini, 2011, 48; Board of Governors of the Federal Reserve System and the Office of the Comptroller of the Currency 2011; BCBS 2009). These regulations require, among other things, that such departments be organisationally independent from the front office. That is, model validation quants should report to a separate authority within the bank than that which oversees the front office quants and traders.

While regulators prefer model validation departments to remain wholly separated from the front office, this is infeasible in practice due to both the tacit nature of quant expertise, as well as the social influence of the front office throughout the bank as a whole. Roger, who at one point worked as a head of model validation, explained that he faced a tension between two competing needs whilst working in that role. On the one hand, he had to ensure that his model validation quants were intellectually 'close enough' to the activities of the front office to provide meaningful oversight and advice with respect to model selection and calibration, given the inherently tacit nature of these activities.[27] On the other hand, he also had to ensure that the team demonstrated a sufficient degree of separation from the front office to comply with the demands among regulators for independence between the two groups. Roger explained that his bank's regulators preferred to see a visible 'paper trail' of adversarial 'back and forth' between the two groups (via, e.g. email correspondence), whereas in practice, model validation quants need to work somewhat collaboratively with those in the front office to understand the choices made by front office quants. Theresa, a quant who has worked in model validation for a number of years, also highlighted the necessarily collaborative nature of model validation work. She explained in an interview that effective model validation, in her experience, requires agreement and consensus with the front office quants:

> If I need to validate a model, I need to work with front office quants to understand the model. Usually, you are going to find some limitations on the model. You need to discuss that with the front office, right? Make sure they agree....And I guess typically people work together. There is sometimes a tendency for front guys to not to want to get bothered with some stuff, right? (laughs) But generally people are reasonable.[28]

Thus despite the formal organisational independence of banks' model validation departments, the highly tacit nature of model building and calibration would suggest that front office quants possess an asymmetric advantage when negotiating

Matching the market 53

with model validation teams, who rely upon front office quants to understand their technical choices.

Some quants that were interviewed, however, provided a much less optimistic view of model validators' capacity to appropriately govern the activities of the front office, due to the political power of traders and other front office staff within banks, as well as the comparatively low status of model validators compared to front office quants. In an email, Aaron, for instance, described the influence of the front office as 'tentacular' throughout the bank as a whole, and that the model validation department faces considerable pressure to 'play ball' with the front office. Aaron explained that while validators are encouraged by the front office to discover programming errors in a model's implementation (which might create losses for the traders), critiquing the *type* of model used, or how it is calibrated, is heavily frowned upon, as doing so can cause the bank to lose trades to its competitors. As a consequence, according to Aaron:

> Everybody knows that the job of a validator is a thankless one, and subject to enormous pressures. Therefore bright quantitative people do not go for this job (they go for the front-office job, where there is money, status, and kudos.) This creates a self-fulfilling prophecy: indeed, very often the model validators (who are not from the top drawer to start with, and have had very little experience) fail to see the wood for the trees, miss the commercial point, etc. For the principled ones, life is hell.[29]

Conclusion

This chapter has examined some of the day-to-day working practices of front office derivatives quants: the physicists, mathematicians, and engineers who build models and pricing infrastructure that are used within dealer banks to both hedge and track the changing fair value of banks' derivatives positions. Rather than focussing on the historical development of the models used by quants, this chapter has focussed on an important modelling practice known as 'calibration', which concerns how the mathematical parameters of banks' models are assigned specific numerical values, thereby allowing the model to make calculations. In developing algorithms to calibrate these models, quants must balance several competing criteria of what constitutes a satisfactory model: most notably, those of traders, who require models capable of effectively hedging banks' derivatives positions, and fair value accounting standards, which require models that minimise the use of information that cannot be directly 'observed' in the markets. To manage the potential conflicts that arise from trying to satisfy these groups, bank regulators have required dealers to create independent 'model validation' departments, staffed with their own quants, to provide oversight of the choices made by quants in the front office. Yet governing these choices is made difficult by several factors: first, by the fact that calibration (and model building in general) is not easily reducible to simple rules, but instead depends upon the tacit knowledge

54 *Taylor Spears*

and even subjective judgment of quants; and second, that model validation quants often lack the power and influence necessary to challenge the decisions made by quants and traders in the front office. In developing this account of modelling, this chapter has attempted to sketch an outline of a sociology of financial modelling that simultaneously acknowledges the importance of tools, models and infrastructure in the constitution of present-day financial markets, but which foregrounds the tacit knowledge and subjective judgement of the builders of these market devices.

How might we understand these findings within the broader context of the social studies of finance (SSF)? Traditionally, the SSF has been primarily concerned with how material artefacts, tools, and calculative devices constitute and shape social interaction within markets. This focus largely stems from the SSF's grounding in actor-network theory. However, as Pickering (1993) notes, actor-network theory conceives of human and material agency as being essentially *interchangeable*. In this view, machines can be 'substituted' for humans (and vice versa), a view that implicitly underlies the SSF's traditional focus on how models and other market devices increasingly mediate social interaction within markets. This notion of interchangeable agency may be true in the case of simple artefacts. But as Pickering notes, it is difficult to imagine any number of humans effectively 'substituting' for more complex tools such as telescopes, particle accelerators – or in the present case – derivatives pricing models. Rather than human and material agency being interchangeable quantities, Pickering effectively argues that they are instead *complementary*, and that human and non-human agency are deeply intertwined. Applied to finance, this suggests a shift to paying closer attention to the agency that quants possess in representing the value and risk of financial instruments, and the efforts that are made to shape and govern their actions both by the dealer banks that employ them, as well as outside regulators and accounting authorities. By foregrounding the routine working practices of quants and the tensions that arise over the governance of their practices, one can examine how these financial professionals both contribute to – and are shaped by – an increasingly financialised economy.

Acknowledgements

The research leading to these results was funded by the European Research Council under the European Union's Seventh Framework Programme (FP7, grant 291733).

Notes

1   A derivative is a financial instrument whose value is dependent upon the price of one or more underlying assets or interest rates. A swap is a particular type of derivative whose value depends upon the movement of a particular market interest rate, typically Libor (the London Interbank Offered Rate).
2   The largest derivative dealers are members of an industry group known as the G16, which currently consists of: Bank of America - Merrill Lynch, Barclays, BNP Paribas,

Citigroup, Crédit Agricole, Credit Suisse, Deutsche Bank, Goldman Sachs, HSBC, JPMorgan Chase, Morgan Stanley, Nomura, Royal Bank of Scotland, Société Générale, UBS, and Wells Fargo (Mengle 2010; Cameron 2011).

3 The ASA's financial statements for the year ending 31 December 2014 note that for its interest rate swap, 'Fair value is derived from quotes from a dealer or broker, where available. Models used in valuing such agreements consider the contractual terms of and specific risks inherent in the instrument, and inputs used typically include yield curve, instrument volatility, repayment rates and assumptions concerning nonperformance risk'.

4 Portions of this chapter are drawn from the author's PhD thesis, *Engineering value, engineering risk: what derivatives quants know and what their models do*, University of Edinburgh, June 2014.

5 The term 'front office' refers to the portion of a bank focussed on sales and trading, in contrast to the 'middle office' and 'back office', which tend to govern and support the activities of the front office.

6 All names used in this chapter are pseudonyms.

7 The G16 consists of the following banks: Bank of America, Barclays Capital, BNP Paribas, Citigroup, Credit Suisse, Deutsche Bank, Dresdner Bank, Goldman Sachs, HSBC, JPMorgan Chase, Merrill Lynch, Morgan Stanley, Royal Bank of Scotland, Société Générale, UBS, and Wachovia.

8 Unlike exchange-traded derivatives, over-the-counter derivatives are privately negotiated and traded directly between market participants.

9 Interview with John in London, 8 October 2012.

10 FAS 157 (the relevant US accounting standard), for instance, specifically requires that 'Valuation techniques used to measure fair value shall maximise the use of relevant observable inputs [...] and minimise the use of unobservable inputs'. Both sets of accounting standards also articulate a three-level 'fair value hierarchy', which classifies fair value estimates based on the degree to which the inputs to a fair value calculation are directly observable via quoted market prices. See: IFRS Foundation (2013, sec. 36) and Financial Accounting Standards Board (2006, sec. 21B).

11 See, also, MacKenzie and Spears (2014), who discuss the impact of this practice on the development of the Gaussian Copula family of derivatives pricing models.

12 Unlike so-called 'exotic' derivatives, which are highly customised instruments that are designed to meet the particular needs of a market participant, quants and traders refer to standardised derivatives that are bought and sold regularly as 'vanilla' (Andersen and Piterbarg 2010, 697).

13 Interview with Daniel in New York, 11 April 2012.

14 Interview with Paul in London, 13 March 2012.

15 Interview with Nathan in London, 3 July 2012.

16 See Donald MacKenzie and Spears (2014) and Rebonato (2013) for more detailed discussion of the impact of the practice of 'day one P&L' on traders' modelling practices.

17 Interview with Robert in London, 12 March 2012.

18 Andersen and Piterbarg (2010, 22.2.2), for instance, examine how models are used to produce 'P&L Explain' reports in their recent textbook on interest rate modelling.

19 Interview with Paul in London, 13 March 2012.

20 See, among others, Rebonato (2004, 18), Andersen and Piterbarg (2010, 299), and Bjork (2009, 376).

21 Interview with Paul in London, 13 March 2012.

22 Interview with Oscar in London, 4 July 2012.

23 Interview with Stephen in New York, 11 April 2012.

24 Interview with Paul in London, 13 March 2012.

56 *Taylor Spears*

25 Interview with Aaron in London, 16 March 2012.
26 Interview with Roger in Palo Alto, 14 August 2012.
27 Interview with Roger in Palo Alto, 14 August 2012.
28 Interview with Theresa in London, 8 July 2015.
29 Email correspondence with Aaron, 24 August 2012.

3 Buying it

Financialisation through socialisation

Natascha van der Zwan

Financial markets are built around shared understandings of similarity and difference that inform who gains access and who is excluded. They are the territory of the investor, a particular subjectivity whose characteristics reflect widely held beliefs regarding the legitimacy of the financial marketplace (Preda, 2005). The idea of "who gets to invest where and when" is not just embodied by particular social groups (Leyshon and Thrift, 1996), but also embedded within the organisational structures of financial institutions (Ortiz, 2014b) and the collective imagination of financial professionals (Ho, 2009). Yet, the understanding of the financial sector as a bounded field does not preclude movement across or interactions with the outside world. In fact, recent scholarship has emphasised the interactive character of the finance sector (Vargha, 2011). This chapter builds on these studies by analysing how the field of finance is constituted through its interactions with outsiders.

Distinct from scholarship that focusses on the organisations of professional finance, the study presented here hopes to "open the black boxes of global finance" (MacKenzie, 2005) from the perspective of an outsider, namely organised labour. This "outside in" approach reveals the dialogical process by which financial market access was negotiated by Wall Street professionals and their interlocutors from the American labour movement. The chapter presents the attempts by the AFL-CIO's (American Federation of Labor and Congress of Industrial Organizations) Industrial Union Department Committee on Pension and Benefit Fund Policy to establish its own employee buyout fund to participate in the market for corporate control during the late 1980s. While developing the plans for the Employee Partnership Fund (EPF), the Committee reached out to financial professionals within its network and asked for advice on how to organise a labour-friendly investment fund. Over the course of 3 years, committee members and Wall Street bankers discussed how organised labour could set up a fund that would attract the interest of professional investors.

Although a minor instance in the 1980s markets for corporate control, the case of EPF offers two broader insights on the financialisation of the American political economy. First, the correspondence between organised labour and financial professionals exposes the social boundaries separating the financial sector from the industrial economy. Sociologists have used the concept of boundary work to describe the interpretive acts that actors undertake to distinguish "us" from "them" (Lamont and Molnár, 2002: 171). In this case, the Committee on Pension and Benefit Fund Policy

58 Natascha van der Zwan

performed boundary work, when it strongly rejected Wall Street's buyout practices, setting it aside from "honourable" labour union activities. In turn, Wall Street bankers who were invited to comment on organised labour's plans also engaged in boundary work. They formulated the preconditions under which an outsider like organised labour could transverse the social boundaries separating finance from the industrial economy and enter the "imaginary community of market actors" (Preda, 2005: 148).

Second, by accommodating the bankers' suggestions for the buyout fund, financial sector norms and practices slowly diffused through organised labour's project to create its own financial intermediary in opposition to the corporate raiders of the time. When the EPF went to market, its design no longer reflected organised labour's critical project, but rather resembled a standard buyout fund. This "mimetic isomorphism" (DiMaggio and Powell, 1983) was rooted in the bankers' belief that value creation was dependent on the alignment of interests between fund organisers and fund investors. Their ideas followed the central tenets of agency theory with its concern for managerial discipline and shareholder value (Jung and Dobbin, 2013). The case of the EPF thus fits within the larger story of the financialisation of the American political economy, characterised by the adoption of shareholder value-oriented practices by non-financial actors and organisations (van der Zwan, 2014).

The outline of the chapter is as follows. Section 1 will describe the leveraged buyout and its role within the market for corporate control. Sections 2 and 3 present the case study of the Employee Partnership Fund. Section 2 presents the early plans of the EPF, as conceived by the Industrial Union Department's (IUD) Committee on Pension and Benefit Fund Policy in 1988. A rejection of mainstream buyout practices, such the maximisation of return and value extraction from the firm, strongly resonated throughout these early plans. Section 3 shows how these critiques of finance largely disappeared from the proposal after the IUD Committee adopted Wall Street's suggestions for revision. The chapter ends with a reflection on the mechanisms of financialisation. The case study shows how financialisation does not only proceed through the "colonisation" of the industrial economy (Chiapello, 2005), but may also occur through the socialisation of critical outsiders into the world of finance. The brief history of the EPF therefore warrants a closer attention to the role of critique within the financialised political economy.

The case study presented in this chapter is based on archival research conducted at the Kheel Center for Labor-Management Documentation and Archives at Cornell University. Various drafts of the project proposal, meeting notes and internal memos, officials' correspondence and other primary documents related to the EPF were drawn from the Jacob Sheinkman records from the Secretary-Treasurer's and President's Offices, 1970–1996 (hereafter: JS records) to create a historical reconstruction of the EPF project. The JS records are part of the larger collection of the American Textile and Clothing Workers Union, present at the Kheel Center archives. A site visit to the archives took place in February 2014.

Financialisation through socialisation 59

1 Leveraged buyouts and the market for corporate control

One of the major developments associated with the financialisation of the American political economy during the final quarter of the twentieth century has been the reorientation of the goals of the modern corporation from the realisation of growth to the maximisation of shareholder value (van der Zwan, 2014). Providing the academic justification of this new understanding of the firm were agency theorists like Michael Jensen and Eugene Fama, who in the 1970s argued that managerial capitalism had undermined the position of the shareholder within the firm. Rather than serving the firm's true owners, its shareholders, by maximizing its value, corporate executives had only served their own interests by keeping firms large and salaries high (Jung and Dobbin, 2013). Agency theory prescribed that the corporation be reduced to its "core competencies" by selling off divisions and cutting costs to maximise profits. It also proposed a realignment of managerial and shareholder interests by tying executive compensation to financial performance, for instance through stock options (ibid.).

Financial market actors enthusiastically adopted agency theory's core principles. Institutional investors, such as pension funds and mutual funds, embraced the notion that active ownership could remedy the negative effects of lacklustre management on firm performance. Their growing influence followed the expansion of occupational pension plans during the post-war period. As more and more workers began to save for their future retirement, pension funds acquired more capital in need of investment. Traditionally, pension funds invested in fixed-income assets, such as government bonds. By the 1980s, however, increased funding needs and a liberalisation of investment regulations provoked a shift in pension funds' investment practices with corporate equities becoming the dominant asset class (McCarthy et al., 2016). With large ownership stakes in America's biggest corporations, institutional investors had a strong self-interest in incentivising management to adopt pro-shareholder policies.

The new financial orientation of the firm did not only influence its internal management of the firm, but also how firms were bought and sold. Between 1981 and 1988, a wave of mergers and acquisitions, many of them hostile, took corporate America by storm. Instead of passively owning shares in public corporations, corporate raiders would acquire entire corporations with the explicit purpose of becoming actively involved in their management. The general idea behind a buyout is that "ownership matters" (Erturk et al., 2010): firms have the potential for profitability, but the current owner is not able to extract those profits. To improve the financial performance of the firm, an ownership change is warranted. The goal of corporate raiders such as Carl Icahn or T. Boone Pickens was to extract as much value from the corporation as possible within a short period of time. To this end, they would target large industrial conglomerates, undervalued by the marketplace, and separate their divisions before selling them on. It is estimated that around a third of the 1980 Fortune 500 had disappeared by the decade's end (Davis, 2009b: 34).

A major impetus to the market of corporate control was a financial innovation called the leveraged buyout. A leveraged buyout is a financial technique through

60 *Natascha van der Zwan*

which a group of investors acquires a corporation by borrowing money and using the assets of the corporation as collateral. In 1981, leveraged buyouts had represented only a small share (4.6 per cent) of the mergers and acquisitions market in the United States. They quickly gained popularity, however, and by the end of 1989 leveraged buyouts had accounted for 26.8 per cent of mergers and acquisitions (Brancato, 1989: 5). Among these was Kohlberg, Kravis and Roberts' infamous buyout of RJR Nabisco at $24.8 billion in 1988, the largest in history. The RJR Nabisco buyout quickly became the symbol of an overheated buyout market: with increased competition in the takeover market that spurred prices for takeover targets, bought-out companies became burdened with massive amounts of debt which they were increasingly unable to service. This resulted in a growing number of bankruptcies by the end of the decade (ibid.).

Much of the popularity of the leveraged buyout could be attributed to new financing techniques, in particular the usage of high-yield bonds or junk bonds, and their preferential tax treatment. The typical capital structure of a leveraged buyout transaction combined debt provided by commercial banks and insurance companies with equity financing provided by institutional investors, often through a limited partnership fund. Leveraged buyouts commonly followed the "rule of 70–30," with 70 per cent of the purchase price financed by debt and 30 per cent by equity. Interest payments were tax deductible to both lender and borrower (Clark, 2009). Commercial banks were eager to finance leveraged buyouts, as growing stock markets and rising interest rates had reduced other opportunities for corporate lending. Banks and insurers saw their role in the buyout market greatly reduced, however, after Michael Milken at investment firm Drexel Burnham Lambert began to market junk bonds to finance leveraged buyouts. These low-rated, but highly profitable bonds made megadeals such as the RJR Nabisco takeover possible. With the collapse of the junk bond market in 1989, the leveraged buyout craze also came to an end (Kaufman and Englander, 1993).

In several respects, leveraged buyouts represented the dominant economic ideas of the decade. Leveraged buyouts solved the problem of the separation between ownership and control by placing the acquired firm directly under the control of the new owners. Direct ownership allowed the new owners to closely monitor management. Debt repayments imposed another form of discipline on corporate managers: because cash flows were not commonly sufficient to service outstanding debt, value would be extracted from the firm through restructuring. Firms were commonly sold again after 3 to 5 years (Clark, 2009). Additionally, the relationship between the buyout fund manager and outside investors was also organised as to prevent agency problems. Most commonly, a limited partnership was established, in which liability resided with the fund manager or general partner. The general partner would run the daily operations of the fund and make the investment decisions. To align the interests between general partner and limited partners, the general partner would typically receive a 20 per cent performance fee on top of his 2 per cent annual management fee (Erturk et al., 2010).

To organised labour, the market for corporate control posed a major threat. Union federation AFL-CIO estimated that in the course of just a few years

Financialisation through socialisation   61

leveraged buyouts had resulted in more than 90,000 lost jobs. The retail sector had been a particularly popular target for corporate raiders. "The largest employer of the United Food and Commercial Workers Union is now KKR – Kohlberg, Kravis and Roberts, an investment firm specializing in leveraged buyout deals," AFL-CIO President Lane Kirkland testified before the U.S. Senate Finance Committee. He urged the senators to take legislative action (Kirkland, 1989). Meanwhile, initiatives within the labour movement were developed to use pension funds' ownership stakes in American corporations to workers' advantage. In addition to shareholder engagement and other types of financial activism, labour leaders wanted to expand their own investment activities in the corporate economy (van der Zwan, 2011). Among these was the Industrial Union Department's initiative for a worker-friendly leveraged buyout fund.

2 Imagining the employee partnership fund

Already in the 1970s, Peter Drucker had argued that workers indirectly owned large shares in American corporations through their pension funds, which they could leverage to their own political advantage (Drucker, 1976). Taking this idea to heart, the Industrial Union Department of labour federation AFL-CIO created a Committee on Pension and Benefit Fund Policy. Throughout the 1980s, the committee met periodically to discuss how pension savings could be invested in workers' interests. Besides the creation of a union-initiated investment vehicle, the committee also considered, among other things, strategies of proxy voting and shareholder activism. Jacob Sheinkman, secretary-treasurer (1975–1987) and later president (1987–1995) of the Amalgamated Clothing and Textile Workers Union (ACTWU), stood at the helm of the Committee. Additional members included other union presidents, such as Lynn Williams of the United Steelworkers of America and Sigurd Lucassen of the United Brotherhood of Carpenters. Future AFL-CIO President John Sweeney (1995–2009) was also a member of the committee in his capacity as the president of the Service Employees Industrial Union.

Sheinkman's chairmanship was not coincidental: the founder of two labour banks in the 1920s, his union had previously employed financial activism in its organising campaign against textile firm J.P. Stevens. Sheinkman himself had developed a personal interest in the question how unions could "use their rights as stockholders" (Sheinkman, 1979: 15). By January 1988, Sheinkman et al. had produced a draft proposal for "a trade union investment" vehicle together with William (Bill) Patterson, ACTWU's Director of Corporate Affairs. The authors explicitly positioned the fund as an alternative investment vehicle to regular buy-outs funds. According to the authors, the investment fund would serve companies that combined long-term economic stability with "honourable trade-union-based labour relations policies." It explicitly rejected the short-term profit maximisation celebrated by corporate raiders: the fund would not be "burdened with the multimillion dollar salary and bonus requirements of the conventional investment banking world" and would promise investors "something less than rate of return maximisation." It would invest in the industrial economy, in unionised firms constituting the "economic base on which those depositors rest." The fund would support a wide range of business activities, such as the purchase of plant and equipment for modernisation, the purchase of business assets to increase market share, or to assist in the creation of employee stock ownership plans or management buyouts to avoid takeovers by external parties ("A trade union investment vehicle," January 31, 1988).

The proposal for the union investment vehicle reflected a broader understanding among American union officials that traditional labour politics—organising, collective bargaining, lobbying—was no longer sufficient to represent their members' interests. Increasingly, union officials began to see that the workplace and the financial system were not at opposite ends of the political economy, but were closely intertwined domains: in the financialised economy, jobs and wages had become highly dependent on investor behaviour. As the authors noted: "Unions now recognise that they must address questions of investment and finance in order to be able to address their traditional concerns for job security and terms and conditions of work" (ibid.). They hoped that if organised labour adopted financial techniques, they could use them to workers' advantage. The proposed trade union investment vehicle was therefore part of a "capital strategy for organizing." If organised labour could help restore profitability at a bought-out firm, they could prove to other employers that unionisation made financial sense. Firms had to compete "on the cost of capital, not labour", or so the proposal read (ibid.).

Within a year, the plans for the investment fund had developed further. Now called the Equity Partnership Fund (EPF), the fund would assist employees in buying out their own corporations through the use of employee stock ownership plans. Employee stock ownership plans are a type of retirement plan that allow employees to purchase shares in their corporation on a tax-deferred basis. Employee stock ownership plans are very similar to leveraged buyouts: shares are purchased through a fund, which borrows money from a bank to make the acquisition possible (see Figure 3.1). Every time an employee contributes to the fund,

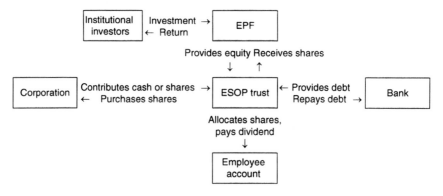

Figure 3.1 Financial flows in the Employee Partnership Fund.

Financialisation through socialisation 63

the fund pays back part of the debt. The moment the loan is repaid, employees become owners of the stock and receive dividend payments. According to the proposal authors, labour unions were much better suited than corporate raiders to establish successful employee stock ownership plans. After all, unions could count on employees' loyalty to help improve the firm's financial performance ("Draft for Equity Partnership Fund," February, 1989).

Although in existence since the 1920s, employee stock ownership plans gained new momentum with the passage of the Employment Retirement Income Security Act in 1974. Under the Employee Retirement Income Security Act, both the principal loan and the interest payments tax had become deductible. What's more, lenders providing capital for the employee buyout were only taxed on half of the income that the employee stock ownership plans generated. Lenders could therefore offer lower interest rates for employee buyouts than for other loans, making them attractive to corporations in need of capital for large investments. Employee stock ownership plans also became a new line of defence against corporate raiders, after the Polaroid Corporation staved off a hostile takeover bid by raising its employees' shares in the corporation. Between 1980 and 1989, large corporations like Avis ($1.75 million) and Proctor and Gamble ($1 million) initiated employee stock ownership plans, while investment banks such as Drexel Burnham Lambert and Goldman Sachs set up teams to explore these new opportunities for profit (Bernstein, 1987; Farell and Hoerr, 1989).

Through the EPF, Sheinkman and co-authors hoped to solve two common problems associated with employee buyouts: (1) employees' lack of capital, forcing them to take substantial wage and benefit cuts to finance the employee stock ownership plan; and (2) their lack of control over the corporation. Taken together, both problems often resulted in a situation whereby the new employee-owners would carry the financial risk for the corporation's performance without having a strong say in business matters. The EPF would provide financing for a small part of the buyout sum, the rest of which was to be borrowed. In exchange for the equity, the fund would receive an ownership stake that would be several times larger than its actual investment, preferably in preferred stock "paying very generous dividends" ("Draft for Equity Partnership Fund," February 1989). At the same time, the authors wrote, the fund would serve as a "friendly partner with labour" and help workers gain a say in the selection of CEO and seats on the board of directors. If all went well, the authors noted, the EPF could be bought out after 5 to 10 years, "leaving the Fund with a very good return and employees in control of the company" (ibid.).

To govern the fund, participating unions would share responsibilities with a professional banker. Union officials would take seats on the fund's board, but the daily management of the fund was to be subcontracted to an independent banker. Although the participating unions would alert the fund manager of possible buyouts, ultimate investment decisions relied solely with the fund manager. Independence was necessary, according to the authors, because "the fund manager will have to have the authority to take or leave a deal based purely on its economic merits" (although the proposal added that "obviously, the fund should never do a deal which would put it at odds with organised labour, or open it to charges of bad faith"). An advisory board of investors would set the investment policy in broad terms, but the EPF would limit itself to long-term investments of around 5 to 10 years. Potential investors should therefore expect high returns, the authors wrote, but had to be "willing to wait a number of years to realise those returns" (ibid.) Long-term investors, such as pension funds and foundations, were therefore among the likely target group for the fund.

Furthermore, the EPF was to be structured as a so-called blind pool. In a blind pool, the limited partners are passive investors: they don't decide on which deals are made, but only commit capital to the fund. Investment decisions lie solely with the general partner. To attract limited partners for the EPF, it was imperative that the general partner had the kind of professional reputation in the financial community that organised labour lacked. After all, unions were "not parties with whom typical investors are used to doing business at all" ("Draft Proposal Employee Partnership Fund," November 4, 1988). Lazard Frères, Drexel Burnham Lambert or American Capital Strategies were considered good candidates for general partner due to the firms' prior involvement with employee buyouts (ibid.). In personal correspondence, both Sheinkman and Patterson expressed a strong preference for Lazard Frères.[1] The bank had a close relationship with the American labour movement, having assisted unions with large employee buyouts at—among others—Weirton Steel and LTV Steel. "I think the Lazard name and the fact that we and other unions trust them makes them a natural choice to run the fund," Bill Patterson wrote to Jacob Sheinkman (Patterson, 1989).

3 Selling the employee partnership fund

Coming up with the idea for an employee buyout fund was one thing. However, selling it to unions and other potential investors was quite something else. Earlier labour-oriented investment vehicles had not always been able to gain the necessary financial support and, at times, had become the target of aggressive anti-union organisers. The EPF initiators therefore had to walk a tight rope, making sure that support from Wall Street professionals was not gained at the expense of the unions whose investments they sought. The Committee on Pension and Benefit Fund Policy proved to be an ideal vehicle to bring both sides together. The Committee could reach out to Wall Street professionals via Sheinkman's contacts, while using its membership to gauge interest within the labour movement. In February 1989, the EPF proposal was sent for commentary to the "most disposed" unions represented on the Committee, such as the UMWA (United Mine Workers of America) and the USW (United Steelworkers). Several Wall Street firms—including Drexel Burnham Lambert, Kohlberg Kravis Roberts and Shearson Lehman Hutton—were also asked for their response (Sheinkman, 1989).

Only the responses from Drexel Burnham Lambert and Shearson Lehman Hutton, the two big rivals in the leveraged buyout market, were included in the archives. The documents reveal that both firms were critical of the initiative, questioning the fund's ability to attract investors and banks' willingness to provide the capital required for

Financialisation through socialisation   65

the transactions. Both the blind pool and the employee stock ownership plan were unpopular investment tools, the documents read; the former because investors had no say in how their money was spent, the latter because investors regarded these plans as strategies of last resort for failing firms (Acosta, 1989; Drexel Burnham Lambert, 1989). Because successful employee stock ownership plans were still few and far between, they first needed "to educate the marketplace" on the desirability of this tool before raising capital. The presence of some success stories, Drexel staff noted, might reduce the "natural scepticism that investors might have toward an organised labour-sponsored fund" (Drexel Burnham Lambert, 1989).

Suspicion towards the unions also informed the commenters' suggestions for the fund's organisational structure. Because managers might fear political interference from the unions, it was important that the board was completely independent from the labour movement and not—as was the case in the earlier proposal drafts—composed of labour officials, both Drexel and Shearson emphasised. "If political pressure is allowed to influence the investment decisions," the Drexel staff wrote, "no reputable fund manager will be retained and the EPF will have no credibility" (Drexel Burnham Lambert, 1989). According to the representative from Shearson Lehman Hutton, the unions needed to think carefully about how much capital they were willing to commit: at least 25 per cent of the pool to show they were serious, but less than 50 per cent to avoid conflicts of interest (Acosta, 1989). The Drexel staff suggested a commitment fund. In a commitment fund, investors would put up a small amount of capital to pay for the daily operations of the fund, but would only contribute to the investments on a deal-by-deal basis: "If an investment opportunity is good, the necessary funds will be plentiful and available quickly" (ibid.).

Sheinkman and Patterson rewrote the proposal once more. The board of union officials disappeared from the proposal and was replaced by an advisory committee. The reference to union ownership of the investment company was also removed; instead, it stated that the company would be "supported, but not owned" by organised labour ("Request for Proposal: Employee Partnership Fund," 1989). In addition, investments would be based on "sound economic criteria, insulated from any pressures to act otherwise." The authors explicitly acknowledged possible scepticism towards labour movement, expressing the hope that collaborating with a "well-known, large firm" might overcome "any investor scepticism as to the fund's purpose" (ibid). Other aspects of the EPF, such as the structure of the fund or the choice of fund manager, they deliberately left vague to avoid alienating the unions whose seed money they sought. After all, an internal memorandum stated, "for unions to provide the up front [sic] money creates heightened labour expectations and invites intervention in the operation of the fund" ("Issues of EPF working their way towards resolution," 1989).

Still, the committee's ultimate goal of establishing worker-friendly buyouts did not completely disappear from the proposal. In June 1989, the committee sent out its formal request for proposals to sixteen investment banks and other financial firms. "[We] solicit your interest," the letter read, "[in a fund] to help workers and their unions compete in capital markets" ("Request for Proposal: Employee

66 *Natascha van der Zwan*

Partnership Fund," 1989). The authors expressed the hope that the fund would appeal to investors "interested in transactions which produce long-term returns through growth and increased productivity, rather than transactions designed to maximise short-term returns using break-up strategies" (ibid: 1). The authors listed five criteria for future investments: (1) strong labour-management partnership in the restructured company; (2) sensitivity to jobs; (3) respect for existing collective bargaining structures; (4) promoting worker ownership; and (5) providing the necessary return for the fund (ibid). Majority employee ownership, mentioned in an earlier draft, no longer appeared on the list ("Issues of EPF working their way towards resolution," May 19, 1989).

Despite its initial criticism, Drexel Burnham Lambert made a formal bid for the EPF in August 1989. The investment bankers proposed a $100 million commitment fund, with a Drexel subsidiary responsible for its management. Limited partners would need to commit at least $2.5 million, of which 20 per cent had to be fulfilled at the start of the fund. The manager would raise 5 per cent of the capital. In return, he would receive a 2 per cent fee and 20 per cent of the net gains, but only after the limited partners earned a 10 per cent return on their capital. An investment committee of five members (three from investors, two from Drexel) would determine the investment policy. In addition, an advisory council of seven labour officials served the manager. The authors also suggested a union task force, which would assist local unions after the buyouts were completed. Citing the $5 billion of transactions in employee-owned firms DBL had been involved in in the past 5 years, the authors expressed their hope that it could continue working with the union leaders on this project (Cogut and Flanagan, 1989).

6 months later, Drexel Burnham Lambert declared bankruptcy. The infamous Wall Street firm became the subject of a large-scale U.S. government investigation into securities violations. Michael Milken, the dethroned king of the junk bond, was indicted for 97 counts of securities fraud and insider trading. Amidst these scandals, a growing number of defaults caused a sudden drop in the value of junk bonds. Many critics, including a growing number of investors, wondered out loud if leveraged buyouts had not saddled America's corporations with too much debt. In 1989, a record number of corporations defaulted on their debt, at a total amount of $8.1 billion. A year later, the defaults further increased to $18 billion. Meanwhile, Wall Street firms were faced with big losses and began to let go of thousands of employees. As one journalist wrote: "... debt is becoming a dirty word and raiders have lost their prestige" (Greenwald et al., 1992).

In this new economic context, Sheinkman and Patterson selected Eugene Keilin and Ron Bloom as the EPF's general partners. The two men had been involved in the development of the EPF as employees of Lazard Frères, but had left the company to start their own firm. By the time they joined the EPF, Keilin and Bloom had already amassed considerable experience with employee buyouts at Weirton Steel (Keilin) and LTV Steel. With the aim set on employee buyouts at companies valued between $100 and $500 million, the men hoped to make between 10 and 20 deals within 5 years (*Wall Street Journal*, 1989; Swoboda, 1990; Bernstein, 1990). They approached public and private pension fund managers to gauge their

Financialisation through socialisation   67

interest in joining the EPF. "We believe the Fund offers an attractive investment opportunity," Bloom wrote the New York State Comptroller's office, "[a]s well as an opportunity to enhance productivity, protect domestic employment and encourage employee participation by facilitating transactions involving employee ownership" (Bloom, 1991). Similar letters were sent to local and national unions as well as several public employee retirement systems.

Despite the declining popularity of leveraged buyouts, Keilin and Bloom remained optimistic that the fund would garner enough interest from investors: "The EPF proposal is currently under intensive review in New York and California," Bloom reported back to the Committee on Pension and Benefit Fund Policy in February 1991, "[a]nd we are hopeful that these major state funds will agree to participate in the EPF." Still, Bloom admitted, "this project has not moved to completion as quickly as we hoped, but it came on the market when the economy was in decline and buyout funds were in disfavour" (Industrial Union Department Executive Committee on Pension and Benefit Fund Policy, 1991). His words were prescient: CalPERS (California Public Employees' Retirement System) and other pension funds declined to participate in the EPF. The archival documents do not reveal what happened to the EPF in the following 2 years, but in August 1993 the fund was again on the agenda of the Industrial Union Department Committee. In the meeting notes, we read the following diagnosis of why the EPF failed to launch:

> A few years ago, our committee developed a model for a pool of capital that would be invested in employee owned [sic] firms. The model flowed from an intensive staff investigation of how the leveraged buyout craze could be turned to our members' benefit. Unfortunately, the EPF hit the "market" just as the buyout era peaked and investors active in such undertakings were retrenching. Another factor that made it hard to complete the fund was the lack of a substantial number of successful employee-led buyouts at unionised firms.
>
> (Industrial Union Department Executive Committee
> on Pension and Benefit Fund Policy, 1993)

The historical records do not offer further insights in what happened to the EPF after 1993. In 1996, Bill Patterson became the director of the AFL-CIO's newly created Office of Investments, which would coordinate labour's activities in the area of corporate governance. Eugene Keilin and Ron Bloom continued their partnership for another year, after which both moved on to other projects, while Jacob Sheinkman continued as ACTWU's president until 1995. What the records do show is that the committee's effort to make American finance more labour-friendly was made in close cooperation with professionals from the very industry it hoped to reform. In order to set up the fund, labour officials had to rely on the expertise that these professionals could provide. The historical records show how much emphasis labour's financial advisors placed on the need for credibility and political independence. To launch the EPF, organised labour had to conform to

68 *Natascha van der Zwan*

the professional standards of the financial industry in order to prove that labour's financial activities had to be taken seriously. As a result, the proposal for the EPF lost its critical edge as it tried to appeal to investors' sensibilities for risk aversion and competitive returns.

4 Conclusion: beyond financialisation as colonisation?

The Employee Partnership Fund never came into existence as the labour-friendly financial intermediary that would transform the market for corporate control from within. Still, its brief history offers a glimpse of the processes that transformed the American political economy during the 1980s. Unlike actual hostile takeovers by corporate raiders, the case of the EPF is not a typical narrative of financialisation, involving "the capture of resources by finance in the broadest sense" (Chiapello, 2015: 15). Instead of financialisation as a "colonisation" of the corporate economy (ibid.), the term socialisation might be more accurate to describe the gradual process through which organised labour adopted the norms and attitudes of the finance sector in its EPF proposal. The finance sector is a social system with its own cultural norms, behavioural attitudes, and knowledge base. Sharing a commitment to these norms, attitudes, and knowledge creates the trust necessary for financial transactions with a high degree of uncertainty.

The years-long correspondence between the Committee on Pension and Benefit Fund Policy and Wall Street bankers also reveals the latter's strong suspicion of the EPF as a union-initiated enterprise. The bankers' advice on how to organise the fund suggests that credibility and trust are preconditions for the pursuit of value. The bankers' suggestions centred on two elements of the fund: (1) a removal of organised labour from the investment decision-making within the fund; and (2) a greater financial commitment from organised labour. If put in practice, the suggestions would have led to a paradoxical situation: to show the unions were serious partners, they had to increase their investment, yet without gaining a say in the decision-making process. Here, the bankers followed agency theory's prescription to create a common financial interest between organised labour and other investors. At the same time, their suggestions enlarged their own possibilities for enrichment. After all the general partner of the fund, one of their own, would be paid an annual management fee in addition to his performance-related fee. The general partner therefore stood to gain financially, even if the fund itself performed poorly (Erturk et al., 2010).

The committee's adoption of the bankers' suggestions complicated its relationship with its members. The unions had a very different view of value than the bankers centring on workers' contributions to the financial performance of the firm. They justified labour's involvement in the market of corporate control by claiming that unions were better equipped to gain the workers' loyalty necessary to realise a return on investment. This worker-oriented notion of value stands in stark contrast to investment bankers' own workplace culture with its high insecurity, but also high rewards. As Karen Ho (2006) has shown, investment bankers projected their own experiences of being expendable in the pursuit of value

Financialisation through socialisation 69

onto the workforce of the corporations they acquired. The legal retrenchment of shareholder value maximisation in the Employee Retirement Income Security Act, the lack of control over single-employer pension funds, and the absence of broad political support from union members have been mentioned as additional obstacles preventing the realisation of 'pension fund socialism' in the United States (cf. McCarthy, 2014).

Still, the question of how to make the finance sector more responsive to the needs of citizens has not lost its relevance since the takeover wave of the 1980s. On the contrary, mass ownership of pensions, home mortgages, and other financial products has resulted in ever more complicated webs of interdependence between workers, firms, and the finance sector. Yet, following Davis (2009: 32) this democratisation of finance is a representative democracy only, channelled through intermediaries over which citizen-owners lack control. Some authors (Engelen, 2006; Block, 2014) have therefore argued for the development of social investment funds outside of the financial mainstream. The case of the EPF, however, shows that the lack of attention to investment goals besides the maximisation of return is not just a function of the structure of the finance sector. A true socialisation of finance, therefore, starts with a more fluid understanding of who constitute legitimate and credible investors rather than upholding the social boundaries that separate the finance sector from labour and other segments of the political economy.

Note

1 ACTWU's affiliate, the Amalgamated Bank, was also considered as a general partner. But, so the authors noted, it lacked experience with employee buyouts and was therefore less qualified than other candidates for general partner (ibid.).

4 Financial logic and bankers' institutional entrepreneurship

The politics of the "zombies" debate in bankruptcy proceedings at the Commercial Court of Paris (2000–2005)

Emmanuel Lazega, Lise Mounier and Sylvan Lemaire

Businesses of all kinds usually try as much as they can to participate in the regulation of their own markets. Social control of economic exchanges and regulation of entrepreneurial activities have therefore created a political struggle between states, business, and consumers. This struggle intensifies in an organizational and market society where the state privatizes even its regalian functions. For business, one way of participating in this joint regulatory activity is to take advantage of this privatization and quietly exercise control in public institutions, for example institutions that solve conflicts among economic actors and discipline entrepreneurs. The financial industry is a powerful, but often discreet set of actors in this exercise of control. The question addressed in this chapter relates to how this notoriously "dual" (economic and political) industry, especially bankers, participates in this joint regulatory activity. This chapter argues that it does so by investing heavily in institutional entrepreneurship and looks at some of the consequences of this strategy.

This blurring of the boundaries between government and economic sectors does not mean that privatization of a state function is a form of "deinstitutionalization"; it is rather a form of imposition of private professional logics in public official decision making, combined with the accumulation of organizational clout. To show this, French "consular" institutions, in particular commercial courts, provide an interesting case in point. These institutions are a specific example of blurred boundaries between politics and finance, between public and private. In one court in particular, the Tribunal de Commerce de Paris (TCP, i.e., Commercial Court of Paris) on which this chapter focuses, the financial sector has achieved physical and epistemic domination that verges on institutional capture. Here finance is more than merely an economic sector. Banks in particular are shown to be shadow regulators and discreet policymakers. They perform these roles of discreet regulator and policy maker by importing into government and the political sphere—with the approval of the state—their own appropriateness judgments and epistemic toolkit. The latter are the core of the collective pragmatism (Lazega, 2011) of the bankers when they make judicial decisions.

The politics of the "zombies" debate   71

In the social sciences, exogenous regulation of markets (by the state) and self-regulation (by business) are usually examined separately. This leads to strong simplifications in the comprehension of the social organization of markets, and thus of the organizational and market society. The notion of joint regulation—borrowed from Jean-Daniel Reynaud (1989) and extended to the context of the relationships between the state and business (Lazega and Mounier, 2002, 2003a, 2003b, 2003c)—and the study of its institutional forms help prevent this simplification. The consular institutions on which this chapter focuses are part of a complex system of cooperation between the French state, local meso-level institutions, and civil society individuals (Chatriot and Lemercier, 2002; Lemercier, 2003), thus precisely a system of joint regulation. They represent a specific way of sharing the costs of regulation and social control of industrial activity and markets (Falconi et al., 2005), in particular by mobilizing, on a voluntary basis, the knowledge and experience of the economy accumulated by business and labor (Lazega, 2003, 2011).

In particular, the analysis of work and professions in the financial sector has to deal, at some point, with joint regulation in the judicial work on bankruptcies as a structural dimension of the organization of business. In all countries, this area of judicial work involves the centrality of banks as the main creditors in market economies. In France, to understand the logic of the joint regulation of bankruptcies, it is necessary to understand the organization of consular commercial courts. The first sections of this chapter briefly describe this organization and the notion of collective pragmatism that characterizes joint regulation by its consular lay judges. A theoretical framework is provided, based on an approach to judicial decisions that does not separate the organization of markets from the judicial organization that makes such decisions about the financial balance of firms. The focus on bankruptcies as they are managed by the TCP shows how the financial sector, by achieving multidimensional domination of that court, participates in the above-mentioned blurring of the boundaries between politics and finance. The data used to substantiate this argument is based on a sociological study of this court (see Box 4.1).

Section I presents consular justice in France as an institution involved in the joint regulation of markets. Section II identifies a variety of pragmatic and political logics related to bankruptcy work carried out by consular judges. Section III shows how their decisions focus on eliminating "zombies," i.e., companies that should be dissolved based on the principles of market economics, but that are "artificially" kept alive by various kinds of support. In the case of the TCP, this joint regulation raises tense questions related to conflicts of interests in which bankruptcy judges are entangled, especially when they come from the financial sector. The "dirty work" of bankruptcies, as presented by various categories of consular judges at this court, is a good illustration. Section IV uses as an analyser a document, written by a former president of the TCP, jointly with a former minister of finance, that describes the discreet political strategy that they jointly designed and used during the financial crisis of 1992–1997 when the French banks themselves were the zombies. This conclusion shows that this document provides a rare and published moment of truth that, when the bankrupt companies are the banks themselves, the articulation of the financial and political logics emerge more clearly in the analysis of consular work carried out by the professions of finance. The conclusion shows that, although fieldwork for this study dates back to 2000–2005, it is relevant to bring back its results in the context of 2016–2017.

Box 4.1: Sources

Compared to the majority of other commercial courts, the Commercial Court of Paris (TCP) is particular in that it is much larger: it holds a higher number of specialized chambers and hears more cases than any other. The TCP alone deals with 10–20 percent of the commercial disputes that arise in France (arbitration not included). It differs furthermore in the diversity of sectors represented by its judges as well as by having a larger customer base. The judges' level of education is often very high (X, ENA, HEC, Sciences-Po*, doctorate in law). However only half have had any judicial training. The majority of them are no longer businessmen or entrepreneurs in the traditional sense of the term, but rather executives or former senior managers of large companies.

The empirical research consisted of three waves of in-depth interviews, conducted face to face with all of the consular judges of the court. The first wave was conducted in Autumn 2000, based on the list of the 157 judges of that year, to which 10 persons were added—the "wise men" of the court (former judges who make themselves available to advise more novice judges, and knowledgeable leaders of the association of consular judges). For the second wave, carried out in 2002, a list of 197 judges was compiled. This new list combined the judges from the first wave (either still working at the court or having left it) with newcomer judges who had been elected in the interim period. The third wave of interviews took place in Autumn 2005, with a list of 234 judges including those in activity in 2005 (166 judges) and those who participated in the previous interviews and/or had been elected since 2002. The research reports on these waves of fieldwork papers and chapters are available at the Law & Justice Research Mission of the French Ministry of Justice and other scholarly publications.

Here this study ends with the presentation and analysis of a text commenting on the financial crisis of 2008. This text was co-published by a former president of the court and by the minister of finance who were in office at the same period of time. In the text they summarize the strategy, which is still in use, that they adopted in order to manage the financial crisis of 1992–1997.

Prestigious French Higher Education Institutions

I Consular (public/private) justice in France

In France, it is in part the role of the commercial court to resolve conflicts between economic actors and to exercise discipline on the entry, activity, and exit of markets, in particular managing commercial disputes and bankruptcies. These jurisdictions, peculiar to the world of commerce, have existed for four and a half centuries and are particularly relevant for the study of this dual regulation. It was one of the only institutions that weathered the French Revolution of 1789 almost unchanged, while having been fundamentally called into question on a regular basis from its very inception. It is a shining example of an intermediary institution whose existence is difficult to justify in theory (from a classical legal and political viewpoint) and yet which has always been well established in practice, both in response to a claim from the parties concerned and from the state.

For a very long time the state has shared its judicial power in this court with the local business community, which is represented by the consular judges who work it. These judges, who willingly see themselves as representatives of "economic civil society," are voluntary, i.e., not paid for their work. The consular judges can, however, be both a court judge and get paid by the company that employs them outside of the court. Consular judges are judicial. They have the same powers and prerogatives as career judges, i.e., judges in ordinary courts, and are also subject to the same rules of abstention and recusal, as laid out in the French New Code of Civil Procedure (Articles 339 to 341). They are elected for a mandate of either 2 or 4 years (for a total maximum duration of 14 years) by an electoral body consisting of judges already in service and employers' association representatives at the chamber of commerce in their community. They can be candidates for this election after having first been sponsored by an employer's union and pre-selected by a committee from the very same chamber of commerce, as is the case in Paris. In theory, these two "sister" consular economic institutions (the chamber of commerce and the commercial court) are mutually supportive in this tight social control of markets and they maintain close ties with one another, as they have been doing for many centuries (see for example Hilaire (1999); Hirsch (1985); Lemercier (2003, 2007); Kessler (2007)). Through this institutional solution, control costs of the market economy are shared by the state, the industries or the companies, and the individual judges. In theory, however, every judge acts as an individual judge, without the specific mandate of a sector of the economy.

In the implementation of this social control, the specific value of the judges' commercial experience and their knowledge of the economic world is attached with a certain amount of pragmatism in their decision making. This pragmatism is often collective (Lazega, 2003, 2011) and reflects the fact that this institution is supported by an entire inter-institutional system. It thus represents a real consular "regime" that politicians may well have a vested interest in preserving. The Code of Commerce itself was indeed written by the president of the TCP in 1807. Another more recent example of this was the significant contribution made by the first female president of the TCP to the promotion and formulation of a new bankruptcy law in 2006.

Therefore, from the point of view of some sectors of the economy, consular judges are regarded as more than mere judges. In effect, they can be regarded as

74   E. Lazega, L. Mounier and S. Lemaire

"institutional entrepreneurs" (DiMaggio, 1988). This term is here understood in the sense of actors who, in order to defend their regulatory interests, act–and have sufficient resources—to maintain, modify or create institutional solutions and structures, whether by instrumental and strategic calculation or by ideological or moral convictions, which are themselves more or less institutionalized (Lawrence, 1999; Lawrence and Phillips, 2004). Consular judges uphold militant beliefs regarding the functioning of the economy and act both in their own name and on behalf of companies and the employers' organizations who sponsored them at the time of their election. They promote "sensitivities" and specific functional rules in the business world. These are also "judicial entrepreneurs" in the sense of McIntosh and Cates (1997)— in particular those who come from over-represented sectors (notably banks and the construction industry). This observation invites political sociology to rethink public policy based upon a review of this consular, hybrid, and joint regulation regime.

A pragmatic institution of joint regulation of markets

In France these private disputes are dealt with by a variety of different commercial courts, which are located in different cities, each with a defined geographical remit. Article L.411-1 of the French Code of Judicial Organization defines commercial courts as specialized first instance jurisdictions whose specific competence is to settle commercial disputes between natural and corporate trading "persons," i.e., between companies but also, for example, between a company and an individual consumer who is engaged in a commercial act. Furthermore, the Commercial Courts are now competent in insolvency matters (judicial recovery or liquidation) and, more recently, in the prevention of bankruptcy.

Such a joint regulatory system is justified by the actors in several ways: as a less costly and speedier form of justice than a system that calls upon career judges; as having experienced judges who are trained to understand the problems faced by companies and the behavior of company executives, particularly in matters of insolvency and bankruptcy; as having an understanding of the idiosyncrasies of the different sectors of the economy, designated as "customs"; as having the ability to rapidly unlock the systems and adapt laws and regulations in the ever-changing world of business : customs are sources of law (*Les usages sont sources de droit*, an expression often used by consular judges). It is upon these justifications, among others, that the claims to joint regulation are based.

In fact, elected consular judges perform what is usually considered to be a regalian function of the state. This somewhat anomalous case of joint regulation is an extreme form of "co-regulation" (Grabowsky and Braithwaite, 1986: 83), which is understood to be a form of self-regulation by the industrial organizations that the state has approved and to which it lends a part of its sanctioning powers. This institution, however, suffers nevertheless from a certain lack of legitimacy. The parties involved have only a limited amount of confidence in the impartiality of a court's decisions, especially in the commercial courts in smaller towns. They fear that the judges of these smaller courts have the ability to exercise judicial control over their own competitors and this lack of legitimacy repeatedly comes to light as an issue in recurrent attempts to reform these commercial jurisdictions.

Collective pragmatism, customs, and judgments

From the perspective of the notions of dispute, sides, respect of the adversarial principle, and the obligation to judge in law, consular justice does not theoretically diverge from the law. Nevertheless, some elements of "practical" commercial procedure observed ethnographically, and that experienced business lawyers teach at the Ecole de Formation du Barreau de Paris (i.e., Paris Bar Association School), make it possible to determine the context in which pragmatic reasoning begins to take on its meaning. Much of the reasoning of consular judges is based on precedents; however, the jurisprudence remains opaque (as in all first instance jurisdictions in France). Very often, commercial disputes are not foremost a question of justice, but rather a question of renegotiation of contracts based on the decision of the court. It is often frowned upon by consular judges if lawyers are summoned without prior attempts at finding an amicable solution. They feel a sense of closeness to the litigants: they value that the parties appear in person (especially for the pleadings); they like to ask them questions using non-legal language. Hence, the lawyers fear any uncontrolled reactions from their clients during these interactions. The judges also seek alternatives: subsidiary demands that help the parties to reach a compromise, stressing where both parties are in the right, explaining to the unsuccessful party why they lost.

In this context, pragmatism is, in practice, affirmed by the judge as the evaluation of the consequences of their decisions on the functioning of the economy: prime importance is attached to the consequences of the rule of law, precedents, decisions, and institutions on the realm of facts. A decision is considered pragmatic in that it combines the judge's knowledge of the economy and of management with his or her knowledge of law and jurisprudence. In practice, this produces judgments that are based on a synthesis of law, management, and economics, but that also calls upon the customs of the business world, common sense, and the judges' sense of "fairness."

In the judges' minds, these pragmatic judgments are often based on "sensitivities" (*sensibilités*) and individual experiences. However, this pragmatism is not just an individual characteristic as it is also associated with more collective norms of the business world. There are many non-legal conventions and criteria that consular judges resort to in order to make their judgements, notably when these judges have strong discretionary powers. In the area of bankruptcy, strong political positions are used to make decisions in matters of liquidation and/or judicial recovery and, for the latter, whether it be a case of cession or continuation. This issue is as topical as ever due, for example, to ongoing restructurations in the banking sector in the western world.

II Politicizing the judiciary by promoting financial collective pragmatism

The financial sector is clearly overrepresented at the Commercial Court of Paris, in both absolute and relative terms. Between 2000 and 2005, 29 percent of the consular judges came from the financial sector (38 percent if insurance

76   E. Lazega, L. Mounier and S. Lemaire

companies are included in the financial sector), whereas these sectors represented 5.1 percent of the workforce in the Paris area (Ile-de-France). Each year this sector—which has at least one person paid full time to watch what goes on at these consular institutions and seek potential recruits—puts up dozens of candidates for the positions of consular judge in the commercial courts. Finance expends great quantities of resources in commercial litigation and bankruptcies. Consequently, it is willing to invest in the political and regulatory process and it is in its interest to try to structure the court in a way that will increase the influence of its own norms and practices rather than those of other sectors. Its priorities (e.g., upholding the value of assets, eschewing both excessive financial support or sudden cut-offs in lines of credit, high sensitivity to the repercussions of business failures on the economy at large) are thus likely to be promoted with insistence as ready-made solutions in this kind of commercial court, to be permanently taken into consideration there in connection with all kinds of legal disputes and bankruptcy cases. Promoting a financial logic in this institution takes organizational clout (Lazega, Mounier and Brandes, 2011; Lazega and Mounier, 2012). For example, there is a concentration of bankers in specialized (and closed to the public) bankruptcy chambers. With these strategies finance shows how it has been able to "capture" a pragmatic judicial institution, a target for bankers as judicial entrepreneurs. This pragmatism, individual and collective, characterizes joint regulation in general and shows the necessity to look at the financial logic, in particular that of bankers, in their bankruptcy decisions without dissociating the organization of markets from how the judicial organization operates with respect to the financial balance of companies.

Institutions of joint regulation thus appear to be the locus of a struggle to exert influence upon the construction of the shared frame of reference, which is required if their members are to be able to describe and interpret facts in a consistent way. In this "epistemic" and normative competition between sectors, banking and finance (often, but not always formally organized to do so) are in a position to promote their own readily identifiable occupational sensitivities and pragmatism, their own collective representations, customs, justice criteria, and conventions. Empirical research brings to light a relationship between career, sector, and the sensitivity commercial court judges draw upon in making decisions in which they have a great amount of discretion (Lazega and Mounier, 2009).[1]

For example, judges with a law degree and members of the banking and finance world tend to be more interventionist (than all commercial court judges taken together) in cases of conflicts between boards and minority shareholders. In such disputes they are more inclined than other judges to decide in favor of the board. They are thus less hostile than other respondents to judicial intervention in the internal affairs of a company. On the other hand, they tend to be much less interventionist than their colleagues in contractual disputes. Lastly, they are less "punitive" than their average colleague with respect to awarding so-called "moral" damages resulting from unfair competition of the sort that may disrupt (supposedly natural) market mechanisms.

The politics of the "zombies" debate 77

In contrast, the reverse is observed for judges coming from the building sector. The latter are likely to be less interventionist than their colleagues in intra-organizational cases opposing the board to minority stockholders. They are much more interventionist than the other judges in inter-organizational litigation between parties to a contract on a given market. Judges representing the building sector are also more punitive in awarding damages.

By systematically sending senior managers with legal education to the Commercial Court of Paris, the financial sectors have achieved physical and epistemic domination of that court: bankers with a law degree are consistently the most central, if not super-central players in the advice network in this court (Lazega et al., 2009). This domination is not necessarily well tolerated by non-bankers. Bankers' social integration into the court is weaker than that of judges coming from other sectors, precisely because the banking sector's strong presence or "position" (in Flemming's [1998] sense) is resented by others, and even sometimes proves counterproductive in terms of influence. At the time of our study, the financial sector was indeed perceived by judges from other sectors to be either defending its own corporatist interests or trying to replace the state once the latter began withdrawing from direct control of the economy. As a response to this very critical reaction, one president of the court, himself a former banker, dismissively declared: "Shopkeepers hate bankers."

III Bankruptcy work as politically dirty work: the "don't feed the zombies" controversy

More generally, this resentment is related, in part, to the fact that when a company faces bankruptcy judges, it is usually the case that its bank has decided not to support it any longer. Banks evaluate business creditworthiness based on several factors, including legal structure, business age, business credit ratings, company revenues, personal credit scores of the entrepreneurs, and finally the social network of the entrepreneur; even the social relationship of the entrepreneur and the bank manager can be a decisive factor when seeking credit (Uzzi, 1999). In France, a cat and mouse game between the entrepreneur and the bank manager revolves around the fact that jurisprudence of the Cour de Cassation (the highest French court) allows entrepreneurs to sue their own banks either for "abusive support" (*"soutien abusif"*) or for "abusive termination of credit" (*"rupture abusive de crédit"*), or both. Knowing that, entrepreneurs try to get banks heavily involved, to strongly implicate them in their business so as to be able to sue them and their deep pockets in case the business goes bankrupt. Bank managers walk a fine line between both demands. This creates a strong micro-economic incentive for banks to be present at the court and to send in representatives of their industry who will side with creditors when dealing in bankruptcy proceedings.

By eliciting the discourse of consular judges about bankruptcy, it is possible to flesh out a central controversy within and outside the courthouse, a controversy coined the "don't feed the zombies" debate. The zombie is a metaphor used by bankers and economists for a company that is a "living dead", i.e., neither alive nor dead, no longer making profits but not willing to give up and declare bankruptcy. It threatens both banks and the market economy by "distorting the competitive arena." To do this, a module in the interviews with the judges asked them about their personal opinion and criteria for how best to manage insolvency proceedings using liquidation vs. a recovery/administration plan, and when using the latter, selecting between selling the company ("cession") or continuing with the same owners and managers ("continuation"). Discourse analysis did not need much subtlety to tease out, beyond the technical dimensions of these decisions, their political—if not militant—dimension. In spite of the lack of room in this text, it is worth showing the color of this discourse with short quotations when summarizing its content and variations among the consular judges of the TCP.

When analyzing the arguments developed about recovery plans, the court can be considered to be divided into three categories: two opposing minority groups and one majority that "pragmatically" mixes the views of the minority groups. The views of the two "extreme" minority groups were for the most part divergent on the issues related to bankruptcy proceedings: preference for either a cession (takeover, for example) or a continuation, importance of purely legal criteria, cost of cession, safeguarding employees, reimbursement of liabilities, etc. These opposing views are founded on very different visions of the role of consular justice with respect to recovery plans and representations of the functioning of the business world, i.e., what they consider to be appropriate or not in general commercial practices. In the middle, the largest of the three groups is pulled between these two opposing orientations, adopting an apparently more neutral position, while here and there borrowing aspects that they agree with.

The first group of judges is thus characterized by their propensity to take into account the social impact of their decisions both at the level of the employees about to be fired and at the level of the directors of the companies in difficulty. They favor continuation plans on the grounds that they would provide more guarantees to save employment, which they consider to be the main objective of any recovery plan, including the continued employment of the same management. Throughout the discourse, the entrepreneur who runs his/her company is viewed as a highly-valued figure, a genuine source of wealth creation, the lifeblood of innovation, and the foundation of an economy centered on industrial creation. As such, he/she must be protected against attacks from financiers, whose aim is only to increase their profits regardless of the company's added value. In this conception, the task of consular justice is to preserve the company, notably by favoring continuations, which are perceived as a source of economic life. Here the judges strongly condemn those amongst their colleagues who place too much emphasis on a company's accounts—this must be linked to the fact that the members of this group are mainly themselves former company managers, notably coming from the construction, services, and industrial sectors.

The following are some typical examples of the discourse from this category of judges:

The politics of the "zombies" debate 79

Judge A: A part of the court is in fact very considerate: it truly does try to save the company. That is abundantly clear. I've known this ever since I was in bankruptcy chambers, it truly is their goal. The priority is to save the company, along with the former manager.

Judge B: I personally favor continuations if they safeguard jobs; and cessions if the new buyer keeps the staff on; but that is just my political stance.

Judge C: The idea is that keeping a company alive is preferable to letting it die. Therefore, if in any doubt, recovery plans are always preferred, especially continuation plans.

Judge D: In cases of cessions, beware of sharks and vultures amongst the buyers. There are plenty of them around.

Given their opposing views, members of the second group maintain a clear preference for systematic liquidation and, in some cases, for cession plans on the grounds that they are economically more viable than continuation plans: they can generate cash that the company needs. Furthermore, they constitute a sort of "electric shock" for the company, as they are more conducive to radical reorganizing of the business. Moreover, in contrast to the first group, the judges in this group are not preoccupied with the preservation of the social dimension of the company. They hold that employees cannot be a fundamental aspect of the consular judgment, since it represents only a secondary aspect of the company—giving it more importance would only lead, irremediably, to the failure of the recovery plan, which will rapidly result in liquidation. Therefore preference must be in favor of a company's creditors, for two reasons: first, creditors are considered to be the source of a company's economic dynamism. Second, they are also companies in their own right and can be affected by their clients' difficulties—in the worst situations creditors themselves can go bankrupt if their clients do not pay them back what they are owed, which in turn also leads to redundancies. The role of the judge must be restricted to the preservation of the interests of creditors as their investments play a key role within the global economy (capital is reinjected into other companies), promoting a dynamic movement of financial flows. This viewpoint tends to characterize judges with a background in the banking and industrial sectors, who dominate this group both in terms of numbers and influence.

Amongst the typical remarks from this category of judges:

Judge G: It is utterly essential to avoid intensive care.

Judge H: The question "Is this not going to upset the social order?" is something that I really feel strongly about. For me, social order is competition. If I put this in extreme terms, a company that is no longer performing has to be liquidated. If companies in difficulty are killed off, there'll be no more companies in difficulty! I'm almost not joking here: in the jungle or in the savannah there are no sick animals because all sick animals die off. The problem of sick animals has therefore been eliminated, as they have all died!

Judge I: As a banker I can tell you that bankruptcy is just a phase in the life of a company. Companies are formed, they live and they die, just like humans. So therefore if you apply this to financial analysis, you are going to have a certain amount of companies that die out, it's the functioning of the economy. The point is that it doesn't get out of hand. You then of course have the problem of staff which is now a significant issue but it must be treated separately, in particular through career switches.

The third group comprises the majority of judges and is split between the divergent orientations of the two smaller groups. Its position is based upon a thorough examination of the particularities of each individual recovery plan. It advocates a solution that is meant to combine the interests of all of the parties involved (managers, workers, creditors)—a solution believed to be possible. From this point of view, the judge can theoretically favor neither continuation nor takeover—in the same way that he/she cannot take the side of either the employees or the creditors. Indeed, both the prospect of staff redundancies and the writing off of debt obligations are measures that must be considered as possibilities: they are a legitimate part of the (difficult) reality of the market economy and they can therefore not be exempt from consular intervention. Accordingly, allowing takeovers often constitutes a difficult consular decision, insofar as they bring about layoffs and exclusion of the entrepreneur/company creator, whom many judges are nevertheless willing to support. Coming from the business world, many of the judges in this group empathize with the managers in difficulty and have a tendency to favor them.

The following are examples of typical discourse from this category of judges:

Judge J: What really matters is the future of the company and the benefits to society. But in truth there are no key factors, it's on a case by case basis. So should the situation occur where safeguarding the staff is paramount or the *stability* of the provisional recovery plan, the only certainty is that whatever the prevailing element ends up being, it must guarantee the durability of the business.

Judge K: It's common sense, in order for a takeover plan to work out, two things are required: firstly, the company has to be truly viable and secondly, it cannot be done by recklessly damaging the interests of the creditors or the employees. There has to be something in it for everyone. A continuation plan, during the judicial process, allows the manager to have a bit of a "spring clean" within the business, if he needs to lay off some staff or if he needs to renegotiate his contracts with his suppliers etc.

Within this third group, a sub-group of judges nevertheless stresses the need to develop decision strategies to combat a broader economic trend, i.e., the increasing concentration of wealth and power of decision in the hands of large financial groups. A strong criticism of financiers' logic emerged from their discourse,

The politics of the "zombies" debate   81

which was observed in conjunction with some benevolence towards the entrepreneur, whom they consider to be the true creator of wealth. These judges are particularly attuned to the personality of the company boss or the potential buyer. As a result the will, business experience, and know-how of the entrepreneur play an important role in the formation of their judgements.

IV Saving the financial zombie

Thus, the "zombie" debate brings out deep ideological beliefs, conventions, professional disputes, and political rhetorics of the judges with respect to the life and death of companies, as articulated with their own careers. This case also shows how the work of financiers extends financial logics and pragmatism beyond the boundaries of the financial sector. The political dimension of these choices permeates the discourse and practices of all consular judges dealing with bankruptcy proceedings. This level of politicization, however, is intrinsic to the politically "dirty job" itself. The next section looks at how the TCP and consular judges reach a much higher level of politicization in their discourse and practice of bankruptcy. It is based on a narrative by a former president of the TCP, a narrative that reflects a "moment of truth" in the discourse of consular judges, and that was published a year after the 2008 financial crisis. This shows that when banks themselves are caught in insolvency proceedings, politicization reaches its highest levels and the zombies debate takes a different dimension. After citing at length a section that shows how this president of the TCP coordinated with the minister of economics and finance to both slow down bankruptcy proceedings in exchange for specific investments reflecting government industrial policy, this section looks at the institutional context that supports this institution precisely because it is capable of such discreet political activity (Box 4.2).

This former President of the TCP, Michel Rougier, recounts in an article on the financial crisis of 2008 how he had gone about saving the French banks during a previous crisis between 1992 and 1997 (which had also been triggered by the bursting of a real estate bubble). This earlier crisis, although less spectacular than in 2008, nevertheless posed the threat of collapse for the large French banks. The former President of the TCP, along with the Minister of Finance and the Economy in office at the time, partook in a debate about the role of the banks during the crisis. His account is based on his experiences as president at the time of this crisis.

Box 4.2: Excerpt from the article by Edmond Alphandéry, Michel Rougier, and Patrick Pélata (2009), Qu'attendres des banques? Le Journal de l'Ecole de Paris, vol. 78, pages 8–16.

Michel Rougier

Between the summers of 1992 and 1997, I asked myself daily, and occasionally at night, the question that brings us here tonight: What is to be expected from banks? To answer this, we need to establish the two given meanings of the verb 'to expect': "What do we expect?" expresses a requirement, whereas "What can we expect?" expresses patience. It is somewhere between these two that my speech will meander.

The crisis of 1992–1997

What we experienced between 1992 and 1997 was a crisis of "promised revenues," much like today. This crisis had begun at the end of the 1980s in the commercial and real estate markets in the United States and London. In France, it took the form of a crisis of promised revenues linked to the exchanges of realestate transaction promises that had begun circulating in very high quantities. Upon his appointment as Minister of Finance, Edmond Alphandéry blocked the free circulation of these sales agreements, which had become a form of hidden securitization of epidemic proportions. Given the significant valuation slump that is observed when property markets turn, the banking system proved to be totally incapable of bearing the corresponding cost.

The prospect of planned legislative elections in March 1993 and the impending political changeover did little to ease the management of the crisis. From September 1992, the commercial court found itself on the front line as there was no longer anyone in the political class who was able to make the necessary decisions. And yet the situation was serious: not only were the banks affected, but also the three main insurance companies (Union des Assurances de Paris - UAP, Groupe des Assurances Nationales - GAN and Assurances Générales de France - AGF).

Patience

Faced with this economic and political collapse, we quickly realized that it would be impossible to expect everything from the banks and that rather, we would have to learn to wait for them, whatever pressure from public opinion we faced. This pressure was, however, very strong: the main criticisms were targeted at the Crédit Lyonnais, but we also helped to settle ideological scores between the supporters and adversaries of the central bank

We were confident that if we could leave the enormous property assets acquired by the banks, for which they had not yet found any buyers, for just a few years in these banks' hands, we would be able to resolve the crisis as the privatization of insurance companies would result in the emergence of a new property market. We did indeed succeed in postponing the first liquidation of a significant bank, the Pallas Stern, until 30th June 1995. If this collapse had happened two years earlier, it would have undoubtedly caused a real systemic crisis similar to the collapse of the Lehman Brothers in 2008. However, in 1995, the warning beacons were well placed and the collapse did not bring about any serious consequences. The property market was already starting to re-emerge from the ashes. American companies rushed to France to buy in earnest, often without seeming too concerned about what they were buying, i.e., properties or debt. Sang-froid and the ability to remain patient paid off in the end.

Demand

At the same time we put the second strand of our plan into action, which, conversely, consisted in setting for the bank very strong expectations within a very specific area—the preservation of two industrial sectors which seemed to us essential to protect. The first being the transportation sector and the second being the press, upon which depended the advertising, printing, and pulp and paper industries. We did not compromise on this point and imposed on the banks to extend all the necessary credit to these sectors. This was not a simple task and in some cases we needed to resort to coercion. We noted that under these circumstances politicians by and large left us on our own: they obviously thought that the judge's imperium would be more effective when dealing with banks than any pressure that they would exert.

The current situation

In order to get us out of the current crisis, we are again going to need to know how to apply the two meanings of the verb to expect ....

As far as the consular judges within the commercial court are concerned, President Rougier is the president "who saved the French banks." His account brings to light another political dimension of the work of the commercial judge in France. It is here particularly interesting as it illustrates the institutional ecology and supports from which the commercial court benefits, the continued existence of which depends on an entire institutional system.

V The consular court, an institution at the crossroads of multiple political interests

Indeed, provided that the state is not considered to be a monolithic organization (Laumann and Knoke, 1987), this institution represents a vested interest for a number of actors. For politicians in general, management of bankruptcies is delegated to the "independent" judges whose "imperium would be more effective when dealing with banks." For the minister of economy and finance, the consular court represents, beyond just a simple instrument for awarding moratoria, a discrete industrial policy tool, i.e., "the preservation of two industrial sectors." Based on the delegation of the "dirty work" (in the sociological sense of Everett Hughes) of managing crises and bankruptcies by means of restructurations, it makes it easier for them to play for time and prolong any procedures until the effects of the crisis have been sufficiently mitigated. For the minister of justice (still on a very low budget compared with many other ministries), it delivers considerable savings in terms of the salaries that would have to be paid to career judges if another institutional solution were put in place. Companies are able to rely on this institution that offers a self-contained normative space, a form of justice taking pragmatically into account the constraints of the business world: speed, awareness of market customs, easy instrumentalization compared with the generalist justice of the Tribunal d'Instance (Court of First Instance), and encouragement of contractual renegotiations between the parties rather than dogmatic implementation of the law. It is also used as an institutional tool to convey new ideas of business self-regulation to the legislative powers in the early stages of lobbying campaigns. From this perspective, based on the idea that "customs are a source of law" (*les usages sont sources de droit*), the consular commercial court proves to be a source of legislative innovations and legitimacy in the promotion of these innovations within the political system. It is a place for the formulation, testing "prototype norms," and maturation of new rules for an economy in constant evolution. Lastly, further to the ministries, trade associations, and companies, it is worth mentioning the consular judge associations. These help the consular judges who operate this institution on a daily basis keep their convictions and personal commitment (see above for examples of quotes concerning bankruptcies).

Unlock and capture: banks as shadow regulators and discreet policymakers

Although our research dates back to 2000–2005, it is relevant to bring it into the context of 2016–2017. In France and in other Western nations, this context is characterized by a proliferation in the number of bankrupt businesses and banking restructurations, whereas the system itself has changed little since 2000. The continued relevance of the handling of large banking collapses, as managed during the 1990s, is that they are still today administered in three ways: in courts, politically (organization of "consolidation" by the ministry of finance), and financially (recovery of collateral by central banks)—although the latter has seen much change since the 1990s. The restructuring of the French banking sector however is ongoing and the question of conflicts of interest remains as relevant as ever.

More generally, our theoretical framework and definition of joint regulation insists on the necessity to examine bankruptcy work without dissociating the organization of markets from the judicial organization making decisions about the financial balance of companies. Thus, by looking into the discourse of consular judges at the TCP, the dual dimension of the zombies debate emerges, stressing one or the otherside depending on whether the zombies are industrial or financial companies. The blurring of the boundary between politics and finance appears to be an outcome of the blurring of underlying boundaries between executive, legislative, and judiciary powers altogether. The story of how the zombie banks themselves were saved shows that this blurring of the boundaries by institutionalized brokers such as consular judges is often convenient for both politicians and the financial industry. Once collective pragmatism has been instituted, once it has opened the door to exogenous influence from sectorial norms, it becomes difficult to separate the pragmatic judgment of an individual judge from the corporate

The politics of the "zombies" debate   85

regulatory interests he or she necessarily represents to some degree. Moreover, the specialized institution can only be captured by a shadow regulator (Huault et al., 2012) because it has been sustained for centuries by the social milieu that has been constructed around it: commercial court judges, with all their heterogeneity, are the primary recruiters of new judges and they are also often likely to be relatives or friends of new judges (Falconi et al., 2005).

Lastly, the fact that privatization of state functions is not "de-institutionalization," but rather a gradual replacement of statutory institutions with institutions that operate on the hybrid, consular model and redefine the boundaries between public and private, points to the wide overlap between politics and economic sectors and to the importance of rethinking public action on the basis of a neo-structural critique of such consular regimes, as much as on the basis of a conventionalist and regulationist economic sociology (Lazega, 2003). Based on this analysis of the work and professions of finance in the bankruptcy minefields, sociologists of the economy and the law are much more attentive today to the norms surrounding institutions such as commercial courts than are specialists in law and economics (Ayres and Braithwaite, 1992; Swedberg, 2003). With the zombies debate, research on notions such as self-regulation, co-regulation, and joint regulation goes far beyond the usual divide between hard law and soft law. It brings in neo-structural analyses that show how financial sectors have achieved epistemic domination of such institutions of joint regulation. The debate is inextricably ideologically and institutionally political because banks are shadow regulators and discreet policymakers importing into public institutions—often with help from the state itself—appropriateness judgments and logics that were designed for their private practice. Theories and methodologies that can be promoted by such an economic sociology of law and joint regulation have yet to be further developed (Lazega and Favereau, 2002). In this area much remains to be done.

Note

1 These results are based on in-depth interviews and jurisprudential exercises on real life cases, as correlated with biographical and career data for these judges (Lazega and Mounier, 2009).

PART II

Passing through boundaries

Financiers as intermediaries in conversion
to financial logics

Introduction

Financialising economic activities

Donald MacKenzie

At one of the bleakest moments of the global banking crisis, the commentator Martin Wolf wrote: 'Finance is the web of intermediation binding economic agents to one another, across both space and time' (Wolf, 2008). That role means that nearly all complex, extensive, modern economic activities are to a degree financialised. There is much variation, however, in *how* they are financialised (financial logics are plural, not singular), the *extent* of their financialisation and the *cost* (monetary and non-monetary) of that financialisation.

A classic example of different logics comes from Neil Fligstein's research on the financialisation of US corporations. Fligstein (1990) identified what he called '[t]he finance conception of the modern corporation' (1990: 15), which was driven by managers' desire for growth in a context in which takeovers of direct competitors were restricted by antitrust laws. The senior managers of conglomerates such as Textron and Litton Industries acquired companies in a wide range of industries, whose activities they could not plausibly direct in substantive detail, so they managed them as financial entities. Even as Fligstein was writing, however, that conception was declining fast, succumbing to the rise of what Fligstein came to call the 'shareholder value conception of control' (Fligstein, 2001: 149). Proponents of 'shareholder value' argued that corporations should not aim to diversify: they preferred 'lean', focussed firms in which managers were incentivised – especially by granting them stock options – not to pursue growth as a goal in itself (as the conglomerates had), but to maximise profits and therefore increase share prices. Diversification, suggested the supporters of 'shareholder value', was best achieved not by corporations themselves but by investors spreading their holdings across multiple firms.

Finance has, of course, expanded markedly as well as changed its nature. In the US, for example, financial services grew from 2.8 per cent of GDP in 1950 to 8.3 per cent in 2006. The two most important areas of growth were in collective investment vehicles such as pension funds and mutual funds, and in consumer lending – most notoriously, of course, the large-scale expansion of 'subprime' mortgage lending (Greenwood and Scharfstein, 2013). Simultaneously, however, financial intermediation did not manifest any consistent long-term tendency to become more efficient or less costly, despite the huge growth in its scale and the massive improvements in information technology underlying finance. In a

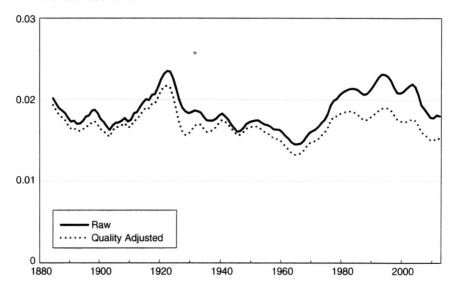

Figure II.1 The unit cost of financial intermediation in the United States, 1884–2012.
Data courtesy Thomas Philippon. For details, see endnote 1 and Philippon (2015).

striking – indeed, a shocking – analysis, Philippon (2015) finds almost no reduction in the unit cost of financial intermediation in the US from the late 1880s to 2012: see Figure II.1.[1]

The analyses by Fligstein, Greenwood and Scharfstein and Philippon are US-focussed and at a high level of generality. A fuller understanding requires more diverse and more detailed case studies – especially of the *work* involved in financialising economic activities – of the kind to be found in the chapters that follow. The chapter by Laferté and Diallo examines a bank's efforts to persuade well-to-do French farmers to go beyond their traditionally materialist views of economic life, and to diversify their 'patrimoine' (a term that in French has connotations of heritage as well as wealth) into financial instruments. Although Laferté and Diallo are not explicit on the point, it is very likely that this diversification involved persuading farmers to invest in mutual funds charging high fees, thus contributing to the continuing high unit cost of financial intermediation (Bazot, 2014) finds costs in Europe similar to those in the US). The efforts to reshape farmers' preferences were cultural as well as economic: the bank on which the chapter focusses offered them not just financial products but also evenings at the opera!

Ravelli takes up the second of Greenwood and Scharfstein's two main forms of the expansion of finance: expanded consumer lending. Examining subprime mortgage lending in Spain, he finds practices that were just as irresponsible, even predatory, as in the US. He also finds, however, organised resistance in post-crisis Spain that has no full analogue in the US.

Finally, Ducastel and Anseeuw examine a form of financialisation that is only just beginning to be examined by researchers: the financialisation of farmland.

They provide rich, persuasive detail on the work (not just legal and cognitive, but also political) involved in transforming land into a financial asset.

Note

1 The unit cost of intermediation is the total amount of intermediation services divided by the cost of those services. To calculate the total amount of intermediation, Philippon adds together the sums of money involved in four broad financial activities: the total amounts held in bank accounts and similar 'safe' deposits; the money lent to firms and the value the market gives their shares; the money lent to households; and the total value of corporate mergers and acquisitions. He works out the total cost of intermediation by adding up the profits and staff salaries of the entire gamut of financial intermediaries: banks, investment-management companies, insurance companies, private equity firms and so on. The lower line in Figure II.1 is Philippon's estimate of the unit cost corrected for the changing aggregate level of the difficulty of the task of intermediation. For example, investing wisely in start-ups involves more screening and monitoring – and is thus intrinsically more expensive – than buying the shares of established corporations with lengthy track records.

5 The financialization of the private wealth of farmers

Is it the work of the banks?

Gilles Laferté and Abdoul Diallo

This chapter describes the changing nature of the economic behavior of farmers in contemporary France based on their financial practices. These changes can in part be understood through the work of the banking institutions engaged with the agricultural world.

Indeed, sociological literature rarely portrays French farmers as being driven by a capital-focused, bourgeois relationship to the economy. The success of work on the end of peasants by Henri Mendras (1971), the declining proportion of farmers in the French countryside by Pierre Bourdieu and Patrick Champagne (Bourdieu, 2008; Champagne, 2002), and miserabilist cinematic representations of farming aesthetics among the French elite (as analyzed by Bessière and Bruneau, 2001) have all contributed to the perception that contemporary French farmers' economic behavior is characterized by a peasant mentality. The modernity of their era subjecting them to a particular socialization, they are supposedly still somewhat behind, forever trying to catch up with a capitalist ethos originating in the bourgeois milieu (Weber, 2001; Elias, 1991) that is still thought to be a social asset of people with the highest cultural capital (Bourdieu et al., 1963; Lazarus, 2012).

Without focusing directly on the changing nature of the farming ethos – such a study would require long-term research with a group of farmers, recording any changes in their discourse on economics and capital—our study seeks the connection between the image that farmers' bankers have of farmers' economic mindsets (their relationship to time, risk, savings, consumption, and so on) and the actual practices of farmers in handling assets. To do so, we have to understand how institutions (in this case, banks) guide social groups through the transformation of their economic practices through the establishment of services and products and financial socialization work, shifting them toward a world of bourgeois sensibilities. The underlying hypothesis of this paper is therefore that practices promoting financial assets are integral to the dissemination of a calculating and capitalist mindset, as embedded in these practices.

The normalization of the economic socialization of farmers, understood as aligning their mindset to a calculating managerial rationale, began very early with the spread of accounting tools in the nineteenth century (Joly, 2015). French farmers benefited from an early socialization to the banking system with the development of the sector-specific bank Crédit Agricole during the first half of the twentieth century, marking a widespread increase in banks' influence on farmers in

The financialization of farmers' wealth 93

the 1950s (Gueslin, 1984). Banking transactions for credit and cash-flow management are part of farmers' everyday experience as business owners, which equips them with above-average financial literacy. Moreover, a number of contract and insurance strategies related to harvests are changing their relationship to time, which was historically perceived as cyclical and random but is now understood as more linear and probabilistic (Joly, 2011). Likewise, in recent years farmers have been reducing the proportion of their crops they deliver to cooperatives and are acclimating to financial mechanisms. Agricultural counsellors, traders, and cooperatives offer training and guide entry into the MATIF (the French grain futures exchange). An economic mindset promoting enterprise, strategy, anticipation, and the abstraction of accounts, all geared towards standard economic thinking, has become widespread everyday activities for French farmers, especially among those producing cereal crops (Anzalone, Barraud-Didier and Menninger, 2012).

This study is based on two types of data: statistical data derived from the Household Wealth Survey to understand asset management practices, and interview-based research with bank employees in an agricultural region to gather professionally qualified representations of the economic behaviour of farmers (see box). In the studied agricultural region, grain farmers are involved in a process of *embourgeoisement*, defined in reference to a social group, household, or individual, as "a process of accumulating capital, first and foremost economic but also cultural, social and symbolic, that creates upward social mobility through the recognition of the legitimacy of a social order and the lifestyle of the dominant group" (Laferté, 2014: 46). Through their embourgeoisement, exemplifying the economically successful side of French agriculture, our farming informants appear to be somewhat advanced in the process of financializing agricultural accounts. Does this mean that we should conclude that farmers' behavior is fully aligned with that of the economic bourgeoisie, the professions, executives, and business people?

To answer this question, this chapter will first review the representations that bankers specializing in an agricultural clientele have of farmers' financial behavior (I). This will be followed by two contradictory observations: the continued existence of an asset structure that is still specific to farmers, and the more recent financialization of farmers' assets at a faster pace than for other occupational social categories (II). Farmers now have financial toolkits superior to those of executives and comparable to people in the professions. It will then be important to explain these observations by considering the development of farmers' financial assets as the result of fairly widespread banking initiatives in the French population at large, and ultimately as the product of the very visible hand of bankers (III).

Sources

This study is based on two types of data. The first set comes from French public statistics from INSEE,[1] taken from the surveys entitled "Financial Assets" in 1986 and 1992 and "Household Financial Wealth" in 1998, 2004, and 2010 that describe households' financial, real estate, and professional assets. The nomenclature of financial assets has changed over time, sometimes complicating comparisons between surveys. Likewise, despite the increasing size of the sample (from 5,000 to 20,000 households), the data does not allow us to work on a localized scale. Furthermore, the sharp fall in the number of farmers makes it impossible to differentiate between farmers with small, medium, and large holdings (except for the 2010 survey), even though their lifestyles vary greatly (Bessière et al., 2014). INSEE statistical data was treated by Abdoul Diallo.

This statistical data is joined by an ethnographic study begun by Gilles Laferté in 2007 in a part of the French region of Burgundy specializing in livestock and grain farming (Laferté, 2013). The study was focused on farmers' lifestyles and banking transactions, through interviews with farmers (50 interviews), local bank counsellors, and branch managers (20 interviews) as well as observations in bank branches. The study was continued at the regional Crédit Agricole headquarter branch, which provided data on the asset portfolios of its clientele according to the various services, socio-professional categories, and geographical areas concerned. Several interviews were conducted with the managers of the regional branch's "Private Banking" service, and then at the national headquarters with the designers of Crédit Agricole's private banking services' financial products, accountants specializing in agriculture, as well as within the Cerfrance network , the first network of Accounting Agencies for French Agriculture, at the local and national levels. The authors heartily thank the staff and institutions that opened their doors to us. The study's archives are available for consultation on the authorization of MSH (Maison des Sciences de l'Homme) Dijon.

I Bankers' representations of their farming clientele

France's agricultural clientele is largely managed by a single bank, Crédit Agricole. Even after the liberalization of the banking system in 1984, the "Green Bank" (a frequently used nickname for Crédit Agricole) still manages to hold on to 70 percent of the market after the end of its longstanding monopoly over the distribution of subsidized loans and assistance for setting up a new farm business (Neveu, 2007). Crédit Agricole's rural branch counsellors are very familiar with this clientele, which has historically been its core customer base and is still an honored clientele in most rural areas.

Farmers in France are obviously very heterogeneous, varying with their technical specialties and geographical location. A winegrower from the Champagne region has very little in common with a sheep farmer from southern France. With reference to the financial behavior of farmers, a financial product designer at the Crédit Agricole's "Private Bank"[2] describes farmers' relationship to financial capital as follows:

> Well, actually, it depends on the farmer, because if you are talking about grain farmers then they have quite a high level of understanding of financial

The financialization of farmers' wealth 95

markets, and what's more they call on us for insurance coverage on their crops...so they do possess financial reasoning, that's pretty obvious. We speak to grain farmers about derivative products, about raw materials....so they're the first type of farmer, they're on the ball with everything, we offer them something, they sign up. But then you have the livestock farmers...they are quite far removed from what is happening on the financial markets, they don't have the same reasoning. Winegrowers are the same, of course they are going to know their vines and if you speak to them about tax optimization they'll be all ears but they're not experts in the financial markets.

> (Manager of the private banking services of several regional
> Crédit Agricole branches at the subsidiary Amundi,
> a company offering asset management and
> financial product development for Crédit Agricole)

In spite of these internal variations among farmers, this high-ranking banking executive outlines some common traits within the agricultural socio-professional group:

And it's true that for them, they are already people of the land, and for them property is real, tangible, and won't change … .Yeah, with farmers, it's crazy. … It's like their farms they see every morning, they think that they are going to stay part of their capital, something will remain even if there's a possibility that their credit rating will be reduced by 50 percent, but then that's not something that they really think about, for them I think it's related to their line of work. It's really striking in their case.

Another banker, the private banking division manager of a regional Crédit Agricole branch, has thoughts along the same lines.

In agriculture, I've noticed that farmers do not like to lose. I mean, for risky investments there's really got to be assets, and only then will I begin to move on that kind of action. Or else there is some passion involved but I'll only play with what I can afford to lose. And I don't put everything on it in hopes of making infinite gains. They know that trees don't grow to the sky.

> (Senior executive at a regional Crédit Agricole branch,
> private banking manager)

From the bankers' perspective, farmers are still preoccupied with tangible materialism and are still reluctant to pursue the most dematerialized and speculative forms of financial investment. Farmers' economic view of their private capital can thus be characterized by a greater desire for profit (in comparison with salaried workers, particularly in the public sector), a real difficulty envisaging a loss of capital (in contrast with executives and professionals), a sense of financial value, a hatred of taxes (like many business owners), a prudent approach to the future and the economy, and a materialistic relationship to enrichment, a behavior that is particularly noticeable among livestock farmers. These economic traits of farmers

96 *Gilles Laferté and Abdoul Diallo*

would explain their historical reticence regarding financial assets and their preference for property, a tangible asset belonging to the owner and similar to inherited real estate, historically central to agricultural enrichment.

Farmers, now a diversified asset class

Given such discourse from banking professionals, what are farmers' actual financial practices? They can be distinguished by three characteristics: a high level of capital heavily leaning towards business assets, a financial structure that is less risky than those of other wealthy social categories, and being latecomers to the financial products market.

Substantial wealth and significant business assets

French farmers undeniably form a wealthy class, particularly those from large-scale farms, who today are one of the social categories with the highest accumulated capital in France. In 2003 the median farmer's wealth was four times greater than that of the median wealth of all French households (Bessière et al., 2012). These disparities are mirrored in the 2010 survey. Laborers have a gross average wealth of 43,257 euros, while the median for farmers is 291,297 euros, rising to a median of 779,470 euros for large-scale farmers (with a mean of 972,673 euros), therefore a ratio of 1 to over 18 between laborers' and large-scale farmers' capital (or a ratio of 1 to 8 if using the mean instead of the median)! Nationally, the capital of large-scale farmers is three times greater than that of all farmers, highlighting the disparities in this socio-professional group. While the median of the assets of all farmers as a group (291,297 euros) is higher than that of mid-level occupations (198,896 euros), that of large-scale farmers (779,470 euros) is now more than double that of executives (326,028 euros) and is even significantly greater than that wealth category *par excellence*, the professions (median of 555,925 euros). Large-scale farmers make up 40 percent of all farmers in France and 92 percent of farmers in the area studied (according to the 2010 census). Even large retailers have a lower median, with an asset median of 676,886 euros (but a higher average, demonstrating the greater distribution of wealth among large retailers: 1,617,246 euros as compared to an average of 972,673 euros for large-scale farmers).

Comparing both to other wealth categories and independent business owners, farmers' asset portfolios tend to favor business assets. Looking more closely, this corresponds to a balance of land, farm building, and farm equipment ownership. In 2010, 48 percent of farmers' capital was comprised of business assets, a figure which rises to 65 percent for the farmers of large holdings (with a mean of 616,224 euros). The moment when a farmer ceases his professional activities, known as transmission, is a pivotal moment in his financial life, as he receives a large sum of money from the sale of buildings, machinery, and land to his successor.

> The difference that exists today between farmers and tradesmen or retailers, which can be seen in rural or urban settings for that matter, is the issue of

Table 5.1 Household asset portfolios, 2010

Number of households concerned: 14,958	Assets		Form of assets			Risk Index	
	Mean	Median	% Financial	% Real-Estate	% Business	Mean	Median
All households	**258,958**	**150,177**	**21%**	**65%**	**14%**	**1.24**	**1.17**
Farmers	491,343	291,297	18%	34%	48%	1.26	1.22
of large-scale farms	*972,673*	*779,470*	*14%*	*21%*	*65%*	*1.32*	*1.29*
former farmers (retired)	*260,853*	*152,857*	*28%*	*49%*	*23%*	*1.21*	*1.00*
Tradesmen, retailers, and business owners	612,057	319,820	20%	48%	32%	1.33	1.29
small independent business owners	*553,255*	*313,631*	*13%*	*45%*	*42%*	*1.27*	*1.22*
large independent business owners	*1,617,246*	*676,886*	*19%*	*37%*	*45%*	*1.53*	*1.50*
Executives, higher intellectual occupations	510,881	326,028	24%	65%	11%	1.39	1.38
the professions	*911,443*	*555,925*	*27%*	*52%*	*21%*	*1.44*	*1.45*
Mid-level occupations	238,445	198,896	20%	76%	4%	1.24	1.20
Basic employees	139,257	76,045	19%	77%	4%	1.15	1.00
Laborers	118,433	43,257	15%	81%	3%	1.13	1.00
Other, non-working population	77,797	6,017	25%	68%	7%	1.11	1.00

Source: INSEE-Household Wealth Survey 2009–2010.

accumulated capital. A retailer or a tradesman might give up his customers but that is a far cry from a farmer's potential to realize business capital gains, and this is obviously what shapes their long-term thinking: "My assets, they are my pension...." Retailers and tradesmen aren't remotely coming from the same capitalist perspective.

(Chief Strategy and Skills Officer for Cerfrance, the leading accounting network for farmers in France)

Relative to this high concentration of professional capital, farmers conversely possess fewer real-estate assets (excluding agricultural buildings, counted among their business assets) than wealthy social categories, with median property assets at 121,190 euros for farmers as a group and 156,432 for large-scale farmers more specifically, compared to 284,124 euros for the large business owners, 354,004 euros for the professions, and 253,478 euros for executives and the higher intellectual occupations. Likewise, farmers actually possess less financial wealth relative to their overall assets, a phenomenon that is heightened for farmers of large holdings (14 percent of large-scale farmers' assets are financial, compared to 18 percent for farmers as a whole, and 28 percent for retired farmers). However, given large-scale farmers' very high level of asset accumulation, the sum of their financial wealth (130,865 euros) is actually slightly higher than that of executives and the intellectual professions (117,995 euros).

So, while this data supports bankers' representation that farmers possess more tangible assets (business and property assets) than other asset-based social categories, it should be noted that they no longer see real estate as the sole path to increasing wealth, as they once did. In the area we studied, agricultural land, which has a yield of approximately 3 percent (90 euros per hectare in rental for 3000 euros per hectare to buy), is no longer farmers' preferred asset. Land represents illiquid capital and is constrained by 9 or 18 year leases: "When land is leased, it's worthless, because in any event, you can only sell it to the person renting it from you" (retired farmer, 180 hectare farm, without successor). This system is the fruit of land-use policies designed to make land an economic tool ahead of being a means of financial accumulation (Laferté and Sencébé, 2016). "I put everything into a life insurance policy, it is tax-free, 4%, and the capital is much more liquid."

A less risky asset portfolio

Ranking the financial wealth of households in a risk index (from 1 to 3) built with the help of bankers in the studied zone,[3] assigning a risk rating to each risk-bearing financial product category, reveals that risk aversion decreases as financial wealth increases. Once banking customers have begun investing in standard products they may move on to riskier products. However, risk-taking also correlates with socio-professional categories. Here, too, we find that the discourse of bankers also places farmers, including large-scale farmers, among the most risk-averse of those with a similar level of wealth. For example, farmers of large holdings maintain

The financialization of farmers' wealth 99

less risky financial structures than executives and intellectual professionals (1.34 compared to 1.39 on a scale of 1 to 3), despite being the farming group most socialized to risk and having higher financial assets than executives. Furthermore, the risk index of farmers as a whole is barely higher than that of mid-level occupations (1.26 compared to 1.24), despite the fact that farmers possess double the financial assets. Of all the wealthier categories, farmers are the most risk averse.

However, beyond farmers' particular economic mindset, bankers emphasize that the great fluctuations in agricultural markets encourage farmers to invest their savings in safer investments because they are looking for a guaranteed revenue, while a professional or tradesman would not hesitate to choose risky products for optimization, safe in the knowledge that his professional activity guarantees an income. It is therefore economically logical for a farmer to rely on less risky products, knowing that he bears a greater risk in his professional activity. Farmers' aversion to risk on the financial market should not necessarily be attributed to a very different ethos, but rather be seen as a consequence of professional risks specific to farming.

Recently caught up on financial assets

Financial products began to spread to the greater public in the 1980s. The financial assets of French households, which represented 144% of their gross disposable income in 1978, had increased to 360% by 1999 (Ministry of the Economy, 2002). This was mainly because of financial supply, with the banking liberalization laws of 1984 and the creation of OPCVMs (Organizations for Collective Investment in Transferable Securities) joining the classic "Livret A" passbook products and securities (stocks and bonds). Public policy measures indeed played a decisive role in structuring financial institutions and shaping market architecture (Fligstein, 2002; Bourdieu, 2003). This financialization of household assets was achieved in particular through the development of life insurance. In 2002, 40 percent of households held life insurance policies, an investment that is particularly low-risk when drawn up in euros. By contrast, since the financial crisis a sharp decrease in transferable securities has been observed in the financial portfolios of French people (the percentage of people holding transferable securities dropped from 28.3 percent in 2004 to 24.3 percent in 2010). Financial actions have given over to passbook accounts, retirement savings, and life insurance (in euros, primarily composed of bonds), stifling the activity of private banks looking to sell more sophisticated products. This consequence of the financial crisis is receding today.

It should be noted that farmers, as part of this general trend, are newcomers to the world of financial assets. Indeed, the extent of farmers' investment in financial products in 1986 was similar to that of laborers and mid-level employees, whereas in 2010 it was at a level comparable to that of business owners (see Figures 5A.1 through 5A.5). This level of investment is nevertheless inferior to that of executives, who benefit from a larger range of products. Initially farmers were content to invest in diversifying real-estate assets (despite their high capital) and only recently—in the last 20 years and particularly the last decade—have

100 *Gilles Laferté and Abdoul Diallo*

farmers begun to be more receptive to financial products. While over the last decade French households as a whole have shown a clear shift away from financial savings products (particularly equity products), farmers have continued to invest in them (the percentage holding of transferable securities has risen from 42.3 percent in 2004 to 47.3 percent for farmers, while it has decreased from 42 percent to 23 percent for retailers and tradesmen, from 50.3 percent to 36.7 percent for executives, and from 62.1 percent to 51.2 percent for the professions). It is evident that farmers have rapidly become highly receptive to financial assets, regardless of the financial crisis. How, then, should we understand this late arrival, which not only contrasts with the population at large but occurs in spite of the financial crisis?

II Financializing farmers' assets: banking work

As one of the biggest farmers in our study summed it up:

> We make a very good living. We make more than doctors or surgeons and what's more, we capitalize on it. A doctor will at best have bought two apartments, his chalet in the mountains, whereas us, we have houses, land, forest.
> (Grain farmer, 55 years old, 850 ha farm)

The interviewed farmers belong to the most economically advantaged social categories thanks to their income and their assets. It nonetheless seems like a stretch to consider their new investment in financial products as an automatic consequence of the embourgeoisement of large numbers of farmers. Indeed, taken as a whole, farmers' incomes have certainly increased in recent decades relative to other social categories, now above the national French household average, but they are usually below the levels enjoyed by the highest wealth categories. Taking the year 2010 as reference (bearing in mind that French farmers average income triennially), farmers' incomes range widely according to their specialization, with an average farming income of 12,400 euros per household on farms specialized in raising cattle (25,000 euros for the total household income, including revenue from non-farming activities), compared to 39,300 euros for farms specializing in field crops (59,500 euros for the total household income), thus giving an average ratio of 1 to more than 3 between livestock and grain farmers (for more detail on the calculations, see Delame, 2015, table 8: 41). The average income for French farming households (38,200 euros) is thus slightly higher than the average income for French households (35,200 euros in 2010[4]). Their income places livestock farmers considerably below the average national household income, at the same level as mid-level employees (26,500 euros in 2010). Grain farmers' incomes put them at nearly double the average national income, at the same level as executives (62,200 euros in 2010) but below the professions and senior corporate executives. In a manner of speaking, farmers are the least financially endowed members of the wealthier social categories and still stand out in the bourgeois world of financial assets.

The financialization of farmers' wealth   101

After eliminating the hypothesis of a huge savings surplus linked to higher recent incomes, the idea remains that the financialization of farmers' asset portfolios results from the proliferating supply of financial products offered by banking institutions. Although Crédit Agricole has long financed farming by distributing credit while shunning the question of savings (Gueslin, 1988), over the last decade the "green bank" has developed a policy of developing agricultural savings.

> We realized that throughout our customers' lifetimes we were financing, contributing to development, doing whatever was necessary to keep them happy and ultimately they weren't investing with us because of some independent wealth investment advisor, or the Rothschild family or whoever, because you know it looks good to be with the Rothschilds, or with the insurer who says "come with me" and steals all the fruits of a lifetime that we helped to grow. So we said, "hang on, we are going to take our rightful place." And ... why did we introduce a private bank? Because at first view "Crédit Agricole" doesn't exactly scream "I'm an investment expert," y'know. There's "credit" and there's "agricultural," that's where we were at.
>
> (Senior executive in a regional branch of Crédit Agricole, in charge of the private bank)

Crédit Agricole developed its private banking brand a decade later than the large European bank networks (Herlin-Giret, 2016). The creation of private banking and targeting its own wealthy customer base was intended to increase its intake of funds from investors in order to comply with more demanding regulations (Basel 3).[5] The effects today are significant.

> Well ... it must be 10 years now that we have been talking about the private bank at Crédit Agricole. It's true that we started after everyone else, we got a late start. I think that the distribution of portfolios to the regional branches was only completed about two years ago. But when we look at the statistics it's clear that in spite of having started after the others, we remain the leader in terms of client volume, including our private banking brand ... .Yes, about ten years, Aquitaine launched the first one, but I'd say it's only really been, say, five years since Crédit Agricole took on the private banking niche, with active public relations.
>
> (Manager for the private banking services of nine regional Crédit Agricole branches from the subsidiary Amundi)

In the studied regional bank (with 450,000 customers, the leading bank in a region composed of four administrative departments with a population of 1.4 million inhabitants), 6 percent of customers (25,000) were categorized as "high-end"[6] and accounted for 50 percent of its deposits. Moreover, spurred by an increase in economic and financial disparities (Piketty, 2014), the private banking market has been growing at a regular annual rate of 6–7 percent, whereas the rest of the market has been saturated ever since the general public's conversion to banking.

102 *Gilles Laferté and Abdoul Diallo*

In Europe, the high-end concentrates the last possibilities for banking market growth. Since the 2008 creation of the private bank within the regional bank under study (with 40 employees and 5,200 customers in 2014, but ultimately hoping to offer the service to all of its 25,000 high-end customers, also known internally as "asset" customers), the high-end customer base alone is responsible for 94 percent of the increase in liabilities. The creation of the private bank brand corresponds to internal plans to develop the asset management activities of wealthy customers banking at Crédit Agricole.

The private bank brand ushered in several new services: branch-level advising by wealth management counsellors, each assigned to serve multiple branches (26 counsellors managing 200 customers each) and a private counsellor for larger asset portfolios (7 counsellors managing 120 customers each); at the regional bank headquarters, a concierge service run by two technical experts for addressing banking difficulties or more specific demands, as well as two financial counsellors specializing in portfolio management (in which customers authorize counsellors to fully manage parts of their portfolios according to their chosen risk level); and an advisory service (a telephone platform specializing in stock market advice, where customers are advised on investment options instead of delegating the choices). In addition, two experts in agricultural and viticultural business transfer are available to better assist in transforming business wealth into private wealth through bank products at the time of retirement and/or sale of the farm business, a pivotal moment in the financialization of farmers' asset portfolios.

The private bank's sales force has been left free to identify its future customers. It is thus up to them to find receptive customers with an active approach to their assets. The extent of the network's farmer-focused efforts can be measured with a funnel plot to compare the sociological profiles of the bank's regional customer base to its "assets" and private bank clientele. While farmers represented 3 percent of regional bank customers in 2014,[7] they make up 12 percent of the high-end customers, 19 percent of the wealthiest customers and 21 percent of the private bank's customers. Conversely, retired farmers make up 13 percent of the wealthy clientele but only 3 percent of the private bank's customer base. By retirement age, financial choices have already been made so it is unnecessary to approach them. Small business owners and active farmers (before passing the farm to someone else) are over-represented in this population (the average age for private bank customers is 54 years old compared to 68 for the wealthy customers). Among the working employed, this data also makes it possible to measure the effort expended on people employed in executive positions.

In the studied region and in French rural areas in general, this new private banking brand has mainly benefitted farmers. Rural areas have a disproportionately high percentage of working class residents, and so Crédit Agricole is the only local banking institution to offer such a service for high-end asset management, a service that was historically found in big cities (Herlin-Giret, 2015). In fact, by creating the private banking brand, a significant number of farmers were offered a new kind of service from their bank. Crédit Agricole has mooted plans

The financialization of farmers' wealth   103

to democratize the private bank but it still needs to fine-tune the proposal by first addressing the embourgeoisement of banking relations.

III The work of bank counsellors

Indeed, today Crédit Agricole is orchestrating a new banking relationship that is developing both within the bank and in its agricultural clientele. "The private banking customer, especially a farmer, needs to go to the agency and feel truly welcome as a high-end customer. Today there's still some work to be done in some regions" (Manager of the private banks of nine regional branches of Crédit Agricole for its subsidiary Amundi). On Crédit Agricole's side, a particular effort has been made to recruit and train counsellors for its private bank. Since the Crédit Agricole group's purchase of the largely urban and bourgeois bank Crédit Lyonnais (which later became LCL), a bank accustomed to dealing with wealthy clientele, a large number of counsellors were laid off. Similarly, a number of independent asset management counsellors have also been hired:

> And so, because there were some deficiencies on the private banking side, Crédit Agricole took some counsellors from LCL because LCL's private banking services have been on the market for a long time. We require that our counsellors have a good level of economic and financial understanding, and they've got it to spare.
>
> (Ibid.)

The appeal of hiring asset management specialists is that it offers another facet to the commercial exchange, no longer focusing on the sale of products in the very short term (as is the case in standard retail banking relationships), but instead on the overall analysis of customers' wealth management:

> Because the financial advisors ultimately follow the rationale that "I have an open architecture approach, therefore I've got offers from Crédit Agricole, BNP, Société Générale [other French banks] and basically I'm going to sell, I'm going to offer my customers the best solutions…." They are already in this mindset, "I'm going to seek out the best for my customers." And that's where Crédit Agricole wants to lead its private banking counsellors. It's "don't start out by what we have to offer, listen to your customer, make him talk about what else he has elsewhere," etc., listen to him and lay out his plans before speaking to him about what's available, because the main focus is not what we have to offer. And so this is the direction in which we're pushing the group now in 2015.
>
> (Ibid.)

It is about understanding all of the customers' plans for their assets and offering them personally adapted solutions, and getting them to bring their assets back to Crédit Agricole's financial products as needed.

104   *Gilles Laferté and Abdoul Diallo*

In addition to these external hires there have been internal promotions to agency director and co-directorships and agricultural and professional counsellors, the most highly skilled positions in classic bank branches. They attend economic, financial, and fiscal training, and both their skills and their presentation are subject to regular evaluation. It is also important that the new hires possess the requisite social skills to feel at ease during interactions with upper-class customers. "There are some things that go without saying. You're not going to welcome customers of so-called 'exception' into these plush premises without being appropriately dressed, you have to be just like them. And that can take some work" (Ibid.). The aim is to demonstrate to Crédit Agricole's wealthy customers that they will truly gain in terms of advice. Crédit Agricole has consequently asked one of its subsidiaries specialized in financial products, Amundi, to devise the broadest spectrum of financial products possible in order to adapt its services to meet all potential demands. For the management of Crédit Agricole, it is important to change the culture of the bank's counsellors, who were historically less favorable to transferable securities that they judged to be too risky:

> I think it's true that at Crédit Agricole our way of thinking is "pay attention to the risks we make the customer bear," so alright for the return, but with some oversight of risk. That is obvious for the Crédit Agricole side. On the LCL side we're like "yeah ok, we shouldn't make the customer take too many risks, but I've got to run a private bank and with private banking, if you want a good return, you need unusual things to offer".

> (Ibid.)

Crédit Agricole is looking just as much to develop its relationships with the customers themselves. For its most promising agricultural customers, the bank has set out to increase its outreach opportunities by organizing thematic days teaching customers how to optimize financial assets, take better advantage of tax exemptions, and minimize income and wealth taxes. These events (called "*patrimoniales*") take place in breakfast or cocktail party settings in upscale hotel dining rooms over a glass of champagne. The marketing department emphasizes on the special invitations that guests must bring their invitations to enter the event. Farmers, who compared to many other professions have more free time (particularly in winter), are the most partial to this kind of meeting. Thus financial socialization seems to go hand in hand with bourgeois socialization. Crédit Agricole is developing a program known as "*club millésime*" (vintage club) or "*club privilège*" (privilege club) depending on the regional bank, a clubby environment available exclusively to private bank customers, who, in addition to these training sessions, receive invitations to public events (concerts, classical music, cinema, soccer matches) with a VIP-labelled spot reserved for members of the "club." For example, as a donor to the opera located in the regional capital, the regional branch may request that some club members attend performances, dress rehearsals, the dressing of the stage, or a presentation by the company director.

Becoming a customer of the private bank therefore means benefitting from both better financial advice and social opportunities enshrined in the world of bourgeois meaning in order to emphasize their value: "It is not possible to convey a high-class image by dealing with customers with a neighbourhood bank image. It's just not possible" (Ibid.).

Just as Crédit Agricole socialized farmers to the salaried workers' vacation experience by organizing group tours in the 1980s, today it is accompanying its agricultural clientele in the embourgeoisement process in order for them to better financialize their assets.

Conclusion

The creation of Crédit Agricole's private banking services 10 years ago is a good indicator of the financialization of farmers' assets after a long lag behind the widespread financialization of the rest of the asset-bearing public. Large-scale farmers' embourgeoisement certainly runs into a supply-side effect. The transformation of banking now gives a range of upwardly mobile social groups access to previously inaccessible services and products and makes it possible for them to financialize their asset portfolios while ensuring an adequate level of equity for the banks. Banking work brings about the financial socialization of social groups whose economic behavior has historically been far from that of the bourgeoisie. Such financialization is one of the economic transactions particular to the bourgeois worldview.

These developments in banking have thus had significant consequences in return. They indeed tend to increasingly separate the asset dimension of farming from its economic dimension, and promote transmission for the benefit of the potential buyers as well as for siblings who stand to inherit the non-agricultural assets in compensation (Bessière, 2011; Anzalone and Purseigle, 2014). Through asset accumulation and accruing financial savings (especially among those with the highest incomes), contemporary banking is contributing to the current spread of "speculative" economic behaviors and the capitalist ethos and is modifying many social categories' relationship to assets, which used to be based in land and real estate. There is no doubt that all social groups are dematerializing assets to some extent. It is becoming increasingly difficult to speak of a "farming mindset" in relation to the economy. The guidance of banks has led today's farmers to be confronted with the most abstract, technical, and complex forms of asset management that used to be solely reserved for smooth transactions in financial counselling firms and large urban and bourgeois banking institutions. Just as with financialization in the strictly economic sense, this ongoing process should lead farmers to acquire distinctive forms of social capital, financial skills, a calculating mindset, a disposition to abstract thinking, and bourgeois interactional skills—in short, non-formalized cultural capital, which other wealth categories more often acquire through social reproduction in the family and through their studies.

Appendix

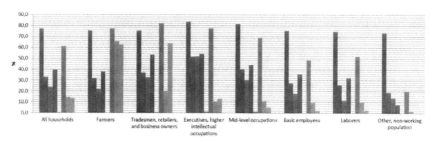

Figure 5A.1 Rate of ownership of financial and non-financial assets in 1986.

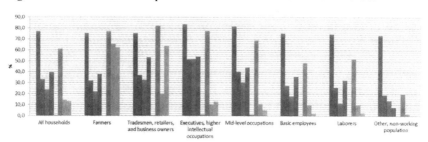

Figure 5A.2 Rate of ownership of financial and non-financial assets in 1992.

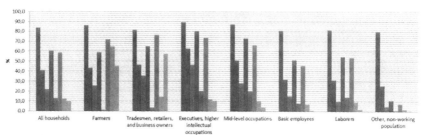

Figure 5A.3 Rate of ownership of financial and non-financial assets in 1998.

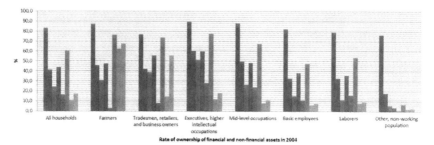

Figure 5A.4 Rate of ownership of financial and non-financial assets in 2004.

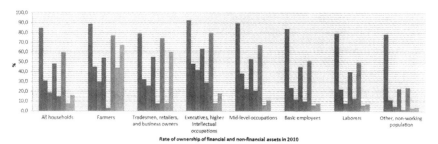

Figure 5A.5 Rate of ownership of financial and non-financial assets in 2010.

Notes

1 Institut National de la Statistique et des Etudes Economiques (National Institute of Statistics and Economic Studies).
2 The "Private Bank" mentioned here is the private banking division of the Crédit Agricole group. More generally speaking, a private bank provides personalized and sophisticated services, and often asset management advice, to individuals with a high net worth.
3 To construct this index we asked banking counsellors to classify the financial products specified in the wealth survey into three categories: Group 1, the least risky: passbook account, personal equity plan, savings bonds, term deposits, company saving plan; Group 2, moderate risk: employee savings plans, popular retirement savings plans, voluntary retirement, life insurance, capital stock, debt obligations; Group 3, the riskiest: share savings plan, listed shares, unlisted shares, mutual funds, property funds, unlisted shares outside of trading accounts.
4 Source TRD03—average annual disposable income of households according to the socio-professional category of the household reference person.
5 Basel 3 is the third installment of the Basel Accords. This is a global, voluntary regulatory framework on bank capital adequacy, stress testing, and market liquidity risk. It was developed in response to the deficiencies in financial regulation revealed by the financial crisis of 2007–08 (Baud and Chiappello, 2015).
6 The marketing department identifies three levels of high-end customer: the first (HE1, 3,481 customers in 2014), referred to as "wealthy customers," have capital valuing over 500,000 euros in the bank's care and/or an annual cash flow of over 2000,000 euros; the second level (HE2, 9,734 customers), known as "dynamic customers," are under 65 years of age and have capital valued between 150,000 and 500,000 euros and/or a cash flow of 100,000 to 200,000 euros; the third level (HE3 9,430 customers), known as "traditional customers," are over 65 and possess capital exceeding 150,000 euros and/or a cash flow of over 100,000 euros.
7 Data by socio-professional categories of the regional Crédit Agricole bank.

6 Financial backlash

When local bankers face social protest

Quentin Ravelli

In 2007, at the peak of the financial crisis in the United States, Spanish minister of finance David Vegara repeatedly said that *subprime* mortgages—loans contracted by borrowers who could not repay them—simply didn't exist in Spain.[1] Even after 2008, when the crisis had hit Spain strongly, many Spanish experts still believed the country had maintained a financial structure immune to the credit crunch. Economists Angel Berges and Alfonso Garcia Mora (Berges and Mora, 2008), of the consulting group *Analistas Financieros Internacionales* (AFI), among others, desperately concocted arguments to support their view. They said Spanish banks had not transformed mortgages into toxic financial products, mainly because the existence of two separate banking networks— deposit banks and commercial banks—had preserved the financial sphere from systemic collapse. They believed that the numerous *cajas de ahorros*, or savings banks, rooted in local and regional household economies, had not indulged in commercial activities like Santander or BBVA (Banco Bilbao Vizcaya Argentaria), powerful commercial banks searching for rapid and high returns on investments.

In retrospect, this view is pure economic mythology. The few far-seeing Spanish economists who intended to forewarn the population of the financial risks now feel they suffered the same fate as Cassandra.[2] Securitization of mortgages, a financial practice consisting in pooling different types of debt to sell their related cash flows to third parties, developed slowly in Spain in the 1990s and flourished in the 2000s, during the real estate bubble. According to a BBVA research group, a total volume of 428,000 million euros of securitization bonds were issued from 2000 to 2007, almost 71 percent of which were backed by mortgage assets (Roibás Millán, 2014: 3). At the other end of the subprime chain, there were more than 604,489 foreclosures due to mortgage delinquencies since the beginning of the crisis.[3] In a country of 46 million inhabitants, this gave Spain a higher foreclosure rate than that of the United States, England or Ireland.

This dissemination of financial products into domestic economies, which led Spain to social protest and political change, didn't just take place in the headquarters of international banks and hedge funds purchasing Spanish mortgage-backed securities. Of course, such a secondary mortgage market was necessary to *sell* these loans on international markets, to transform them into liquid commodities. But these mortgages also had to be *originated* in local branches of *cajas de ahorros*, or savings banks, in a primary market where lenders provide money to borrowers so they can buy homes. The tremendous increase of this primary market was driven by the profound social transformation of savings banks. *Cajas de ahorros* were liberalized and began to sell doubtful mortgage credits, *larga manu*, until the housing bubble burst. Their branch managers were at the forefront of the liberalization process in the 1990s, of the credit boom in the early 2000s, and of the social crisis after 2008, when customers began to hold bankers responsible for their risky loans. For 20 years, this profession stood at the very heart of the capitalist system's contradictions.

This shifting social role can help us understand better the economic crisis and its social consequences. It should also show that a financial market is not a matter of liquidity and symmetric information, but is made of domination, political choices and even social movements—and bankers actively play a role in generating and fighting against these movements. Not only do markets suppose a social architecture, they are *made* of social relations of power. A branch manager, or *director de oficina*, at the head of the local office, has to make sure the branch employees under his responsibility (tellers, lending officers, product specialists...) are performing their jobs optimally in terms of approving loans, applying credit scoring rules, building links with the local community, and dealing with customers who can't pay their loans. Even if they need the approval of their hierarchy, branch managers are responsible for the main financial operations at the bank, including default payment, and are an essential cog between customers and bank executives of regional offices who will take, later, the important decisions concerning insolvent borrowers. As mortgage loans underwriters, they have to obtain and review credit reports and proof of income of potential debtors, to sum up the risk of default, and to decide to either reject or approve the loan.

In Spain, the role of branch managers is stronger than anywhere else for a simple reason: in 2008, the concentration of bank branches (1004 branches per million of population) was the highest in the world, when compared to Italy (716 branches per million), the United States (350), France (445) or Germany (163) (World Bank). Branch managers of savings banks, diffusing the ideology of homeownership, were targeting new customers within local communities where the granting of credit, as well as individual private property, was scarce. Financial products made their way into low-income, working-class and immigrant communities. However, after a few years of financial crisis, branch managers began to face the collective popular anger of over-indebted *subprime* customers who felt they had been cheated—*estafados*—and organized politically to force banks to cancel their debts. After a short history of subprime lending in Spain (I), this chapter will show the key role played by branch managers in the liberalization process (II), then the unexpected social "firewall" they had to maintain against social movements after 2008 (III).

110   *Quentin Ravelli*

Methodology: managers' representations and participant observation of banking practices

This chapter relies on a series of 12 interviews with bankers conducted from 2014 to 2016, and on long-term direct observation from 2011 to 2015 in citizens' groups of bank customers. All bankers interviewed had worked for more than 8 years in a savings bank and had been branch managers for several years between 1985 and 2012. They worked in Cataluña, Madrid province, Andalusia and the region of Murcia, most of them in the countryside in the first years and later in urban or suburban areas. Their ages ranged from thirty-six to sixty-three. The oldest didn't hold specific degrees or diplomas, but had climbed the professional ladder due to professional opportunities that their employers offered, and according to specific policies that some banks, like Banco Popular, still maintain. Five of them, the youngest, had a degree in economics or law, completed by a Master of business administration in human resources for two of them. The interviews sought to reveal representations of banking practices: ideologies, moral conflicts, professional trajectories, and the moment when managers noticed important changes in their work habits.

These interviews were compared to participant observations at the "Platform of Mortgage Victims" or Plataforma de Afectados por la Hipoteca (PAH) (Fernandez Garcia and Petithomme, 2015; Gonick, 2015), a grassroots organization founded in 2009 in Barcelona and, 2 years later, in Madrid. Widely known in Spain, it now has more than 240 groups in different cities. Many other "plataformas", sometimes of different political colors, are also fighting against evictions, sometimes with more radical ideas and strategies, but the PAH is the largest, and its former leader in Cataluña, Ada Colau, after several years of organizing, was elected Mayor of Barcelona in May 2015. The observations were made in the offices of several cajas de ahorros, where groups of afectados—the victims of mortgages—used to renegotiate their loans with branch managers. On a macrosocial level, apart from statistics established by the PAH, the chapter includes data by the Central Bank of Spain, the Instituto Nacional de Estadisticas, the Ministries of Finance and Housing and the Consejo General del Poder Judicial, the constitutional body governing all judiciary powers in Spain and one of the most reliable and detailed sources of information about foreclosures.

I   From *obra social* to *hipotecas basuras*: a short history of Spanish subprime loans

Spanish savings banks, as defined by the 1835 law, were self-financed, non-profit institutions accepting very low deposits placed into "mounts of piety"—pawnshops—to make small loans to the underprivileged. This type of banking, as well as the name "*monte*," came from Italy: in 15th century Italy, Franciscans had developed charitable lending activities to fight against usury, considered

When local bankers face social protest   111

as unethical. Spanish savings banks kept this charitable vocation which was called, in the 1920s, an *obra social*. The term described a financial activity oriented toward social welfare and agricultural projects, essentially rooted in each *caja*'s local area. Savings banks were prohibited from opening new branches outside their province. Under the Franco regime, this principle of territoriality was maintained, regulation reinforced and supervision of savings banks transferred from the Ministry of Interior to the Bank of Spain (Comin and Torres, 2005). In 1977, restrictions were lifted and *cajas* slowly began to act as commercial banks. However, until 1988, they kept relatively low interest rates, were not involved in complex financial products, and still couldn't open new branches outside their local territory. The role of local branch managers, inherited from the Francoist regime, was still more political and social than commercial. All this radically changed in the late 1980s and early 1990s.

The liberalization of banking practices

In 1988, *cajas* were authorized to operate outside their local areas by law.[4] They opened new branches all over Spain, began to increase their profits, and to develop new financial products oriented toward the construction business and primary mortgage markets. On July 7, 1992, securitization was authorized by law in Spain: foreign institutions could buy Spanish mortgages and savings banks could finance their lending practices on international financial markets.[5] In the act's preamble, the legislators explained that the specific goal of this legislation was to reduce the price of home financing. One year later, in 1993, the first Spanish Special Purpose Vehicle (*fundo de titulización*) was registered by the *Comisión Nacional del Mercado de Valores* (Martín, 2014: 15), the government agency responsible for financial regulation of stock markets. A secondary mortgage market was born. Spain was following, decades later, the example of the United States, where the federal government had created in 1938 a state-sponsored agency, Fannie Mae, to build the first residential mortgage-backed securities market (Fabozzi and Modigliani, 1992; Angelides, 2011). After 7 years of relatively slow development, this new financial practice fuelled a credit boom (Blanco Garcia and Carvajal Molina, 2001). As a result, many foreign banks, often globally renowned, purchased mortgage credits in Spain.

As this new financial market grew, its products underwent a series of radical transformations. For decades, they had been sold to middle class families, whose stability was of utmost importance for the balance of the Franquist regime. They were now becoming products of mass consumption designed for everyone. In the early 2000s, brokers and financial marketers began to focus on low- and very low-income families (Palomera, 2014) with whom savings banks' branch managers had few, if any, prior commercial relationships. This brought about a lengthening of loan terms. The average term changed from 10 or 20 years to 30 or 40 years and even to 50 for certain *cajas,* such as Kutxa, as a retired branch manager from Cataluña recalled during an interview. Solvency requirements—debt-to-income ratio, professional status, proof of solid guarantors among relatives—were dropped and undocumented loans began to flourish, as two managers

112 Quentin Ravelli

who had worked in working-class neighborhoods in San Blas, East of Madrid, and Los Rosales, South of Murcia, testified. Last, but not least, adjustable-rate mortgages (ARMs) prevailed. This type of loan depended on fluctuations of the Euro Interbank Offered Rate (Euribor), a rate used to fix interest rates in the Eurozone, which is based on the trading activity of 57 European banks. As the Euribor rate went up in the 2000s, many families couldn't keep up with the augmentation of their monthly repayments. Thus, the ups and downs of international finance directly affected the day-to-day life of Spanish domestic economies, and loans began to be considered as toxic commodities.

As we can see in Table 6.1, the metamorphosis happened rather quickly. The Central Bank of Spain, who explicitly considered in 2008 that "direct or indirect exposure of Spanish financial entities to *subprime* is almost inexistent"[6] began to change its economic categories. According to these reports, from 2005 to 2010, the "doubtful household loans"—most of them home mortgage loans underwritten in savings bank branches under the managers' supervision—increased by 655 percent.

These figures give us a hint of the magnitude of the financial collapse. If most economists didn't see it coming, it is mostly because the social characteristics of subprime loans were obscured. The daily work of bankers, as well as the relationship of domination and asymmetric information it implies, the role of construction workers and of low-income immigrants were simply not taken into account. Seen from above, the financial crisis was cut from its social processes and historical developments. Now that the wound is wide open, we can look at it from a different perspective.

Banks' social networks and the social embeddedness of financial markets

Between 2000 and 2008, many branch managers were recruited in new branches, most of them opened outside the savings banks' local environment (Tortosa, 2015). According to the Central Bank of Spain, during these 9 years the number of local offices opened by financial entities increased by 16.2 percent, from 39,391 to 45,775. While the number of commercial banks branches slightly decreased, from 15,811 to 15,577, new *cajas* really blossomed: there were 19,268 branches in 2000 and 24,707 in 2008, which means their volume increased by 28.2 percent.

Table 6.1 Doubtful real estate loans vs. total credit (basis 100 in 2005)

Year	Total Credit	Doubtful Household Loans	Doubtful Construction Loans	Doubtful Real Estate Loans	Total Doubtful Housing Loans
2005	100	100	100	100	100
2006	125	113	86	112	111
2007	146	169	154	260	173
2008	155	655	1032	3157	820
2009	152	969	1531	5292	1248
2010	153	1113	1920	7177	1506

Source: Banco de España and Gentier (2012)—Banco de España, Financial Stability Reports, 2009–2014.

In 9 years, 5,439 new savings banks branches opened at an average rate of 604 new branches every year.[7] Thousands of new branch managers were hired according to their ability to develop new markets in remote areas. They were an essential engine of this new financialization machine. To conquer new market shares, this financial labor force heavily relied on the real estate business, and more particularly on large scale mortgage lending, securitized and then sold to other entities.

However, this *subprime invasion* couldn't have happened so quickly if the former financial structures had really been "anti-risk." Far from preventing liberalization processes, they have actively hastened them. Savings banks' deep networks, their *obra social*, as well as the strong links built over the years between local elites and bank managers, contributed to a strong social "embeddedness" of financial power (Polanyi, 2009), which is necessary for credit markets (Uzzi, 1999), as well as for any other market (Fligstein, 2002). The wave of new branch managers in the 2000s generalized and commercially instrumentalized a type of long-lasting paternalistic relationship based on home ownership and inherited from the dictatorship (Naredo, 1996; Coudroy et al., 2013: 20; Gonick, 2015). To definitely bury the reminders of the Spanish revolutionary wave of the 1930s and the risks of a politically organized working-class, José Luis Arrese, first Housing Minister, said in May 1959: "We don't want a society of proletarians, but a society of proprietors." To some extent, the centralized power of the Franco dictatorship, and its political use of savings banks, prepared the financialization of the real estate sector, even before banks began to assume an aggressive role. If the social "relation of credit" always develops in the long term (Bottin et al., 2009; Bourdieu et al., 1963), then this sense of long lasting moral obligation, generated by savings banks' social influence, paved the way for credit lending generalization.

Among the ideological tools that were used to encourage hesitant buyers to purchase, the idea that "*la vivienda nunca baja*"—"home prices never go down"— was frequently mentioned by bank managers, many of whom honestly believed their customers would be able to resell their properties a few years later for three or even four times what they had paid. Indeed, the average price per square meter of new apartments had skyrocketed: from 326 euros in 1985 to 2,905 euros in 2007 (source: Tinsa).[8] Instead of considering this increase to be a symptom of the financial bubble, a historical aberration, it was naturalized and used as a universal law of the market. "As home prices had been going up since the Transition [in 1975] we all thought it could go on forever," said one branch manager who had worked in *cajas* in rural areas of Castilla La Mancha, and then in Madrid.

II From *obra social* to subprime lending: the metamorphosis of savings banks managers

According to branch managers, the liberalization of savings banks led to a profound transformation of their occupation in the early 1990s. Those who were hired in the 1970s or 1980s felt as if they had joined a public institution, where financial practices were regulated by customs, repetitive tasks, and bureaucratic rules by which they had to abide. Relations with customers, as well as relations

114   Quentin Ravelli

between colleagues, other branches, and regional head offices were producing and reproducing the same habits and obligations. Geographical limits between each branch zone were to be respected, as were the social boundaries between distinct categories of clients. Some branch managers—maybe in hindsight exaggerating some aspects of their former occupational lives—talk about a "ritual" and compared their former social status with those of a school teacher, a postal employee, or even a rural clergyman. However, at the end of the 1980s, and the beginning of the 1990s, this situation changed and managers began to feel the effect of a corporate "double-bind."

Increasing pressure and increasing autonomy

The central headquarters exerted increasing pressure to obtain higher margins, implementing standardized credit scoring, while the rules were loosened or even removed, which opened a disturbing space of occupational freedom. More pressure, fewer guidelines: "You had to sort it out for yourself looking for new customers" said one branch manager, who had worked for Caixa from 1967 to 2010. The Spanish expression for "sort it out for yourself"—*buscarte la vida*—literally means to "find your own life." It insists on the solitude and autonomy associated with this increasing pressure:

> Local branch offices, in charge of all credit operations, were subjected to a great deal of pressure that was always more intense. They had to do business. They had to increase on their balance sheets their assets, as well as their liabilities, deposits, as well as loans, because they had business objectives to fulfill every year. This was in contradiction to the security and the quality of operations....There are several levels of approval: the branch, the regional office, and the territorial direction. If you had a classical mortgage, there's no problem. However, when the loan is over 80 percent of the value of the house, or maybe even 85 percent, you have to get area approval. In theory, the risk you take will be rewarded.

Interestingly enough, this branch manager's career direction was not a promotion from "field" to "headquarters." On the contrary, he wanted to quit his job as a market analyst in the central office, to work as a local branch manager in the early 1990s in a mid-sized city of Cataluña. He experienced change from both sides and remembers the strong feeling of having been dropped in a "small and aggressive private firm" whose manager—himself—had to take care of everything:

> My office, which used to be part of the branch, was transformed into a center of profit, a center of costs and benefits. The branch manager was responsible for everything—growth, benefits, business, and clients. They said: "You have to increase the number of credit cards, the number of clients." In the first place, there were quality checks, and the central services called people to know if they were satisfied. There had to be quality objectives, for

everything, for life insurance. You were playing a game. Every office had a distinct goal that depended on whether you were in a zone with many corporations, in an industrial area, or if you had to deal with the middle class, or if you were in a commercial area. To increase the profit, you had to choose the way you needed to go. If not, the director was fired.

He had only four to five employees and around 2,000 customers, 500 of whom were "regular and important," 1000 who were usual customers, and 500 others who were called "open breaches"—*abrir brechas*—which meant they belonged to new categories of customers, to social groups unfamiliar with financial products. These more experimental customers often had profiles that wouldn't have met underwriting standards for attributing loans in the early 1980s. Their debt-to-income ratios wouldn't have been sufficient, they didn't have the proper documentation or their work wasn't sufficiently stable. These precarious conditions were obscured by the ideology of the "home prices can't go down" which supposed that in case of economic difficulties, the owner could always resell their house with a nice benefit. Low-income immigrants could therefore be subordinated to financial experimentation and were offered "new products" that central services issued. Among these were very long-term and variable loans, most of the time linked to the Euribor. This was a way to shift the financial risk abroad, preparing future systemic damages. It also greatly transformed the "social meaning of money" (Zelizer, 1994) in Spanish society and, especially, in rural communities. It became less and less linked to *savings*, and more and more connected to *investment*, as though a venture capitalist's spirit had pervaded the lowest strata of popular classes.

> People who would have rented a small flat ten years earlier now were buying a big apartment, and people who would have bought one home earlier could now buy two, or three houses, as investments. And we all sincerely thought you just had to sell everything a few years later to get a profit even if you lost your job.
>
> (A branch manager)

According to an activist from the Mortgage Victims Platform (PAH) who obtained a cancelation of her loan, "the branch managers who convinced her to sign up to her loan also convinced her that the idea was not only to *live in a home* but to *make money out of it*."

To achieve their goals, the branch managers often had to "steal" customers from other *cajas*, and even from other branches or regional offices of the same savings bank. Tactics with which to enrol new credit card holders and, often, new mortgage borrowers, became part of the "game," as explains a branch manager who opened two new branches for Caja Madrid:[9] "Now you had to play according to new rules that your parents would have disapproved of. You had to play it aggressively, to extend your field, to find new customers." Previously, each office had its own area, which others had to respect. However, in the beginning of the 1990s, these borders began to become blurred. A process of deterritorialization

116   *Quentin Ravelli*

was taking place. This involved the implementation of competition between people who had previously viewed themselves as complementary. This competition between operating offices also involved competition between employees to find strategies that would produce results exceeding those of other offices. Each *caja*, originated in a region, often bearing its name—Caja Castilla la Mancha, Caja Madrid, Caja Cataluña, etc.—began to extend its operations over all of the national territory in order to increase its market share. And the introduction of computerized credit scoring standardization, thanks to calculative risk management technologies, already described in the U.S. context (Poon, 2009), contributed to a new relationship with customers. According to a retired branch manager from Murcia:

> What is strange is that even if you had a lot of levels of approval, three or four I think, nobody really felt responsible for the underwriting. ... The software was doing it, you just had to feed it with the data. At least that is the way I felt.

The responsibility of the customers' solvency, or insolvency, instead of resting on bankers' shoulders, became a sort of technological entity without consciousness. The sense of financial responsibility was absorbed by computerized systems.

'Los capturados': *targeting low-income immigrants*

This new situation led to constant innovations to extend credit access to new populations, such as immigrants from Latino-American countries, Romania, and Morocco. The latter often lacked the necessary income for loan approval, but arrived in Spain in great numbers as construction workers during the real estate bubble. In the 4 years before the crisis, Spain produced more houses than Germany, France, and Great Britain combined.[10] This flourishing business rested on unskilled workers' employment. Consequently, the anti-immigration laws were loosened for a few years (Sánchez Jimenez, 2005: 96),[11] and the number of foreigners rose from 923,000 in 2000 (2.28 percent of the population) to 5.2 million in 2007[12] (11.3 percent of the population). Accordingly, banks began to develop marketing strategies targeting immigrant populations. In 2005, Caja Madrid created a commercial department to stimulate credit borrowing by migrants. In 2007, it signed an agreement with the Council of Europe Development Bank to devote 190 million euros to "foster homeownership and integration of low income foreign workers."[13] Following Caja Madrid, other savings banks, such as Banco Popular, developed similar strategies. According to a manager of the latter bank, this marketing "segment" was thought to be financially interesting, which turned out to be a wrong bet in many cases.

> It is a segment which has a level of specialization, and a financial culture that is rather low, so to speak. For this reason, and also because the risk to the bank is higher, we could have a higher pricing policy. This segment was considered—at least, this is the way we saw it—to be better payers [*tenía*

un compromiso en el pago muy grande], as they were people who were accustomed to owing nothing to the bank because, in their countries, banks were important institutions.

This moral obligation to reimburse the loan—the *compromiso en el pago*—was strong, not only because a credit relationship with banks was less frequent in Morocco or Ecuador than in Spain, but also because recent immigrants often had the desire to become law-abiding Spanish citizens, a will to "integrate," and a stronger submission to any type of institutional power. Some scholars even argue it was part of the "europeanization" of Spain (Gonick, 2015). The dream to succeed, to become the owner of a home, and to be able to pay for it on one's own was all the more acute as these workers had durably endured job market and home buying exclusion. In these booming years, many traditional representations of social logics, like the association of immigration to poverty, blurred the eyes of bank managers. A branch manager, who was working for Banco Popular, recalls that in those years his own social status and financial privilege came into question. "I was seeing immigrants who had arrived in Spain one year before and had higher wages than mine, as branch manager. A concrete worker! Who was making 5,000 euros a month!"

Apart from very rare situations, this representation of the wealthy construction worker is highly exaggerated, deformed by the bankers' lenses. Most concrete workers, even if they were skilled workers in large corporations at the peak of the construction business, could hardly earn more than 2,500 euros with extras, working Saturdays and even Sundays, which was still a lot more than a mason. As for branch directors, most earned around 3,000 euros a month, although it could be much more in large branches in the main cities, and only 2,000 euros or less in small rural branches of minor *cajas*. Instances in which an unskilled worker was earning more than his branch bank's director were infrequent, despite the myth. However, during the real estate bubble, some unskilled workers managed to create their own businesses, and operated, for a few years, small construction corporations. Only then could they earn significantly higher incomes than the average branch director.[14] These short-lived entrepreneurs, as well as their employees, were interesting customers for bankers. However, when the real estate bubble burst and the annual volume of the construction business dropped to 40,000 houses a year,[15] many of these new customers lost their jobs, and couldn't repay their loans.

Generally speaking, the new clients arising from this immigration wave, who had been "captured" by the bank—*capturados*, according to the term used by informants—had low incomes and needed to be convinced within their community. One of the practices, as revealed by observations and discussions with mortgage borrowers, was called the technique of *avalistas encadenos*, or "chained guarantors." It involved asking solvent borrowers, when they were signing a loan agreement, to be the guarantor of insolvent customers, who had no guarantors. A recently arrived Ecuadorian mason, living alone in the outskirts of Madrid, without any friends or relatives in Spain, could see this proposal as a gift from

118 *Quentin Ravelli*

the bank, even if it was only a way to diminish the potential delinquency rate. Chains of financial obligations, with all the risks they carried, were created in order to extend the credit market. Another practice was financing more than 100 percent of the price of the house. This meant that the customer could receive cash immediately after signing the loan: borrowers from the PAH frequently mentioned proposals by bankers to offer them "envelopes" of a few thousand euros, included in the loan, as a mark of gratitude. These formal and informal practices, fostered by the reorganization of banking structures, dramatically changed the role of bank branch managers. They contributed to both globalization and atomization of financial work—while accelerating the collective reaction of angry customers.

III Under pressure: the political role of bank managers facing social movements

According to Carruthers and Stinchcombe, the increase of financial "liquidity" is underpinned by the development of a "crowd of knowledgeable buyers" (Carruthers and Stinchcombe, 1999) who understand the commodities they buy. In the case of Spanish *subprimes*, liquidity of commodities was clearly a major objective in the liberalization of mortgage markets. But more than the accurate knowledge of the commodity, it is the ignorance of its real nature that played a leading role: when signing up, many mortgage borrowers didn't understand the complexity of their contract. The tremendous increase of mortgage loans in volume relied on a very low level of economic literacy. But when they did try to understand—sometimes years later, when facing harsh economic conditions— they often considered the clauses as being abusive—*clausulas abusivas*. The "floor clause," the "Euribor clause"[16] and the "non-disclosure clause"[17] are among the most controversial. This major shift in customers' relations to financial knowledge triggered new representations of bankers, and a strong sense of discontent. In addition to the four representations of bankers described by Lazarus—the trader, the judge, the counsellor, the saviour (Lazarus, 2012)—a new one emerged: the scammer. Branch managers often had to deal with this representation that often violently pops out during physical confrontation with empowered mortgage borrowers.

"It isn't a crisis. It is a fraud"

Of course, one of the tasks expected of branch managers has always consisted of dealing with unsatisfied customers. Sometimes, blackmail or physical threats can disturb the quiet routine of the bank clerk. However, these tense situations were rather easy to handle until the end of the 2000s, as they were the exceptions and involved only an individual customer, or his family, who frequently was dominated, intimidated, or lacked proper information. The balance of power shifted after February 2009, when the *Plataforma de Afectados por la Hipoteca* (PAH) was created in Barcelona and, in the following years, in many places throughout

When local bankers face social protest 119

Spain—first in cities like Madrid, Murcia or Valencia, and then in smaller towns all over the country. This social movement, by far the strongest in Spain since the beginning of the crisis, significantly changed borrowers' perceptions of their bank and, therefore, the role of bank managers, who became the targets of popular discontent.

Nowadays, in many working class neighborhoods, where evictions are rife, such as Carabanchel, south of Madrid or Nou Barris, north of Barcelona, militants often act in two phases. First, they organize a demonstration in front of the building of the borrower threatened with eviction. Then, if the mobilization is successful and policemen are unable to evict the borrower out of his home, they go to the local bank branch and attempt to negotiate collectively with the branch manager. When fifty angry people rush into the bank, shouting "si, se puede" or "si Bankia es nuestra, sus casas tambien,"[18] the bargaining power of the *afectado* changes, as the bank manager is physically dominated and often frightened. However, when such an incident occurs, the bank's hierarchy—the regional manager in contact by phone or email with branch managers from regional headquarters—may prefer to negotiate with the militants than to tarnish its public image. Activists try to get the branch manager to convince his superiors to obtain a cancelation of the loan in exchange for the apartment—*dación en pago*—or debt restructuring—*restructuración de la deuda*—or even a cancelation of a percentage of the debt—*quita*.

Branch managers as firewalls against social movements

Needless to say, most branch directors don't openly talk about these situations where they are often called *ladrones*—"thieves"—or *sin verguenzas*—"shameless"—by mortgage borrowers who feel they have been cheated. But participant observation in local banks shows how managers react when 40 or 50 activists storm into the bank branch and ask for a cancelation of the loan, while the regional headquarters insist the loan has to be repaid, one way or the other. Caught between popular anger and executives' orders, branch managers are forced to develop diplomatic skills, to be socially creative, and to learn different tactics to neutralize the social movement even if they have never been trained to do so. One of the tricks they use is to stall for time. When the activists enter the branch, they can wait, remain in their office, or let the bank clerks deal with the first wave of anger. They may ask their employees to tell the PAH they are out of office for the day, or to explain they are waiting for new reclamation sheets—*hojas de reclamación*—and can't do anything until these forms arrive from the head office. Doing so, they are waiting for the activists to get tired, or to display violent behavior, so that the police will intervene.

During one action at a bank branch in the working-class neighborhood of Carabanchel, in February 2015, the director, a woman of approximately forty years, had to face a group of 55 people surrounding the branch and then storming into the bank offices. This group was asking for the cancellation—*dación en pago*—of the mortgage loan of an Ecuadorian woman with two children. She was only working part-time as a housekeeper, and had been abandoned by her

120   *Quentin Ravelli*

husband, a mason who had lost his job. This woman, assisted by her lawyer from the Spanish Communist Party, couldn't repay her loan and was threatened by the bank with expulsion from her home while still having to pay her debt. Many *afectados por la hipoteca*, or mortgage victims, outraged by this situation, were siding with the Ecuadorian woman. They were supported by PAH activists and by *Indignados* from the local assembly of Carabanchel. They shouted in the branch, scared bank clerks and customers, transformed the documentation and advertizing posters into tiny confetti thrown over the heads of the employees, who looked paralyzed. They asked for the branch manager to come over and negotiate with them. The tactic of the branch manager, far from addressing the activists' demands, consisted in doing nothing for approximately 20 minutes, without letting the activists know she was the director. During all this time, a faithful bank clerk under pressure refused to talk to the activists. Then, the branch manager waited for three policemen to enter the bank, while 15 others were protecting the entrance to the branch. A final tactic was to stay close to her employees without revealing who she was, until PAH activists agreed to leave the branch in exchange for an appointment with the seemingly absent branch manager. Only then, in her office with the *afectada*, her PAH lawyer, and other members of the PAH, did she reveal she was the branch manager.[19]

Acting as firewalls protecting the banks' interests, branch managers must develop many social skills to combat their own fears and have the courage to talk with activists. Some of them do this despite a feeling of being morally wrong in their actions. This was the case of several bank managers who mentioned having had a sense of discomfort, and felt they should have sided with the *afectados*. One of them even politically agreed with the activists, but didn't want to talk about it.

Conclusion

In two decades, Spanish semi-public savings banks have been transformed into private for-profit corporations supplying financial markets with raw materials and diffusing complex financial products among popular classes. Mortgages were provided even to their most precarious segments: unskilled construction workers and low-income immigrants. In many cases, home mortgage borrowers were working directly or indirectly in the construction business. From this perspective, the "*ladrillo* economy," or "brick economy" (Ravelli, 2013), which amounted to 25 percent of growth domestic product, appears as a closed Fordian regime of capitalist accumulation where consumers and producers of houses were the same social group. In this socio-economic organization, small local savings banks were a key stone directly connected to the most powerful global financial institutions.

In Spain, the fundamental contradiction leading to financial collapse was that this system was based on what appears to be an artificial financial market. But this market, although artificial in the sense that it was excessive, was not an abstract financial force attacking the society from outside. It was sustained by the multiplication of local savings banks massively distributing loans that couldn't be repaid. Branch managers, actively marketing mortgages toward new customers, and responsible for their underwriting, were a strong and essential link in this chain. The dramatic change of their social role precipitated the macrosocial transformation of the Spanish economy. Local elders maintaining social cohesion, and sometimes compared to teachers, police officers or clergymen until the late 1980s, they were asked to act as innovative bank executives looking for new market shares in the 1990s and early 2000s. And when the bubble burst, the strong link became a weak link targeted by social contestation: savings banks had to maintain social order but had lost their credit as reliable institutions.

Notes

1 For instance: "Vegara: inyección BCE es adecuada y problema 'subprime' está focalizado EEUU," *ElEconomista.es*, August 10, 2007 [http://ecoaula.eleconomista.es/empresas-finanzas/noticias/260203/08/07/Vegara-inyeccion-BCE-es-adecuada-y-problema-subprime-esta-focalizado-EEUU.html].
2 Fuertes discusses six years of "peregrination of Cassandra" (Fuertes, 2010). Similar economic mythologies related to the financial crisis can be found in other countries, like the United States or France (Lebaron, 2000 and 2010).
3 Consejo del Poder Judicial (2015), *Memoria sobre el estado, funcionamiento y actividades del consejo general del poder judicial y de los juzgados y tribunales en el año 2014*, p. 252: 25,943 *ejecuciones hipotecarias* in 2007, then 58,686 (2008), 93,319 (2009), 93,636 (2010), 77,854 (2011), 91,622 (2012), 82,680 (2013), 80,749 (2014). Statistics established on July 22, 2015.
4 *Ley 26/1988, de 29 de Julio, sobre Disciplina e Intervención de las Entidades de Crédito.*
5 *Ley 19/1992, de 7 de julio, sobre Régimen de Sociedades y Fondos de Inversión Inmobiliaria y sobre Fondos de Titulización Hipotecaria.*
6 Banco de España, *Informe de Estabilidad Financiera*, Banco de España, n°15, 11/2008, p. 28.
7 Banco de España, *Boletín estadístico*, Junio 2008, p. 78.
8 *Índice Inmobiliario de la Sociedad Española de Tasación* (TINSA). The inflation can't explain such a tremendous increase, as it remained every year under 10 percent after 1985, and under 7 percent since 1992.
9 Caja Madrid, later called Bankia, was one of the largest savings banks most exposed to toxic loans.
10 Ministro del Fomento.
11 Spain, *Ley Orgánica 4/2000, de 11 de enero, sobre derechos y libertades de los extranjeros en España y su integración social.*
12 Instituto Nacional de Estadistica.
13 http://www.elmundo.es/elmundo/2007/12/12/suvivienda/1197462415.html.
14 One mason, who had come from Romania during the boom years, showed me proof of income and was earning, after he had created a small construction business with more than five full-time workers, between 4,000 and 6,000 euros a month from 2006 and 2007, before going bankrupt.
15 Source: Ministerio del fomento.
16 The *clausula suelo*, or "floor clause," stipulates that the monthly repayment of variable loans indexed to the Euribor can follow the Euribor—according to the "Euribor clause"—only when it rises, but not when it falls below a certain level (e.g., 3 percent). This means that the customer has the inconvenience of the variable rate without the advantages.

17 This clause stipulates that the savings bank doesn't have the obligation to notify the borrower when the mortgage is sold to another financial entity.
18 "If Bankia belongs to us, its houses belong to us too"—*Si "Bankia es nuestra", sus casas tambien!*: transformation of the commercial slogan of the bank—"Bankia belongs to you".
19 This sequence was filmed and can now be seen in a documentary on the Spanish crisis: *Bricks* (Ravelli, 2016).

7 The assetisation of South African farmland

The role of finance and brokers

Antoine Ducastel and Ward Anseeuw

> Farmlands provide an attractive risk-return combination over time thanks to a strong appreciation of land coupled with competitive cash returns. Also commodity prices are likely to rise, hence increasing profitability, because of the increasing supply deficit (due to a growing global population) and negative supply impacts (due to climate change). We believe that pension funds and private investors should consider farmlands as an alternative investment to include into a well-diversified investment portfolio.

This quote concludes a flyer entitled: 'Benefits of agricultural asset classes in managing investment portfolios' prepared by a specialised South African asset manager. Such statements could surprise as farmland is not a traditional component of a 'well-diversified investment portfolio' unlike bonds, equities or even urban properties. However, perceptions are currently changing and farmlands tend to be more and more promoted as an 'emerging asset class'. The promotion of such innovative assets must be understood as an uncertain process driven by specific entrepreneurs spatially and temporally situated, rather than a natural and ineluctable expansion of the financial realm. Indeed, farmland 'brokers' (Bierschenk *et al.*, 2000) play an active role in structuring and mediating demand and supply; on the one hand, they select and frame the farmland offers, on the other hand, they raise and channel international and/or national demands. In addition, they play a key role by converting and transforming capital and resources from these two different arenas. Through their actions, these intermediaries set up the instruments and cognitive frameworks for this 'emergent asset class' (Bessy and Chauvin, 2013). Rather than promoting an existing product, they tend to produce a new asset, converting farmland, already framed and considered as a commodity (Li, 2012), into a financial asset. As stated by the fund A's manager in a commercial flyer: 'the objective remains to not only become the most successful food producer in South Africa, but almost more importantly, the most valued food producer'.To be recognised as an asset, a particular good, service or activity must be framed to fit with financial market requirements and values. An asset is based on specific beliefs: that it can generate a positive cash flow in the future, preferably outperforming the average profits on financial markets, and is liquid enough (Orléan, 1999). On specific devices this can be evaluated and compared with others according to

124 *Antoine Ducastel and Ward Anseeuw*

standardised benchmarks. This financial valuation (Vatin, 2013) is not a natural given but is rather produced by particular actors or group of actors in a specific social environment. Indeed, the production of this asset is embedded in specific societies and social structures. Farmland brokers, for instance, are engaged in a translation process between global investors on one side, and local agricultural sector on the other. While this farmlands' transformation has been observed in several countries (see Daniel, 2012; Larder *et al.*, 2015; Gunnoe, 2014), this chapter focuses on the South African version of this global transformation.

This chapter endeavours to understand how an emerging group of South African intermediaries are currently trying to shape, or reshape, farms as investment opportunities for institutional investors, i.e. as an asset class. Progressively, these financial entrepreneurs tend to empower themselves as a financial sub-industry with their own expertise, instruments and procedures. Yet, at the same time, they compete with each other in this market in structuration as they try to impose their own conception of farmland. These intermediaries channel capital, instruments and imaginations from the global financial markets to the South African landscape. By analysing their daily management, their interactions with investors, farmers, workers and government, this chapter aims to understand the concrete issues and challenges related to the 'assetisation' of farmland. This approach is in line with other meso-analyses of the 'financialisation' process focusing on the social construction of specific financial markets such as the future markets of agriculture (Cronon, 1991; Williams, 2014).

To do so, this chapter analyses specifically two investment funds, fund A and fund B,[1] which are exclusively dedicated to farm investments in South Africa. Both started investing in the late 2000s. In 2014, fund A had 22,336 hectares of which 3,050 hectares were irrigated, 3,859 hectares were dry lands mainly for grain production, with the remaining land used for pasture or grazing; fund B had 1,490 hectares of fruits and vegetables, all under irrigation.

Through these two South African case studies, an uncertain process of farmland 'assetisation' is highlighted, i.e. the attempts to 'unlock financial value' from farmlands, and particularly its groping and failures. Indeed, if the farmland brokers mobilise instruments and procedures from other sub-financial industries, they face constraints and resistances that transform it. Therefore, the innovative strength of the financial industry and its adaptive capacity are illustrated. To do so, this chapter will first present the actors engaged in these innovations, describing them as promoters of South African farmlands as a 'new' financial product (I). Thereafter, the chapter will focus on the production process of this emerging asset class (II).

Methodology

The data presented in this chapter has been collected mainly through participant observations, during two 'internships' undertaken with the two South African asset management companies. From May to June 2013 and then in June 2014, for three and four weeks respectively, time was spent at these companies' head offices in order to partake in their every-day work. This allowed, together with the investment officers and back-office employees, to become familiarised with their daily activities, to interact informally with employees and to participate in strategic and commercial meetings.

In addition, from 2013 to 2015, 14 asset management companies' directors, investment officers and agronomists were interviewed, sometimes several times. During these semi-directive interviews, company and managers' backgrounds, the asset management company's' daily activities and the originality of farmland as an asset class were discussed.

In parallel, six different farms were visited, in four different provinces, managed by these two asset management companies. During these one-day visits, managers were interviewed about their daily work, their relation with head office and – as much as possible – the farm worker relationships and conditions.

Finally, 'grey literature' from the two asset management companies was also collected, i.e. minutes of the investment committee or the valuation committee, commercial flyers for potential investors, annual and quarterly reports regarding both financial and social performances.

Thanks to the above (interviews, observations, grey literature), comparisons between the different companies could be conducted and core elements regarding the management of farmland investment in South Africa were identified.

I The promoters of South African farmlands as a 'new' financial product

The asset management industry in South Africa and its asset classes

From the 1980s to the 1990s, deregulation policies and the end of the Apartheid regime boosted the development of the asset management industry. It was mainly related to the opening-up of the South African economy, resulting in South African conglomerates being listed on stock exchanges abroad (particularly in London) and in the introduction of foreign companies and investors in the country (SAVCA, 2015), and to 'black economic empowerment' programs promoting 'black' shareholders and directors into South African firms (Freund, 2007). Shareholders value principles rapidly became the core matrix of firms' structuration and strategies, with asset management companies playing a key role in the 'deconglomerisation' of the South African economy and the transformation of its racial configuration (Ibid.).

In this context, major commercial banks, linked to the mining conglomerates, created the first independent asset management companies in the early 1990s. They raised funds from institutional and individual investors in order to invest into local firms (SAVCA, 2015). Later on, in the 2000s, investment funds and asset management companies specifically dedicated to farmland and agriculture

126 *Antoine Ducastel and Ward Anseeuw*

emerged as challengers in the South African asset management industry. They developed in South Africa as well as in the rest of the continent: at the African level, Laura Silici and Anna Locke identified 27 private equity funds or firms dedicated to agriculture or agribusiness (Silici and Locke, 2014). Lauren Thomas counted 12 private equity funds in Southern Africa (Thomas, 2012). Finally, Antoine Ducastel mapped and analysed 15 funds or firms engaged in agriculture and farmland managed from South Africa (Ducastel, 2016).

These companies occupy a particular position at the margin of the South African asset management industry. They are often created by entrepreneurs coming from the mainstream asset management industry, mobilising their economic and social capital to promote this new asset class. Regarding the major actors of the asset management industry investing in stocks or in private equity, these asset managers are relatively small in relation to both their capitalisation and the size of their teams. For instance, the asset management companies A and B both have four executives and asset management company B manages US$41.5 million.[2]

The asset management companies dedicated to agriculture are in competition upstream, to raise capital from institutional investors, and downstream to invest their capital in farmland or agricultural companies. As such, they design and frame their financial products according to the requirements of their potential investors. The farmland financial market is therefore segmented depending on the identity of the investors. For instance, while development financial institutions invest mainly into small and medium agricultural companies, pension funds invest more in farmland. Several fund managers target South African farmlands but they differ regarding the agricultural production and the financial valorisation model, as will be shown through two case studies. Indeed, both asset managers put a specific group of investors, i.e. pension funds, with a particular 'asset class', i.e. South African farmlands; however, the concrete forms of intermediation diverge according to the profile of managers and investors illustrating the many conceptions of 'farmland' and 'asset' that are coexisting and competing.

The farmland's coalitions: the matching between a demand and an offer of capital's valorisation

Funds A and B raise capital on financial markets and channel it toward investment opportunities identified, thus progressively building an 'asset portfolio'. To better understand these financial vehicles, their similarities as well as their differences, it is important to detail both the investors' and the asset management's construction and trajectory, and the relationships and interactions between these two actors.

Regarding the investors, capturing their profile is important to understand the capital allocation of the funds and their governance. Indeed, the source of the capital, mainly related to their liability structures (Aglietta and Rigot, 2009), weighs significantly on their investment policy, and thus on their choice and expectations regarding agriculture.

The first case study, fund A, was set up in 2008 and is quite atypical in the industry as it has only one investor. It is structured by a major American endowment fund that is investing in this fund as part of its 'natural resources' portfolio along with other investments all over the world in agriculture, but also logging and renewable energy. In 2013, this natural resource asset class accounted for 13 per cent of a large and diversified portfolio dominated by equities. The second vehicle, fund B, started in 2010; its two main investors are a leading South African insurance company and a South African Government Employee Pension Fund. Other minor institutional investors joined the fund, mainly smaller pension funds. Pension funds, endowment funds and insurance companies are all long-term investors (Aglietta and Rigot, 2009) looking for stable return investments to reward their subscribers. As such, they implement diversification strategies through investments in asset classes that are not correlated with one another (Campbell, 2011). South African farms become an attractive investment for these investors as a result of such diversification strategies.

Investors entrust their capital to a management company that implements the projects. Fund A is managed by a South African 'agro-financial' services' company, which was initially fully dedicated to agricultural commodity trading but got progressively more involved in the management of farm and other agro-industrial assets on behalf of foreign investors. In parallel, they manage a similar fund for a European industrial investor, investing in soybean crushing plants in South Africa. Fund B's daily management is overseen by a fund advisor specialising in agriculture and farm investment under the supervision of a major South African 'alternative asset' management company, i.e. real estate, currencies or 'development equities'. Fund B and its manager also manage a 'Swazi Fund' with farms and agricultural infrastructure in Swaziland. They are currently raising funds for an African fund with a similar mandate.

These management entities adopted standard pyramid organisation, as is common in the asset management industry. There are one or two senior partner(s) at the top in charge of investors' relations and deal negotiations. They are supported by several financial analysts who perform financial modelling and data analyses, especially prior to the transactions during the due diligence processes. There is also a back-office, under the supervision of a chief financial officer, which monitors and audits asset balance sheets. While at these three management levels, individuals all have financial backgrounds, both fund management companies hired agronomists in charge of the supervision of the farms' operations, consultants for environmental and social governance or legal and tax issues and operating companies for the farm production.

These management companies are thus mostly producers and managers of financial models as any other asset management entity; however, in order to fit the agricultural and farming issues into their models, they tend to integrate – although marginally – agricultural and other expertise. On one hand, these companies claim a field experience and a deep network in South Africa and its agricultural sector, affirming their essential role as gatekeepers to the country and its agricultural value chains. On the other hand, they claim their embeddedness in the financial industry, mobilising generalist financial professionals. As such, they occupy a strategic position between 'the bush' and the 'board room':

And me, my job is to…to structure all this. The agronomist can't do it. When he writes, he writes too technical, which confuses everybody. I, I speak to people who are…who have a financial background, and who don't know anything about agriculture. So, it's the story you tell. You have to tell: it's this, it's that. You don't have to infantilise, but you need to make the story digestible.

(Interview with fund B financial analyst,
Cape Town, 23 March 2015)

Finally, an investment fund is basically the alliance of these two types of collective actors, the manager and the investor(s), each with their own interests and beliefs. To formalise these partnerships they set up 'securitisation vehicles', both registered in Mauritius as 'limited life companies', with a 10 to 12 year life span, in order to benefit from tax optimisation mechanisms.[3] A shareholders' agreement and an investment policy define and frame the structure and the mandate of these securitisation vehicles. On one hand, the shareholder's agreement defines specific procedures and standards in order to protect the investors' rights: an investigative 'due diligence' process prior to the investment, side letter[4], external audit, remuneration system by profit sharing[5] etc. On the other hand, the investment policy defines the fund's mandate regarding the type and the size of the targets, the geographical scope of the fund and a general business plan using, for instance, value ranges and ratios.[6] Finally, an investment committee composed of a mix of independent directors, investors' delegates and senior managers ensures the procedural requirements and makes the final decisions.

According to these different 'cocktails' of expertise and relationships, the management companies commit to different financial sub-fields and asset classes and take different paths –different investment policies – to farmlands' investments. Fund A looks more like a venture capital fund, buying a farm/company and trying to improve its cash flow in order to increase the firm's value; meanwhile fund B seems closer to a real-estate investment trust which owns and rents buildings and offices in global cities (Renard, 2008). In other words, while fund A invests in farms as an economic asset, fund B invests in farmland as a physical asset. More concretely, both funds target exclusively South African farms, but they differ regarding the type of crop they are investing in: 'cash crops'/grains for fund A; 'permanent crops'/fruits for fund B. Both fund managers rely on farmland appreciation in order to reward their investors at the end of the fund life. Such appreciation is planned according to market dynamics and macro-economic trends on one hand and development programs implemented on every single farm by fund managers on the other hand.[7] At the same time, they also mobilise two different cash flows to get a higher return for their investors: fund A is directly engaged in agricultural production, capturing agricultural incomes; fund B leases its farms to large operating companies[8] and as such earns a monthly rental.

Another example concerns the social and environmental dimensions of their respective investments. Indeed, asset management firm B, is an active member of the 'Global Impact Investing Network',[9] a global association set up by investors and asset managers in order to develop specific metrics to value the 'social return'

The assetisation of South African farmland 129

of their investments, in other words to establish a correlation between the capital invested and the social and environmental production of a farm or a company (Chiapello, 2015). Therefore, they offer to their investors the ability to 'unlock' both financial and social value from farmlands, while asset management firm A only focuses on financial performances. As such, these fund managers mobilise different know-how and expertise from different emerging financial sub-fields or communities on the global stage.

Rather than constituting a unique and standardised financial channel to South African farms, these funds are diverse, built around the plurality of the investor/manager relationships. However, they are all engaged in the same production process of a specific asset class. In such a process, managers play a key role at the interface of two different arenas.

II Toward the production of the asset: from South African farms to a financial asset

The production of an 'asset', i.e. the attempt to 'unlock financial value', relies on the active work of shaping and promoting by intermediaries who aim to attract financial flows. This work can be described as a translation process from a particular good, service or activity inserted in a specific environment to a reliable and sustainable investment for financial markets and actors. For this translation, intermediaries will mobilise a set of techniques and instruments (Lascoumes and Le Galès, 2007). Such production processes are embedded in the broader social and political environment. Indeed, the ability to mobilise these instruments relies on specific policies and social structures that are historically and spatially situated.

South African farms, as well as other agricultural assets on the African continent, are currently the object of such a translation attempt. Therefore, the production of an emerging asset class through the specific case study of South African farms will be analysed focusing on the intermediaries' role. Three different modalities of such translation can be identified for this research concomitant to the following realities: first, intermediaries have to manage the characteristics and constraints surrounding agriculture production to 'unlock the value'; second, they have to build an information flow toward investors, which relies on recognised standards and benchmarks; finally, this shaping work is faced with social, political and cultural resistance which managers have to deal with.

Leveraging South African farms: toward a profitable and predictable bundle of assets

To be recognised as an asset, a good or an activity must be considered by financial markets as liquid (Orléan, 1999) and as generating a predictable positive cash flow. South African farming faces several inherent risks, such as natural risks and international markets volatility that have historically discouraged private investments from outside the sector because of its random returns. Indeed, the farming cash flow looks particularly unstable from one year to another, and the mitigation

130   *Antoine Ducastel and Ward Anseeuw*

of these specific risks is a decisive step toward the 'assetisation' of South African farms. The mitigation of agricultural risks and the making of profitability by farmland brokers rely on the mobilisation of specific instruments, expertise and procedures. From the case studies described in this chapter, three specific instruments are highlighted that seem to play a crucial role in the asset production process in the South African farming sector for both risk mitigation and 'value creation'.

First, in order to mitigate the natural risks (flood and drought), both fund managers set up geographical diversification strategies. Geographical diversification relates to the acquisition of farmland in different areas in the country with different agro-ecological characteristics and different crops or varieties. As for the diversification of the 'optimal investment portfolio' theory (MacKenzie, 2006), the objective is to dissolve the specific risk from one asset by a global mitigation in the portfolio based on the complementarity between assets and the returning force to the mean (Aglietta and Rigot, 2009). Therefore, fund A holds five farms in four different provinces, while fund B has four farms in four provinces. However, such farms diversification policy is not as standard for bonds or stocks and its implementation is quiet a subjective process:

> You just come across a deal, and you think, oh Eastern Cape, I haven't done that much yet. Fit the model. Fit the...it is an interesting deal from a mandate perspective, return, and it is also a kind of diversity. So you run with it. The next time, you find a farm which is directly next to it, then you might think, OK, how much...do we get a kind of concentration risk here? Then you'll probably say, OK, let's not do it. Or you say OK, it is a stable, marginal increase. It is still within.... a proper diversity.
>
> (Interview with fund B's senior partner,
Cape Town, 16 March 2015)

Second, they both engage in 'farming corporatisation' and the development of 'network organisations' (Goldberg *et al.*, 2012), as they gather several farms, enabling economies of scale, as well as facilitating management and risk control. Fund A's manager uses South America's farm business model as its objective:

> The investment premise is based on a similar model to the commercialised agricultural investment companies in South America with the adoption of no-till technology, GMOs and precision farming. Through the pooling of resources and expertise, the business generates substantial economies of scale and influence.[10]

Because their farms are dispersed (see previous point), the challenge for the fund manager is to implement a control system from a distance. In order to do so, they implement a hierarchical organisation, several report procedures, stringent budget control and financial incentives. In addition, they rely on software such as 'Google Earth Pro' to track the farm's performances and to monitor the operations.

Third, through the separation of property and productive activities fund B's management company implements the 'operating company-property company' model (Opco-Propco), which exists in other industries such as the hotel or retail industries, in the farming industry (Burch and Lawrence, 2012). As such, this fund promotes and supports a specific conception of the farm as a 'bundle of assets' (Capron, 2005; Krippner, 2012) which characterises the firm's design in the financial industry, especially in the private equity industry. The farm is considered here as the sum of independent assets: property title deeds, water rights, a 'biological asset' – the soil and a flow of commodities – grains. Each asset would be marketable, so managers 'unlock financial value' from these farms through 'bundling' and 'de-bundling' strategies.

Farms as a standardised and benchmarked asset

A financial asset is also shaped and assessed through a set of standardised benchmarks with key indicators on its 'historical' returns, on its variance and covariance (the beta) or on the market risk premium. Such benchmarks allow institutional investors to compare and evaluate their profitability and their complementarity in their portfolio. This 'commensuration', i.e. 'the translation of different qualities into a common metric that can support, for instance, decision-making' (Styhre, 2013), is a central part of the managers' work to attract financial capital.

These benchmarks and calculations are borrowed from corporate finance analysis and aim to model a specific investment on the medium-/long-term through a discounted cash flow. This accounting framework introduces the value of time in the valuation of transactions and assets (Chiapello, 2005). The production of this information flow is a central part of the fund managers' role and success as they endeavour to translate a specific environment/investment into 'global financial language'. Indeed, the managers' skills and dexterity in dealing with these models and implementing them in new activity areas are central issues in their competition to channel capital flow from institutional investors. Once validated by the investor(s), they guide the managers' action and constitute the benchmarks of their evaluation.

A discounted cash flow model actualises in present value an investment cash flow over a discounted period (Dufumier, 1996). This financial evaluation is realised before any investment is made, and re-actualised regularly during the project's lifespan. It is used as support for both the decision by the manager/investor as to whether the investment is profitable, and for the evaluation criteria by investors in the asset markets. It is a representation device of the productive world, as well as a control device (L'Italien *et al.,* 2011).

The hazards characterising the agricultural production challenged such projections as the discount cash flow valuation is based on the stream of future incomes. Future contracts and other risk mitigation mechanisms allowed investment funds to implement such calculation. Nevertheless, other challenges emerged for the farm's valuation. Farms in the South African agricultural sector are valuated according to the comparable sale approach which gives a value to a specific farm according to 'similar' transactions in terms of localisation and usage. Such valuation methodology is the norm in the agricultural sector and is used and recognized by both farmers and their financial partners, i.e. commercial banks or agricultural services companies, as a reliable estimate of farmers' collaterals.

In 2013 fund B's management team raised concerns to their investment committee about the comparable sale methodology. As a property fund, they adopted the methodology to value the fund at the beginning; but they reasoned that such methodology does not take the future stream of revenue and their potential increase properly into consideration. They pointed out three challenges regarding the undervaluation of new orchards by the comparable sale methodology:

> Young orchards have (1) a longer remaining productive life; (2) have newer varieties that are more tailored to current market demand; (3) are characterised by higher yields and/or lower production costs.[11]

In addition, as fund B had been particularly active on the South African farmland market, they realised that their valuator used previous transactions to benchmark the new ones. Finally, they raised questions about the comparability of two farms, even located in the same area and producing the same crop, as they often have a different risk and return profile.

The challenge for the fund B management team was mainly to highlight the impact of its expansion programs on the farm value in order to make visible its capacity to 'create – or unlock – financial value'; the comparable sale methodology mainly reflected the market fluctuation. In reaction, the fund set up a valuation committee composed of the management team and the major investors, and at the same time, mandated a third-party valuator to test a discounted cash flow valuation of its farmland. The issue around farm valuation methodology illustrates the attempts to import a valuation framework that directly participates in the 'value creation' (Boussard, 2013) and the legitimation of the financial industry. In addition, these investment funds contest, although still only marginally, the commercial banks' monopoly on farmland fair price valuation.

The establishment of this framework, or its non-establishment, also constrains and frames the practices and strategies of financial brokers. For instance, as mentioned earlier, fund A acquired farms with cattle and decided after several discussions between the management and the investor to keep running such activity. The fund manager had to realise a bi-annual discounted cash flow valuation of every single asset, as done by classic private equity funds. However, they quickly faced unexpected difficulties starting with the impossibility of building a dynamic cash flow model for cattle. Indeed, thus far, the valuation of cattle remained on productivity per capita or per hectare maintaining a parallel accounting system in the fund A balance sheet. Because of these difficulties in translating cattle production into financial language fund A is currently selling all its livestock.

As noted, standard modelling is primarily used by investors to arbitrate between different investment opportunities in agricultural value chains, and also between different asset classes. Managers specialising in South African agriculture participate actively in the double movement of deepening the financial market with the inclusion of 'hybrid goods' (Aglietta and Rigot, 2009) as new asset classes, and

The assetisation of South African farmland   133

by connecting the different national markets through the production and diffusion of worldwide recognised benchmarks (Vallée, 2011).

Depoliticisation of the asset

A financial asset is structured on a standard flow of modelling and calculation. But, to 'unlock financial value', asset promoters have 'to conform' social reality to these flows. Indeed, managers undertake a neutralisation, or a depoliticisation, of the farms in order to fit them into the 'bundle of assets' conception. Such work is particularly visible when they have to deal with social or political issues surrounding their farms, as they often have to face stakeholders who embody and defend other, often incompatible, conceptions of farmland value. This sometimes produces a distortion and a diversion of their approach and can interfere with the managers' relationships with the investors. Such confrontation sheds light on the political dimension of the production of an asset and how the 'ferryman' (Pezet and Morales, 2010) manager turns into a political entrepreneur.

Among others, one concrete example from the field is the case of occupiers on fund A's farms. During the apartheid era, farm workers, particularly in the Mpumalanga and KwaZulu-Natal provinces, were allowed to live on the farm on which they worked as 'labour tenants'. In 1997, the Extension of Security of Tenure Act[12] conferred formal residential rights to these (former) workers and their families. This act includes a set of rights and duties for these 'occupiers' and for the owners (e.g. security of tenure, access to services, no commercial use of the land, an income of the occupier under the prescribed amount of R5000), while leaving a margin of manoeuvre for the two parties to negotiate and organise their daily cohabitation (Sibanda and Turner, 1999).

Fund A had acquired several farms with occupiers.[13] Gradually, such cohabitation generated tensions between the new farm owners and the occupiers.[14] The issue with the occupiers progressively interfered in the relationship between the American investor and the South African manager of the fund. Indeed, the investor became more and more anxious about this concern, seen as a potential source of mobilisations and contestations. This concern regarding the investor's reputational risk was particularly strong after another farmland fund operating in southern Africa was targeted by an activist campaign against land grabs. As one of the United States' main university endowments was the investor of this fund, the students of this university mobilised and sought its divestment from the fund.[15]

The fund manager tried to implement different strategies to 'clean' what they considered to be the fund's 'best asset'. They started by implementing an identification/registration system for all the occupiers and their family members on the farms and introduced a code of conduct to be signed by all occupiers. They also implemented a 'livestock permit' to register the different owners and a three-step warning system in case of abuse of the code of conduct by the occupiers. They also proposed removing all the occupiers to another piece of land, outside the farm, with official property titles. But, the occupiers refused the proposition,

134 *Antoine Ducastel and Ward Anseeuw*

arguing that the land was far away from services and useless for grazing. At that point, they were facing increasing concerns from the investor, therefore the manager proposed to group these farms and to list the grouping as a property fund on the Johannesburg Stock Exchange. They argued that in this case, the international investor would become one shareholder, among others, in the listed fund. Such a strategy aimed to dissolve the individual responsibility of the investor into the collective ownership of the market.[16] Regarding the manager's perspective, it allows them to keep control over the operation on one hand, and to balance the investor's power on the other hand. The proposition was rejected by the investor by virtue of its monopoly strategy, so the manager finally had to sell these farms, and the fund mandate has been reoriented toward smaller and more intensive farms such as permanent crops farms.

This example illustrates some of the difficulties faced in the translation process between an international investor and a local manager, and the misunderstandings that may arise. While the manager attempts to valorise its indigenous capital to minimise such issues, the investor seems more concerned about reputational risk, especially in its home country. Such a gap reflects the different positioning of these actors and gives a concrete example of intermediation difficulties.

Through the implementation of various initiatives and policies to regulate the presence of occupiers on farmland (e.g. through a code of conduct and livestock permits), a fund manager tends to become a political entrepreneur. In fact, to 'unlock financial value' from an agricultural asset, they have to mitigate the political and the social issues surrounding farmland and agriculture in South Africa. Indeed, they push for a 'disembeddedness' (Polanyi, 2001) of their farms to materialise the 'bundle of assets' conception. Paradoxically, even if they claim a purely financial approach through the 'asset-fiction', they find themselves engaged in particular forms of 'cross-regulation' (Bessy and Chauvin, 2013) alongside other public and private actors.

Conclusion

To conclude, three main points have to be highlighted.

First, even though South African farms still represent a minor asset class, the investment funds and companies focusing on them are diverse, as illustrated by the two case studies. This diversity can be explained by the specific interactions and power balances between investors and portfolio managers. Fund managers structure and brand their financial products according to the investors' characteristics and a potential new asset class must fit into it. Beyond the divergence in the funds' statuses and investment policies, such financial vehicles are 'living' products. Indeed, the interactions and confrontations between both parties during its lifespan affect the funds' forms.

Second, South African farmlands are far from being standardised assets, and their markets, rules of competition and cooperation are not yet institutionalised (Fligstein, 2001). As such, fund managers compete to impose their own farmland(s), with different natural and social characteristics, as the most legitimate asset. While they are collectively engaged in an emancipation process and the

The assetisation of South African farmland 135

structuration of a separate sub-field, they compete within this arena in order to define the most legitimate forms of capital. Therefore, an asset is not only recognised and assessed according to its good financial returns which are outperforming market performances, but rather because financial entrepreneurs frame and promote it as such with the aim to legitimise their position in the financial field.

Such strategies are spatially and historically situated. Indeed, these financial vehicles mobilise specific institutions and instruments at the national level, from the financial industries, in order to valorise farmlands. The funds thus borrow tools (as well as staff) from other sub-financial industries, as a repertoire of available resources, and endeavour to produce a coherent framework which gives South African farms a 'financial value' and to respond to financial criteria, such as, for instance, the optimal investment portfolio theory (Markowitz, 1952).

From this specific configuration, managers are able to implement financial analysis tools to produce a standardised informational flow. By producing these recognised benchmarks, managers allow institutional investors to evaluate these agricultural assets and potentially integrate them in their portfolios. As an asset is a particular value, this valuation process is at the heart of the process of assetisation. As seen here above, such valuation must be understood as an evaluation and a valorisation (Vatin, 2013), which relies on standardised benchmarks recognised by the financial markets. This commensuration is a support instrument for decision-making but especially a comparison tool as an asset acquires a value only when compared with others.

Third, these benchmarks are not enough to produce an asset; managers also try to 'neutralize' the political and social issues related to agriculture and farmland in South Africa by 'extracting' the farms from their social fabric. Claiming a purely financial and corporate approach, they find themselves engaged as political entrepreneurs, implementing 'corporate policies' or collaborating and negotiating with different actors in order to protect, or increase, the 'financial value' of the farmland.

This chapter illustrates the failures and groping of such attempts. Fund A disposed of several farms in response to sparse mobilisations from local occupants on farms, global activist organisations and students in the United States. This disposal shows that the financial industry, at least this endowment fund, took critics into consideration. But rather than abandon this or future attempts to integrate South African farmland in its portfolio, it now looks for a different kind of farm where the commodification process has been completed. The attempts to integrate South African farms as an asset class into financial markets illustrate the cognitive and political work which asset categories undergo. Polanyi had already shed light on the 'land-commodity fiction' which was an attempt to subordinate land to industrial societal needs (Polanyi, 2001). However, he underlined the existence of 'society's self-protection' movements curbing this dynamic. Today, one wonders if this 'land-asset fiction' will fully materialise through the subordination of farmland to the needs of the financial industry? And if so, will this be done through the heteroclite coalitions, mentioned earlier, embodying society's counter-movement?

Notes

1 One of the conditions allowing me to observe those funds from the inside was to preserve their anonymity.

2 In comparison, for instance Ethos Private Equity, one of the leading South African asset management companies on the private equity market, investing in the industry and retail sectors, has more than 20 executives and manages US$510 million just in its fund IV (SAVCA & KPMG, 2015).

3 GBC1 regime – which offers a harmonised corporate and income tax of 15 per cent, tax exemption on dividends and a set of bilateral double taxation agreements.

4 This is an agreement between the fund manager and an investor that outlines different terms that will apply to the investor's investment in the fund, giving the investor some flexibility to go outside the terms of the fund's legal document.

5 Both funds adopted the manager's remuneration standards from the private equity industry known as 2/8/20: 2 per cent of the asset value under control as management fee; a hurdle internal rate of return fixed at 8 per cent; and 20 per cent of benefits as profit sharing.

6 For instance, fund B cannot invest less than 50 million Rand per farm (3.5 million Euro) and its final portfolio should include at least four farms. Fund A targets farms above 1000 hectares.

7 In their table grape farm in the Northern Cape, fund B's manager is currently increasing their production area from 12 to 73 hectares. Overall, 30 per cent of this fund's capital (R136 million) is dedicated to the farms' improvement.

8 Such contracts are signed on a 10-year basis with a remuneration corresponding to 8 per cent of the annual farm value including inflation.

9 In addition, this fund manager is also a member of the United Nations working group 'Principles for Responsible Investment'.

10 Fund A, commercial flyer, 2013.

11 Fund B, evaluation committee report, 2013.

12 RSA (Republic of South Africa). Extension of Security of Tenure Act 62 of 1997. Pretoria. Government Printers.

13 Most of the farmers in the eastern part of South Africa have to deal with these occupiers' issues.

14 These occupiers own cattle who graze on the farm and managers have accused them of putting the cattle on their grazing land, threatening their own cattle with disease contamination. Furthermore, the access to their family graves, situated outside of their area, has become a source of tension when a manager endeavours to control and regulate this access.

15 Oakland Institute, Vanderbilt University Divests from "Land Grab" in Africa, 13 February 2013. http://www.oaklandinstitute.org/vanderbilt-university-divests-land-grab-africa.

16 Thereby, the financial markets' notion of 'public' challenges the notion of 'public good' as a use by those who live or work on it.

PART III

Crossing boundaries

Individual careers as vehicles for financialisation

Introduction

The financialisation of finance:
The transformation of the French financial elite

Sabine Montagne

This section, consisting of three chapters, is devoted to the trajectories of agents, corporate executives, directors and financial journalists, who all contribute to the spread of shareholder value in France and are, as such, active agents in financialisation "à la française". These three chapters refute, in their own way, intuitive assumptions that one is tempted to make by basing the reasoning on an analysis of the financialisation of the US. The three texts strive to demonstrate that the French financialisation agents are not newcomers as were the American raiders of the 1980s (Guilhot, 2004) or Anglo-Saxon investors introduced by the French privatisations of the 1980s and 1990 (Morin and Dupuy, 1993; Morin, 1998), or even new generations of elite trained in business schools now converted to Friedman-style economics and modern financial economics (Fourcade and Khurana, 2013; Whitley, 1986). Although these changes would have certainly taken place later on, they cannot account for the dynamic at work among the elites in the 1950s.

Chapter 8, written by P. François and C. Lemercier, defends two theses that appear rather counter-intuitive at first sight: on the one hand, that the first phases of financialisation were established between 1950 and 1970, when the financier portion of the economic elite was already in the most powerful positions; on the other hand, that the second phase of financialisation, during the years 1980–1990, grew due to "old" financiers being converted to new ways of doing business thanks to specific professional socialisation. These results were obtained by comparing the trajectories of three cohorts (1956, 1979 and 2009) composed of the leaders of 120 of the largest listed companies and of 210 people who served on at least two of their boards of directors in 2009. The analysis confirms the relative stability over time of the characteristics of these leaders in terms of academic training and crossing of state functions. However, it highlights a division, between financial and non-financial careers, that has not yet been identified by the literature. Already active in the first financialisation era, this division appears to be directly correlated with the shareholder orientation of business management (measured by dividend distribution) in the years 1980–1990. So, to understand the second financialisation era, there should be less focus on describing the reorganisation of the morphology of the elite than on clarifying the conversion conditions of their financial fraction to shareholder value ideology. One must investigate in particular the places where this conversion was made. Going through a function

140 Sabine Montagne

in a finance department or in an investment bank, rather than a commercial bank, becomes additional experience required for access to positions of power, while the Ministry of Finance was the third place for socialisation into the new shareholders' doxa of the corporation from the 1980s.

Chapter 9, written by V. Boussard and S. Paye, highlights the French specificity by following the career paths of three cohorts (1985, 1995 and 2005) of graduates of one of the leading French business schools, HEC. Once again counter-intuitive, the analysis of data shows no major increase in the number of financial positions of the three cohorts. Financial professions do not represent an increasing share of the careers of economic elites. However, the nature of financial positions held by the sample of graduates has changed between 1985 and 2005: the proportion of corporate finance positions has declined in favour of jobs in financial services, capital markets and auditing. Financialisation, therefore, consisted of a transfer of staff between jobs, within financial activities. Finally, access to corporate management positions has not been facilitated in a linear way by an early financial career. Career profiles that achieve the summits of corporate power remain highly contrasted between cohorts. Unexpectedly, the 1995 cohort massively favours passing through marketing/sales positions, while the other two actually favour passage through financial positions, but in a differentiated manner, since it is corporate finance that is preferred by the 1985 cohort and market finance by the 2005 cohort. The cohort study, therefore, invalidates the idea that a financial career path will become a springboard to leadership positions.

Chapter 10, written by A. Machut, questions the consistency of French financial journalism. Do these financial journalists have the same characteristics of commitment, even of activism, as other journalists, which make it impossible to get journalistic legitimacy? The question is even more relevant as, unlike the US, the UK and Germany, France does not have a long tradition of financial journalism. From the analysis of the profiles of 171 individuals – LinkedIn, entered in the database in 2015 – and interviews, the chapter shows the high frequency of moving back and forth between non-financial press and financial press jobs (35%), the banality of their multi-activity (32%), and their exit to financial jobs (39%) even after a hierarchical ascent. These features and the various ways to enter the profession reflect the difficulty of building a professional segment based on a relatively sustainable career model and regulated independently from the financial world's standards. Therefore, banks are able to attract those journalists with a shaky future and problematic professional identity. The task of analysing financial news, therefore, slips from news media to financial institutions, which helps to create a diffuse area of financial information largely under the control of the finance sector.

These three chapters do not analyse the French financialisation as a process of quantitative expansion of financial staffs and separation of their activities from non-financial activities. The French financialisation is, rather, a conversion of financial agents (to the ideology of shareholder value), the transformation of financial transactions and business (from corporate accounting to trading, brokerage, and mergers and acquisitions) and the monitoring of financial information by banks. This section, therefore, gives way to the work on itself that the financial sector had to do to pass from just the financier stage to "financialised", to use the distinction made by E. Chiapello (2014). The financialisation described here echoes described by E. Chiapello (2014) as a process if gradual colonization. Through the use of techniques and methods, which are not only financial but also "financialized". This research program moves the traditional focus on the effects of financialisation, due to the growth of the power and wealth of financial (often taken-for-granted) actors, towards the issue of the financialisation of these actors.

8 The second financialisation in France, or how executives and directors with unchanged financial careers promoted a new conception of control

Pierre François and Claire Lemercier

How far do the careers of managers and directors matter for contemporary financialisation? They may be related in two ways. Change in the careers of managers and directors can be seen as a consequence of financialisation: the growing importance of financial activities and the increasing power of financial firms imply that financiers are now more likely to get to top positions in the main firms. Therefore, financialisation can be seen as one of the main streams that are reworking the economic elites (Mizruchi, 2013). But changes in careers can also be seen as a cause of financialisation. If some actors (for example, former chief financial officers) who seldom reached the top of firms are more and more central, they are more likely to promote financial logics in the firms they now run. In this regard, changes in careers can be seen as one of the key mechanisms that might explain the financialisation of firm strategies (Zorn, 2004).

In this chapter, we will discuss these two main ways to relate the careers of members of the economic elite and financialisation, focusing on the French case. We will more precisely focus on the CEOs of the 120 largest publicly listed French firms, as well as on the 210 persons who sat on at least two of their boards in 2009 (the two groups partly overlap). We will show that the financialisation of French firms did not change the main divides that structure the French economic elite. The sociology and history of French elites has long pointed to the impressive stability of the origins and education of CEOs, and especially the role played by a few schools in operating this reproduction under the guise of Republican elitism. Accordingly, elite schools channel careers into two separate groups: those who go through the top schools and the highest offices in the administration, and those who, after graduating from slightly less prestigious schools, directly join firms (as regards CEOs, Bourdieu and de Saint-Martin, 1978; for a review of the literature, Joly, 2007; on the French elites more generally, Bourdieu, 1989). Our study confirms that the CEOs of the 21st century do not differ much from their predecessors, and that a large minority come from the administration, but it also puts forward a different divide, which has been undermined by this literature: that between financial and non-financial careers. Financiers have always been there, at least from the 1950s on. The growing importance of financial activities

The second financialisation in France   143

and logics within French firms has not spectacularly changed the structure of the French economic elite.

And yet, the stability of this structure does not imply that the careers of directors or top managers played no role in the process of financialisation. We find, indeed, that the dividend yield of each firm, which can be considered as a proxy of its orientation towards shareholder value, is significantly correlated with the presence of financial careers among its multi-positioned directors and/or CEO (François and Lemercier, 2016; such a correlation did not exist in 1979). This correlation holds, all other things being equal, whereas, for example, the type of shareholders or the position of the firm in the network of interlocking directorates has no independent effect. Financial careers (as defined below in "Data and methods") therefore matter for financialisation in France: they seem to produce a specific "conception of control," as defined by Fligstein (1990). According to him, conceptions of controls are shaped by careers, and in turn, have an effect on the strategic choices of firms.

However, in order to make that point, we have to consider careers in much more detail than Fligstein did. He doesn't elaborate much on how he coded the background of his CEOs so as to assign them one conception of control (production, sales or finance). This coding scheme has something to do with the department of the firm in which they worked before becoming CEOs, but those (sometimes a majority) who worked neither in production nor in sales or finance, and those who moved from one of these departments to another, are not discussed. Nor does Fligstein greatly consider the fact that many careers spanned several firms or even sectors. On the contrary, we have carefully reconstructed and taken into account such preliminary steps of the careers. This process, which is presented in the "Data and methods" section below, is key to our investigation of the – limited but significant – changes in financial careers since the 1950s and the – much more impressive and influential – changes in the associated conception of control.

Our first result is presented in the first part of this chapter: whereas financial careers appear strongly associated, in the late 2000s, with the adoption of shareholder value, they do not, at first glance, represent a new path to the boards and CEO seats. Change in orientation towards shareholder value happened due to the *conversion* of a classically selected, trained and experienced elite, not to the *invasion* of a foreign, or more generally different, elite. The French story is, therefore, different from that told by Fligstein (1990) and Zorn (2004) about the rise of chief financial officers to the top of industrial US firms: the financiers, who happen to play a decisive role in the adoption of a new conception of control, are not very different from their predecessors of 30 or 50 years ago (see similarly Davoine and Ravasi, 2013, on a much smaller sample of French firms and shorter time span). It is also different from the revolution that happened in small European countries such as the Netherlands or Switzerland (Heemskerk, 2007; David *et al.*, 2012), with the rise of a foreign or international elite deserting the classical national career paths. It was after having travelled along the same career paths that the French financial elite apparently weighed in favour of shareholder value. In the second part of this chapter, we zoom in on the careers of these financiers so as to

144 *Pierre François and Claire Lemercier*

specify in which context of work this conversion is likely to have happened: we find possible loci of change in specific banks and in the offices of the Ministry of Finance, as well as in the financial departments.

Box 8.1: Data and Methods

Our analysis originates with the firms listed in SBF120 in 2009, that is, broadly speaking, those with the highest market capitalisation (more precisely, those firms chosen by Euronext among the 200 highest market capitalisations). We excluded the few firms that were not based in France from our calculations. For 1979 and 1956, we used historical reconstructions of an equivalent of SBF120 (provided by Euronext for 1979 and by Le Bris, 2001 for 1956). To list the CEOs and board members and gather basic information on firms, including the way they presented what they did, we used the following sources:

- for 2009: information provided by Euronext, complemented by the public reports of firms (found online in 2010) and *Guide*, 2011;
- for 1979 and 1956: a directory published for investors, *Annuaire Desfossés*, years 1980 and 1957.

We coded our firms as financial or non-financial on the basis of the objective of the company as presented in such sources, which leaves room for interpretation. Among financial firms, we included banks, insurance companies, investment companies, and those real estate companies that, as far as we could understand, derived more turnover from leasing than from renting or erecting buildings.

For each firm, we selected the CEO, or a reasonable equivalent for firms with a different structure of governance (in rare cases, more than one person had to be selected). In addition, we selected all members of at least two boards in SBF120. Our definition of boards and directors was very inclusive. We considered as board members the members of *conseils d'administration*, *conseils de surveillance* and *conseils de censeurs*, as well as the two to five top members of the executive committee (mostly *directeurs généraux*), even when the source did not explicitly state that they were also members of boards.

We tried to gather information on more than 60 variables for the CEOs and multiple directors – the total number of persons in this population was 216 in 1956, when there was comparably little interlocking, 282 in 1979 and 283 in 2009 (the structure of interlocking directorates was very stable between the last two dates). We lack most information for about 110 cases in 1956 (a cohort we only use here to assess that, in spite of changes in historical context as well as in sources, careers still appear remarkably similar to later ones), but just 55 in 1979 (20%) and 25 in 2009 (less than 10%).

Some of our variables are positional; that is, they describe the firms in which the person was a CEO and/or multiple director at the time of observation, and the position of this person in the network of interlocking directorates. The other variables are biographical: we looked for information mostly in *Who's Who in France* (for 2010–2016, 1993–1994, 1979–1980, 1971–1972 and 1957–1958) and additionally in other sources for those we had not found there (LesBiographies.com and *Guide*, 2011 for 2009; the World Biographical Index System and the online database Leonore for 1956; exhaustive lists of graduates of the elite universities Polytechnique and Sciences Po were also used for all dates).

We defined as CFS (for "career in the financial sector") those who had worked as employees (from low-level to CEO, but excluding mere board members and similar positions) in the financial sector before our observation; some of them had also worked for non-financial firms. The financial sector was defined on the basis of the names of firms where the person was employed, firms being classified as explained above. There were 105 CFS in 2009 (37% of our population). We defined as CFF (for "career including financial functions") those who had worked in financial departments/functions, for example as chief financial officers, internal auditors, and so on. There were 84 CFF in 2009 (30% of our population); some of them were also CFS.

More generally, we tried to identify all the functions held in firms before reaching the top executive level (that of *directeur général*); we classified them as production (engineering, R&D, etc.), marketing (sales, etc.) and financial, as well as (in addition to the classification in Fligstein, 1990) legal, human resources, management of a plant (or bank agency, etc.), of a product line (or sector inside the firm) or of a geographical area (director for Europe, etc.). Consulting was also coded as a separate function and career step. Such a scheme produced several binary variables allowing us to define CFF, careers involving production functions, and so on. It also produced an additive variable describing the number of different functions experienced before reaching the top of the firm: just one type (e.g. one or several positions related to production); two or more (e.g. several functions in marketing, then director for Europe, then top executive manager); none (e.g. coming from the administration to directly become a CEO); or "only general functions." This fourth case describes careers in firms that began not at the CEO level, but in the immediate environment of the CEO, for example as secretary of the board or personal adviser of the CEO.

Further details and descriptive statistics are given in François and Lemercier (2016). All the results that we present here are based on comparisons between dates, or between financial and non-financial careers, that are significant in terms of Chi2 at the 5% level. The idea of a main divide between CFS and others is based on specific multiple correspondence analysis (a version of the method that accommodates missing data: Le Roux and Rouanet, 2004).

146 *Pierre François and Claire Lemercier*

I Financial vs. non-financial careers: the main divide in the French economic elite

Most of the studies on the French economic elite focus on CEOs and on industrial firms, and generally reconstruct variables on their background, as opposed to their early careers. They therefore undermine the most striking divide within our population of CEOs and multiple directors of industrial, commercial and financial firms: that between non-financial and financial (which we call CFS) careers. Moreover, this is true for the 1956 and 1979 cohorts as well as the 2009 cohort, whereas secondary divides differ. Former officers of the Ministry of Finance who afterwards worked in the financial sector were, and are, more similar to former managers of banks or insurance companies without any administrative or political experience than they are to the engineers in the state nobility.

Box 8.2: French elite educational institutions

A large proportion of our population is made up of graduates of very specific French institutions called *grandes écoles*, that is, elite "schools," a higher education system in competition with universities, which includes both private and public institutions. In our population, the main ones are Sciences Po, a semi-private university with an interdisciplinary curriculum focusing on law, economics and social sciences (created in the late 19th century to emulate the London School of Economics); ENA, the "national school for administration," often entered after Sciences Po, which leads directly to the highest ranks of the administration; and Polytechnique, an elite scientific school in which the top graduates join the Ponts or Mines corps: groups of elite engineers who supervise, for example, energy, transportation or urban planning for the administration.

Our CFS, therefore, include careers that began either in the administration or in the private sector. What has so significantly distinguished CFS from other careers, from the 1950s to the 2000s? This divide has to do with social origins (those with CFS are more often Parisian-born, and their fathers had elite occupations even more often than others), education (in law, in Sciences Po and/or more recently in economics, rather than in business or engineering schools), the type of administrative careers for those who had one, the type of entry-level positions in firms and the position in the interlocking directorates network. When CFS passed through the administration, it was in a few specific departments of the Ministry of Finance; they joined firms later than the engineers of the state nobility, in their forties rather than their late twenties; and they worked more often on the personal staff of ministers, especially the finance minister or the prime minister. As for early careers in firms, CFS, coming from the administration or otherwise, went straight to the top of firms more often than others, whether by direct entry at the top executive

The second financialisation in France 147

level (from the administration or as heir to a family firm – possibly smaller than an SBF120 firm, of course) or by working solely around the CEO, as opposed to working in a specific department of the firm.

A French or even "Latin" model of careers of top executives has sometimes been described (Davoine and Ravasi, 2013) as involving an important mobility both between firms and between functions in firms, especially as contrasted with the German model. Managers would be "catapulted" from outside into firms and easily move between functional departments. What we show is different: some French executives are indeed catapulted, but they reach the top directly, and it happens mostly in finance. Multi-functional careers are a different story; they more often happen inside one firm and do not involve the financial sector. There have been some recent changes in this general pattern: our 2009 cohort, on average, exhibits more complex career paths than in the previous decades, probably produced by a new way to select and promote so-called high-potential managers. For example, the former CEO of the cement producer Lafarge explained that he established "a secret, pre-established plan [to train future top executives]: 4 years in this operational department, 3 years in that far-away country, 2 years in the headquarters, 3 more years running a major subsidiary, and one day access to the executive committee" (Lecerf, 1991: 55). Yet even in this new context, CFS careers remain simpler than non-financial careers, and 32% of them still led directly to the top, or only went through the entourage of a CEO (as opposed to 16% among non-CFS). Those are the over-schooled, supposedly polyvalent "providential men" whom the same Lecerf advised avoiding: many of his colleagues apparently still praise them. On the contrary, the CEOs studied by Fligstein (1990, 280–7) apparently almost never had such straight-to-the-top trajectories (his "general" category, which is much broader than ours as it includes, e.g., the direction of a plant, covers only 6%–17% of his population in each period). The existence of a conception of control driven by such direct careers would deserve further investigation. Lack of experience inside a specific department of the firm, plus experience alongside the CEO and/or board (probably implying, in recent years, frequent contacts with the main shareholders), is likely to encourage an orientation towards shareholder value.

This divide between CFS and other careers is, to a certain extent, the transposition to the space of top managers of the opposition between financial and non-financial firms. Yet CFS are not only found on the boards and in the CEO seats of banks, insurance or investment companies: their presence matters in large firms more generally. Indeed, one of their other peculiarities is the fact that they are sought after by non-financial companies, both as CEOs and as multiple board members (Table 8.1). In 2009, 18 out of the 103 non-financial firms of SB120 (as well as all the financial firms) had a CEO who had previously worked in finance.

Therefore, if we loosely define as "financialisation" the fact that "finance influences non-finance," it could be argued that one of the important channels of this influence in contemporary France is the movement of former managers of banks to CEO and multiple board positions in the largest industrial and commercial firms. This, however, was already very true in 1979 (not in 1956), as shown

Table 8.1 Financiers on boards

Cohort	CFS (%)			Non-CFS (%)		
	Only sitting on boards of financial firms	Sitting on boards of financial and non-financial firms	Only sitting on boards of non-financial firms	Only sitting on boards of financial firms	Sitting on boards of financial and non-financial firms	Only sitting on boards of non-financial firms
1979	28	49	23	6	21	48
2009	9	41	50	0	11	89

Note: "Boards" include CEOs and members of executive committees.

in Table 8.1, and by the fact that, in 1979, 20 out of the 79 non-financial firms of SB120 also had a CEO who had previously worked in finance. This leads us to our main puzzle: if the careers in the French economic elite, and the preferences for such careers on the boards of the largest firms, changed so little between the late 1970s and the late 2000s, then how could they influence financialisation?

II From the first to the second financialisation: loci of conversion

In many ways, when 1979 is compared with 2009, similarities are more striking than changes: both now and then, we find the same divide between CFS and other careers, the same peculiarities of CFS, and the same tendency of non-financial firms to favour CFS in the choice of their CEOs and multiple directors. These similarities may seem surprising, since the 1950s–1970s, perhaps especially in France, generally thought of as a time of industrial growth, admittedly with the beginning of a crisis in heavy industries in the 1970s, but certainly with little independent influence from financial markets, or even from banks, which are often described as uniformly state-owned or closely controlled by the administration (see, for example, Coriat, 2008). Yet this narrative deserves an important qualification.

In many respects, a first financialisation can be considered to have happened in France from the 1950s to the 1970s. It was not based on market finance or shareholder value, and therefore, it cannot be confused with the current financialisation. However, it involved the birth or quick expansion and diversification of very large financial firms, their higher-than-ever centrality in the network of interlocking directorates (the average degree centrality of financial firms was 7.5 in 1956, 11 in 1979 and 10.5 in 2009), and a much larger number of CFS in our 1979 cohort than in 2009. In fact, the very number of financial firms in SBF120 in 1979 is striking: 39, vs. just 12 in 2009. Thus, finance was already very much present and powerful in the late 1970s, and some of the central players in the contemporary financialisation were already among our sample of firms. Indeed, the financial firms that matter today are not young, whereas many in 1979 were less than 20 years old. For example, Eurazeo, one of the leading French investment funds, evolved from Eurafrance, already part of SBF120 in 1979, which, in turn, had been created by the partners in Lazard frères, a key non-listed merchant bank of the 1960s. Lazard frères was already 100 years old at that time, and its partners still control Eurazeo today, together with Crédit Agricole.

However, stressing the similarities between 1979 and 2009 should not hide the differences between some of the features and (even more) causes of the first and second financialisations. The financial firms were much more specialised in the late 1970s than 30 years later. They are less numerous in SBF120 in 2009, but much larger, since they have mostly absorbed specialised finance, which thrived in independent companies (with interlocks or minority shareholdings by the main banks of the time) in 1979. Some of the characteristics of the first financialisation differ deeply from those of the second. Therefore, comparing the two helps

150 *Pierre François and Claire Lemercier*

to better describe the latter: not as a sudden intrusion of finance into an industrial and/or statist world (as in Coriat, 2008) but as a change in the shape and stated mission of financial firms, as well as in the objectives of financial and non-financial firms.

As for its causes, the first financialisation, that is, the growth and growing influence on industry of some financial firms, can be related to specifically French roots. One of these can be found in the fiscal policy promoted by the French government, which aimed at favouring investment in building; hence the development of firms that specialised in the financing of the building industry, often in dependence on large banks. Another cause of this first financialisation was the reconversion of old firms to financial activities: some colonial firms (e.g. Compagnie du Cambodge) reinvested the sums they got as compensation when they had to leave the French Empire, and became investment funds. The beginning of the crisis of heavy industries also prompted owners of capital to exit (sometimes selling their firm to the French state) and reinvest in portfolio firms (such as the companies controlled by the Wendel family). Thus, the first financialisation had very French causes. These no longer operated during the second financialisation. Still, this new process is not completely foreign to the history of the French elites. It has been imposed by people whose resumes generally look the same as those of their predecessors, but they have adopted different ways of thinking about the aims of their firms. To make sense of this conversion, we could put forward a general atmosphere, something that would have convinced the actors through their readings, interactions with foreign executives, and so on. This would, however, not explain why firms with more CFS and CFF in their boards offer higher dividend yields than others. By zooming in on our career data, we can be more specific about the likely loci of conversion – perhaps those in which such readings and encounters mostly took place.

Finance departments

If one first turns to the usual suspects that have been convened as hypothetical loci of conversion, it seems that neither changes in the education of the top managers and directors of French firms, nor their (temporary) migration, can explain their conversion to financial logics. The conversion of the French economic elite is not likely to have happened during their education. There is no doubt that the curriculum of the main institutions where they have been trained (especially Sciences Po and ENA) has changed a lot in the last decades (Kolopp, 2013), but our population was not exposed to this change: we are talking here about people who were born in the 1930s and 1940s, and whose education took place between 1950 and 1975, that is, during the first financialisation, at a time when the elite French schools were teaching Keynesianism and the prominence of the general interest. The shift in the strategies of French firms did not come from abroad either. More precisely, if it came from the adoption of foreign ideas, this did not happen because of the weight of foreign shareholders, who remain a minority (François and Lemercier, 2016), or that of foreign top executives or multiple directors: a mere 8% of our

The second financialisation in France 151

2009 cohort were born outside France, and fewer than 20% of CFS (interestingly, even less than for non-financial careers) included a period abroad.

Another classical way to explain the rise of shareholder value, the growing importance of financial functions in the career of those who run firms, deserves further attention. We have not yet come back to our CFF, but their increased frequency is the main change in our database between the first and second financialisations. Of course, there were internal auditors and chief financial officers before, but they rarely became CEOs or multiple directors. We find 5% of CFF at most in 1956. There were 14% in 1979, but they were mostly found in the specific, arguably non-central position of representing the same firm (often an insurance company) in the seat specifically assigned to this company in several boards. They were managers, but not top executives of their own firms; interlockers by accident, so to speak, not specifically sought by the receiving firm but mere representatives of a shareholder.

On the contrary, 30% of our 2009 cohort have held financial functions. Among those 84 persons, 57 were chief financial officers; 27 worked as internal auditors, in the management control or accountancy department; and 32 were financial analysts, or in charge of mergers, participations, and so on (many went through several of those functions). They entered such positions at extremely different times, from 1962 to 2008 (for 70%, between 1975 and 1993). What we are considering here is thus not a precise moment of conversion; it is, rather, a specific type of function that is likely to induce a specific view of firms (Fligstein, 1990). As the aforementioned former CEO of Lafarge stated (regretfully), "the top executive of 1992 has to be comfortable with finance, and it is a big difference with that of before 1970," who could be content with having a financial department specialise in such matters. Such a change was required because executive committees had to take part in maintaining good relationships with shareholders and in public debates about the firm's performance (Lecerf, 1991: 62). Indeed, the CEO of Lafarge in 2009 (also a director of the electricity company EDF), Bruno Lafont, entered the firm as an internal auditor in 1983 (after 1 year in the Ministry of Finance). He was the son of a doctor, born in the wealthy suburbs of Paris, and had graduated from both ENA and a prestigious business school. He then climbed to the top, not only through the function of CFO, but also, in a perfect echo of Lecerf's "secret plan," after having run subsidiaries and the Turkish branch of Lafarge.

However, what is striking in the French case, and differs from Fligstein's thesis that CFF may be considered as vehicles of a new financial, as opposed to a productive or commercial, view of the firm, is that financial functions come as a *complement*, not an *alternative* to almost all the previously existing career paths. We find people having held financial functions even among CFS (although in smaller numbers, because many of the latter were still promoted straight to the top); among the state nobility as well as in purely private careers; and many of them have also held positions related to production or sales. Three quarters of SBF120 firms now have at least one CFF on their board, and this, as well as the presence of CFS, seems to influence their orientation towards shareholder value. Yet those CFF have very little else in common; they come from business schools

152   *Pierre François and Claire Lemercier*

slightly more often than non-CFF and have had a little more experience working abroad for foreign firms, but even those features only describe 20%–25% of them. What we find here is therefore not a new profile, but a new addition to some careers in all the old profiles. Yet it is likely that this type of experience, now required, shaped attitudes towards shareholder value and the firm more generally. As in the US, financial departments have probably been one important locus of conversion; but this conversion shaped values more than careers themselves.

For the state nobility: the Ministry of Finance

Finally, whereas the early career profiles of CFS changed very little, we can document some changes in the exact organisations that employed them to discover likely loci of conversion.

While the rise in numbers and positions of CFF is the single important change in our career data from 1979 to 2009, what conversely changed the least is the profile of those CFS who first worked in administration. They graduated from ENA and worked in the Ministry of Finance, especially as inspectors (N = 16 among CFS in our 2009 cohorts) and/or in the Department of the Treasury (N = 14) or Budget (N = 6). Many of them spent some time working in the personal staff of the finance minister (or one of his under-secretaries, or the prime minister, or the president; N = 32). They then, often directly or almost directly, became CEOs of a firm, frequently a state-owned or formerly state-owned company, before moving to the private sector proper. As we have seen, they had been trained long before the curriculum of ENA included a socialisation to the new rules of finance: their conversion must have happened after their graduation. Gérard Mestrallet is a good example of such a career, virtually indistinguishable in its general shape from similar ones in the early 20th century (François and Lemercier, 2014). The Parisian son of a "merchant," he typically graduated from Sciences Po and ENA (less typically, also from Polytechnique) and worked in the Treasury Department in 1978–1982, then in the staff of Minister of Finance Jacques Delors at the time when the socialist government first envisioned turning to financial markets for the public debt. Then he directly joined Suez, was soon in charge of industrial affairs among the top executives, and became the CEO in 1995. He had the firm focus its business on utilities, but used various financial techniques to do so. At the end of the 2000s, he was the chair of Paris Europlace, an organisation aiming at the promotion of the French financial markets – as well as the CEO of Suez Environnement and a board member of GDF Suez and Saint-Gobain.

Along with Mestrallet and Gilles Benoist, whom we will shortly meet, no fewer than three other CEOs and/or multiple directors in our 2009 cohorts, Paul Hermelin, Philippe Lagayette and Charles-Henri Filippi, had been part of Delors' staff. Four additional top executives of the late 2000s had worked for Delors' under-secretaries (e.g. Laurent Fabius, in charge of Budget) during the same key years, in 1981–1984. Lemoine (2016) gave a precise account of this period, when the socialist government decided that financing the public debt on the international financial markets was the only possible option – and that the largest French firms should also resort to market finance rather than banks. The fact that this period was a turning point could explain the surprising weight of its veterans at the top of the largest French firms, 25 years after.

In fact, conversions also happened before and after the Delors period in the Ministry of Finance, and more precisely, in its Treasury Department. Lemoine's study also documents this point, making sense of the careers of our CFS who worked in the Treasury in the 1970s or 1990s. This department has been key to the diffusion of the idea that financial markets are legitimately essential for the economy. As early as the late 1960s, the Treasury, which played a central role in the regulatory, bank-based French economic policy of the time, had begun to question the rationale of such a policy. By the late 1970s, the men in charge there were convinced that changes had to occur. When they eventually convinced the socialist government, they presented their thesis as a technical requirement, not a matter for political debate. Daniel Lebègue is an emblematic case here. An advisor of Prime Minister Pierre Mauroy in 1981–1984, he was not a socialist: he had worked in the Treasury department since 1969. He left the administration in 1987, at 44, to directly reach the top of the bank BNP. In 2009, he was a member of the boards of Scor and Technip. In interviews with Lemoine, he stressed the fear of the early 1980s: France was at risk of being humiliated by the IMF or by lenders in the Gulf countries. There was a "Treasury thesis" on this problem of the public debt and on the virtues of financial markets generally; it was independent of personal political preferences and spanned the decades before and after the turning point. What we find is that French firms of the 2000s, when they exhibit an interest in former public officers as CEOs or multiple board members, very much draw from this pool.

In addition to the Ministry of Finance itself, a likely locus of conversion is *Caisse des dépôts et consignations*, a state-owned financial institution closely connected to the ministry, which is supposed to help cities, departments and regions in their investments. In the 1980s, it also had to rapidly adapt to the rules of the financial markets. 12 of our CFS worked there (nine were part of the French nobility, three were not): no other single firm employed as many people in our cohort. Gilles Benoist, for example, the son of a "top manager of a corporation," was born in Paris, graduated from Sciences Po and ENA and worked for the Ministry of Internal Affairs, then became the chief of staff of Jacques Delors. He afterward joined the *Caisse*, where he worked for 11 years. At that time, the *Caisse* faced the opening of competition in the banking sector and the "big bang" of financial markets in France. It had to adopt new strategies of investment. It chose to adapt to the changes occurring at the time in the financial markets (Lavigne, 1991), for example by contributing to decompartmentalising their segments. In 2009, Gilles Benoist was the CEO of an insurance company and sat on the board of Suez.

For the private careers: from commercial to merchant banks

Few non-state nobility careers in our sample begun at the *Caisse*. Where, then, did the conversion take place for those? In our 1979 cohort, the most common trajectory went through private, commercial banks, especially but not only Suez and

154 *Pierre François and Claire Lemercier*

Paribas, which neither specialized in merchant banking nor directly provided retail banking. Among 147 CFS in our 1979 cohort, 66 worked for this type of bank. They had established relationships with industrial firms akin to what is generally described as "the Rhineland model" (Lamard and Stoskopf, 2015): long-term, close partnerships including loans, the buying of a substantive amount of capital, multiple shared directors and an influence on industrial strategies. The case of Philippe Malet provides a good example. Born in 1925, the son of a member of the *Ponts corps*, he graduated from Polytechnique and entered the even more prestigious *Mines corps*. After working in the Ministry of Industry and in the staff of President de Gaulle, he joined Suez in 1963. There, he was in charge of the relationships with industrial companies that Suez invested in. He became closely involved in the strategies of many industrial firms: Compagnie des Mines de Huaron, Compagnie de Mokta, Société Lille-Bonnières et Colombes, Compagnie des Salins du Midi, Compagnie Lyonnaise des eaux, and so on. In 1979, he sat on more boards than anyone else in SBF120 firms.

The typical CFS career paths in our 2009 cohort, while they have the same general shape, went through quite different financial firms. Merchant banks appear much more often than in 1979 (25% of the 2009 CFS worked there, as compared with 12% of the 1979 CFS). This is especially the case with Lazard and Rothschild, two banks that were still partnerships when our future CEOs and directors worked there. As much as the *Caisse des dépôts*, they are very likely loci of conversion to shareholder value, and to market finance more generally: 10 of our CFS worked for Lazard and 10 for Rothschild. Lazard has been, for a long time, at the heart of financial innovation: as soon as the early 1950s, André Meyer, one of the main New York partners of Lazard, set up a structure that contributed to defining the business model of modern investment funds (Reich, 1986). At the same time, the New York branch of Lazard developed the business of consulting in mergers and acquisitions, such as the buying of Jennings Radio by ITT in 1961, helping to build the large conglomerates that flourished in the 1960s in the US. Lazard New York was also one of the most aggressive firms in reactivating the policy of hostile takeovers at the beginning of the 1960s. After the Second World War, all these financial practices had been invented or reactivated in the US, but they were well known by Parisian partners, who often spent months in New York to complete their education in the field. One of the first hostile takeovers launched by Lazard in 1964, on Franco-Wyoming, was appraised by Michel David-Weill, who later became the head of Lazard. The Parisian heir of a Lazard partner and a graduate from the French high school in New York, then Sciences Po, he had joined the firm at 29, already as a junior partner. In 2009, he was a member of the boards of Danone (food) and Eurazeo (finance).

However, such innovations were not easily adopted in France, at least in the first decades that followed. The hostile takeover of Antoine Riboux's BSN, advised by Lazard (together with Paribas and Neuflize), against Saint-Gobain failed in 1969 because of the opposition of other major Parisian financial institutions (Orange, 2006). It was only later that such techniques were legitimised and taught to new firms by those who had (re)conceived them in the 1960s. For example, Antoine Bernheim was one of the main advisers of Bernard Arnault in his conquest of

Boussac, in the early 1980s, and of LVMH a few years later. He was also one of the only members of both our cohorts. The son of a Parisian lawyer, he studied science, then law at university and, at 30, became a partner in a real estate firm belonging to his family, before working for Lazard, then for an insurance company. In 1979, he sat on the boards of the retail chain Euromarché, the investment fund Eurafrance and the real estate company Sefimeg; in 2009, at 80, he was still a director of the financial firms Bolloré and Eurazeo and the non-financial firms LVMH (luxury), Havas (media) and Ciments français (cement).

Like the careers of those two heirs, most of our CFS including a span at Lazard were purely private. Rothschild, however, offered a slightly different path, from the most prestigious parts of the state nobility (and often ministerial offices) through a merchant bank to the top of financial and non-financial firms. For example, Nicolas Bazire, a graduate of ENA, was the chief of staff of Prime Minister Édouard Balladur; he joined Rothschild when Balladur lost the presidential election in 1995. Four years later, he became the managing director of LVMH, in charge of mergers and acquisitions. In 2009, he sat on the boards of Carrefour (retailing), Suez Environnement, LVMH and Atos Origin (digital media). Just like the *Caisse*, Lazard and Rothschild are two of the main places where financiers were socialised to the new conception of control that now dominates the firms they run.

Conclusion

The financialisation of French firms and the careers of their top managers and directors are causally related in an asymmetric way. The financialisation of firms did not disrupt the main career paths and internal divides of the French economic elite. The differences between the social properties of financiers and those of non-financiers have structured the field of the economic elite for decades, arguably in a much stronger way than divides usually underlined in the literature. This enduring divide has not been significantly modified by the adoption of the shareholder value. The relationship goes very much the other way around, since the financialisation seems to have been brought about by the conversion of old financiers to new techniques. Therefore, the French story is very different from the US trajectory as drawn by Zorn (2004): if a new conception of control came to be adopted, this was not because those who went through a new financial function eventually succeeded in reaching the top of the firms. It was because some financiers, whose biographies look very much like those of 25 or even 50 years earlier, converted to new ways of doing business, then imposed them on firms when they reached the top of their careers. Our careful observation of careers helps to identify the loci of their conversion. It did not happen because they were trained in different ways, or because they went abroad, but in specific places and times: the French Ministry of Finance in the early and mid-1980s, the *Caisse des dépôts et consignations* when the public bank had to learn and shape new rules of the game, and Lazard and Rothschild when the financial techniques (re)invented in the US in the 1960s were imported in the 1980s. Of course, conversions also happened elsewhere, but those organisations were certainly the main incubators of the new conception of control.

9 Financialisation through the trajectories of business school graduates in France

Valérie Boussard and Simon Paye

Most of the time, financialisation is understood as "the tendency for profit making in the economy to occur increasingly through financial channels rather than through productive activities" (Krippner, 2012). Financialisation is therefore a shift in the social structure as financial capital becomes predominant (Bourdieu et al., 2003), and many works have shed light both on the process giving birth to this new balance of power and on its consequences for the economy. Amongst these works, some have pointed out a new model of corporate control wherein financial actors as institutional investors have gained power over managerial or corporate actors (Lazonick and O'Sullivan, 2000; Useem, 1996). Some other works have underlined that financialisation cannot be explained without taking into account the transformation of managerial and corporate actors themselves. In this perspective, Fligstein and Brantley showed that the finance conception of control "originated with executives trained in finance methods who had been primarily financial officers in their company" (1992: 287). As it appears in the inquiry of F. Widmer (2011), financialisation of the Swiss machine industry is related to a change in corporate elites. Managers with backgrounds in business administration or in finance expertise have taken a more central place in top management and boards since the 1990s and opened the doors to investors while they were supporting the finance conception of the firm.

These works account for financialisation by showing two intertwined changes related to the role played by economic elites. On the one hand, they show that financial elites have embraced new roles. Indeed, financial actors such as investment banks or investment funds now offer occupations and careers to elite graduates (Useem, 1996; Godechot, 2001; Ho, 2009). These occupations (traders, asset managers, investment bankers) are in line with the financial capitalism that marked the end of the 1980s and the emergence of shareholder value as a new financial logic (Fligstein, 2001). On the other hand, they underline that corporate elites have been recomposed. Financial roles within corporations have become a new way to achieve corporate careers, as financial background plays a more central part in top executives' profile (Davis and Useem, 2002; Zorn, 2004; Zorn *et al.*, 2005). Focusing on the role of economic elites in the financialisation process opens up a set of new questions addressed to the understanding of financial capitalism. The first question is whether these new financial occupations

Trajectories of business school graduates 157

actually played an increasing part in economic elites' careers. Do they appear to be desirable career prospects for graduates of schools that, in each national context, traditionally shape ruling elites? Such a phenomenon would go on to result in the role of the economic elites being recomposed. To what extent has this role moved from specialisation in operational functions (production, organisation, commercialisation), which characterised industrial capitalism (Chandler, 1977), to a specialisation in financial matters, thus taking into account the increasing role played by financial flow in the flow of goods and services? A first hypothesis can be drawn: financialisation runs parallel to a shift in economic elites, which hold more financial occupations than in the past.

Financial occupations themselves also evolved. Alongside traditional occupations focused on the management of financial flow within businesses (finance directors or chief financial officers, financial controllers, treasurers, etc.), often known as "corporate finance", occupations relating to the management of financial products on capital markets appeared (traders, brokers, investors, etc.). The activities of consulting and financial intermediation in conjunction with the sale of businesses or financial products also played an important part in banks at the expense of the traditional activities of deposit and financing. At the same time, the activities of auditing and financial consulting in valuating businesses as financial assets (stocks, etc.) or as underlying financial assets also increased significantly outside the banking sector (auditing firms, legal practices, etc.). In opposition to traditional corporate finance dealing with financial flows, where financiers are supposed to "count beans", the bunch of new occupations developed a finance turned towards the market, where financiers are seen as "value hunters" (Boussard and Dujarier, 2014), in line with the "shareholder value" logic. Whether involved in capital markets, financial services or auditing, these financial occupations share the same conception of capital as a commodity in itself, which has to be valuated and traded, whatever its shape (stocks, assets, loans, currencies, etc.). Capital is an opportunity for speculation and profit rather than a means for a corporation to produce commodities. From this perspective, these financial occupations could be called "commodified finance". The question raised is whether this commodified finance creates alternative job prospects for elite graduates. Do elite graduates choose financial occupations oriented towards capital markets, such as traders, brokers, or investors, rather than financial occupations oriented towards the control of the corporate financial flows, such as financial control or accounting? Do elite managers in "corporate finance" or in other top managerial positions embrace positions in commodified finance in the course of their careers? As a result, beyond the evolving role played by finance in the careers of graduates, the second hypothesis is that commodified finance has taken a more central place in elite graduates' careers.

Another set of questions concerns the modalities of access to top executive roles in the economic sector and their transformation. As noticed by Fligstein and Brantley (1992), the study of financialisation intends to clarify "who controls the Large Modern Corporation". In other words, has it become necessary to move through roles in finance in order to access top executive positions in a firm? As such, this transformation would take into account another way in which economic elites have been recomposed, in terms of their structure. The way in which top executive positions are accessed would thus have changed, which could parallel different biographical characteristics of the new business ruling elites (Ramirez, 2003; Lagneau-Ymonet, 2008). Beyond this, the fact of business ruling elites being recomposed could also explain different ways of foreseeing how modern corporations are governed, namely, with a more financial focus (Fligstein and Brantley, 1992; Davis and Useem, 2002; Davis, 2005; Zorn et al., 2005; Widmer, 2011). According to Fligstein and Brantley, "[t]he finance conception of control originated with executives trained in finance methods who had been primarily financial officers in their companies" (1992: 287), suggesting that financial roles are followed by access to executive roles. Therefore, a third hypothesis poses that a financial background, specifically a background in commodified finance, has become a major springboard to top executive positions.

To address these three hypotheses, this analysis has focused on the careers of graduates of one of the French elite higher education institutions, a Parisian business school, the École des Hautes Etudes Commerciales de Paris (HEC). This school specifically positions itself as the equivalent of an international "business school", training future senior executives and directors of the French economy, and it is identified by different statistical studies as among the places from which graduates can access top executive positions (Dudouet and Grémont, 2009). This school has followed the international trend in business education, delivering courses in finance oriented to the capital markets since the end of the 1980s. New financial actors in France such as investors and international investment banks have focused their recruitment process on this school as one of the French elite schools, alongside the École Polytechnique (X), the École Centrale and Sciences Po.

This school has collaborated with former students to compile a yearbook of alumni; as such, there is reliable data providing the names of all graduates year by year. This data allowed three cohorts of graduates (1985, 1995 and 2005) to be defined so as to carry out an analysis of the transformation of career patterns.[1]

The comparison of data on the careers of each cohort was carried out based on three main questions. First, what is the share of financial roles in these careers, and how does this share evolve depending on the cohort and the period in the career? Second, what are the positions that tend to most often lead to top executive positions, and what part does a financial role play in these? Third, which financial positions play the more central role in both these phenomena?

Contrary to the first hypothesis, data show that the share of financial roles has not risen over the period. The share of financial roles is stable and stands at 25% of all positions over the first 17 years of the career of all cohorts (I). But this surprising result is then qualified by looking more in detail at the distribution of roles within finance. In line with the second hypothesis, amongst financial roles, commodified finance is the role which has risen the most, while other roles, such as corporate finance, have fallen (II). Regarding the access to top executive positions, financial roles act as a springboard, as forecast by the third hypothesis, but not in a linear way over the time. If finance was the privileged step to entering the

Trajectories of business school graduates   159

ruling elites for the 1985 cohort, it lost its appeal for the 1995 cohort, for which marketing and sales positions were the first gate to top executive positions. The young 2005 cohort tends to continue to use marketing and sales as a springboard to top executive positions, but finance has regained its major role in this process (III).

Box 9.1: Sources

The dates of the three cohorts were chosen to avoid cohorts whose careers would have started at times significantly affected by economic and financial crises. Indeed, it is known that the context surrounding the start of a person's career has a significant influence on the rest of this career (Parodi, 1999; Oyer, 2008). The cohorts chosen were therefore taken between three different crises: the second oil crisis at the end of the 1970s, the economic crisis at the very beginning of the 1990s, and when the dotcom bubble burst at the very beginning of the new millennium.

Measuring how the financialisation of careers has evolved consisted in comparing the occupational careers of the three cohorts of HEC graduates. The HEC yearbook of alumni was revealed to be insufficient, since it did not allow tracing the job history of every graduate, as data was generally not up to date. As compared with data from the HEC graduates' yearbook, online CVs happen to be more reliable, as they are more regularly updated by individuals. After interviews and observations were conducted in a recruitment agency specialising in finance, it became apparent that the LinkedIn social network is the most complete for finance, as compared with other networks such as Viadeo or internal systems set up by recruiters. Analysing careers based on CVs has been shown to be a relevant data collection for statistical analyses. Yet, the information is self-declared and can be subject to interindividual variations (Dietz *et al.*, 2000). Overall, most CVs uploaded onto LinkedIn are in line with standard practices of how people report information about themselves. With regard to incomplete CVs, the choice was made not to complete them using other sources, so as to ensure that career data do not mix information generated and diffused for different purposes.

Data collection was carried out during summer 2011. Out of a total population of 1110 graduates, 510 CVs were considered sufficiently informed for the present analysis. Retrieved CVs in PDF format were parsed by an algorithm to feed a longitudinal database. According to manual tests performed on the resulting data, coding errors concern at most 10% of the careers. Even though these coding errors should not affect the distribution of functions over time, for they are equally present in the three cohorts, data interpretation must be done with due care, and further enquiries will be needed to cross-check empirical results. There turned out to be an uneven distribution of cohorts, increasing from 23% of CVs analysed for the cohort of 1985 to 39% for the cohort of 1995 and 67% for the cohort of 2005. These samples were checked using data from the target population, based

160 *Valérie Boussard and Simon Paye*

on the most recent position that the graduate is known to have had, as well as his/her gender. The three samples do not differ greatly from entire cohort populations. Major imbalances are (1) a slight over-representation of men in the 1995 cohort of the sample (+3%) and (2) an over-representation of people working in trade and industry (+8% for the 1985 cohort, +6% for the 1995 cohort and +3% for the 2005 cohort).

Each career was defined as a sequence of year-long time units corresponding to the occupied job positions. The resulting database thus allows career patterns and transitions to be compared between these positions, distinguishing between financial and non-financial roles.

All three individuals presented in Table 9.1 belong to the last cohort, whose members graduated from HEC in 2005. Individual no. 520 has not included information on his online CV about his occupational status in 2005; hence, his sequence starts in a state from which data are missing (code 0). The rest of his career comprises a two-year sequence in the sector of consulting (code 8), followed by four years with executive roles (code 5). The online CVs of individuals 521 and 522 allowed their entire career to be coded. After a short episode in corporate finance (code 1), individual 521 moved to audit (code 4) for about two years, and started a role in consulting, where he stayed until the year the data was collected. The third individual, 522, started in the organisational sector (code 7) before moving into an executive position.

There was a considerable process involved in coding these roles, based on titles that differed greatly from sector to sector, company to company and cohort to cohort (the same list of responsibilities can change name depending on the date; for example, the term "directeur financier" ("finance director") has gradually been replaced by the English abbreviation CFO).

With regard to variables, arranging the job titles into categories involved following an iterative process that resulted in nine groups of occupational roles, comprising one code for a top executive position outside of finance (senior executives), four codes for financial roles and four codes for non-financial roles.

"Top executive positions" include all positions that involve decisions on the allocation of company assets. They include positions of people who define themselves as owners or who serve on the board of directors, and people who define themselves as "president", "vice-president" or "chief executive officer" of companies. Top executive positions within the financial sector, such as partners in a financial auditing firm or partners in investment

Table 9.1 Three career paths in the sequence data

ID	Cohort	Year 1	Year 2	Year 3	Year 4	Year 5	Year 6	Year 7
520	2005	0	8	8	5	5	5	5
521	2005	1	4	4	8	8	8	8
522	2005	7	7	7	5	5	5	5

banks or investment funds, were not taken into account in this category, but were coded within each corresponding financial role. The term "top executive positions" thus ensures that top executive positions in industrial companies or the services sector are isolated, in order to examine whether or not individuals with these positions have previously been in financial roles, whatever hierarchical positions they have held.

Financial roles are broken down into roles in "corporate finance" (finance directors or chief financial officers, management accounting, financial assessment, treasury, etc.) on the one hand and roles in commodified finance on the other hand, including "capital markets" (trading, arbitrage, investment, etc.), "financial services" (mergers and acquisition, leveraged buyout, etc.) and "audit".

Non-financial roles are broken down into "organisational" (logistics, information systems, project management, etc.), "marketing/sales" (product management to head of division, etc.) and "consulting".

Additional variables for each graduate are people's age ("proxy" calculated based on the cohort), sex (based on the first name) and employment sector (finance, consulting, other, media, trade and industry) for the year 2011.

Tools and methods from sequence analysis were used to compare careers patterns of the three cohorts (Blair-Loy, 1999; Blanchard et al., 2014). All computations and graphs have been made using the R statistical software environment and the package TraMineR for sequence analysis (Gabadinho et al., 2011).

Three sources of bias have been taken care of. First, information is sometimes lacking on the CV about some years (generally at the beginning of a person's career), especially for older cohorts. As such, the "frequency" of missing values varies considerably across cohorts, with more of them in the 1985 cohort. To reduce this bias, it was decided to remove missing data when calculating the overall share of finance in careers. Second, so as to avoid bias linked to variations in censorship of longitudinal data across cohorts, the solution adopted was to compare matched lengths of time. Careers in the 2005 cohort are 7 years long. Therefore, to compare between the three cohorts, focus was put only on the first seven years of careers. For comparison between the 1985 and 1995 cohorts, the focus could be extended to the first 17 years of careers. Third, occupational categories were harmonised so as to ensure comparability of job titles between cohorts. It is indeed important not to perceive a context as changing, when in fact, all that is changing is simply a job title. Inversely, it is also important to be aware of the changing context, even if the name remains the same.

I A stable share of financial roles across cohorts

As could be expected, the financialisation of the economy should go hand in hand with a financialisation of business elite careers, that is, with a rise of financial roles in professional trajectories. Actually, no dramatic shift has occurred over the period, the overall proportion of financial roles in careers having remained relatively stable for the three cohorts[2] (Figure 9.1).

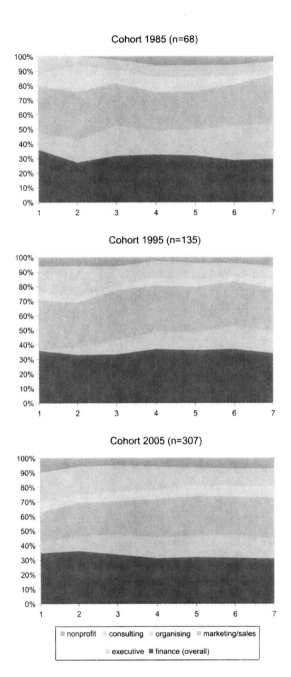

Figure 9.1 Overall proportion of financial roles in careers.

Trajectories of business school graduates 163

On the other hand, noticeable shifts have occurred with regard to other job roles. The proportion of top executive positions in careers has decreased significantly, while the proportion of commercial or consulting positions has increased. This result seems to illustrate the evolution of the job market of business school graduates, in line with the creation of multinational corporations made up of numerous divisions (Chandler, 1977; Di Maggio, 2001), creating many positions in senior management, on the one hand, and the increasing role played by the consulting sector (MacKenna, 2006), on the other hand. There are fewer graduates in the 1995 and 2005 cohorts than in the 1985 cohort who access positions that are strictly executive.[3] But the positions were coded in such a way that the size of the organisations and wages in question are not taken into consideration. As such, this evolution could indicate that there are now fewer graduates who are bosses running small organisations, but more who are employed in a position of great responsibility in a large company.

Financial episodes seem to take place more often at the beginning of careers. The share of finance seems to decrease over time for the three cohorts (Table 9.2). At the start of the careers, this share seems to remain relatively stable over time: in the three cohorts, about 35% have joined a financial role one year after graduating. But the proportion of financial roles in the middle of the careers (year 7, and especially year 17) shows more variation. There is a notable increase of the share of financial roles in the 7th and 17th years of careers between the first and the second cohort (from 30% to 34%).

Besides looking at year-by-year shares, a calculation of the overall share of financial roles over the whole time period was done (this share is reflected by the surface of the dark grey area in Figure 9.1). Results (Table 9.3) confirm the pattern identified above: the role played by finance has remained relatively stable over the years. Financial roles represent about one third of the career time of HEC graduates of all three cohorts. The slightly higher share of finance for the 1995 cohort (35% against 31% for 1985 and 33% for 2005 for the first 7 years, and 30% against 25% for 1985 over a 17-year period) does not allow any strong statement about a possible stronger influence of finance for those who graduated in 1995.

Table 9.2 Percentage of individuals in financial roles 1, 7 and 17 years after graduating (missing values removed for percentage calculation)

	1985 Cohort		1995 Cohort		2005 Cohort	
	Percentage	*Valid cases*	*Percentage*	*Valid cases*	*Percentage*	*Valid cases*
Year 1	36	25	36	64	35	245
Year 7	30	54	34	129	31	307
Year 17	19	65	23	135	N/A	N/A
N	68		135		307	

Interpretation: Out of 25 individuals in the cohort of 1985 who provided information about the first year of their career, 36% were occupying a financial role.

164   *Valérie Boussard and Simon Paye*

Table 9.3 Overall distribution of professional sectors over 7 and 17 years

	First 7 years			First 17 years	
	1985	*1995*	*2005*	*1985*	*1995*
Finance (overall) (%)	31	35	33	25	30
Executive (%)	19	11	13	33	23
Marketing/sales (%)	30	32	25	26	27
Organisational (%)	9	4	7	7	6
Consulting (%)	7	13	16	5	9
Non-profit (%)	4	5	7	4	6
N	68	135	307	68	135
Missing data (%)	36	18	5	21	8

Interpretation: For the cohort of 1985, the overall share of financial roles stands at 25% of all positions over the first 17 years of the career.

Data suggest that financialisation of the economy has not been accompanied by significant shifts in the weight of finance positions in HEC graduates' careers. In other words, contrary to the first hypothesis, financialisation has operated without any major increase in the number of financial positions in the careers of business school graduates.

II Beyond stability, the rise of commodified finance

To understand this surprising result, there is a need to look in more detail at the distribution of roles within finance. The data give evidence of rising and falling trends, suggesting that the global stability of the share of finance in careers actually conceals a reconfiguration of its different components. In other words, financiers have not become more numerous over time, but they have taken a different profile.

Finance has been broken into four sub-sectors: corporate finance, financial services, capital markets and audit. The overall proportion of each of these sub-sectors (and of other job roles) over the first 7 years of careers[4] (Figure 9.2) allows a "scissor effect" to be identified within the four financial roles.

Whereas the proportion of corporate finance roles decreases significantly between the first and the second cohort (20% to 12% for the first 7 years; 19% to 11% for the first 17 years, see Table 9.4), the proportion of commodified finance (the three other roles, taken together) rises from 10% to 22% for the first 7 years and from 6% to 20% for the first 17 years (see Table 9.4).

The proportion of roles in corporate finance over the first 7 years of careers has halved between the 1985 and 2005 cohorts, while other financial roles have doubled (financial services and capital markets) or tripled (audit).

Even within commodified finance, several trends are noticeable. The 1995 cohort is chiefly characterised by the importance of financial services (9% for the first 7 years), while the 2005 cohort distinguishes itself by a prevalence of capital market roles (14% for the first 7 years).

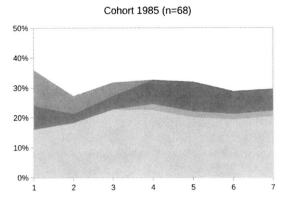

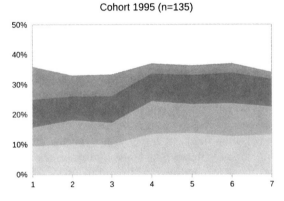

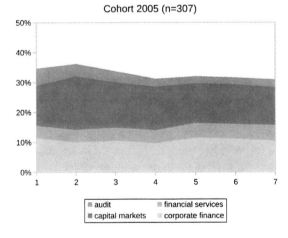

Figure 9.2 Overall proportion of each sub-sector (and of other job roles) over the first 7 years of careers.

166 *Valérie Boussard and Simon Paye*

Table 9.4 Overall distribution of professional sectors over 7 and 17 years (missing values removed for percentage calculation)

	First 7 years			First 17 years	
	1985	1995	2005	1985	1995
Corporate finance (%)	20	12	11	19	11
Financial services (%)	1	9	5	1	9
Capital markets (%)	7	9	14	4	8
Audit (%)	2	5	3	1	3
N	68	135	307	68	135
Missing data (%)	36	18	5	21	8

Interpretation: For the cohort of 1985, the overall share of corporate finance roles stands at 20% of all positions over the first 7 years of the career.

We tried to account for these changes by specifying whether they were due to variations in cohort participation in financial roles, or to variations in the duration of financial roles. Unfortunately, because of differing levels of missing data in the three cohorts, both participation rates and duration measures are biased and thus cannot be used in this study. Nevertheless, these approximate measures of duration and participation globally follow, rather than contradict, the trends presented in Table 9.4.

Our data suggest that financialisation does not imply a growing number of financiers, but rather, a reconfiguration of finance, therefore confirming the second hypothesis. Over time, HEC financiers are more and more likely to occupy positions in commodified finance rather than in corporate finance. The typical financial career for the 1985 cohort is a succession of corporate positions focused on financial flows control, as exemplified by the career of Laurence M. (see Box 9.2). The typical financial careers for the latest cohorts include successive positions in banks and/or financial services firms and occupations that are more oriented towards shareholder value generation, like Stéphane E. or Chawki C. (see Box 9.2), who deal with equity markets and assets optimisation.

Box 9.2: Different trajectories in finance

Laurence M., who graduated in 1985, has been a CFO for the last 6 years for a French industrial business, subsidiary of an international group, after being an auditor for 4 years for one of the four leading companies (PWC) and a financial controller for 13 years (for two separate industrial businesses). Her career has been entirely in corporate finance, after a start in auditing.

Stéphane E., who graduated in 1995, pursued a career in commodified finance, in the field of financial services. After working for a French merchant bank in London for 4 years, he joined a little merchant bank in Paris, specialised in capital-raising solutions for the new economy, for

Trajectories of business school graduates 167

3 years. He then became a partner in a financial services company, which offers equity financing and strategic advisory services (2 years), before becoming director of mergers and acquisitions for a large French media group.

Chawki C.'s career, which started after he graduated in 2005, is yet another example of a financial career. Again, we are talking about a career in commodified finance, but this time in the field of capital markets. After being a trader (equity and credit arbitrage) in London, 5 years for a German bank and then 1 year for a Swiss bank, he became wealth manager for an English bank in Switzerland.

III Financial roles as springboard for top executive positions

Nevertheless, what are the impacts of these structural evolutions of finance on the profile of top executives? To what extent have employment experiences in finance become determining in the access to the highest positions in firms?

Our data confirms that a significant proportion of HEC graduates effectively gain access to top executive positions. The overall share of these positions in careers decreased between the 1985 cohort and the 1995 cohort (from 19% to 11% for the first 7 years; 33% to 23% for the first 17 years), and later seemed to stabilise (Table 9.3). Not surprisingly, within each cohort, there is a year-after-year increase in the proportion of these positions (see Table 9.5).

This year-after-year increase is coupled with a decrease in the share of organising and consulting roles. As such, this could suggest that organising and consulting roles act as entry ports towards top executive positions. If this is verified, it would contradict the third hypothesis, that in a financialised economy, financial responsibilities act as springboards towards executive roles. To identify the part played by financial roles in this process, focus is now put on the trajectories of individuals before they access their first top executive position. This entails using for Figure 9.3 an alternative timeline from the previous figures in this chapter. Individual sequences are synchronised[5] according to the year of the first top executive position (Figure 9.3).

Figure 9.3 gives us a hint as to what happens before joining top executive positions. Financial roles undoubtedly are one important springboard, along with

Table 9.5 Percentage of individuals in top executive positions during the first 7 years after graduating (missing values removed for percentage calculation)

	Year 1	*Year 2*	*Year 3*	*Year 4*	*Year 5*	*Year 6*	*Year 7*
1985 cohort	12	15	20	16	18	23	24
1995 cohort	0	5	10	12	12	16	16
2005 cohort	8	10	14	14	15	15	14

Interpretation: 24% of the cohort of 1985 were occupying a top executive position by the seventh year of their career.

168 *Valérie Boussard and Simon Paye*

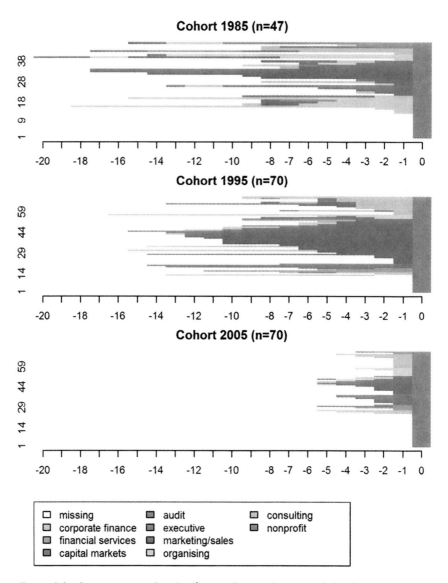

Figure 9.3 Sequences synchronised[5] according to the year of the first top executive position.

marketing/sales and – especially for the second cohort – consulting. A focus on the year immediately preceding access to executive functions provides a more accurate insight into the most prevalent springboards. Modal values in Table 9.6 shed light on which job roles have played the biggest part for each cohort. For the 1985 cohort, positions in finance (overall) account for 37% of all springboards;

Trajectories of business school graduates 169

Table 9.6 Proportion of individuals in financial roles 1 year before accessing top executive positions (missing values removed for percentage calculation)

	1985 cohort	*1995 cohort*	*2005 cohort*
Direct access after graduating (%)	8	0	29
Finance (overall) (%) of which:	37	14	23
Corporate finance (%)	24	4	5
Financial services (%)	0	5	6
Capital markets (%)	13	4	11
Audit (%)	0	2	2
Marketing/sales (%)	32	58	20
Organisational (%)	8	5	9
Consulting (%)	8	23	15
Non-profit (%)	8	0	3
N	47	70	70

marketing and sales accounts for 58% for the 1995 cohort; and finance accounts for 23% for the 2005 cohort.

These results suggest the existence of three typical patterns. Executives from the 1985 cohort come primarily from financial roles in corporate finance, such as Laurent T. (Box 9.3), who is a former CFO. For the graduates of 1995, top executive positions are massively accessed through roles in marketing/sales (and, to a lesser extent, consulting). Top executives have climbed the ladder of corporate hierarchy from responsibilities in sales or marketing to management of business units, such as Amaury D., who had never held financial positions before becoming CEO (see Box 9.3). In comparison with previous generations, the 2005 cohort sees more diverse pathways leading to executive functions. Significantly fewer executive holders of this cohort come from roles in marketing/sales. On the other hand, the influence of commodified finance is stronger: almost 20% of executive functions were accessed from financial services, capital markets or audit roles. Top executives are most of the time founders or presidents of private companies after having held positions in banks, funds or financial services firms, as did Marc M. (see Box 9.3).

Financial roles have not yet re-established the extent to which they acted as springboards for the cohort of 1985, but commodified finance plays an increasingly significant role, while corporate finance has a minor role (compared to its previous role for the cohort of 1985).

Box 9.3: Three different ways to access executive positions

Laurent T., who graduated in 1985, became CEO of a French insurance company in 1997, after having joined the company in an executive position (chief underwriting officer). Before that, he held a position in business finance for two consecutive insurance companies. After his first position as

> a CEO, he held two other executive positions in another insurance company before becoming CEO once again, for another insurance company. He then created a medical services company in 2008, followed by an education services company.
>
> Amaury D., who graduated in 1995, became CEO (managing director) in 2009 for a French agro-food company, subsidiary of an international group, after a relatively linear path in sales and marketing within another agro-food company: product manager, group manager, brand manager, followed by marketing director.
>
> Marc M., who graduated in 2005, with an additional law degree, was first a counsellor for the French Ministry of Finance, then a lawyer for an international law firm, and finally an investment banker at Lehman Brothers (until October 2008). In 2008, he became managing director for a large French brand of ready-made clothes before creating a fashion and jewellery company in 2011 and an artistic creation agency in 2013.

The flows between financial roles and executive functions have therefore changed drastically. As regards the overall part played by financial roles, the data suggest a U-shaped pattern: the proportion of financial roles is significant for the cohort of 1985 (37%), then decreases to only 14% for the cohort of 1995, before increasing again to 23% for the cohort of 2005. A more detailed analysis shows that for the 1985 cohort, the part played by financial roles as springboards is mainly attributable to corporate finance (24%). Its influence decreases dramatically for the 1995 cohort (4%) and remains at the same level for the 2005 cohort (5%). The type of career of Laurent T., a former CFO, is rarely to be found in the 2005 cohort. In comparison, although the part played by roles in capital markets decreases between the first and the second cohort, it is relatively stable from the first to the last cohort (13% and 11%, respectively). Finally, roles in financial services and audit, which do not grant access to executive functions for the 1985 cohort, do play an increasing part in the following cohorts.

Note that the data shown hitherto are affected by a temporal bias related to the fact that individuals in each cohort have been in their career for different lengths of time. To remedy this problem, the solution was to restrict the comparative analysis to equal lengths of individuals' careers (7 and 17 years). This accounts for the variation of inflows towards top-executive positions (Table 9.7).

Between the two first cohorts, the part played by financial roles as springboards tends to diminish, and between the two last cohorts, it reinstates itself. As shown by Table 9.7, financial roles account for 27% of all springboards to executive positions for the first cohort. Their share then decreases to 7% for the second cohort, and then rises to 28% for the last cohort. Figures calculated from a 17-year perspective (from 32% for the first cohort to 11% for the second cohort) tend to confirm the same falling trend between the first and the second cohort. The opposite trend is observable for marketing/sales roles, for which the springboard effect reaches its maximum for the cohort of 1995. At the same time, it is interesting

Table 9.7 Patterns of mobility towards top executive positions

| | 7 years | | | | | | 17 years | | | |
| | Cohort 1985 | | Cohort 1995 | | Cohort 2005 | | Cohort 1985 | | Cohort 1995 | |
	Moves	*%*	*Moves*	*%*	*Moves*	*%*	*Moves*	*%*	*Moves*	*%*
Missing	6	40%	9	31%	5	9%	8	18%	13	16%
Finance (overall) of which:	4	27%	2	7%	15	28%	14	32%	9	11%
Corporate finance	1	7%	1	3%	3	6%	7	16%	2	3%
Financial services	0	0%	1	3%	4	7%	1	2%	4	5%
Capital markets	3	20%	0	0%	7	13%	6	14%	2	3%
Audit	0	0%	0	0%	1	2%	0	0%	1	1%
Marketing/sales	2	13%	10	34%	14	26%	13	30%	37	47%
Organisational	1	7%	1	3%	6	11%	2	5%	4	5%
Consulting	1	7%	7	24%	11	20%	3	7%	14	18%
Non-profit	1	7%	0	0%	3	6%	4	9%	2	3%
All moves towards executive positions	15	100%	29	100%	54	100%	44	100%	79	100%
Headcount in the cohort	68		135		307		68		135	

Interpretation: Over the first 7 years of career, 15 moves towards executive positions have happened in the first cohort. Almost one-third of them came from finance (27%).

172 *Valérie Boussard and Simon Paye*

to note that consulting roles become means of accessing top executive positions, which is particularly significant for the cohort of 1995 (24%), whereas their role is only minor (7%) for the cohort of 1985.

These analyses show that the part played by financial roles as means of accessing top executive positions does not increase significantly over time, but of all financial roles, it increasingly seems to be those of commodified finance that have the most bearing on this. This shift in the role of finance could render the transformation of corporate control noticed by N. Fligstein (1990, 2001): corporate finance as a springboard to executive positions could be a hint at the selection of managers of firms on the basis of their allegiance to a finance conception of the firm, for which "the firm is a collection of assets earning varying rates of return" (1990, p. 239). Indeed, financial controllers and CFOs play an important role in controlling the capital allocation and its return. On the contrary, top executives with a commodified background could indicate selection of managers on the basis of their allegiance to the shareholder conception of the firm. This conception leads to seeking value creation through placing assets and equity in the markets. In this capital market-driven conception of control, graduates with a commodified background have more advantages than their corporate finance colleagues. The persistence of this pattern through the three cohorts could be the sign of a rise of the shareholder value conception of the firm in France since the end of the 1980s, in parallel with the decrease of the finance conception.

Yet, this increase in the role of finance is not linear. In this sense, the financialisation of business elites has not been a straightforward process since the 1980s. The succeeding stages involved in building a top executive career reveal the surprising role of marketing/sales. Indeed, following Fligstein's perspective would lead to hypothesising a decreasing role of marketing/sales background for accessing top executive positions. Instead, marketing/sales plays a central role for the three cohorts, even for the 1995 cohort, where a central role of commodified finance was expected. The reason why the transformations of French capitalism occur through a resurgence and a maintaining of what resembles a sales and marketing conception of control (Fligstein, 1990) has not yet been clarified. It requires further investigation.

Conclusion

Financialisation in France thus does not appear as a linear trend of rising importance of finance in business executive careers. It corresponds, instead, to rising and falling trends in the part played by the different financial roles. On the one hand, the importance of corporate finance in careers has decreased both in terms of overall share and as a means of accessing top executive positions. On the other hand, roles in commodified finance have become increasingly significant and seem to have become established as a new norm for reaching dominant positions in the business field. This trend within finance could indicate a shift in the transformation of financial corporate control in France. Moreover, unpacking the finance background of top executives, between corporate finance and

Trajectories of business school graduates   173

commodified finance, could give tuned indicators of the rise of the shareholder value conception.

The role played by marketing and sales for the second cohort at the end of the 1990s is rather unexpected. Following Fligstein's perspective (1990), the finance conception of control displaced the sales and marketing conception during the 1960s and early 1970s. The data shows neither a displacement of sales and marketing by finance nor a delay in this displacement. It suggests, rather, a more complex evolution, as if the sales and marketing conception had played a role after the finance conception, and then had been incompletely replaced by the shareholder conception. This gives further credit to the idea that financialisation, in France, does not follow a linear process.

There is now a need to account for differences in involvement in financial roles amongst the HEC graduates. Further enquiries are needed in order to determine whether sex and complementary higher education credentials are correlated to specific pathways in or out of finance. Another perspective for investigating the role of finance as part of the making of business ruling elites is to analyse its position within the different career stages of a top executive career rather than merely focusing on its presence the year immediately before access to top executive positions. Moreover, corporate finance is expected to have changed (Zorn, 2004) but the present inquiry does not allow us to quantify this change and the shift in the way CFOs endorse their role over time.

These results open up two questions. First, is there a similar rise of commodified finance in other contexts? The empirical scope of this study is restricted to graduates of an elite business school. In this sense, financialisation is grasped as a process taking place in business elite careers. What happened in less elitist career systems, such as bank middle-ranked financial workers (see Chapter 11), or large corporations employing graduates and undergraduates from a wider pool of schools and universities? Second, what does the concept of commodified finance bring to the understanding of financialisation? What do the three financial roles gathered in this unique category share beyond the conception of capital as a commodity? To what extent do these different specialisations in Finance share a shareholder conception of control? What are the consequences of such a conception for the way top executives with a commodified finance background control the firm they own or manage? The beginning of an answer to the last question can be found in Chapter 1, presenting the representations of firm that financiers employed in financial services (specifically, mergers and acquisition services) share.

Notes

1   Initially, five cohorts were going to be analysed (1975, 1985, 1995, 2005 and 2011). It turned out that the cohort of 1975 could not be used due to lack of data about the graduates. The cohort of 2011 was not analysed either, since insufficient time had passed in the graduates' careers, but this cohort could be used in future research. The same type of graphical representation was used for comparing the 1985 and 1995 cohorts taking into account the first 17 years of careers (not shown here). See Tables 9.2 and 9.3 for summarised results.

174 *Valérie Boussard and Simon Paye*

2 The same type of graphical representation was used for comparing the 1985 and 1995 cohorts taking into account the first 17 years of careers (not shown here). See Tables 9.2 and 9.3 for summarised results.
3 Figures can be found in Table 9.3.
4 Again, the same graphical representation over the first 17 years of careers for the 1985 and 1995 cohorts is not shown here. See Table 9.4 for summarised results.
5 This operation of sequence synchronisation is discussed in detail in Colombi and Paye (2014).

10 "I didn't leave financial journalism, I left classical journalism"

Careers and commitments of French financial journalists at the time of financialisation

Antoine Machut

In Great Britain, the criticism of the submission of financial journalism to financial logics, to the detriment of journalistic quality, is a fairly old one.[1] Howard J. Carswell already deemed financial journalism to be too boring in 1938, saying it was too closely linked with the New York Stock Exchange index. This way of doing things avoided telling another narrative, which could have revealed the power financial markets had over the well-being of citizens and hidden the way they were fixing prices and control the economic market (Carswell, 1938). By sticking too closely to the financial market, financial journalism produces information that can deter most of the population, even if they are rich enough to place their savings on the financial market. 35 years later, Chris Welles deplores what he describes as a "bleak wasteland". This renowned financial journalist deems the financial journalism of his time to be a specialised "pallid and boring" journalism, incapable of regulating business activity to spur corporate "social responsibility" (Welles, 1973). The proliferation of stock market crashes and financial scandals since the end of the 1980s has led to a new critical examination of financial journalism. Following the subprime crisis, numerous works have attempted to explain its inability to account for the events that should have heralded the crash. They show that financial journalists are focused on a micro-economic coverage of finance, neglecting the "critical and holistic" view (Manning, 2013). The extremely tight control that banks exert on information limits journalistic work, which is already constrained by internal editorial operations (how to sell a "story" based on obscure financial derivatives?). The premise of these criticisms is that financial journalists should act as "watchdogs", as guardians of the public interest. However, this does not make consensus among financial journalists, whose professional ethic is based on legal requirements and the inevitable effects of the media on financial markets. The impact of their writings should forbid them from reporting rumours, whereas some of their specific rights, such as protecting sources, are only justified by a duty of participation in defending the public interest (Tambini, 2010). At the time of Enron's bankruptcy, Gillian Doyle (2006) already pointed out that even if journalists are barely bound to the idea of defending the public interest, it does not prevent them from maintaining a critical position towards financial professionals, or from defending common standards of journalism, such as objectivity.

176 *Antoine Machut*

Another perspective to understand the links between finance and journalism is given by the sociology of finance: it shows how financial journalists fully contribute to the building and operating of financial markets, and does not consist in a priori opposition of the two sectors. In this framework, journalists participate in the "public expression" of the fundamental value of ratings agencies or financial assets, by relaying the "market consensus" (Charron, 2010). The work of financial journalists is also important in the introduction of new financial products, under the "social supervision" of the promoters of these products (Oubenal, 2015). The legitimacy of financial journalists to financial professionals, who often give the former little recognition, is far from established. Journalists are seen more as secondary interlocutors, who can be useful for financial analysts in search of notoriety.[2] In the European foreign exchange markets, for example, they do not constitute an important source of information for traders (Oberlechner and Hocking, 2004). The elite of financial journalism manages to be considered as legitimate in spite of this: the giants Bloomberg and Reuters have benefitted from internationalisation and recent technological advances, and are an established part of the material infrastructure of financial markets. They contribute to a "circular circulation" of financial information and can transform rumours into events.[3] Equally, the legitimacy and influence of financial journalists are strongest in the titles that are most read by financial professionals: analysing the *Wall Street Journal*'s "Abreast of the Markets" column, Dougal *et al.* (2012) showed that its editors had a direct effect on the short-term yield surplus of the Dow Jones: the simple fact of naming it improves the predictive capacity of the model. Likewise, it is possible to identify "bearish journalists" and "bullish journalists". These are the most specialised media, and those most integrated into financial work. At the end of the chain, financial journalists of the mainstream press can be considered more like intermediaries between the financial markets and the small shareholders, non-integrated into financial institutions.

From this perspective, financial journalists play a direct role in the formation of the "market opinion", built on consensus of analysts. It points out that analyses that propose to evaluate the degree of independence of financial journalism presuppose the existence of a boundary separating a journalistic social group from a financial social group, the former trying to defend their autonomy from the latter. However, such a boundary is not apparent. It might be more relevant to consider financial journalists as elements in the division of financial work. This is the hypothesis that I will develop in this chapter, based on a longitudinal study of the careers of French financial journalists. Before this, I will provide more information regarding the case of financial journalism in France.

The French case and its historical specifics

Financial journalism was marginal for a long time in France. Economic journalists disregarded it after 1945 in the context of an almost non-existent stock exchange activity: financing the economy relied heavily on support from bank loans. Besides, social protection was financed by redistribution rather than market capitalisation.

Careers of French financial journalists 177

However, private capitalisation intermediation increased in comparison with state redistribution as the national economy became increasingly open to foreign competition (Lagneau-Ymonet and Riva, 2011). The resurgence of the financial press in the "field" of journalism has accelerated significantly since the 1980s. This period was characterised by financial deregulation and by the emergence of a social group of executives as the main readership privileged by the press (Duval, 2004). From 1984 to 1986, privatisation increased the number of direct shareholders from 1.5 million to 6 million, quadrupling it in 2 years. In this context, the press gave more space to financial information. This was characterised by greater visibility of general economic newspapers, with distribution growing by 270% from 1985 to 1995. This growth was parallel to that of national news dailies, which increased by 285% in the same period (Cazenave, 1997). This historic trajectory led to the development of a very fragmented financial press. In France, no particular publication stands out,[4] and the average age of the financial press in 1993 was 38 years (Henno, 1993). Conversely, one newspaper has dominated for a long time in the United Kingdom, the United States, and to a lesser extent Germany: the *Financial Times*, the *Wall Street Journal* and the *Handelsblatt*, which were created in 1888, 1889 and 1946, respectively. The dominant positions in the field of French journalism are held by economic papers, or economic columns, which have gained prestige since the 1980s compared with others (social and environmental in particular). Despite the intertwining of "economic news" and "financial news", newspapers maintain a clear distinction between "economy" and "finance", relegating the latter to themes that are both micro and very practical. However, the way journalists choose to work in financial journalism remains mysterious. On the one hand, it is possible to assume that journalists in the financial press have more opportunities to find a stable job in the context of great uncertainty in the journalistic job market (Devillard and Rieffel, 2001, Leteinturier, 2014). On the other hand, it is also possible to make the hypothesis that for those who are trained in finance and have significant professional experience in the sector, financial journalism is not only an opportunity but also an objective to fight for.

To what extent do careers of financial journalists contribute to the creation or weakening of a boundary between journalism and finance? What makes people commit (or be committed)[5] to financial journalism? Is this commitment sustainable? This chapter proposes to answer these questions by analysing the professional trajectories of financial journalists. This will allow us to measure the porosity between journalism and finance by focusing on the frequency with which people pass between these two sectors. It will also give some evidence on the sustainability of financial journalism. Eventually, it allows us to clarify the way in which people adjust continually to the arrangements of their employment and manage to maintain a consistent professional identity. Following the suggestion of Andrew Abbott (1995), this chapter does not focus on a fixed social group ("financial journalists"), but rather, on the boundaries that are drawn and solidified or dissolved over time. In other words, it is about the definition of the financial information "jurisdiction", which can become the exclusive domain of a specific professional group.

178 *Antoine Machut*

This chapter is organised in the following way. First, I measure the frequency of movement from one position to another. The high mobility of financial journalists in the press towards finance relativises the boundary dynamic, of which one assumes journalists to be the initiators (I). Second, the chapter gives an account of the power of attraction of finance over financial journalists and the conditions that lead financial journalists to work in the finance sector (II). Next, it shows that the force of their commitment is strongly linked with the conditions in the journalistic labour market, the conditions surrounding financial activity and the level of education (III). In conclusion, these results demonstrate a great malleability in the boundary between finance and journalism, as a result of the perceived press decline faced with the rising communication practices and networks in the production of financial information. Finally, the thesis of this article is as follows: financial journalists are not committed in the world of journalism as much as in the world of financial information, in which they are driven to redefine their role, leading them to identify with a form of journalism that is closer to finance.

Sources

The data used to analyse the careers of French financial journalists was extracted from the professional online social network LinkedIn in July 2015. Users create a profile, in which they detail their career path and share their information, and in which they "connect" with each other. They also use this network to share their articles and exchange with professionals. The data was obtained by a systematic compilation of information contained in LinkedIn profiles that contain the key words "financial journalist". The data also adds those people who defined themselves as "journalists" but whose employer is a newspaper specialising in finance. In total, the database covers 239 individuals. The information on these individuals was collected from their entry into the job market (training periods were not taken into account) till July 2015. The information gathered on these individuals' careers was recoded to model each career into two sequences of successive "states". The first represents the career as a sequence of positions held, and the second as a sequence of types of employers. The signification of possible "states" is detailed in Annex 1.

Our sample consists of 130 men and 109 women, of whom 31% undertook professional training in journalism, whether or not recognised by the profession, and 20.1% in political science; 41% of the individuals completed specific training in "Economics and Business Administration" (EBA). I therefore distinguish between three sub-groups of people when focusing on education: the first group is made up of 78 people (33%) with a background in "pure" economics-business; the second is composed of 56 people (23%) who trained as "pure" non-specialised journalists; and the third comprises 19 people (8%) who received an education in both economics-business and journalism. The length of careers ranges from 15 to

45 years, with an average of 16.5 years. The population is mostly young, because more than half of them had their first job during or after the year 2000 (51.5% of the sample).

The longitudinal statistical analysis was carried out in three stages. First, I sought to identify the most frequent transitions to know, for example, whether financial journalists are more likely to become editor in chief or to leave journalism. Second, I reduced the complexity and the diversity of the trajectories available to show "trajectory types" and attempted to determine whether there were configurations in which individuals make a long-term commitment to a financial journalism career. To do so, I used the *Optimal Matching Analysis* (OMA) method, allowing the calculation of a matrix of distance between each pair of sequences (Abbott and Hrycak, 1990).[6] This allows me to create a typology of trajectories with five clusters, each of them grouping the trajectories that are most similar to each other while being as different as possible from those grouped in the other clusters. To prevent the construction of the typology from depending on career length, the sample was reduced here to careers that lasted more than 10 years ($n = 171$), and the OMA was applied to the first 20 years. Finally, the probability of following one type of trajectory over another was measured by logistic regression. I include control variables such as education, gender and the period of entering the labour market. Rather than analysing each cohort separately, I prefer to introduce cohorts as independent variables in the logistic regressions applied to each cluster. Thus, I applied five logistic regressions with five different binary dependent variables corresponding to the five clusters. The variable is coded as follows: 1 means belonging to the cluster, and 2 means not belonging to the cluster. The cohort limits were defined in relation to dates that constitute turning points in the history of the financial press, which can influence the recruitment of financial journalists. The first cohort consists of individuals who entered the job market between 1966 and 1978 ($n = 10$), when the Monory law was voted, making investments in the stock market exempt from tax. The limits of the second cohort are from 1978 to 1995 ($n = 91$), a period affected by the public deregulation of the financial markets and the rise of individual shareholdings. The third cohort runs from 1995 until 2001 ($n = 43$) to test the effect that the "internet bubble" had on the recruitment of financial journalists and on the orientation of their careers. The last cohort is made up of individuals who entered the job markets between 2001 and 2005 ($n = 27$).

Finally, the third stage of the study was based on analysis of semi-guided biographical interviews with 19 financial journalists characterised by a variability of trajectories over time. These interviews allowed the employment configurations and processes, already drawn by statistical analysis, to be explained in more detail.

180 *Antoine Machut*

I Unstable commitment of financial journalists

The first noticeable characteristic of financial journalists is their lack of stability. The most frequent transition occurs between financial journalism and another type of journalism, and vice versa (these two transitions are present in 40.2% and 35.2% of sequences, respectively). Often, these transitions are not definitive, but correspond to a back and forth movement: in 20% of the careers analysed, individuals went from journalism to financial journalism, to finally return to journalism. In the same way, in 17% of the careers, individuals went from financial journalism to journalism and came back to financial journalism. This tendency is confirmed by the multi-activity indicator that I inserted into the database: almost a third of individuals (32.2%) had another job alongside their financial journalism work, at least once in the course of their careers. This lack of stability in financial journalism careers, which does not contribute to a great segmentation of the journalistic world, is quite original. Surveys of journalistic specialities in France usually show a high level of commitment to one speciality to gain journalistic legitimacy.[7] The second most common type of transition shows an exit from the media sector, and confirms the logic of low commitment in financial journalism. In 23% of careers, there is a movement from financial journalism to executive jobs in the private sector, and in 15.9% of careers, there is a movement towards executive positions in finance. Transitions between the media sector and the finance sector are equally frequent in the other direction, that is, from finance to financial journalism (13.8%). In comparison, internal upward mobility is rarer: movement from financial journalism to a position of editor-in-chief occurs in only 15.5% of sequences.

II The erosion of journalistic careers: the exit towards finance as a response to the decline of the press

The aim of this section is to summarise the conditions under which financial journalists maintain or modify their commitment. Despite frequent transitions, long-term commitment to financial journalism is relatively frequent. 51% of the careers analysed represent a career model corresponding to the creation of a "professional segment" with a long-term commitment to financial journalism ("Professional Segment" and "Upward Mobility" class, Figure 10.1).[8] This model shows a form of rapid hierarchical upward movement towards an editor-in chief role (18% of careers of this type) or a form of "upgrading" towards financial columns in newspapers perceived as more prestigious in the economic or generalist press (25%). But this sustainability does not indicate a high level of vocation-like commitment. This is perceived, first, in the heterogeneity of the ways of entry: half of these individuals began their career in some form of occupation other than financial journalism. Generally, it is either journalism (23%) or a position in the financial sector, often as a consultant or financial analyst (14%). More interestingly, a number of journalists end up leaving their function in financial journalism after approximately 10 years to find a position in finance, including after having been editor-in-chief in a financial column or newspaper. Long-term commitment in financial journalism, often initiated by opportunity and subject to the instability of

Careers of French financial journalists 181

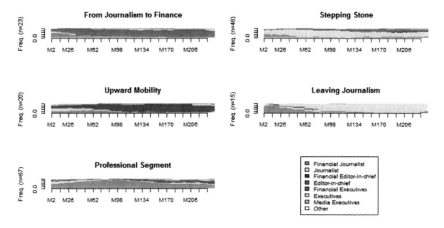

Figure 10.1 Distribution of positions held by individuals according to the class to which they belong, month by month.[9]

the journalistic labour market, does not prevent people from making these "exits" towards finance.

The Gauthier case[10] is particularly illuminating here. After finishing his studies in finance-economy in 1999, he had the opportunity to do an internship in a weekly newspaper dedicated to stock market advice, which had the potential to lead to a permanent employment contract. After 7 years, he entered the market column of a large political and economic daily newspaper, and became head of the column until the liquidation of the newspaper, which forced him to leave. Here, he describes how he left the press for a career as an editorial consultant for financial management companies:

> I worked as a freelance journalist for [economic daily newspaper], I had files left and right and then … but actually the problem is that that's not what makes you a living. [...] What you are paid for papers is ridiculous, and when you effectively have the possibility of being paid either 60 or 80 euros in the press [or] 250 at a corporate, well it's a quick calculation [...] And so at some point, during those two years, [...] I started to think about a work project, but a little more structured than what existed until then, actually dedicated to management companies since that was the population that I knew extremely well, since they made up part of my interlocutors when I did my market papers [...] so I considered doing that alone until I met my current employer, just like that a little by accident, or actually not really by accident because I had known him for ten years, and showing him my project he says to me "you know I'm interested because I have this fund services company" [...] and he said to me: "listen I will give you carte blanche".

The decline of the press sector, as it is perceived by individuals who, like Gauthier, lose their jobs following the bankruptcy of their newspaper or a drastic reduction

182 Antoine Machut

in editorial staff, is determinant in the process of leaving financial journalism. This decline does not only take the brutal form of redundancy, but also results from a less clear distinction between journalistic practices and communication practices. In the past 15 years, banking institutions have reinforced their channels of communication and their control of journalists' work. They have systematically used public relations specialists to distribute their press releases, which easily find their place in journalistic routines. This reinforcement includes calling to order financial journalists who look for other sources than banks' PR to obtain information. Increasingly, banks take direct control of the production of editorial content and decoding of financial news and thus create opportunities for financial journalists whose skills fit this type of work: arranging and ordering relevant information, making technical subjects more comprehensible via a specific angle, telling a story, commenting on events, and so on. Under these conditions, leaving financial journalism for a financial editorial position seems to be a "natural" step, or even a form of promotion that allows financial journalists to revive their career, rather than ending it. This is illustrated very clearly by the way those who have left their jobs relativise the change that this "line-crossing" means and maintain the relationships with their old financial journalist colleagues:

> In fact I write papers. What I do is like writing papers. I mean I follow the news, I am aware of the current events, the statements, the figures that are just in, so in fact, honestly, I apply exactly the same methodology that I used to apply when I was a journalist. And finally when I write for the client, what I do is like writing exactly the same papers as before except that there is just one source. [...] In any case, editing now ... journalists need seven–eight arms to cover the central banking news, bring it back to a social issue, and then go into the results of [the gas and oil company] Total, well, now it's a bit of a mess [...] I do a little bit of PR management but then they're my mates because I've worked with around 60% of the economic journalists working today.
>
> (Gauthier)

Exit strategy is therefore a way of breaking free of the declining press world while continuing to do valued work for which specific skills have been developed. Moreover, movement towards the financial sector does not necessarily mean disowning one's journalistic identity. The case of Frédéric[11] illustrates this very well:

> I didn't leave financial journalism, I left classical, traditional journalism [...] I'm in news content, I mean I produce serious content linked to the news, with an editorial line, a narrative thread, for brands. So actually I am still a journalist. Journalists don't consider me to be anymore, but that doesn't matter, I'm very happy with it. [...] The big difference, yes I'm not independent, I'm not going to ask the competition their advice, I'm not going to go ... trying to make trouble, I'm not going to investigate. But you can talk about an economic and financial journalist, a noble journalist, but it's ... my impression is that barely 10% of people do that. So between being in the 90% who are journalists and who suck up more or less ... to everyone, without really

Careers of French financial journalists 183

being able to demonstrate where are the stakes and being on the other side of the barrier with more tools and means, and promoting messages, bah [he sighs], I'm having fun, my journalistic curiosity is more satisfied here, and I have great projects to manage.

The perceived decline of the press sector also leads financial journalists to relativise the previous boundary that is supposed to separate them from people working in communication. Matthieu is editor-in-chief in a stock market weekly magazine. The way he answers when asked how he sees the coming years, after describing heavier and heavier constraints on his job, is very illuminating:

> I'm growing a bit weary of this job, which is ... because I've worked in it and I've been in it for a long time, and today no doubt I would want to try something else ... try something else. We kind of go round and round in circles after a while, and given the constraints I've just told you about. Q: And ... do you imagine, for example, you could work for generalist press? A: No, if it's ... no no. [...] The generalist press, the problems I've described to you, interest in things that aren't important, this tendency is even more significant now [...] We're constantly doing story telling. Newspapers have become a sound box for communications strategies. Q: If you had to change path now, which sector, which job would it be for? A: I have no idea for the moment. Certainly still in the finance domain. Always finance, I don't know, I don't know. Perhaps in financial communications, go to the other side. Become the one whispering in the journalists' ears.

Here, the position of financial editor-in-chief seems to be a "dead end" for a career from which he must escape. This strongly relates to Chris Welles' argument (1973). This reputation plays on how individuals expect their careers to go. Franck summarises his main motivation to leave the press after 7 years of activity: "I did not want to become an old journalist."

III The role of stock market activity and training in the organisation of careers in journalism

The particular context of the "Internet bubble" reveals another crucial dimension of the relationship between journalism and finance at the time of financialisation; namely, how stock market activity pressured the labour market and career development of financial journalists. First, there has been less possibility of hierarchical upward movement in financial journalism since the late 1990s. Among the journalists who permanently occupy a financial editor position in the analysed careers, 75% entered the job market between 1966 and 1995. This is probably due to more intense competition for editor positions since the 1990s, in contrast to the previous period. Due to the rise of individual shareholders, a lot of financial newspapers were created, while general press and politics newspapers were eager to revitalise their stock market columns. As a consequence, prospects were more open for individuals who engaged in financial journalism.

184   *Antoine Machut*

Second, the recurrence of financial crises has had an effect on career opportunities in the press for financial journalists. Phases of stock market activity put more or less constraint on individuals' commitment towards financial journalism. Thus, individuals who entered the labour market during the upward phase of the "Internet bubble" are five times less likely to pass quickly from journalism to finance.[12] On the other hand, they are more likely to stabilise in the financial journalism sector, or to move on to non-specialised journalism ("Stepping Stone" class[13]). In other words, the formation of the Internet bubble did not reduce the movement from journalism to the financial sector, but rather, delayed it. This reveals the opportunity effect represented by the "Internet bubble". Many websites were launching financial information sections to meet the need of content generated by the development of "technological values" on the stock market,[14] and the written press was expanding its financial sections. Many graduates in Economics and Business Administration (EBA) who entered the labour market in the late 1990s were attracted to financial journalism, even though they had not planned to enter these careers themselves.[15] Many of them tell how they have had positive responses from the financial press, even though they did not receive any positive answers from financial firms. This population is the most likely to leave the profession when the journalistic labour market deteriorates, enjoying their more appropriate background for working in the finance industry, reinforced by years in the press. Unsurprisingly, they are seven times more likely than others to quickly switch from journalism to finance (class "From Journalism to Finance", Table 10.1). At the same time, the rise of this type of training also contributed to the segmentation of the world of journalism by limiting traffic between a specialisation in finance and other topics. Individuals trained in EBA are indeed two times less likely to flow into the world of the press by de-specialising ("Stepping Stone" class, Table 10.1). Finally, the transitions between journalism and finance mainly concern careers in the financial press.

Otherwise, many aspiring journalists without an EBA degree have seized the opportunity offered by the financial press to get a job quickly and to de-specialise, thanks to the creation of web editors throughout the press. But these favourable conditions disappeared with the bursting of the Internet bubble, which seems to have helped to curb this springboard logic. The low representation of members of the 2001–2005 cohort in the "Stepping Stone" class attests to this. The trajectories that started just after the bursting of the Internet bubble are more likely to lead to a quicker exit from journalism, particularly towards the finance sector (Table 10.2). The period that followed the crash of 2001 is also likely to speed up the erosion of the commitment towards financial journalism described in the previous section. Mobility opportunities within the world of journalism were reduced after the crash of technology stocks in 2001, mainly because the mainstream press had no more reason to have specialised finance editorial teams in their newspapers: the first consequence of a financial crisis for the press is a drying up of financial advertising, which eventually reduces resources from financial items.[16] The second consequence is to deprive the press market of its main readership: according to an estimate reported by the newspaper *Les Echos*, the stock market lost 2.3 million individual shareholders in France between 2008 and 2012.[17]

Table 10.1 Odds ratio obtained by means of logistic regressions, for each cluster[18]

Variables	Clusters									
	From journalism to finance	p-value	Stepping stone	p-value	Upward Mobility	p-value	Leaving journalism	p-value	Professional segment	p-value
EBA	7.25	0.004**	0.41	0.06	0.51	0.30	0.40	0.16	1.44	0.34
Journalism	1.6	0.58	1.42	0.44	1.17	0.79	0.28	0.12	0.93	0.87
EBA+ Journalism	0.35	0.39	1.56	0.62	1.30	0.84	0.00	0.99	0.98	0.98
Cohort 1966–1978	0.00	0.99	1.94	0.36	1.24	0.81	0.00	0.99	1.59	0.51
Cohort 1995–2001	0.20	0.04*	1.55	0.30	0.50	0.30	0.60	0.29	1.23	0.60
Cohort 2001–2005	1.48	0.50	0.57	0.35	0.65	0.60	1.88	0.64	1.35	0.52
Women	0.69	0.69	0.61	0.76	0.55	0.27	0.41	0.14	1.9	0.05

** Statistically significant at .01
* Statistically significant at .05
. Statistically significant at .1

186 Antoine Machut

Table 10.2 Representation of the cohorts in each cluster (%)[19]

Clusters	Cohorts				
	1966–1978	1978–1995	1995–2001	2001–2005	Total
From Journalism to Finance	0	15	5	26	13
Stepping Stone	40	26	33	15	27
Upward Mobility	20	14	7	7	12
Leaving Journalism	0	9	14	4	9
Professional Segment	40	35	42	48	39
Total	100	100	100	100	100

Finally, the only strict dividing line between journalism and finance is in setups where individuals gain rapid access to the position of economic or general reporter, or in cases where the financial press is only one employer among other newspapers. Of the 46 careers of the "Stepping Stone" class, only one landed in a job in finance. It thus seems that low involvement in financial journalism is the price to pay for actually "protecting" journalists from the gravitational pull of the financial world.

Conclusion

This chapter shows that financial journalism has difficulty in gaining the commitment of individuals. It is sensitive to the attractions of other professional worlds – journalism and finance, in the first place, and the private sector more generally. In the end, 51% of the careers that I analysed correspond to a type of trajectory that spreads across financial journalism, but do not perfectly converge,[20] since a significant number of them, about 10%, eventually led to a position in the finance industry. 27% of careers present mobility logics within the world of the press, which means a low commitment to financial journalism. Finally, the logics of quick "exit" typify 22% of the careers, of which 13% move to finance.

The sustainability of financial journalists' commitment is also affected by the degradation of conditions in the journalistic labour market, which improved temporarily under the influence of the Internet bubble. Since the 2001 stock market crash, the line that separates general from financial journalism strengthened with the bursting of the Internet bubble and the end of the opportunity effect, while the line that separates journalism and finance continued to blur, with journalism receiving a growing number of EBA graduates. The beginning of this chapter showed the apparent tensions between a "world of journalism" and a "world of finance". The analysis I conducted demonstrates that the opposition between these two worlds is largely artificial, given the strong divergence of the professional trajectories of financial journalists and the strong power of attraction that finance has on these individuals. It would probably be more appropriate to speak of a world of financial information, in which the skills of journalists are sometimes, paradoxically, more valued by financial institutions than by the press. More broadly, financialisation is part of an erosion of the journalists' commitment, or even their "burn out" (Reinardy, 2011), which causes them to redefine their skills and invent new professions such as content or community managers (O'Donnell *et al.*, 2016). The norms and rules of the financial information world deserve to be clarified. But the weak capacity of financial journalism to independently regulate the standards imposed by the world of finance is clear. A thorough study remains to be done around the assumption of adoption by financial journalists of an ideology of transparency, as advocated in finance, and their help in legitimising the domination of economic activity by financial markets.

Annex 1: Encoding methodology

Code	Description
FinJou	Financial journalist.
Jou	Journalist non-specialised in finance. This includes "economic" journalists.
FinEic	Financial editor-in-chief. This category also includes the column writers.
Eic	Editor-in-chief (excluding those with financial speciality).
FinExec	Executive in the financial sector. Often "producer of editorial content", "financial consultant" or "responsible for financial communications".
Exec	Executive in other sectors than the press or finance.
MedExec	Executive in the media sector. Typically, "managing editor" or "publication manager".
Other	"Publisher", "parliamentary assistant", and so on.

In cases of multi-activity, we favoured the first activity that the user put in, while adding a multi-activity indicator.

Notes

1 A preliminary version of this chapter was presented at the "Finance at Work" International Symposium, which took place in Paris on 9–10 October 2014. I would like to thank the participants and the reviewers who commented on this version. This work is also part of a sociology thesis underway at the Pacte laboratory (CNRS, UMR 5194), financed by a Rhône-Alpes regional doctoral research grant.
2 We can refer here to the accounts of financial analysts gathered by Jacques-Olivier Charron (2010). They show that the research bureaus that are most open to the media are generally the least influential in the world of finance.
3 Oberlechner and Hocking (2004) notably show that traders and journalists cite each other mutually as primary sources of information.
4 The daily newspaper *Les Echos*, although founded in 1908 by the Servan-Schreiber family, has seen development punctuated by success, but globally erratic, affected by the 1929 crisis, and then ceasing publication during the war.
5 In this chapter, we use the word "commitment" in its interactionist definition; that is to say, to characterise the succession of choices made by individuals in a given social world during their career and the way they maintain reasonable continuity (Becker, 1960).
6 The data collection for this research has been funded by the Scientific Committee of the Institute of Political Studies (University of Grenoble, France) and was carried out by Jean-Marc Francony with the help of Gilles Bastin. The analyses and the graphics

188 *Antoine Machut*

were done using R software with the package TraMineR. See Gabadinho et al. (2011) and Studer (2013).

7 This is, for example, the case for journalists specialising in health issues (Marchetti and Champagne in Benson and Neveu, 2005), the environment (Comby, 2009) and social journalists (Lévêque, 2000).

8 The most representative career of this trajectory type contains a sequence of 11 years of financial journalism.

9 Note: graphs represent the distribution of positions held by individuals according to the class to which they belong, month by month. The x axis shows the number of months passed since the beginning of their career (each mark corresponds to 12 months, or 1 year). It reads as follows: in the class "From Journalism to Finance", 55% of individuals held a financial journalist position in the first month of their career. In the 20th year of their career, only 20% are financial journalists. Given that some careers last less than 20 years, the percentage of positions held on the right of the graph is not based on the same number as on the left of the graph. This does not show the individual sequences, and therefore does not allow us to deduce the nature of the transitions that occur over each career. These, however, are documented in the discussion of the results.

10 Names have been changed.

11 After his studies in economy and finance, he started in financial journalism at the beginning of the 2000s in radio and a French national newspaper, and then spent 5 years in a reputable financial information agency in London. After around 10 years of this work, he returned to study at a large business school, and was subsequently employed by a communications agency that works most notably for banks.

12 The odds ratios are summarised in Table 10.1.

13 This type of trajectory is the most heterogeneous. Careers that best represent this class consist of brief experience in financial journalism (rarely more than 3 years), which serves as a springboard to a career in journalism. This path also includes a type of freelancers, who work for both the financial press and the general press, and may at some point be hired by one or the other type of employer. But they never "cling" to financial journalism: the average time spent in a financial reporter position in this class is less than 4 years.

14 Online financial information portals such as Boursorama.com, optionfinance.fr, boursier.com and Trader online magazine were all created in the late 1990s.

15 Their proportion rose from 34% of new entrants in the 1978–1995 cohort to 50% in the 1995–2001 cohort and 59% in the 2001–2005 cohort.

16 For the general press, the financial section is what Tunstall called the "advertising goal" as opposed to topics that relate prestige ("non-revenue" or "prestige goal". See Tunstall, 1971).

17 "Stock Exchange: the exodus of individual investors," Lesechos.fr, 4 June 2012.

18 Reading: having trained in EBA multiplies by 7.25 the probability of taking the type of path "From Journalism to Finance". The probability that this correlation is due to chance is 0.4%.

19 Among the analysed career segments, the durations show few variations between clusters, from 16 to 18 years. This finding verifies the fact that the length of considered careers was of very little importance in the construction of the typology.

20 About the concept of "convergence" in careers studies, see Bastin (2016).

PART IV

Internal boundaries

Diversity, segmentation, stratification within financial occupations

Introduction

Is sociology of finance a general sociology?

Olivier Godechot

The establishment of the label *social studies of finance* on the model of *social studies of science* rooted the idea that *social studies of finance* was mainly an application of *science and technology studies* in general, and more specifically an application of the pragmatic approach of Bruno Latour and Michel Callon's research program (Callon, 1998) to the study of finance (Preda, 2001; Riles, 2010). Coined as such, *social studies of finance* should study more specifically how economics, financial theories, market devices and algorithms format and shape the financial markets and their participants (MacKenzie, 2006; Muniesa, 2007). The specificity of the theories, of the technology and of the market devices contributes to anchoring the idea that finance is a very specific domain of social life that requires a specific sociology. However, this representation of *social studies of finance* is both historically incorrect – the diversity of the research done under this label is underestimated – and misguiding. The three following chapters in Part IV – *Internal boundaries: diversity, segmentation, stratification within financial occupations* – of this book show us exactly the contrary. Stéphanie Mignot-Gérard, Constance Perrin-Joly, François Sarfati and Nadège Vezinat study how gender, class and ethnic origins, and moreover their intersection, affect early careers in portfolio and wealth management. Camille Herlin-Giret shows how wealth management stems from intimate and mainly masculine networks between wealth managers and wealthy families, and how managers are not just people who optimize wealth, but also persons helping wealthy families to make sense of their fortune. Finally, Fabien Foureault describes the structure of the financial field for LBO (leveraged buyout) and unveils its profound duality.

Therefore, in these three chapters, we find the most classical concepts of sociology: gender, class, ethnicity, networks and fields. We do not deal with the most esoteric technicalities of finance, such as sophisticated derivatives, brilliant mathematical models or complicated algorithms. There is no claim that dealing with money under its various forms changes the nature of social relations. On the contrary, here we find classical forms of discrimination, of intersectionalism, of embeddedness and of domination within the field. Those results are interesting for a primary reason. Thanks to the tools of general sociology, we learn how finance works. We learn that it works in a different way from the way it likes to put forward, that of an enchanted world of performances, of perfect markets,

192   *Olivier Godechot*

of best prices and of indifference to non-productive personal characteristics. But studying finance brings us something else. It can help us to build better tools of general sociology for understanding society as a whole. Finance can be used as an observatory of society, because social outcomes, which are more fuzzy and mitigated elsewhere, are here much more contrasted. Therefore, finance can help to discover, test and prove the underlying social mechanisms producing those outcomes. For instance, the tremendous level of inequality in financial outcomes, whether it be profits, bonuses, wages, or even prestige and popularity, enables us to establish inequality-generation mechanisms. Hence, finance is good material for understanding winner-take-all or winner-take-almost-all phenomena, market arm's length ties and network embeddedness, market freedom and organisational interdependence.

Among the factors of hierarchisation and domination within a field, social science scholars often focus both on assignation of individuals to categories of unequal value and legitimacy, and on resources accumulated and used by actors. Categorisation fuels group identity and influences distribution in several ways, such as status-based exploitation or opportunity hoarding (Tilly, 1998). Resources, which can be viewed as capital (Bourdieu, 2011), as specific or non-specific assets (Williamson, 1985), or more generally as resources in the resource-based theory (Pfeffer and Salancik, 1978), not only confer prestige and acquisitive power, but also constrain other actors who depend on access to those resources into accepting unfavourable terms of exchange (Emerson, 1962; Cook and Emerson, 1978; Williamson, 1985; Hart and Moore, 1988).

Studying those phenomena in the financial field enables us to investigate the relative importance of categorization, and resources that are exogenous to the financial field and those that are endogenous to it. Classical societal categorization along the dimension of gender or ethnicity, and classical resources such as educational background, family wealth and family social capital, of course, count. But the financial field enables us to contrast the role of these with endogenous financial categorization such as front-office versus back-office identification (Godechot, 2001), or resources accumulated in the activity, such as clients, knowledge or teams (Godechot, 2017).

Finance adds something more. Financial market fluidity enables us, on some occasions, to circumvent the people holding critical resources or those categorized in highly legitimate or illegitimate categories. Markets may annihilate traditional dependencies. But on other occasions, especially in niche markets that remain structurally narrow, or within organizations where relations between actors (for instance, between traders and salespeople) are compulsory, the activity gives a lot of importance to categorical assignation or to resources accumulated. Therefore, finance is the perfect locus for studying some of the fundamental questions of social exchange (Emerson, 1962), such as the relative role of arm's length ties versus embedded ties (Uzzi, 1997), independence and interdependence.

A last reason for studying finance goes beyond its heuristic role in coining better concepts and sociological mechanisms for studying society as a whole. To some extent, finance is ahead of the rest of society on many dimensions: it is at the forefront of the financialization process that also transforms non-financial firms and households. New rationalities, new forms of calculation, new ways of accounting activity, risk and profit, and new forms of incentives are experimented on first in finance and progressively spread out of their original sector. Finance might tell us something about the shape of society to come.

Therefore, there are very good reasons for social scientists to venture into the study of finance and not to leave this domain of social life to its traditional academic disciplines, such as economics and academic finance. But in order for this exploration to be most fruitful, social scientists should avoid thinking of finance as a separate and specific domain.

11 Early careers in portfolio and wealth management

The roles of class, race and gender in occupational segmentations

Stéphanie Mignot-Gérard, Constance Perrin-Joly, François Sarfati and Nadège Vezinat

The relationship between education and labour markets is a central issue for both economists and sociologists. According to the human capital theory (Becker, 1964), individuals who benefit from the same level of education should attain equal social positions and expect similar outcomes on the labour market and equivalent career opportunities. Since then, sociologists have provided ample evidence that education is merely reproducing the inequalities of inherited family economic and cultural resources (Bourdieu and Passeron, 1970). Multiple studies have also highlighted the existence of persistent social inequalities (whether in recruitments or salaries) on labour markets.

Central to these studies are those related to the "intersectionality" theories. Despite the complexities, ambiguities and unstable developments of intersectionality theory (Davis, 2008, McCall, 2005), they broadly refer to the need for investigating the interactions between class, race and gender in building individual identities. The large success of intersectionality theories led them to be applied to various sociological inquiries, including the study of inequalities on the labour markets (Browne and Misra, 2003). Overall, Browne and Misra argue that intersectionality studies on labour markets remain inconclusive because of the diverse approaches of the issue with respect to both the types of labour markets studied and the empirical methods used. Beyond the case of labour markets, there is a large consensus across the literature to point out two shortcomings of intersectionality theories. On the one hand, because they were initiated by US scholars – the United States being marked by the civil rights movements and the country where women studies were born – the studies generally focus on race and gender, tending to obscure the notion of class (Mc Call, 2005). On the other hand, because intersectionality is rooted in Black women theories, a large part of the scholarship aims to give voice to marginalized populations, thus leaving out of its scope the unmarked categories and their own experiences, and hence excluding possibilities of comparisons between the marginalized and the mainstream (Choo and Ferree, 2010).

Although they rarely refer explicitly to intersectionality, the so-called "social studies of finance" also have investigated the roles of race, class and gender in

Early careers in wealth management 195

producing inequalities at the workplace, challenging the Wall Street mantra that "money does not discriminate" (Ho, 2009). While US studies deal mainly with gender inequalities in financial occupations (Blair-Loy, 2001, Roth, 2003), the French scholarship is more akin to exploring the social effects of work segregation. Several authors emphasize the growth and diversification of financial occupations and the parallel growing social diversity among finance employees since the 1990s (Godechot, 2001, Sarfati, 2007, Vezinat, 2012). Those studies indicate that the social mix within financial occupations differs across the financial industry segments: for example, Godechot (2001) notes that only 10 per cent of traders come from the working class (2001:141), while Vezinat (2012) shows that the job of financial counsellor has become more and more accessible to working-class employees. Nevertheless, and quite similarly to American scholarship, the analyses tend to focus on one social factor and omit to investigate the relative influences of class, gender and race on occupational trajectories.

Overall, social studies of finance suffer from the same limitations as those of intersectionality research. First, research that systematically articulates gender with class and race in explaining the segmentation of financial jobs is unusual; rather, it focuses on one or two of these social determinants. Second, the sociology of finance invariably predicts that individuals who occupy the lowest position in one or two social categories – for example, coloured people and women in the finance industry – accumulate disadvantages (Ho, 2003).

In contrast to the latter studies, and drawing on McCall's critique of intersectionality (McCall, 2005), this chapter attempts to contribute to the social studies of finance by systematically analysing and untangling the respective effects of class, gender and race on the jobs occupied by individuals at an early stage of their career in two occupational niches of finance: wealth management and portfolio management. Two arguments are emphasized. The study first shows that the "choices" of those two occupational segments are shaped by race and gender, which play out independently of each other as well as independently of social class. In addition, it demonstrates that class is the major determinant for creating a vertical differentiation within each occupation. As a result, the higher education and professional paths in these fields of finance come to nuance the idea of a cumulative disadvantage of race, gender and social class and to show the different influence of each variable in context.

These arguments are based on the analysis of Master's students' individual trajectories. The population at stake includes students involved in two Master's programmes, one in portfolio management (PM) and the other in wealth management (WM). Both are offered by an Institut d'Administration des Entreprises (IAE), a school of management of a public university located in a relatively disadvantaged area of the Paris suburbs. Both Master's programmes are vocational sandwich programmes, meaning that the students alternate studies and work – they hold a 1-year fixed-term apprenticeship contract during the whole training period. As apprentices in a Master's degree, these students are supposed to enter the labour market by the end of the academic year. In France historically, the majority of higher education programmes in banking and finance have been

196 *Stéphanie Mignot-Gérard* et al.

offered by Grandes Ecoles, either business schools or engineering schools, considered as the elite segment of higher education. Business education is relatively new in French public universities, which opened their first management departments in the 1950s. The IAEs stand behind Grandes Ecoles in terms of prestige; they generally recruit students from middle-class social backgrounds, who cannot easily afford the tuition fees of Grandes Ecoles and do not have the school records to access the elite institutions (Mignot-Gérard *et al.*, 2014).

Sources

The fieldwork was conducted in 2011. The study is part of a research contract between a research centre (the Centre d'Etudes de l'Emploi) and a national association in charge of enhancing the employment opportunities of executives, the Association Pour l'Emploi des Cadres.

The empirical data involves two types of material. First, a database of the students in both programmes between 2008 and 2011 was analysed to compare the characteristics (age, sex, nationality, etc.) of the populations in Portfolio Management and Wealth Management Master's ($N = 119$). The database was built up from the students' enrolment files digitalized in the university software, called APOGEE.

The database helped to characterize the 119 individuals' gender and national origins. In this quantitative study, the national origin was investigated instead of race, because no database on race is available in France. The identification of national origin was elaborated through the analysis of the individuals' surnames (for a description of this method, see Felouzis, 2003, Cédiey and Foroni, 2005, Jobard and Névanen, 2007). The analysis highlights three different types of surname (French surnames, foreign surnames and indistinguishable surnames). By combining variables such as nationality, country of birth and surnames, this database allows us to estimate the number of immigrants and descendants of immigrants regardless of their country of origin.

The second part of the material is composed of individual biographical interviews with 28 students who were attending the two programmes in 2011. More than two-thirds of each cohort were interviewed (the sample depended on the students' agreement and their availability). The interviews were conducted by the four authors, with the same questionnaire, at the IAE during class breaks. Whereas "race" was difficult to trace through the quantitative material, it was possible to make it visible in the qualitative interviews.

The chapter is organized in two parts. In the first part, an educational segmentation is highlighted: despite similar titles, the two Master's degrees lead to different occupations for apprentices; the division of the students is moreover unevenly distributed in terms of race and gender (I). The second part sketches the vertical differentiation that exists within each speciality in terms of both occupations and professional expectations; the better-off students occupy the most prestigious jobs of the labour market (II).

Two master's programs and the horizontal segmentation of the occupational world of finance

Sociological studies on financial occupations generally focus on one specific segment, either "financial counsellors" (Lazarus, 2012, Moulévrier, 2002, Vezinat, 2012), "financial analysts" (Ho, 2003, Sarfati, 2012) or "traders" (Godechot, 2001). The lack of comparative case studies on different financial jobs makes it difficult to highlight the horizontal segmentations that were observed in other occupations (Bucher and Strauss, 1961, Hughes, 1971). This section describes the great variety of activities, occupations and career paths in wealth management and portfolio management. Second, it outlines that both programs are socially mixed, but involve a different representation of women and non-nationals.

Portfolio management and wealth management: close appellations, sharp differences in content

In the school under scrutiny, although their titles are very similar in French (wealth management: gestion de patrimoine and portfolio management: gestion de portefeuille), the programmes actually offer different job opportunities with regard to the nature of the job itself and its related career paths (concrete activities, type of firms/bank departments where students/graduates are hired, type of clients, professional networks and so on).

What do wealth and portfolio managers do and who are their employers?

Wealth managers advise their customers about opportunities to develop their personal or family portfolios. Professionals are experts in financial products and taxation issues. They deal with particular customers and have therefore to be good sellers. Large retail banking institutions hire wealth managers in local offices of retail banks or in subsidiaries dedicated to well-to-do customers, so-called "private banking departments". One can also work as a portfolio manager in independent firms such as small consulting agencies of wealth management, family offices and even single-family offices (private companies dedicated to a single family).

Portfolio managers deal with institutional clients (banks, investment companies and so on). Traders make transactions that need financial knowledge, computer skills and mathematical models. Most portfolio managers work in large investment banks.

198 *Stéphanie Mignot-Gérard et al.*

In wealth management, students work as private counsellors for prosperous individuals (either in small family offices or at major national banks); they are in charge of optimizing their clients' financial assets according to the fiscal rules that apply in their national context. For their part, portfolio managers follow the evolutions of financial markets and the values of different products (stocks, bonds, derivative products) to maximize the financial returns for third parties (either institutional clients or their own company).

The two programmes thus reflect the heterogeneity of banking activities. Rather than competing, the two programmes are indifferent to each other, since they lead to different occupational niches of the banking industry. Therefore, besides the usual and well-known segmentation between retail and investment banking (Godechot, 2017), the study points to differentiated financial activities that extend beyond the banking industry, since they may take place in insurance companies (portfolio management) or independent consulting firms (wealth management).

Class, race and gender across wealth management and portfolio management

The students enrolled at the IAE studies are characterized by the relative homogeneity of their social backgrounds. Most originate from the working or middle class: they resemble "petits-moyens", a category that encompasses individuals "situated in-between the top of working class and the bottom of middle-class" (Cartier *et al.*, 2016).

The individuals' social origins were characterized through the analysis of their two parents' occupations. The better-off among our interviewees do not accumulate various forms of capital (Bourdieu, 1984b); those who have benefited from quite high cultural capital are not granted a high level of economic resources. For example, Antoine's father is an associate professor at the university, while his mother is unemployed. In addition, among the 28 students who were apprentices at the time of this study, only 9 had one parent employed at an executive level; in 6 families out of 9, the second parent held the status of employee or technician. Overall, the sample includes only one family in which both the mother and the father embraced an executive occupation. The 19 remaining students of the sample had a parent who was either a technician or worker, and 12 among the latter were working class. Some accumulate social disadvantages: two working-class students originated from single-parent families. Access to a Master's degree in a rather selective higher education institution thus represents social upward mobility for the great majority of the population of students in question.

Two socially diversified cohorts

By comparing the social origins of the students in the two Master's programmes, we see a relatively mixed social group in both programmes: in Wealth Management, over 16 students, 7 students originating from the working class and 9 from the middle class; in Portfolio Management, over 12 students, 7 from the middle class

Early careers in wealth management   199

and 5 from the working class. The sample is not representative, since these data were accessed through the 28 interviews. It is nevertheless interesting to point it out, for slightly different social origins seem to influence early occupational trajectories (see section 2). This social mix intrinsic to both programmes is all the more important to emphasize that gender and racial origins are, by contrast, not equally distributed in the portfolio management and wealth management cohorts.

More women in Wealth Management, more non-nationals
in Portfolio Management

The analysis of the 119 individuals' characteristics – cohorts 2008 to 2011 – shows that women are more numerous in Wealth (46 per cent) than in Portfolio Management (24 per cent). One explanation probably lies in the gender effect of schooling choices; as shown by Duru-Bellat (2004) in her study of French pupils' trajectories in secondary education, males typically dominate the scientific specializations, whereas females are more numerous in literature, humanities and social sciences. While Portfolio and Wealth Management programs both require a fundamental knowledge of finance, the technical skills that are needed to graduate differ to a large extent between the two programmes, as is supported by the titles of core courses: in Portfolio Management, core courses are "portfolio management", "instruments of portfolio management" and "diagnostic of financial markets"; in Wealth Management, "fiscal policies" and "law" are more central in the curriculum. The academic profiles of our two cohorts vary accordingly: while 57 per cent of the students in Wealth Management hold a baccalaureate with a specialization in Economics & Social Studies, only 39 per cent of their counterparts in Portfolio Management do so; on the contrary, the latter are more likely (41 per cent) than the former (23 per cent) to hold a baccalaureate in Mathematics and Science. The horizontal segmentation between portfolio management and wealth management thus seems to be correlated with gender stereotypes that have been shaped since primary and secondary school.

As far as the issue of nationality is concerned, the collected material indicates that Portfolio Management is more ethnically diverse than Wealth Management; first, the percentage of students who took their baccalaureate abroad is higher in Portfolio Management (13 per cent versus 3 per cent in Wealth Management); second, while no distinction can be made according to the students' nationality or native country, students' surnames that "sound foreign" are three times more numerous in Portfolio Management (21 per cent) than in Wealth Management (7 per cent).

The interviewees' early occupational trajectories confirm that women feel more comfortable in Wealth Management than in Portfolio Management. In Wealth Management, students originating from North or Sub-Saharan Africa were not recruited into private banking departments of retail banks; those enrolled in the Portfolio Management programme generally occupy positions – such as performance analysts – that entail technical and calculation skills. How to account for these findings? Wealth management involves face-to-face commercial relations with well-off clients. The interviewees themselves point out that the majority of their clients are "white males" whose values are quite conservative. By contrast,

200 *Stéphanie Mignot-Gérard et al.*

portfolio management is a typical activity of the globalized economy: financial operations are dematerialized, set up in a common language (English) with alter egos all over the world. The universe of portfolio management is inhabited by the male representation of the trader, often depicted as the warrior in modern times. The only female of our sample who worked as an assistant trader stresses the masculinity of the trading desk and confesses her disillusionment with the job and her desire to move away from it:

> Now, I work with men only. I find it cool to be surrounded by males. There is one Chinese, one Malagasy, one guy from Poland, only one French. I am kind of THE Maghreban female, which they like I think. I feel that I was recruited because there are very few girls in finance. So when you are a girl, I suspect it's easier to get in, because they are machos, they want a girl, like "Come on, let's have a girl as an intern", yes I felt that ... That pisses me off. So I am literally plunged into this masculine universe ... They always talk about women. It's really a men's world. *What kind of job would you like to do in the future?* I would like to work at home. I think it's just great. I met some ladies who have created their own companies and work at home, one is a stylist. She used to sew in her garage, she would work for famous brands, of course she works hard but she has a nice quality of life. I think that's a good option for me in the future, I will be able to combine it with a family.
>
> (Hasna, PM)

By contrast, Laurence, consultant in private banking in the biggest French bank, states that being a woman is not a problem regarding her business relations; it can even represent an advantage with some male clients, even though she needs to protect herself from attempts at seduction. She feels that her age is a stronger handicap than gender to enjoying credibility with clients.

> I spend my days counselling people who are my parents' age. At first, to being credible in front of these elder clients was my major concern. That's why I wear glasses and a tailored suit. And I have always lied on my age. I am 23 but I say that I am 26. ... When you deal with clients who possess many millions, you must command their respect, you must inspire trust. Sometimes when they talk about the stock markets in the eighties, I feel bad ... so I tell them that I can't be all-knowing. *So, being a woman has never been an issue?* Well, with some of my colleagues, sometimes I felt ... Some would say "you are here because you are a girl", I experienced this kind of remark, but I generally try to contest with some sense of humour. On the other hand, some clients enjoy very much meeting with their lady-banker, they come alone, without their wife. So well, I try to keep these relations friendly, I refuse proposals of dinner or lunch, I say that I am not allowed to. I was offered presents too, but nothing inappropriate. I also received declarations of love like "I wanted to tell you that you are charming, your husband is a lucky man" ... I always say that I am engaged.
>
> (Laurence, WM)

Early careers in wealth management 201

The case of Laurence is not isolated; other female students in Wealth Management testify that being a woman might be an issue with colleagues, but to a lesser extent with clients.

By contrast, Hamid, one student originating from North Africa who works as a performance analyst in the same bank as Laurence, suspects – even though he is reluctant to admit it – that his race was an obstacle when he applied for the position of wealth manager in the private banking department:

> I am not a person who is suspicious about racism. If some people are racist, I try to figure out why, something may have happened to them, so when I face a blockage with this issue, I try to move beyond. ... At the X Bank, well I felt this kind of blockage ... At my second job interview, they were talking about my future mission, so I felt very confident, but there was one person more aggressive among the interviewers. After that I felt that I was maybe irrational, I thought it was a "good cop-bad cop" interview. But at the end, nothing happened. Anyway, I don't want to over-interpret this event, I don't want to generalize it too much.
>
> (Hamid, WM)

Hamid's testimony moreover indicates that he was recruited into relatively technical jobs; he anticipates difficulty in attaining a more business-like position in a renowned French bank, and invokes his plan to move abroad, even though he does not clearly reflect on or admit the racial factor as an obstacle to his future career. On their side, women feel uneasy in trading positions, typically male-dominated jobs (Blair-Loy, 2001, Crompton, 1989, Stovel *et al.*, 1996), and more comfortable in occupations that entail direct relationships with a private clientele.

In sum, the study reveals that the nature of the financial product frames the segmentation of the labour market. Personable young women match well with the elegant settings of private banking offices, but they seem less suitable for the rough floors of trading desks. As places where world economic exchanges are made, the latter look more open to welcoming employees from diversified ethnic origins, who experience greater difficulties in attaining jobs that entail business relationships. On the other hand, both specialities involve a relatively mixed social composition of students. And this horizontal segmentation is coupled with a vertical one.

The influence of "class" on the vertical segmentation at the edge of employment

The interviews draw a neat and consensual view of a vertical hierarchy across jobs in each specialty. For the students in Portfolio Management who work in capital markets, the activities related to back/middle office activities are much less valued than those attached to front offices. Similarly, students in Wealth Management assess jobs that take place in the private banking departments of banks differently than those located in the offices of local banks. The chances of holding a job in

202 *Stéphanie Mignot-Gérard et al.*

the most prestigious segments of both occupations are strongly related to the students' social backgrounds.

Vertical division in wealth management: counselling versus sales

The Wealth Management students' employers are either banks or private wealth management consulting firms. A similar vertical differentiation occurs in both organizations depending on the clients' portfolios; in banks, the wealthiest clients are advised in the banks' "private banking" departments (as opposed to local agencies of retail banks); in private consulting firms, they are managed in family offices (as opposed to smaller cabinets en gestion de patrimoine).

Among the students who obtained a 1-year apprentice job in a bank, few actually work as wealth managers. Most of our interviewees are indeed "customer advisors+" for the segment of a private clientele whose financial assets stand in between those of the regular clients and the wealthiest ones (see boxed text below).

The private clientele's counsellors in the French bank industry: a clear hierarchy of occupations

In retail banks in France, the sales jobs are generally divided into three different positions. The first and least qualified position is that of "customer advisor". Applicants to those positions generally hold a Bachelor's degree, and they are in charge of selling basic financial products (credit cards, home loans, life insurance, and so on) to the largest clientele.

"Customer advisors +" have the same tasks and responsibilities, but manage clients whose financial assets are higher (between €20 k and €100 k).

"Wealth managers", for their part, may work either in a bank branch or in specific offices dedicated to private banking. Their clients' assets exceed €250 k. They deal with more sophisticated financial products (stocks, shares, real estate investment trusts, and so on). An additional level of responsibilities (so-called "gestion de fortune") is designed for the upper segment of their clientele (assets > €5 M).

If they assess positively their chances of getting a permanent job in their bank after graduation, the position that they expect to obtain is not necessarily that of wealth manager. According to the students in Wealth Management, becoming a sales counsellor after graduation would depreciate their degree's value. Most are, however, pessimistic about their chances of reaching the occupation of wealth manager straight after university graduation.

The apprentices draw a clear boundary between occupations dedicated to "sales" (customer advisor) and those of wealth management that involve "counselling". According to the testimonies, the higher the clients' assets, the more counselling replaces sales; while sales involves pushing clients to buy standardized products, counselling implicates handling more complex clients' situations and higher creativity in product choices.

> The "sales" dimension is more significant in retail banks. I feel a bit upset by this sales side of the job ... You know, you have to sell X equity savings plans every week. I prefer counselling. In private banking, the job is more qualitative, less oriented towards sales. You need more reflection, it's more complex, I like that.
>
> (Octavio, WM)

Another option for the Wealth Management students is to work outside the banking industry in private small offices of wealth management, a job that includes close expertise in the clients' holdings and allows investment counselling based on a larger range of financial products. However, attaining these jobs requires the development of a personal network, especially in family offices, which deal with a more prosperous clientele and offer more sophisticated financial investment solutions.

A Master's degree in Wealth Management thus covers a large range of concrete occupations with regard to the clientele's financial resources, the range of financial products that may be offered, and the balance between selling and counselling. These differences are to a large extent connected to the functional segmentation between retail banking and private banking.

Vertical division for Portfolio Management students: back or middle offices versus trading

Likewise, the occupations in portfolio management are heterogeneous. In the banking or insurance sector, the students are employed as traders, fund investors or financial analysts. Nevertheless, these general denominations hide a vertical hierarchy that exists between activities. Occupying a position in the front office is more prestigious and more lucrative than working in back or middle offices The most valued jobs are thus the nearest to the sales, that is, in the front office (Godechot, 2017; Ho, 2009).

If many students thus yearn for trading, all recognize that full-time job opportunities remain scarce. Antoine describes below how he became a trader – he is the only one of the cohort who works in a front office. The road to trading was not straightforward; it has involved many steps and rites of passage from the back to the front office:

> I moved from back office to middle office but stayed in the same field – the money market –, where I built a modest network ... and then someone told me "your internship went well, so we'll move you to the middle office." Then, last year I landed on the trading floor as assistant trader. That experience was a real stepping stone. ... This year I was promoted to the front office after my experience in the middle office, so they told me "you're a

204 *Stéphanie Mignot-Gérard et al.*

motivated and serious, so we'll hire you as a trader". At that point every-thing changed: higher responsibilities, higher pressure. The traders, who were nice when I was their assistant, became tough on me. These people are very challenging; their watchword is rigor. As a trader I do not build the products but define the price and inform the client. Of course, at the beginning you make mistakes, and some clashes may occur. I have my own personality so when I received critics about my work, I tried to justify myself, and it was not well received. At the front office, you have to accept to be challenged; you have to listen to your seniors, and learn to shut up. I figured out that it was the normal way ... You have to be tough because the responsibilities are incredibly high. For instance, I now manage a 3 to 4 billions portfolio!

(Antoine, PM)

Antoine's narrative and tone tell how much becoming a trader involved sheer hard work and a level of responsibility that goes far beyond that experienced in back or middle offices. Working in the front office and placing orders directly are the major appeal of the job, somewhat triggered by the sulphurous image of the golden boy. By contrast, all the positions at the back of the trading office are seen as less stressful, but also less valued by the companies and less attractive to students.

My job is called "middle-office benchmark control". I check that the financial instruments in our databases reflect the ones at work on the market, stocks, shares, or options. Because the names of the products may change on the market, some deals made by our traders may be broken and the bookkeeping made at the back office sometimes doesn't match with the market. We do a lot of production for the traders .... *Is there a little bit of innovation in your activity?* Not much innovation, mostly production. That's the reason why I am upset about it.

(Alexandre, PM)

The responsibilities, as well as the intensity and interest of the job and the wages that go along with it, increase with proximity to the market; the level of responsi-bilities goes hand in hand with the prestige of these occupations and thus develops the vertical hierarchies within the occupations.

The influence of social capital on vertical differentiation

Among the students of both cohorts, those who have accessed the most prestig-ious jobs benefit from specific social advantages, either cultural and/or economic capital (Bourdieu, 1984a). For Godechot (2001), the traders who have the best occupational positions are not only those who had the best "scholar dispositions", such as engineers; they also belong to the upper class. What roles does economic and cultural capital play in the IAE students' occupational trajectories?

Early careers in wealth management   205

Contrasted trajectories in Wealth Management

In the Wealth Management class, Mickael and Aurore are employed in the private banking department of the biggest French bank. They both acknowledge that they have reached the highest position in the job market and that they are the "happy few" of the class. Mickael's and Aurore's paths are similar in many respects; both were raised in quite prosperous cities in the west and south of France; they obtained a baccalaureate in Science & Maths, and before enrolling at the IAE, they graduated from a business school involving high tuition fees. Both were offered full-time jobs after graduation, but they decided to complement their initial training, and found their apprenticeship contracts on their own. In the two cases, both parents are employed and one of them occupies an executive position. They equally benefited from family support: Mickael states that he was influenced by his uncles, who graduated from a business school, while Aurore's father always pushed her to work hard at school. Not only do Mickael's and Aurore's gender and race coincide with their occupation (see above), but also, their favourable social environment has probably helped forge their ability to counsel a high-potential clientele.

For his part, Cedric works in a Family Office. His job stands among the most prestigious positions that may be reached in the programme, from both an economic and a symbolic point of view: he earns the highest salary of the cohort, and provides law and fiscal counselling to very well-off families. The cultural capital inherited from his family is important to account for his occupational trajectory. His parents are not particularly upper class, but they share a passion for art: his father has always dreamed of managing an art gallery, and his mother had aspired at an early stage of her career to become an auctioneer. When he was at school, Cedric used to organize cultural trips with friends; he has rushed to art exhibitions and has subscribed to art magazines. Here is how he accounts for his achievement of entering the prestigious auction and art merchant Christie's as an intern:

> So I sent 10 CVs to the 10 different departments of the three best companies: Christie's, Sotheby's and Phillip's. For Christie's, the manager for Europe was in charge of the Jewellery department and I had read an article about him in an art magazine. So I mentioned this article, maybe he was flattered … Anyway he allowed me to meet the HR director in Paris. The internship was just perfect. Actually, I found all my internships through magazines … One day I read an article about the banker who was found dead in his apartment in Geneva … I don't remember his name … Anyway, his lawyer was interviewed and said he had a passion for art. I wrote to him to figure out whether he was seeking interns. I got an appointment and he told me: "I cannot offer you any position here but I am an administrator at the Cartier Bresson Foundation, I can get you in." I was interviewed by the Foundation manager and I got the job! Every time, I got kind of lucky!
>
> (Cedric, PM)

206 *Stéphanie Mignot-Gérard* et al.

The evocation of "luck" might signal that he did not have to struggle too much to build up a career in the art profession. His social background has favoured his capacity to pursue higher education studies, and his passion for art, inherited from his parents, strengthened his position in the occupational sphere that he aimed to reach.

The case of Aurelie illustrates the opposite situation to those of Cedric, Mickael and Aurore. Both her parents are in basic employment at the national French postal services. After the baccalaureate graduation, Aurelie enrolled at the closest university to home, where she completed all her higher education. She did not apply to a business school because of the high cost of the tuition fees. After a "professional bachelor's" in sales, her scholarly accomplishments led her to enrol directly for a Master's degree at the IAE. Now in the Wealth Management programme, she found the apprenticeship contract through the network developed by the IAE. She works in retail banking and is quite unhappy about her situation.

> *So, how is it going for you in the bank where you were recruited as an apprentice?* I am very upset. It is not at all what I was expecting ... At the very beginning, I was supposed to be a counsellor in private banking. Of course, when you lack experience, that's not so easy to get there directly. I agreed with this, and I was happy to start with a lower level job. But the point is that I landed in an understaffed branch, the team has been entirely renewed, the staff is not well trained at all, people are often missing ... so in the end, I spend most of my time at the front-desk.
>
> (Aurelie, WM)

In contrast to some of her peers, Aurelie's family lacks both cultural and economic resources. Her trajectory resembles those of Joaquim and Octavio. Both were raised in industrial cities in the centre of France; their mothers, who hold employee/technician positions, raised them on their own. Their academic records were not good enough to enrol at a prestigious business school, and their families could not afford to pay for a middle-range private school. Instead, they enrolled at university and grabbed small jobs to finance their higher education expenses on their own. Both work as assistant wealth managers but resist taking on the lowly position of customer advisor+.

The contrast in the trajectories of Cedric, Mickael and Aurore, on one hand, and those of Aurelie, Joaquim and Octavio, on the other, shows the influence of a combination of their families' economic and cultural capital. Both forms of capital are converted into an educational capital; the most deprived students experience greater difficulties in enrolling at business schools and/or rely on their own networks to seize the most valued jobs of the market.

Contrasted trajectories in Portfolio Management

Apart from Hasna, the only student of the cohort employed as a trader is Antoine. Being a "white male" is probably an advantage for occupying this position, but not

Early careers in wealth management   207

enough to account for his occupational achievement. It is also worth pointing out that Antoine's father is an associate professor of Mathematics at the university. Coinciding with his father's trajectory, he initially enrolled in a preparatory class to enrol at a Grande Ecole of Engineering, but soon realized that he was more interested in finance than in engineering. He states that he received strong support from his parents during higher education studies. He failed to enter the most prestigious engineering Grandes Ecoles, and thus chose to enrol for a Bachelor's degree in Finance in a Paris intra muros university. He then enrolled at the IAE. Two different factors have therefore played out in his trajectory: his initial higher education background in a preparatory class for a Grande Ecole, and the relatively high economic capital of his family.

At the other end of the spectrum are students who work in middle offices, such as Alexandre or Doriann, who originate from disadvantaged cities in the suburbs of Paris. Alexandre's father is a postman and his mother is a house-worker. His trajectory at the closest university from home follows a similar path to that of Aurelie (see previous section). He is quite happy with his current mission at the middle office because he has learnt a lot in finance, but seeks to reach a job in risk-country analysis; he feels that the only way to make it is to complement his training with a specific programme in risk analysis provided by a Grande Ecole. On Doriann's part, his parents originate from a small Eastern European country damaged in a recent civil war; his father is a truck driver, his mother is unemployed and suffers from cancer. As an apprentice, he works on software that makes connections between the IT and finance departments; he is willing to become a trader, but anticipates that he will need to work abroad to reach his dream, which he is reluctant to do because of his mother's illness:

> If I stay in IT, I will probably make less money than in the heart of finance … Well actually, if I work in IT for financial markets I might earn a lot of money. And it's actually great to enter directly the front office since you have no longer this back/middle office "tag". I unfortunately have this back/middle stereotype. So I would be very happy to get into the market. But I have to be honest, I am not sure that I have the ability to get in. *What would you need to do so? For what kind of job?* Trading! I would love that. … *Do you believe that being a trader is something about passion?* At the start, yes definitely. You have to fit the mould; you need to have high education records, to graduate from specific schools. It's difficult to become a trader. The positions are scarce and with the current economic crisis, you have to stand among the best.
>
> (Doriann, PM)

The vertical differentiation of jobs in the sector of portfolio management is therefore tightly linked with the students' social origins. Consistently with Bourdieu's analyses of the stratification of the French higher education system (Bourdieu, 1989), where Grandes Ecoles represent elite institutions while universities suffer from lower prestige, the interviewees' trajectories show that those who attended

208 *Stéphanie Mignot-Gérard* et al.

preparatory classes to Grandes Ecoles have better professional accomplishments than those who completed higher education in public universities. The cultural capital inherited by the IAE students thus mirrors their paths in higher education as well as their occupational trajectories. Economic capital also shapes individuals' higher education accomplishments. The class factor is all the more important in emphasizing that several interviewees, who may be disadvantaged in their occupational segment because of their race/gender, try to compensate for their handicaps by mobilizing social resources from within or at the periphery of their nuclear family. For instance, Hamid, who struggles to become a wealth manager, confesses that he sometimes uses his family name – his aunt is a European deputy and was a former French Minister of Justice – to be recognized in his professional sphere.

In portfolio management as well as wealth management, differentiated family economic and cultural capitals thus offer contrasted social resources to accomplish professional ambitions in the most valued segments of the occupation.

Conclusion

The public policies of higher education in France in the recent period rely on the assumption that a Master's degree in apprenticeship is the best guarantee of achieving alignment between higher education and employment. The findings of this study bring a nuance to this belief, revealing that the nature of the jobs eventually obtained by students depends heavily on their gender, race and social backgrounds.

In the finance jobs at stake here, and consistently with the conclusions of previous social studies of finance, being a white man from an upper social class is clearly an advantage for access to the highest professions in each labour market. However, by comparing two segments of the financial profession and highlighting their intrinsic vertical differentiation, new conclusions arise. In the first place, the study shows that a priori social disadvantages push in different directions; while being a woman does not fit well with the masculine culture that dominates occupations in portfolio management, it is less handicapping in wealth management; symmetrically, originating from North Africa seems to restrict opportunities in private banking, but to a lesser extent in the dematerialized and globalized market-side activities of finance. Second, it indicates that social class is the major determinant of the ability to seize the most prestigious occupations in both labour niches, regardless of other determinants; economic and cultural capital – which are converted into academic capital – are key explaining factors of differentiated trajectories, even for white individuals in wealth management or men in portfolio management. Moreover, the individuals handicapped by their race/gender in their respective occupational segments develop resistances to this by mobilizing their social capital assets. This conclusion is not only important to raise from a theoretical point of view, but might also be of interest for public decision-makers, who consistently try to moderate race and gender occupational inequalities (Cooke, 2011; Dobbin, 2009): while some labour markets seem rather open to gender and/

Early careers in wealth management 209

or racial diversity, social class remains the major determinant for attaining the most privileged jobs (Lareau and Conley, 2008).

This study, however, comprises one important limitation: when individuals accumulate two or more disadvantages, such as North Africans who originate from the working class (in WM) and women from the working class (in PM), one cannot easily predict which factor is ultimately the most crippling. The interviewees tend to put forward the race or gender factor as the main determinant of their impediments, ignoring the class influence. Three non-exclusive or complementary hypotheses may be drawn here. Either the individuals are reflexive enough to provide the right explanation of their professional trajectory, or their interpretation of their own situation is strongly influenced by the explanations broadcast by the media and the public policies that enhance diversity; a third possible account is that having mixed with upper social classes throughout their academic and professional paths has progressively erased their subjective appreciation of the social stigma.

This study thus raises new issues to be put on the research agenda. First, research should be conducted on Grandes Ecoles graduates; Grandes Ecoles in France have recently opened their doors to a more diverse student body (Van Zanten, 2010). Those individuals' occupational trajectories could inform the extent to which a Grande Ecole allows women to enter front offices, North Africans to become wealth managers, and working-class individuals to reach the most prestigious jobs of the market. At this point, one might also wonder how social class interacts with the two other determinants in the long run: the stigmata of the social background might progressively fade away through professional socialization, while the gender issue might become more salient when women give birth to their first children. Second, the study does not provide any cases of individuals who, despite their multiple social handicaps, seized the best jobs. These "survivors" might exist in the financial industry labour market; identifying them would be an opportunity to better assess the way race, gender and class interact in the long term of the occupational trajectory. One could assume that the feminine gender may compensate for the race issue, or that a double stigma may be reversed as an advantage. In sum, the interrelations between race, gender and class certainly warrant more and further dynamic investigations.

12 Managing fortunes and privacy
Professional rhetoric and boundaries within wealth management

Camille Herlin-Giret

> It is an emotional matter. Managing wealth means managing emotions. And that is precisely why it is so limiting to say, as some organisations do, "it's just technical, it's just technical". [...] At some point, perhaps we should think of it not as managing people's money, but as managing people who have money.

> (A wealth manager)

Wealth management consulting is still a little-known profession,[1] which has yet to be examined in depth. Indeed, it is tricky to differentiate these professionals from other financial specialists – asset managers, branch bankers, lawyers, tax lawyers, mergers and acquisitions specialists, and so on – with whom they work on a regular basis. Having the ability to carry out trading on behalf of their clients, wealth managers are thus most often paid through commissions taken from managing their clients' portfolios, like asset managers. In addition, they also advise clients on various matters related to their entire fortune. They can determine, together with clients, the level of risk they are willing to take on financial markets, assist them with the process of buying a secondary residence or even suggest that they take out a life insurance policy, for which they could then possibly negotiate the terms on their behalf. Wealth managers may also encourage clients to change their matrimonial property regime as well as make donations to their children. Together with a tax specialist, they can set up a complex arrangement to minimize the amount of tax to be paid. They can negotiate sales of artworks or visit vineyards on their client's behalf, should the client discover a passion for fine vintage wines. Lastly, some firms offer a "concierge service" that could take care of opening the villa or sort and process administrative documents. As shown in these examples, the scope of wealth management is potentially quite vast. Like many professional groups, wealth management is characterized as much by the diversity of its activities as by how the profession is practised. A self-employed wealth manager who goes from door to door and combs the Yellow Pages to make a bit of money here and there has, indeed, little in common with a "family officer" who works with clients worth 20 million euros at the very least.

An initial hypothesis was that advisers are first and foremost involved in building up their clients' capital. Asset management – arbitrage trading and asset allocation in the markets on their clients' behalf – would then be the main purpose of their work. Yet the survey reveals that their professional rhetoric focuses on clients' plans and secrets rather than on increasing capital. This rhetoric may come as a surprise. The following chapter deals with these internal divisions within the profession. It analyses the hierarchy of tasks associated with wealth management, and in particular the ambivalent role of asset management. The term *gestion de patrimoine*, translated as "wealth management", is unique to French, as it maintains ambiguity with regard to the work carried out by wealth managers. In contrast, the English terminology establishes a precise distinction between "financial planning", focusing on the client's overall estate plan, and "asset management", referring to financial products management. As a result of this rhetoric that emphasizes working with and guiding people rather than money management, wealth managers can present themselves to clients more as financial planners than as asset managers. An examination of attempts to monopolize certain activities relating to this rhetoric suggests that we should not confine ourselves to a description given in imprecise terms and which advisers appropriate to a greater or lesser degree depending on the relevant practices. In fact, these attempts also reflect an effort to exclude some professionals from the most highly thought-of consulting activities.

To present these results, this first section highlights the fact that the emergence of wealth management as a profession demonstrates the impossibility of establishing a stable boundary between itself and asset management (1). Second, we will show that, in this context, the use of a professional rhetoric that focuses on clients' plans gives advisers various advantages on the wealth management market (2). Lastly, we will study how this rhetoric has led to new intraprofessional inequalities (3).

Sources

Thanks to successive recommendations, 37 interviews were conducted with wealth managers who practised either as self-employed wealth managers (23), in the vast majority of cases after pursuing a career in a bank, or as part of a banking institution (14). The interviews focused on career paths as well as on the concrete activities that make up an adviser's day. Wealth managers treat confidentiality with the highest importance when it comes to meetings with clients (even interns are not allowed to attend). Therefore, despite numerous requests, it did not prove possible to observe these meetings. In addition, the monthly journal *Gestion de fortune* (*Wealth Management*), published between 1991 (the first issue) and 2014, has been investigated. With a circulation of 30,000, this journal, which was first aimed at a professional readership, explicitly focuses on wealth consulting, in contrast to more general journals or very specialized ones regularly read by wealth managers. The interviews and the many stories it publishes have enabled us to examine the conditions in which advisers work as well as how the profession is practised in the various spaces in which it takes place.

212 *Camille Herlin-Giret*

1 A fragile boundary between wealth and asset management

In the 1980s, several professionals with legal, tax and finance expertise tried to determine clear boundaries for what they called "wealth management" to distinguish it from asset management. However, these boundaries were weakened by the fact that it was impossible to close off this new market, and that financial tasks still played an essential role in wealth management.

From interpersonal skills to technical expertise: the rise of wealth management

In the 1980s, wealth management, usually called private banking at the time, was strictly focused on asset management and was quite relegated in banks. In spaces with much grander décor than agencies with store-fronts on the street, private bankers, setting themselves apart mainly through their close ties to the bourgeoisie, received clients whom the bank wished to nurture: "They were well brought up, well turned out, and, well, they knew how to talk", says a wealth manager who went into private banking in the 1970s. Another one, who has also worked in private banking for over 30 years, explains: "We didn't do any sort of wealth management, but we were very courteous to the Countess. And people who were there were perhaps not especially skilled, but they had great interpersonal skills."

Private banking was not highly thought of, but its image was given a boost in the second half of the 1980s with the arrival of professionals who possessed more technical expertise – legal and tax specifically – under a new title: wealth management. In particular, the development of new products promoted the recruitment of younger and more highly qualified professionals, and also resulted in internal training being given on questions of law. As early as 1973, Crédit Lyonnais instituted legal training programmes, run by lawyers, for employees in private management divisions who expressed interest in these issues. Following their training on the tax system, these professionals began to sell their customers various financial packages, tax-exempt products and even life insurance policies (an investment vehicle in which financial products may be held). Poor financial performance has led wealth managers to offer a wider range of products: real estate appeared to provide a way to diversify, and "the idea of making proposals which go beyond a simple portfolio" came to the fore (*Gestion de fortune*, No. 21, 1993). In addition to internal training, the first wealth management degrees were launched in the second half of the 1980s. Created in 1985 in a small provincial town by a wealth manager (the son of a lawyer with financial training), the first degree aimed at bringing law and finance together: "On one side you had banking specialists who sold their clients financial products without paying attention to the relevant aspects of family law, and on the other side you had lawyers who advised their clients on legal solutions which, if they were to be optimised, should have relied on financial solutions which the lawyers did not have the necessary expertise to provide", he explains in *Gestion de fortune* (No. 17, 1993).

Boundaries within wealth management 213

Moreover, the erosion of lending margins in the 1980s led banks to seek out new sources of profit. With the introduction of the Cooke ratio[2] in 1992, activities that did not require many of their own funds presented an attractive option for banks wanting to diversify their activities. Private banking activities, long viewed as not very profitable, thus saw renewed interest. Spurred on by bank executives, many "wealth management" divisions (distinct from asset management divisions) were created in the 1990s. This resulted in the development of an approach focusing on law and tax as well as the recruitment of new professionals. The chairman of a small Parisian private bank states in *Gestion de fortune* that "these two roles [wealth management and asset management] each fall within a particular area of expertise, which is why we have decided to separate them and create two distinct teams of professionals available to our clients" (*Gestion de fortune*, No. 20, 1993). According to the person in charge of creating a wealth management division at Crédit du Nord, "the transition from traditional asset management to wealth management, in the broad sense of the term, is still a goal that needs to be reached by the team. Because, while asset managers remain the primary contact for high-end clients, they will need to extend their areas of expertise to other operations concerning a client's entire estate" (*Gestion de fortune*, No. 6, 1992). The generation filling in wealth management divisions in the 1990s was made up of the first graduates in wealth management. Trained in law, tax and finance, these new advisers, who did not belong to the Parisian upper class, went through university rather than the French *grandes écoles* and entered into the profession with fewer interpersonal skills and more technical expertise.

The dialectic of sales and consulting

In the United States, financial planners, who only deal with wealth strategies, have managed to make their profession an organized one by requiring certification. In France, it is quite the reverse. Patchy regulations and the very limited success of certification – an essential support for the professional community trying to establish social closure of the market (Sarfatti, 1977) – show how weak the control of wealth management by the state is in France. This lack of regulation has led the various professionals who were interviewed to develop a specific discourse that aims to distinguish those providing "genuine" or "good" pieces of advice from the rest. Used to legitimize their activities, this discourse is particularly salient because of numerous cases of fraud that have come to light, such as the Madoff and Bettencourt scandals. This is why wealth managers, during interviews we have conducted, are generally more inclined to try to polish up their image. One way of distancing themselves from other advisers is to base the distinction between "good" and "bad" advisers on the difference between *sale* of financial products and *consulting* services. However, these two elements are often linked in practice, whether through remuneration or through the significant role of asset management activities. There are several ways in which a wealth manager can be paid: through commissions on sales or through fees, as is done in liberal professions. It is only when wealth managers pay themselves exclusively through fees – for *consulting* services and not for sales of financial products – that there is no longer a conflict of

214   *Camille Herlin-Giret*

interest. However, these cases are extremely rare. In interviews with self-employed wealth managers, cases where clients refused to pay fees came up fairly systematically. Those who have most expanded the model separating sales activities from consulting are professionals who imported the term "family office" from the United States. Under this title, they claim to provide high-end, tailor-made consulting services to clients worth at least 20 million euros. However, while additional fees are likely more frequent in these organizations, this is not always the case. A study published in 2009 and conducted together by Deloitte and the French Family Office Association (FFOA) shows that, among family offices, half are paid exclusively through fees, 29 per cent are paid on sales commissions alone, and finally, 21 per cent use a combination of both fees and sales commissions.

In other words, no matter where wealth management is practised or its type of customers, it seems difficult to create a clear distinction between consulting and sales, as, most of the time, wealth managers are remunerated through a combination of both fees and sales commissions. They still make most of their living from asset management, even though they insist on saying that they are primarily doing estate planning. In the highly selective market of clients for whom family offices compete, selling investments for hundreds of millions of euros, just as in the market handling small savings, clients suffer from uncertainty regarding the quality of the service provided. Thus, doubt does not only weigh on private bank or wealth management firms reputed to rely most heavily on trading. Marc, whose fortune is worth about 20 million euros, is a client at various private banks and has also met with self-employed wealth managers on several occasions. He insists on how difficult it is to meet "good" professionals: "Have you met a good one, one you would entrust with your money? Is there one of them who was good? As far as I am concerned, for the time being I haven't met a good one." Very wary regarding services offered, he explains that he is looking for someone who accepts payment exclusively through fees, as he believes he has not yet "come across truly independent people ... because all wealth management firms receive products from their clients which they sell and manage".

The lack of external boundaries within the wealth management market, the combination of asset management and consulting tasks, as well as payments through commissions, do not allow wealth managers to exclude asset managers from trade opportunities. One of the methods used to increase the standing of consulting activities is to adopt a new role that focuses mainly on managing people rather than managing money.

2 Cultivate plans and secrets

Activities solely related to consulting and sales of financial products do not allow wealth managers to set themselves apart from the image of asset managers, which is focused on selling financial products. They regularly try to transform their role by making wealth management projects and clients' secrets the main elements of their work, rather than their portfolio results. This rather unique situation gives wealth managers competitiveness and symbolic advantages.

Wealth planning is paramount

Wealth planning rhetoric relies on a change of situation: wealth managers do not explain to clients how to gain more money, but ask them what they want to gain. Afterwards, they attempt to give meaning to wealth growth rather than being actively involved in the process. In doing so, wealth managers intend to help the execution of wealth planning, from the conception of the plan to its completion. Debbie, self-employed, who went into wealth management after pursuing a career in asset management, tells us "[she] works by making plans". She also systematically asks clients what their goal is: a question that could not be asked in a world where only profit maximization matters. Reluctant to focus on short-term calculations (such as making a certain kind of investment to get a tax exemption), she values long-term thinking, which focuses on investing "for yourself". According to this rhetoric, professionals "should help clients think about the meaning they would like their wealth to have", as one explains in *Gestion de fortune* (No. 141, 2004). It is, thus, directly opposite to the logic of straightforward personal gain. As Finn, a self-employed wealth manager who spent many years in private banking, describes:

> We don't make donations to our children because we wake up one morning and say to ourselves: "There's a tax-saving of 50 per cent on gift tax, I'll make a donation to my children." That's not how we do things. It's stupid and there's no sense of doing it unless it fits into a strategy. And this strategy must be in line with your situation and your particular case.

The three critical elements that characterize wealth planning rhetoric arise here: a specific connection to time, since an adviser must ask and help the client to plan for the future; an inherently conservative dimension, as carrying out plans involves maintaining capital, which is not in contradiction with certain methods of donating or transferring capital (Harrington, 2009); and above all, the necessity of giving meaning to what is planned; in other words, to set goals.

By appealing to the idea of a plan, wealth managers encourage clients to attach precise meanings to specific amounts of money, what V. Zelizer (1992) called to "mark" money. Clients must then claim ownership of cash flows, often arriving suddenly (sales of securities, stock options, inheritance, donations, etc.). Wealth planning rhetoric encourages viewing money as less neutral, marking it so that clients can decide what wealth means to them. Clients' emotional attachment to items they own is viewed here as an essential and positive element of their relationship to money. It must be given as much attention by wealth managers as the effective management of fortunes. Niels, a freelance wealth manager who also first worked in private banking, now advises executives during the process of selling their companies. His method involves a complete immersion in families' lives ("I sleep in their houses, I eat with them, I live with them"). His goal is to find out how money is embedded in family relationships, as well as whether there is any tension surrounding it. In doing so, the idea is to find "the rules of the game, the

216   *Camille Herlin-Giret*

necessary conditions for it to be passed on, and the problems that you are going to have to solve". Niels attempts to supervise and alter how money is embedded in their lives: "I accompany them in these various ways, in order to determine the rules to live by."

The setting and decor must already suggest to clients that their stories and plans are the focus of the interaction, not only the management of their assets. Meetings often take place at the client's home and computer work is done "backstage"[3] (Goffman, 1973) rather than in front of them. In private banking offices, decorative items are chosen to make clients feel at home so that they will unveil their secrets. At HSBC, new offices were created according to the model of airline "lounges" so that banks could receive "their favourite clients over a cup of coffee, sitting comfortably on soft sofas, with subdued lighting" (*Gestion de fortune*, No. 156, 2006). Recently, one of the trends has been to create bank agencies dedicated only to wealth management clients and modelled on apartments to "prioritise the intimacy of the relationships insofar as wealth management requires sharing highly personal information" (*Gestion de fortune*, No. 174, 2007). At Barclays, the idea was to create a "'club' atmosphere, in a friendly yet modern environment", whereas Crédit Lyonnais praises the elegance and "high-standing" of its elegant new premises, but "without ostentatious display of luxury" (ibid.). Clients must "feel that they are wealth managers' equal. That is why the latter receive them in a friendlier and warmer setting like a reception room, rather than in their office" (*Gestion de fortune*, No. 185, 2008). We recognize here some common features with the luxury world in terms of service relationships. R. Sherman (2007), who has conducted ethnographic research in several luxury hotels, highlights how interactions between clients and staff rely on an implied norm of reciprocity, confidentiality and discretion. The dialogue between the two parties also needs to appear spontaneous, like a conversation between equals.

Maintain position and standing: competitive advantages of a wealth planning rhetoric

The changeover from a straightforward wealth maximization logic to a wealth planning one provides wealth managers with some competitive advantages. First of all, as capital gains on financial markets are no longer profitable as in the 1990s, this new role endorsed by wealth managers and based on wealth planning allows them to focus on interacting with clients about their stories and expectations rather than the unsatisfactory performance of their portfolios. Second, wealth-planning logic gives wealth managers a key role. Indeed, they are in charge of shaping and creating a long-term strategy, putting sale of financial products in the background. Time dedicated to developing the strategy is precisely described as the most interesting part of wealth managers' work. Elvis, who manages the wealth management department of a private bank, explains:

> Once the business has been sold, we become financial specialists and manage the assets. But meanwhile, a year and a half, maybe two years, will go

by. This is what makes it an interesting profession. In my opinion, that phase is the one I find very, very interesting, because you finally get to the very heart of the issue. It is a key moment in the CEO [chief executive officer]'s life – they may start out with a new project, or not. There is also a whole family issue, like the protection of family members. Finally, all of these issues abruptly come into play during the sale process.

Lastly, this new mediator role allows wealth managers to be on the centre stage among other financial experts and clients. In a context of increasing division of labour among wealth management departments, especially with the creation of asset-engineering teams made up of experts of all kinds, wealth managers find themselves in both a precarious and an advantageous position; advantageous, since they still remain the "conductors" and main coordinators, as is often mentioned in interviews. Wealth managers hold a key position as the main interlocutors between clients and other experts who, behind the scenes, help implement the strategies they developed in the first place. In other words, they are *structurally autonomous*[4] (Burt, 1992) and prove their usefulness to clients by connecting them with various experts.[5] However, their position is also precarious. If wealth managers do not maintain a certain level of expertise, there is a chance clients could contact other specialists directly.

The detachment from the financial aspect of wealth management to focus on exploring clients' privacy leads to an unusual hierarchy of tasks. In medicine, according to Abbott (1981), professional "purity" depends on the ability to deal with problems from which the human complexities can be removed. Conversely, in wealth management, activities involving more technical skills are quite low-valued, whereas relationships with clients appear to be a standard of professional purity. In trading, "mathematics have historically played a substantial role in legitimating the profession" (Godechot, 2001, p. 195). Even though mathematics is less used in practice today, it remains a highly valued professional skill. In the wealth management world, financial, legal and tax expertise have also contributed to the legitimation of this profession, which was poorly thought of until the 1990s. However, these skills are now overlooked, since they are too closely related to sale of financial products. Nowadays, managing clients' privacy and goals has become favoured over asset management. Nevertheless, not every wealth manager has the ability to hold off or disregard money management. Therefore, we will now explain how the use of a wealth-planning rhetoric fluctuates depending on the kind of firm offering wealth management services and with gender norms. As described below, wealth-planning rhetoric is also discriminatory.

3 Exclusionary rhetoric

Attempts to endorse a wealth-planning rhetoric and to monopolize highly valued activities appear through career turning points,[6] through the division of labour among wealth management departments and through jurisdictional claims[7] (Abbott, 1988). Let's explore the last two points by first analysing the creation of

218 *Camille Herlin-Giret*

a family offices association in the 2000s and then studying the gender division of labour in wealth management firms.

"Families, I manage you"[8]: the French family office association

Founded in 2001, the French Family Office Association (FFOA) – which counts about 100 members today – particularly attempts to further monopolize activities and territories related to a wealth-planning rhetoric. In a study written in 2009 by Deloitte at the request of FFOA, three bases of the profession are defined: "strategic advice", referring to the elaboration of long-term strategy; "operational advice", the technical part of the job, which includes asset management and implementation of plans; finally, "lifestyle and family values" in regard to clients' privacy. Solving potential family conflicts, training new generations and mapping out uses of money make up the various aspects that should be offered by every family office in terms of privacy management. The emphasis on aligning and preserving family interests, as well as managing people rather than managing money, shows how this definition of family office is fully in line with the wealth-planning rhetoric mentioned above.

The creation of an association enables the use of the term "family office" to be regulated. Its importation may have, indeed, generated a risk for "the term 'family office' to be overused in a shallow or uncontrolled way and by a whole kind of different firms, that do not necessarily belong to the true profession" (Camblain, 2008: 198). By being in charge of regulating the profession, the association claims to have become a prerequisite to ensure the quality of services that family offices should be offering.[9] The right to join the association is subject to strict standards. Especially, the family officer has to be paid mostly through fees (at least 70 per cent of their income) and offer the three previously introduced services. For example, FFOA has twice denied membership to Jack, who runs a company whose name includes the term "family office": first, because his firm does not offer a family governance service; second, due to the fact that Jack is paid mostly through sales commissions. Conversely, Derek's is one of the first "family offices" to be accepted into the FFOA. After his graduation from a famous business school, he worked in various private banks and, a few years later, launched his own family office. Derek explains:

> When people say "we are a family office" while they only manage portfolios, I tell them: "No, I'm sorry, asset management is a very nice job but you cannot use the term 'family office'. What you do is different from what a family office does." … Managing portfolios for millionaires or billionaires does not make you a family officer. Family office is not asset management, it's completely different.

However, FFOA's ability to exclude other professionals from activities related to family office does not only rest on rules defined by the association. It is also based on client segmentation. In doing so, the association excludes wealth managers, who, however, claim to have the same professional ethic, by preventing them from being called "family offices", as their clients are more modest than family offices' clients. The significant role of family governance, as well as long-term wealth strategy (vs. technical and operational activities), can also be seen as an elite strategy, based on differences between "upscale" clients who can afford an expensive family office and "wealthy" clients who, implicitly, could only pretend to asset management. The connection between valued activities and a specific group of clients has already been studied (Hughes, 1962, Boussard *et al.*, 2006). This feature appears here through the strong link between a specific kind of client who can afford a family office and what is most valued by FFOA members; namely, the idea of managing people rather than money.

Finally, FFOA may be described as an elitist association on three levels. First, members are required to follow standards defined by the association. Second, only the wealthiest clients can afford family offices' services. In addition to these, we should emphasize that most FFOA members belong to the upper class and often look like their clients. The current FFOA chair is a shareholder of a family business listed among the "top 500" ranking of French fortunes, published every year in *Challenges*. In other words, he is as wealthy as his clients. The founder of the FFOA went to one of the most prestigious business schools in France. He describes that "there was no culture shock between him and his clients" and also explains that his ties to an aristocratic family helped him set up his own family office. Several members are listed in the selective *Who's Who*. This is the case of J. Barré, native of Neuilly, graduate in business law, who, after being a legal and tax lawyer for various corporate companies, turned to wealth management. He is a member of the "HEC entrepreneurs" panel, the FFOA, the French Capital Investors Association and the American Bar Association. He also teaches at Paris-Dauphine University, Paris-Descartes University and the Paris Business School as well as regularly writing articles for *Agefi, Option Finance, Gestion de fortune* and *Le Figaro* (*Who's Who*, 2014). These professionals, more so than other wealth managers, have de facto a large *social reach* (Boltanski, 1973: 9).

When family governance becomes a masculine skill

The first generation of wealth advisers was mostly made up of men, but this is no longer the case. Comparing sex ratios in Master's courses on "Wealth Management" and "Portfolio Management", S. Mignot-Gérard *et al.* (2017) stress that degrees in finance have mostly remained male, while female students are more likely to study wealth management (women make up 46 per cent of wealth management students and 24 per cent of students in asset management). However, women's entry into wealth management firms has also manifested itself through a gender division of labour within firms. Women are assigned to technical tasks, less valued, leaving to men the prestigious role of listening to clients' secrets. This is quite surprising, since the gender division of labour, based on a skill assignment (Bourdieu, 1984a), would, rather, assign men to financial expertise and women to privacy.[10] Such a gender division would thus promote women's access to the most

220   *Camille Herlin-Giret*

valued activities of wealth management. However, women are often in charge of the operational part of the job.

As for women graduating from engineering school, the first women who got to work in wealth management were actually more qualified than their male colleagues, according to a study by C. Marry (2004). Analysing biographical interviews she conducted with women pursuing a career in finance, V. Boussard (2016) underlines the fact that their stories have always been focused on professional events rather than those of family life. The same pattern applies to women working in wealth management, who are mainly recognized by their expertise. For example, here is how this woman working as a wealth manager is featured:[11]

> L. K. exemplifies the success that only a good specialist can have in this position. This elegant brunette, mother of three children, has completed a Master in Business Law and Tax from Paris II and reached the top of the hierarchy when she was only 40 years old. After a career as a wealth engineer, she became "senior adviser". Her success is especially based on her experience in mergers and acquisitions.

This feature also appears in the team presentation of a firm made up of five "senior advisers", including a woman. While the latter is presented with an emphasis on her degrees and her professional career, her colleagues are featured with a set of elements related to their private lives: passions, family life, regional ties or personality traits. Skills commonly associated with feminine or masculine are thus inverted, describing men with horseback riding or family philanthropy and women with "expertise in market strategy".[12]

Gil belongs to the first generation of wealth managers. After a career in a private bank, he set up his own firm. Explaining the implied rules of a good match between a client and a wealth manager, he tells me: "it's got to be the right person for the job. ... You will not similarly approach a luxury goods entrepreneur, and one who sells excavators." The following anecdote deals with an "old ambassador" meeting "a young and extremely brilliant manager, fantastic, widely qualified". The client wanted to switch managers, telling Gil: "I will not tell my stories to a thirty years old girl." Mike, a freelance wealth manager, now works with his "highly educated", "extremely qualified" daughter. Yet he explains:

> When we are in front of a client, my daughter and me, he spontaneously turns to me when asking questions. However, since she is highly technically qualified, once we broke the ice, as he knows he cannot always ask the boss and also that my daughter is completely legitimate, he may discuss his many activities with her. But she will not naturally and easily impose herself to the client.

Older men with "experience", as Mike said, are here opposed to highly educated and "brilliant" young women. The latter are considered less legitimate to listen to clients' stories than men, as if there were a statutory incompatibility between their

Boundaries within wealth management 221

sex and age, on the one hand, and their ability to ply the trade of wealth management, on the other hand (Hughes, 1945).

In the end, despite the reversal of gender norms, we identify the usual gender division of labour. Highly valued activities are performed by men, whereas less valued ones are done by women. Indeed, the latter have had to reach out to assert themselves due to their degrees and expertise.

Conclusion

During the 1990s, wealth management progressively differentiated itself from asset management. However, the difference between these two areas of expertise remained difficult to establish. Embracing a rhetoric that focuses on clients' plans and secrets rather than asset management, wealth managers are bringing forth a new image of their role. This provides insight into powerful speech pushing money management into the background. Financial activities are being symbolically depreciated, even though they can never be delegated, since they represent the most common and efficient way of getting paid. This depreciation provides wealth managers with symbolic and competitive profits. To avoid dealing with clients' discontent and preventing other financial experts from taking their clients, wealth managers focus meetings on clients' privacy instead of portfolio results. However, not all wealth managers succeed in pushing wealth growth issues to the background. Those who have entered the highly selective FFOA not only deal with the wealthiest clients, but also attempt to monopolize highly valued activities. Other professionals dealing with less wealthy clients are then excluded, even though they claim to have the same professional ethic. This attempt also manifests itself regarding the gender division of labour among wealth management firms, leaving men the privilege of building a relationship with clients, whereas women are assigned to less valued activities, particularly technical ones, which allow them to enter the profession.

Notes

1 While many studies focus on institutions that govern the budgetary practices of the working class (especially Zelizer, 1985, Perrin-Heredia, 2013, Plot, 2013), little research deals with professionals managing the money of the wealthy, apart from G. Marcus (1983) and B. Harrington (2009)'s studies of trustees. A *trust* is a contractual relationship, which differentiates the possession and the use of goods. The *trustee* owns a capital he cannot use and provides income streams to a beneficiary.
2 The first Basel Accord (Basel I) was completed in 1988. It sets minimum capital standards for banks in order to prevent them from building business volume without adequate capital backing. This ratio has been called the *Cooke ratio*.
3 E. Goffman defines this as "a place, relative to a given performance, where the impression fostered by the performance is knowingly contradicted as a matter of course" (p. 110).
4 If A knows B and C, their contacts are non-redundant if B and C do not know each other or do not know the same people (except A). According to R. Burt, the lack of relationship between B and C provides A with various network opportunities.

222   *Camille Herlin-Giret*

5 Self-employed wealth managers may use the mediator role in two ways: they are able to connect clients with a large experts' network and also to negotiate on their behalf with banks, asset management companies or insurance companies.

6 For example, after a brief period of work in a sales-oriented wealth management firm, this wealth manager set up his own business, focusing on coaching CEOs during their business selling process. He does not take charge of the entire activities related to money management but supervises "the period of both loss of power and enrichment".

7 *Juridictional claims* is the term for group attempts to control territories of activities. These claims pursue the stabilization of the link between skill sets and a new title defining the group.

8 Excerpt of an interview found in a survey on family offices in *Gestion de fortune* (No. 168, 2007).

9 A charter, written by association members in 2009, documents the whole ethical rules related to the family office (*Gestion de fortune*, No. 200, 2010). The FFOA also publishes books on family offices (Camblain, 2008; Evangelista, 2010) and has several times been mentioned in the press.

10 The *breadwinner* model (Daune-Richard, Devreux, 1992, Crompton, 1999) reports on the association between men and technical aspects on one side, and women and family on the other side.

11 S. Florentin, "Le coach du patrimoine", *Le Point*, 16 December 2004.

12 Overview of a family office team found on its website.

13 The duality of the LBO field

Fabien Foureault

The process of financialization has been the subject of numerous research projects in recent years, with a number of these discussing the strategy changes of large companies that reorient their approach towards "maximizing shareholder value" (Fligstein and Shin, 2007; Davis, 2009). These studies show in particular that the wave of mergers and hostile takeovers during the 1980s played a catalytic role in the shift from managerial capitalism to shareholder capitalism (Davis and Stout, 1992; Stearns and Allan, 1996; Fligstein, 2001, chap. 7). A number of these deals have been carried out using a technique known as the leveraged buyout (LBO).

An LBO is a corporate acquisition technique with debt. LBOs occur when investors purchase a target company using a combination of debt and equity and attempt to improve its profitability before selling it again after three-to-five years. The investors who carry out this type of deal belong to the *private equity* (PE) sector, which seeks to finance non-listed companies. LBOs ultimately result in the relocation of the property and control rights of companies, making them particular cases of merger and acquisition deals. After their emergence during the 1960s in the United States, LBOs began to spread across Europe and throughout the world in the 1980s and experienced a boom in the 2000s. According to American economists and sociologists, LBOs play the role of a *change agent* of capitalism: they enable entire sectors and countries to restructure themselves (Jensen, 1989; Davis *et al.*, 2014), and facilitate the diffusion of a new economic rationale inspired in particular by agency theory (Dobbin and Jung, 2010).

France has not been an exception to this phenomenon, in spite of its peculiar economic model, which is supposed to be particularly hostile towards such practices (Coriat, 2008). The existence and extraordinary growth of LBOs in France is thus paradoxical because it is a priori improbable. To shed light on this paradox, this chapter will study the *agents of change*, namely, the main actors involved in the financialization of French companies, using the LBO field as an example.

The completion of these deals does not solely involve investors, but also top managers of companies, who themselves become investors, and bankers, who are actively involved in the setting up and monitoring of the deal. These deals can therefore be considered as a three-way game. The use of this technique by these three types of actor forms what we call the *LBO field*. This chapter analyses the LBO field at the organizational level, that is, as an "organizational field"

224 *Fabien Foureault*

(DiMaggio and Powell, 1983), focusing on three types of organization: target companies, private equity firms and banks. It is based on the analysis of quantitative data on most deals that were carried out in France in the boom period from 2001 to 2007. The structure of the field is determined by analysing data on market concentration and proximity between actors.

Analysing financial professions through the organizational field is relevant, because organizations provide the daily context in which individuals evolve. Yet, these organizations are far from being homogeneous. The functioning of these organizations as well as their outcomes can therefore not be fully understood without considering their position within the field (Bourdieu, 1999: 3–4). Organizations are also important to analyse financiers *qua* professionals, because they determine the needed skills, set professional standards, influence careers and dictate compensation policies.

This chapter argues that the LBO field is dual in nature. It identifies two main groups of organizations: organizations that belong to "large-scale capitalism" and organizations that belong to "small-scale capitalism". Since organizations structure careers, this dual morphology should also be reflected at the individual level. Indeed, the organizational field seems to formalize two distinct valuation pathways of professional skills: one that operates on a worldwide scale and the other on a local scale. This structural analysis of the LBO field sheds light on the financialization of the French economy. According to our data, this process appears to be far-reaching, as it affects the world of small and local businesses. However, the process is also ambivalent: the same financial technique (in this case the LBO) is interpreted and adapted quite differently according to the actors that use it.

After the LBO field and the actors that comprise it have been sketched (I), its social structure will be described by analysing its vertical and horizontal differentiation at the organizational level (II). The structure of the field at the individual level will also be outlined by reviewing several professional career paths (III).

I Generating the LBO field

In a very broad sense, the LBO field is made up of all of the actors who contribute to the existence and development of this technique: not only investors, but also other actors such as the Ministry of Finance, experts or trade unions. This extensive conceptualization of the LBO field is appealing, as the maximum number of actors would be included, giving the impression of "all-inclusiveness". However, it would be hard to use this definition empirically, in particular with a quantitative methodology, and it would run the risk of regressing towards infinity when selecting the relevant actors. Instead, the choice was to consider the Ministry of Finance, experts or trade unions (for example) as being part of the "environment". If, on the other hand, the LBO is defined as a transaction on the market for mergers and acquisitions, then the LBO field should be composed of all the actors who participate in the deal, both on the sell side (shareholders of the target company) and on the buy side, including the numerous third parties: accounting experts, business lawyers, strategy consulting firms and so on (Boussard, 2015).

The duality of the LBO field 225

A three-way game

Here, the LBO field is defined in a more restrictive sense, since for us, the LBO is an "organizational weapon" (Selznick, 1960). This weapon is used by a new segment of the economic elite ("investors") to transform companies into value-producing machines. As part of this strategy, they mobilize bankers, who provide them with debt. The use of debt helps them increase their purchasing power and magnify return on equity. This is known as "leverage". Debt is repaid using the free cash-flow of the target company. We know from anthropologists – from Marcel Mauss to David Graeber – that debt is not only a resource for financing; it is also a *relationship of power* (Graeber, 2012; Mauss, 2012). In the context of the LBO, the top managers of the target company are forced to generate cash for the company to meet its terms of repayment. In this way, they are directly working for the objectives of the investors. They are working in the shareholders' interests more directly because investors make them invest in the deal. Managers are thus transformed into shareholders. The interests of the two parties being aligned, the organizational weapon of the LBO is supposed to end the problem of "the separation of ownership and control", characteristic of managerial capitalism (Jensen, 1989). Investors and top managers are linked to bankers by the promise of repayment, but bankers are not completely free. If they are not correctly diversified and the company is going sour, they are stuck with an investment that is going to end in a loss. In this game, the three players have their hands voluntarily tied to each other. They have no choice but to comply with the high profitability expectation by streamlining the target company.[1]

LBOs are therefore a three-way game between bankers, investors and top managers, who are all implicated to varying degrees in the structuring and monitoring of the deal. In the following analyses, the LBO field has been restricted to this nucleus of actors, because they have a direct and long-lasting interest in the successful outcome of the deal. We will now briefly describe these three categories of actors.[2] The *bankers* who are involved in LBO deals typically belong to departments specializing in leveraged finance. The sales representatives of these departments are in contact with the structured finance department of the bank, as the loan can often be securitized. Offers sent from these sales representatives to private equity firms are regulated by the bank's loan committee. The *top managers* are the founders or inheritors of the company to be handed over, or they may be the executives of a subsidiary whose parent company wants to disinvest. Target companies are therefore extremely varied in terms of size, age and sector. The thing in common is that they have to generate important and recurrent cash-flows, which are necessary for the repayment of the debt. The average French company that undergoes an LBO is of medium size, from the industrial or distribution sector, based in Paris and operating in a niche market (Foureault, 2014: 62–64). *Investors* are asset managers working in small organizations called investments funds or private equity firms. They are responsible for buying, monitoring and selling the companies that they finance. More often than not, these investors raise money from external institutional investors (pension funds, banks, insurance companies,

226 *Fabien Foureault*

wealthy families) by promising them a minimum level of return. Once this target has been achieved, it is possible for them to receive 20% of the realized gain from the deal, because they own 2% of the private equity fund as "general partners": this is the partnership model. The partners in turn employ investment managers and analysts below them.

Formalizing the field

Now that the relevant actors are delineated, how can the idea of the "LBO field" be operationalized? In France, the notion of "field" is associated with the idea of "field of struggle" and was developed by Pierre Bourdieu (Bourdieu, 1992 in particular; see *Actes de la Recherche en Sciences Sociales*, 2013). The preferred method of Bourdieu and his followers for describing a field is multiple correspondence analysis. The Bourdieusian perspective has regularly been criticized on the grounds that individuals appear "over-socialized" (cf. Wrong, 1961). In theory and in method, individuals (agents) are grouped together according to their common attributes (capital), which they have acquired in their life-course through the process of socialization.

A different perspective puts more emphasis on the actual *relationships* that the actors have with each other and conceptualizes the field as an "action field". For example, Friedberg analyses the social order as a multiplicity of local orders that are structured around relationships of mutual dependence between strategic actors (Friedberg, 1993). For Lazega, the appropriate quantitative method for analysing these systems of interdependence is social network analysis (Lazega, 1994). The data needed for the modelling proposed by Lazega is, however, not at our disposal. Furthermore, the actors are so closely tied to one another in any given deal that it is easier to consider them as linked to the deal itself rather than to one another.

Here, the approach is to formalize an "institutional field", particularly an "organizational field". DiMaggio and Powell define the organizational field as a "recognized area" involving organizations that produce "similar products or services" (1983: 148). Their definition is broader than a definition that would only include organizations in direct interaction or in competition with one another. The criterion used here satisfies this extensive requirement: the organizational field is the set of organizations that participate in the same deals. Following our conception of deals as a three-way game, organizations are restricted to target companies, private equity firms and banks (see Box 13.1).

Box 13.1: Sources

The data comes from professional publications. A total of 1428 LBO deals were listed over the period from 2000 to 2010 by reading *Capital Finance*, a publication created in 1988 to distribute information within the profession in France. It is considered by the actors to be a good source. The sampling method for actors is self-selection through participation in events; as commonly used in social movement studies Biographical information on the individuals was collected using Factiva, a newspaper database. Sources include the following publications: *le Guide des états-majors des grandes sociétés*, AGEFI biographies and *Who's Who in France*. Information was also researched on websites as well as LinkedIn and Viadeo.

To formalize the LBO field defined above, an affiliation network can be constructed in which actors are linked to events. Over the period from 2001 to 2007, 1717 organizations were involved in 943 LBO deals. The procedure set out by Ronald Breiger was followed to create a co-affiliation matrix, in which the cells count the number of events in which the actors have jointly participated (Breiger, 1974). The analysis of co-affiliation matrices has specific problems of interpretation when actors have highly unequal participation rates (Borgatti and Halgin, 2011; Wasserman and Faust, 1994, chap. 8). The participation rate, however, has no significant influence on the calculation of geodesic distances. Analysing geodesic distances highlights the structure of the field independent of the actors' attributes. Multi-dimensional scaling (MDS) is realized on the main component of the co-affiliation matrix, which counts 1184 organizations. This type of analysis, which has a purely descriptive purpose, was used in particular by Laumann and Knoke as well as Padgett (Laumann and Knoke, 1987; Padgett, 2012).

This conceptualization, in which actors are primarily linked to events and not to one another, is similar to theories from authors as different as Schütz, for whom the most basic form of coordination is the joint attention to events;[3] Feld, who holds that individuals develop relations when they participate in the same activity (focus) (Feld, 1981); and Coleman, for whom an actor has power insofar as he or she controls an event in which he or she has an interest (Coleman, 1990: 134). The field is therefore a loose set of actors linked to one another by their participation in the same events in which they have an interest. This analysis thus helps to represent *constellations of interests* that result from the chaining of LBO deals (Scott, 1990).

II Large-scale and small-scale capitalism

The different analyses carried out show that the LBO field is highly stratified: target companies are relatively marginalized, while a small number of banks dominate the market. Private equity firms are in an intermediate position. Moreover, the LBO field is divided into two moieties (rival yet complementary groups), which reflect differences in terms of size and geographical scale, between large-scale capitalism and small-scale capitalism.

Stratification

According to the data gathered, there were around one hundred banks active within the LBO field, several hundred private equity firms and several thousand companies in France in the 2000s. These estimations are in line with those of the French Association of Investors in Capital (AFIC), which represents private equity firms in France, despite some small variations due to the perimeters used for counting.

At a first glance, the market seems very fragmented, as the organization that boasts the largest market share in volume (BNP Paribas) holds only 4% of the market. The Royal Bank of Scotland, which has the highest market share in terms of value, has only 5% of the market. However, if the distribution of these two quantities is examined, a high level of stratification is apparent: 32% of the actors (387 organizations) make up 80% of the market volume, whereas only 11% of the actors (78 organizations) make up 80% of the market value. These organizations dominating the market, here meaning benefiting from an advantageous position due to the asymmetrical distribution of resources (Chazel, 1983). While no one individual actor dominates the market, as may be the case in monopolistic situations, a small group of actors *collectively* dominate the market.[4]

Figure 13.1 shows that market domination is a complex phenomenon: some organizations instigate a large number of highly valued deals, while others carry out a small number of deals that can be of either high or low value.

For ease of interpretation, nine typical organizations have been represented: five banks (BNP Paribas, Euromezzanine, Cial, Goldman Sachs), three private

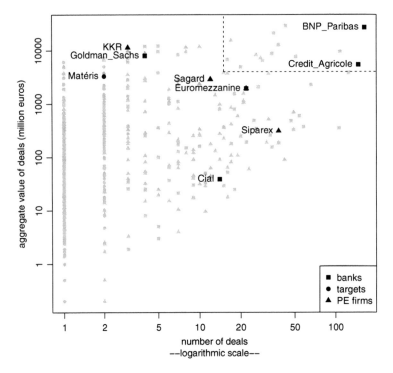

Figure 13.1 Relationship between market volume and market value ($n = 709$).

equity firms (Siparex, Sagard, KKR) and one target company (Matéris). Three observations can be drawn from this diagram. First, three groups of actors are differentiated in terms of strategy. A first group of actors carries out a small number of small deals (Cial, Siparex); a second group also carries out a small number of deals, which are, however, large in size (KKR, Goldman Sachs); a third group of actors can be distinguished by the large number of very high-value deals (BNP Paribas, Crédit Agricole). Second, the target companies appear to be marginalized, as they are involved in only one deal on average (two for the company Matéris represented here). Third, there is a small number of organizations that participate in a large number of very high-value deals, such as BNP Paribas, Crédit Agricole, Axa PE or even the Caisse des Dépôts et des Consignations (Deposits and Consignments Fund). These organizations are actors that are present in most, if not all, market segments. More generally, actors situated in the upper right section of the diagram are those that dominate the LBO field, as defined above.

Actors situated within the dotted rectangle are those that are included in the list of actors in the top 50% market share in terms of both volume and value. Two observations can be made when examining this list. First of all, the majority of these actors are of French nationality, even if a significant number of them come from England. By contrast, none of them are American, which may come as a surprise to the reader given the fact that American private equity firms such as KKR, TPG and Blackstone, as well as American investment banks such as Goldman Sachs, Merrill Lynch and Morgan Stanley, dominate the global LBO market. It is true that these organizations are richer overall than the actors on the list and that some of the deals that they have put together rank among the largest in France, such as the LBO on "Pages Jaunes", a telephone directory provider. However, the superiority of an actor at a local level cannot be inferred from its superiority at a worldwide level. Just like smaller domestic actors, these American organizations are, rather, "challengers", in the sense of Fligstein and McAdam (2012). This status of challenger is indicated by their more recent presence on French territory and by the smaller number of deals that they have carried out there. Counter-examples are Barclays PE and Royal Bank of Scotland, which, despite being non-French organizations, have become heavily integrated into the French LBO market. Barclays PE, for instance, has received several industry awards from the profession, is centrally positioned in the exchange networks and is a prominent member of AFIC,[5] which is not the case for KKR, despite the fact that it has a lot more resources. A second observation drawn from this diagram is that a lot of these actors are well-known French "universal" banks, such as BNP Paribas and Crédit Agricole. Euromezzanine is a fund of French origin, which provides "mezzanine capital", financial instruments hybrids between debt and equity. But the role of the mezzanine provider is close to that of a banker; Euromezzanine was indeed launched in 1991 by a number of large national banks, such as BNP Paribas and Crédit National (which later became Natixis). The private equity firms that are most highly integrated into the French LBO market – in the sense as stated several lines previously – such as Axa PE, Astorg Partners and Barclays PE, were all formed by global financial institutions, in this case AXA, the financial company

Suez and Barclays, respectively. These two observations show that it is these financial institutions, and in particular banks, that are situated at the highest level of the field's stratification system. This contradicts to a certain extent a common representation of LBOs and financial capitalism in France, which perceives them to be a new, exogenous and American force, sweeping in to destroy the French economic model.

Segmentation

MDS of geodesic distances in the co-participation matrix shows how the field is horizontally differentiated (segmentation). As John Padgett explains, this boils down to looking at social structure "from above" and not "from the side", as in the previous section. Figure 13.2 displays the two main dimensions of the MDS.

This figure represents the constellations of interests in the French LBO field in the 2000s. To illustrate significant oppositions, the names of typical organizations have been highlighted (the same as those in Figure 13.1). "Typical" should here be understood in the qualitative sense of shared salient traits and not in the quantitative sense of a modal or average frequency. In contrast to the previous analysis, the field is not structured according to the type of organization: target companies,

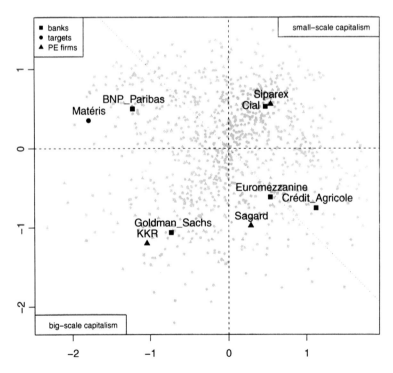

Figure 13.2 Multidimensional scaling (MDS) on geodesic distances in the affiliation network ($n = 1184$).

The duality of the LBO field   231

private equity firms and banks are distributed relatively uniformly across social space. However, it is apparent that the diagram is structured according to a main diagonal, which goes from the bottom left hand corner to the top right hand corner: actors are distributed along this line according to their size, the geographical scale in which they operate and the market segments in which they are present. A second diagonal, more difficult to interpret visually, seems to distribute the actors who are at the same level according to the first line of differentiation, according to their degree of competition: collaborators are close together, whereas competitors are further apart. This second diagonal seems in particular to be structured by two constellations of interests, one centred around BNP Paribas and the other around Crédit Agricole.

At the bottom left are Goldman Sachs and Kolberg Kravis & Roberts (KKR), in contrast to Siparex and Crédit Industriel d'Alsace Lorraine (Cial), situated at the top right: two American actors that both have international presence and considerable financial power (KKR having seven billion euros in assets under management in 2007), in contrast to smaller French actors (Siparex having only 900 million euros). Neither their legal statute nor their age distinguishes them from one another (the two banks were founded in the 19th century, whereas the two private equity firms were created in the 1970s). While the two private equity firms are today located in the most upmarket district of Paris (8th arrondissement), Siparex was started up in the regions (Lyon, where it still has a base). KKR is a symbol of the *gaga 80s* and is headquartered in New York.[6] It was installed on French territory in 2005. Siparex has many regional offices in France (Lille, Nantes, Besançon) and is expanding to North Africa, whereas KKR has offices in Hong Kong and Tokyo. Furthermore, their strategies are also disparate: KKR is a specialist in large company deals, whether they be listed companies or subsidiaries of business groups, while Siparex tends to deal with small or medium-sized companies that are often family businesses and/or in the process of expanding. While KKR is fundamentally activist in nature, taking majority positions, sitting on the board of directors and pushing for restructuring (notably via its consulting subsidiary Capstone), Siparex is less activist, taking both majority and minority positions and cultivating "trust" relationships with top managers, notably via the "Club Siparex", which offers conferences and factory visits.

At the top left are BNP Paribas and Matéris; at the bottom right are Sagard, Euromezzanine and Crédit Agricole. It is unnecessary to focus on BNP Paribas, one of the largest "universal banks", which was born out of the merger in 2000 of the depository bank Banque Nationale de Paris and the investment bank Paribas. It is likewise unnecessary to focus on the case of Crédit Agricole, which is also one of the largest French banks, but which, unlike BNP Paribas, is a decentralized organization composed of a network of regional branches. We have already considered the case of Euromezzanine. Matéris is a former division of Lafarge (its specialty products division) with a turnover of 15 billion euros in 2006. In 2000, three Anglo-Saxon private equity funds (CVC, Advent and Carlyle) bought it out by partnering with its director of strategy, Olivier Legrain. Probably due to its good profile in terms of cash-flow and Legrain's aptitude for cost killing,

232 *Fabien Foureault*

the company did three LBOs (in 2000, 2003 and 2006). At each deal, economic performance increased as well as enterprise value, the amount of debt, and the wealth of investors and managers. When the economic crisis appeared in 2007, the LBO mechanism broke down, and Matéris had to undergo a painful restructuring. Sagard is a French private equity firm founded by the Canadian family Desmarais in 2002 and counts some of France's leading families among its investors (Dassault, Peugeot, Mulliez, Halley, Arnault, and so on). At the peak of LBOs in 2007, the firm was managing almost two billion euros. Sagard's management strategy and communication have an "industrial focus" as its investment committee is composed, in particular, of "captains of industry".

The broadest interpretation of this diagram is that the LBO field is comprised of two moieties separated by the diagonal in dotted lines on Figure 13.2: one moiety grouping the firms situated in the bottom left triangle and the other moiety grouping those in the top right triangle. This division corresponds to a classic distinction between a large-scale or "atlantic" capitalism and a small-scale or "continental" capitalism. "Moiety" should here be understood in the social-anthropological sense, that is, as a system of rival but complementary groups (Kadushin, 1995). As we have shown elsewhere (Foureault, 2014, chap. 2), these two groups are rivals, as each one claims to represent the correct model of LBO and of capitalism more generally: one "serial entrepreneur" model associated with contemporary America, valuing risk and the seizing of opportunities, and one "patient capital" model, valuing the corporation and relationships of proximity. However, these two groups are also complementary, as they collectively cover the whole market. Additionally, they are capable of grouping together in trade associations to act collectively to promote and defend their profession, notably with regard to the state.

III Career paths

Career paths are structured by organizations. A career can be defined as a succession of positions within and between organizations. Consequently, the dual structure identified in the previous section should be reflected at the individual level. This point is illustrated in this final section by a qualitative analysis of professional career trajectories across the typical organizations. Rather than researching information on the hundreds of people identified, attention has been focused on the "representatives" of these organizations. The term *representative* should be understood to mean someone who is at the top of the hierarchy within their company or department. It can be assumed that these individuals, who have reached the pinnacle of their organization, "embody" their position in the field, because the process of internal selection has made them in accordance with the culture of their organization (Boussard and Dujarier, 2014).

The individuals in question have several things in common, which they share with those occupying positions of high social status in global society (Ho, 2009). They are predominantly white males who were aged around 50 in 2007 – with the notable exception of Céline Méchain, a 36-year-old woman in charge of private equity at Goldman Sachs France. They are all highly educated, having all

The duality of the LBO field 233

undertaken postgraduate education, whether in business or engineering schools. However, regardless of whether they are bankers, investors or top managers, they differ in their academic and professional pathways. Even if it is difficult to think in terms of moieties at this stage of research, similar polarities to those that were mentioned earlier can be noted. Three observations can be drawn from the comparison of these career paths.

First, individuals do not seem to be distributed so much according to the level of schooling, but by the international prestige of their establishment. In the large-scale capitalism corner, we have, for example, Jacques Garaïalde (KKR), Céline Mechain (Goldman Sachs) and Chris Spencer (Sagard); all three have obtained diplomas from institutions outside of France. Jacques Garaïalde, notably, obtained an MBA from Institut Européen Administration des Affaires (INSEAD).[7] In the small-scale capitalism corner, we have Bertrand Rambaud (Siparex), who, after having obtained a degree in economic science at the University of Lyon, studied at a management school located there. Second, a line of differentiation can be drawn between those who have had an education or career in England or the United States, or were even born there, from those who have never had this kind of experience. Again in the "large-scale capitalism" corner, Jacques Garaïalde (KKR), Céline Méchain (Goldman Sachs) and Chris Spencer (Sagard) have all worked in London for global financial organizations: Carlyle and KKR; Deutsche Bank and Citigroup; and PricewaterhouseCoopers. Heading back to the "small-scale" capitalism corner, we have Phillipe Vidal (Cial), Olivier Legrain (Matéris) and Thierry Raiff (Euromezzanine), who have all made their careers in France. Philippe Vidal notably worked for the French Ministry of Public Works before working in a local bank, the Société Nancéenne Varin Bernier (SNVB). Thierry Raiff worked for the French Ministry of Agriculture and Olivier Legrain for a large French chemical company, Rhône Poulenc. Third, the individuals seem to differ according to the structure of their career paths. In the "large-scale capitalism" corner, individuals have worked in a larger number of organizations as well as outside of the sector, whereas towards the "small-scale capitalism" corner, the actors tend to have careers within firms. In 2007, at the age of 36 years, Céline Méchain had already worked for three different organizations, while Chris Spencer (Sagard) had worked in five. In the opposite corner, there seems to be more stability. While Philippe Vidal (Cial) has worked in several financial organizations, they all belonged to the same group (the CM-CIC banking group). Likewise, Bertrand Rambaud has only ever worked for two organizations: the first merely changed its name to become the second. The most extreme example of this type of career is that of Jean Bergeret, who has spent practically his entire career working within the Leveraged Finance Department of BNP Paribas.

Thus, there seem to be two valuation circuits for professional skills. These circuits are geographical in nature: one is straddling the Anglo-Saxon world and France, while the other sits in between the French regional capitals and Paris. Two divergent career paths here exemplify these two circuits, that of Philippe Vidal and that of Jacques Garaïalde (Box 13.2).

234   *Fabien Foureault*

Box 13.2: Two divergent career paths

Philippe Vidal (Cial) was born in the French region of Aveyron in 1954. He received a conventional French education in industrial management: educated at the engineering school Ecole Polytechnique, then at the Ecole des Ponts (specialist in engineering, among other disciplines). After spending time in New Caledonia, he began his career in the Ministry of Public Works. At the age of 39, he was appointed as the CEO of the French regional bank Société Nancéenne Varin Bernier (SNVB), a private bank that finances a number of local businesses and whose parent company is the French "universal" bank, CIC. In 1998, he was appointed president of Cial, the Alsatian subsidiary of the CIC based in Strasbourg, a position he held concurrently with the SNVB role to merge the two entities, which would become CIC Est in 2008. He later became deputy director of the CIC, where he was responsible for corporate and investment banking. Described by the press as a "man of values", Philippe Vidal is a member of elitist clubs and is the board member of a subsidiary of a large French industrial group. He is a member of the regional Economic and Social Council for the Lorraine region and a director of an engineering school in the very same region, where he attends long-service award ceremonies.

Jacques Garaïalde (KKR) was born in Versailles in 1956. He holds degrees from the Ecole Polytechnique and the business school INSEAD (MBA). He began his career in 1979 within the Department of Economic Research at Esso (Exxon) before moving to the Boston Consulting Group in 1982. He was a consultant, then associate director, associate director and partner in Belgium, senior vice-president and then partner for France and Belgium. In 2000, at the age of 43, he became the managing director for Europe of the private equity firm Carlyle in London. He was involved with the launching of a large venture capital fund for Carlyle, which collapsed in the dot-com crisis. In 2003, while still in London, he moved into the LBO field, having been employed by KKR thanks to a head-hunter. He oversaw the two largest deals ever to have taken place in France for KKR: the LBO of the company Legrand and that of "Pages Jaunes" (Yellow Pages). In the meantime, he opened the Parisian office of KKR. Considered by the press to be the most powerful Frenchman in the private equity field, he is also a member of elitist clubs. In 2007, he received the "français of the year" prize, which distinguishes French expatriates in London in the fields of finance, industry, sport and show business.

These two career paths illustrate a possible "centrifugal force" formalized by the organizational field and taking the form of the two valuation circuits for professional skills. At the same age, both men started out with a relatively similar education (elitist and generalist engineering school Polytechnique), although one possesses managerial competencies (INSEAD) while the other possesses engineering competencies (Ecole des Ponts). At the outset, one opted for the private (Esso/Exxon) and the other for the public sector (Ministry of Public Works). The career path of the first would lead him to KKR in London via Belgium, and the career path of the second to Paris via the Lorraine region of France. Their individual trajectories thus seem to be structured in the same way as the organizational field, by two geographical valuation circuits.

The two moieties appear to represent two main types of capitalism, including at the individual level. The individuals at the helm of the "small-scale capitalism" organizations, in particular, seem to be instilled with a form of paternalistic ethos. Thus, Philippe Vidal (Cial), who was president of the SNVB, a regional institution created in 1881 by Lorrainian industrialists, is described as being "modern, without losing sight of traditional values".[8] He says he was recruited for his "devotion to the company and its values".[9] The founder of Siparex is Dominique Nouvellet, from Lyon, a former student of the Ecole Nationale d'Administration (ENA) and active within the hierarchy of the Catholic Church. He considers that his conceptualization of the corporation, as a "community of values", dictates the strategy of his private equity firm. This view of capitalism, in which the *corporation* is valued and not the *market*, leads him to criticize the strategies of the organizations situated within the "large-scale capitalism" half as being fundamentally destructive: "the Siparex group has steered clear of the private equity bubble in the United States and in Great Britain and has not indulged in excessive leverage on mega LBOs [...]. It has nothing to do with KKR or Carlyle. When members hear Henry Kravis, founder, shareholder and manager of KKR, claim that the company is a commodity, it makes their hackles rise! In their eyes, a company is everything but that!"[10]

Conclusion

This chapter has analysed the manner in which financial professions are structured by using the LBO field as an example. The field has been defined as a social space drawn by the use of the "organizational weapon" of LBOs, which are financial deals in which banks, private equity firms and companies have a direct and durable interest. The field is vertically structured, with the highest positions in the structure being occupied notably by a small number of banks, followed next by private equity firms and then target companies. The field is also structured horizontally in a moiety system – rival yet complementary groups. From this point of view, the field appears to be dual in nature: it is structured by one main division between a "large-scale" capitalism and a "small-scale" capitalism. The structure of the field at the individual level has also been outlined. The study of several career paths shows that the same structure is reflected at this level. Two valuation pathways for professional skills exist, one of which straddles Paris and the Anglo-Saxon world, the other straddling Paris and other regions of France.

A twofold observation can be drawn from this chapter in terms of the analysis of financialization. On the one hand, financialization appears to be a far-reaching

236 *Fabien Foureault*

phenomenon, as LBO deals, which are considered to be the most radical practices within financial capitalism, affect the world of French small and medium-sized companies just as much as they do the world of large companies. They are even implemented by public actors (such as the Caisse des Dépôts et des Consignations) and small regional private equity firms held by banks or the regional council. On the other hand, financialization is an ambivalent process. It cannot be analysed as an exogenous force sweeping across from the United States to do away with the French model of industrial capitalism. Bédu and Montalban have shown that private equity, as a capitalist model, is not completely identifiable with the "liberal market economy", even though it originates from the United States. It incorporates elements associated with "coordinated market economies", characteristic of Germany: concentration of ownership, bank financing and direct control over the company (Bédu and Montalban, 2013). This is probably why the LBO is compatible with the so-called French model. If a historical equivalent of private equity had to be found, it would be American capitalism from the turn of the 20th century, dominated by "robber barons" (Baker and Smith, 1998). Finally, Paul Windolf demonstrates that American financial capitalism doesn't replace but gets integrated into traditional French capitalism, which is both familial and bureaucratic (Windolf, 1999). This chapter confirms his findings. The tension between capitalist models is reflected, on a smaller scale, within the LBO field via the moiety system.

Notes

1 Employees are not in a more comfortable situation: the repayment of a high debt poses the threat of closing unprofitable sites and threatens the entire company with insolvency. As with nuclear deterrents, all action against the dominant power is pre-empted by the fear of being eliminated from the game – in this case, losing your job (Shleifer and Summers, 1988).
2 These roles/positions can be fulfilled/occupied by individuals or organizations, either consecutively or simultaneously.
3 Quoted by Knorr-Cetina and Bruegger (2002, chaps. 921–922).
4 This observation is reinforced by the fact that these organizations are strongly linked to one another, forming a very dense core.
5 Its president Gonzagues de Blignières was AFIC's president during the 2000s. (For more on networks, please refer to Foureault, 2014, chap. 2).
6 *Gaga 80s* is an expression used within financial circles to refer to the period of euphoria in the markets during the 1980s, in particular with regard to mergers and acquisitions and hostile takeovers. It draws a parallel with the period of the *gogo 60s* (see Montagne, 2014).
7 INSEAD is a graduate business school with campuses worldwide.
8 *La Tribune* newspaper, "Le baron du Cial tire sa révérence" (The Cial tycoon steps down), 29 April 1999.
9 *La Tribune* newspaper, "Philippe Vidal: un homme de valeurs" (Philippe Vidal: a man of values), 30 January 2008.
10 Alain Borderie, *Financer les champions de demain: Siparex, 1977–2008 pour un* private equity *éthique et performant*, le Cherche Midi, Paris, p. 214.

References

Abbott, A. (1981). Status and status strain in the professions. *American Journal of Sociology*, 86(4), 819–835.

Abbott, A. (1988). *The system of the professions. An essay on the division of expert labor*. Chicago: Chicago University Press.

Abbott, A. (1995). Things of boundaries. *Social Research*, 62(4), 857–882.

Abbott, A. (2014). *The system of professions: An essay on the division of expert labor*. Chicago: Chicago University Press.

Abbott, A. and Hrycak, A. (1990). Measuring resemblance in sequence data: An optimal matching analysis of musicians' careers. *American Journal of Sociology*, 96(1), 144–185.

Abolafia, M.Y. (1996). *Making markets*. Cambridge: Cambridge University Press.

Acosta, T. (1989, June 9). Comments on Employee Partnership Fund. JS Records, Box 10, Folder 1.

Actes de la Recherche en Sciences Sociales. (2013). Théorie du champ, 5(200).

Aglietta, M. (2000). Shareholder value and corporate governance: Some tricky questions. *Economy and Society*, 29(1), 146–159.

Aglietta, M. and Rigot, S. (2009). *Crise et rénovation de la finance*. Paris: Odile Jacob.

Alphandéry, E., Rougier, M., and Pélata, P. (2009). Qu'attendre des banques? *Le Journal de l'Ecole de Paris*, 78(4), 8–16.

Andersen, L. and Piterbarg, V. (2010). Interest rate modeling. New York: Atlantic Financial Press.

Angelides, P. (Ed.) (2011). *The financial crisis inquiry report*. Final Report of the National Commission on the Causes of the Financial and Economic Crisis in the United States. New York: Public Affairs.

Anzalone, G. and Purseigle, F. (2014). Délégation d'activités et sous-traitance: Au service de la transmission de l'exploitation ou d'un patrimoine? In P. Gasselin, J.-P. Choisis, S. Petit, F. Purseigle and S. Zasser. (Eds.), *L'agriculture en famille: Travailler, réinventer, transmettre* (327–338). Retrieved from www.edp-open.org/images/stories/books/contents/agricfal/Agricfal_327-338.pdf.

Anzalone, G., Barraud-Didier, V., and Henninger, M.-C. (2012). La distanciation du lien adhérent – coopérative. *Études Rurales*, 2(190), 119–130.

Appelbaum, R. and Batt, E. (2014). *Private equity at work. When Wall Street manages Main Street*. New York: Russel Sage Foundation.

Arrighi, G. (1994). *The long twentieth century: Money, power and the origins of our times*. New York: Verso.

Arrighi, G. (2003). *The diversity of modern capitalism*. Oxford: Oxford University Press.

238 References

Asociación Española de Banca (AEB) (2011). Estados financieros consolidados de los grupos bancarios en España. Retrieved from http://www.aebanca.es/internet/groups/public/documents/publicaciones.

"A Trade Union Investment Vehicle." January 31, 1988, JS Records, Box 10, Folder 5.

Avent-Holt, D. and Tomaskovic-Devey, D. (2013). A Relational Theory of Earnings Inequality. *American Behavioral Scientist*, 58(3), 379–399.

Ayres, I. and Braithwaite, J. (1994). *Responsive regulation: Transcending the deregulation debate*. New York: Oxford University Press.

Baker, G. and Smith, G. (1998). *The new financial capitalists*. Cambridge: Cambridge University Press.

Baker, W.E. (1984). The social structure of a national securities market. *American Journal of Sociology*, 89(4), 775–811.

Banco de España (2011). *Economic Bulletin*. April 2011.

Barth, Fredrik. (1969). Introduction. In *Ethnic Groups and Boundaries: The Social Organization of Culture Difference*, edited by Fredrik Barth. London: Allen & Unwin.

Barthes, F. (1998). *Ethnic groups and boundaries: The social organization of cultural difference*. Illinois: Waveland Press.

Bastin, G. (2016). Gravitation, aléa, séquence: Variations sociologiques autour du concept de carrière. In D. Demazière and M. Jouvenet (Eds.), *La sociologie d'Andrew Abbott*, (195–216). Paris: Editions de l'EHESS.

Batsch, L. (2002). *Le capitalisme financier*. Paris: Repères, La Découverte.

Baud, C. and Durand, C. (2012). Financialization, globalization and the making of profits by leading retailers. *Socio-Economic Review*, 10(2), 241–266.

Baud, C. and Chiapello, È. (2015). Comment les firmes se financiarisent: le rôle de la réglementation et des instruments de gestion. Le cas du crédit bancaire. *Revue Française de Sociologie*, 56(3), 439–468.

Bazot, G. (2014). *Financial consumption and the cost of finance: Measuring financial efficiency in Europe (1950–2007)*. Retrieved from www.parisschoolofeconomics.eu/IMG/pdf/jobmarket-1paper-bazot-pse.pdf.

Becker, G.-S. (1964). *Human capital: A theoretical and empirical analysis*. Chicago: Chicago University Press.

Becker, H. (1960). Notes on the concept of commitment. *American Journal of Sociology* 66(1), 32–40.

Becker, H. (1982). *Art worlds*. Berkeley: University of California Press.

Becker, H., Geer, B., Hughes, E.C., and Strauss, A. (1961). *Boys in white*. Chicago: Chicago University Press.

Bédu, N. and Montalban, M. (2013). Analysing the uneven development of private equity in Europe: Legal origins and diversity of capitalism. *Socio-Economic Review*, 12(1), 33–70.

Benson, R. and Neveu, E. (2005). *Bourdieu and the Journalistic Field*. Cambridge: Polity.

Berges, A. and Mora, A., (2008). Analistas Financieros Internacionales (AFI). Retrieved from www.afi.es/EO/Subprime%20in%20Spain.pdf.

Berk, G. and Galvan, D. (2009). How people experience and change institutions: A field guide to creative syncretism. *Theory and Society*, 38(6), 543–580.

Berle, A.A. and Means, G.C. (1932). *The modern corporation and private property*. New York: Macmillan.

Bernstein, A. (1987, December 14). Move over, boone, Carl, Irv – here comes labour. *Business Week*, 124.

References 239

Bernstein, A. (1990, February 26). Soon, LBO's might be union-made. *Business Week.*

Bessière, C. and Bruneau, I. (2011). La vie moderne de R. Depardon: La beauté de la mort paysanne. *Revue de Synthèse*, 136(3), 448–454.

Bessière, C., Bruneau, I. and Laferté, G. (2014). Les agriculteurs dans la France contemporaine. *Sociétés Contemporaines*, 96(4), 5–25.

Bessy, C. and Chauvin, P.M. (2013). The power of market intermediaries: From information to valuation processes. *Valuation Studies*, 1(1), 83–117.

Bidet, A. and Vatin, F. (2009). Mesure et acteur au travail. In Steiner, P. and Vatin, F. (Eds.), *Traité de sociologie économique*, (689–726). Paris: P.U.F.

Bierschenk, T., Chauveau, J.-P., and de Sardan, (2000). *Courtiers en développement: Les villages africains en quête de projets.* Paris: Khartala.

Bigot, R., Croutte, P. and Müller, J. (2011). *La culture financière des Français.* (Report No. R227), Paris: CREDOC.

Björk, T. (2009). *Arbitrage theory in continuous time.* Oxford: Oxford University Press.

Blair-Loy, M. (1999). Career patterns of executive women in finance: an optimal matching analysis. *The American Journal of Sociology*, 104(5), 1346–1397.

Blair-Loy, M. (2001). It's not just what you know, it's who you know: Technical knowledge, rainmaking, and gender among finance executives. *Research in the Sociology of Work*, 10, 51–83.

Blanchard, P., Bühlmann, F. and Gauthier, J.-A. (2014). *Sequence analysis: Theory, method, applications.* London: Springer.

Block, F. (2014). Democratizing Finance. *Politics & Society*, 42(3), 3–28.

Bloom, R. (1991, February 11). Letter to T.S. Lader. JS Records, Box 128, Folder 3.

Board of Governors of the Federal Reserve System and the Office of the Comptroller of the Currency (2011). "Supervisory guidance on model risk management". Available at:Retrieved from http://www.occ.treas.gov/news-issuances/bulletins/2011/bulletin-2011-12a.pdf. (Accessed: 30 September 2016).

Boltanski, A. (1973). L'espace positionnel: Multiplicité des positions institutionnelles et habitus de classe. *Revue Française de Sociologie*, 14(1), 3–26.

Borgatti, S., & Halgin, D. (2011). Analyzing affiliation networks. In J. Scott & P. Carrington (Eds.), *The SAGE handbook of social network analysis* (417–434). London: SAGE Publications.

Bottin, J., Lemercier, C. and Zalc, C. (2006). *La relation de crédit: Une histoire de longue durée.* Séminaire de l'IHMC-CNRS. Retrieved from http://lemercier.ouvaton.org/document.php?id=154.

Bourdieu, J. (dir.) (2013). Théorie du champ. *Actes de la Recherche en Sciences Sociales.*, 5(200), 1–125.

Bourdieu, J., Heilbron, J. and Reynaud, B. (2003). Les structures sociales de la finance. *Actes de la Recherche en Sciences Sociales*, 1, 3–7.

Bourdieu, P. (1984a). Culture et politique. In P. Bourdieu (Ed.), *Questions de sociologie*, (236–250). Paris: Éditions de Minuit.

Bourdieu, P. (1984b). *Distinction. A social critique of the judgement of taste.* Harvard University Press. Cambridge, Massachusetts.

Bourdieu, P. (1989). *La noblesse d'Etat: Grandes ecoles et esprit de corps.* Paris: Editions de Minuit.

Bourdieu, P. (1992). *Les règles de l'art.* Paris: Seuil.

Bourdieu, P. (1999). Une révolution conservatrice dans l'édition. *Actes de la Recherche en Sciences Sociales*, 126(1), 3–28.

240 *References*

Bourdieu, P. (2003). *The social structures of the economy.* (C. Turner Trans.). Cambridge, UK: Polity Press.

Bourdieu, P. (2008). *The bachelors' ball: The crisis of peasant society in Béarn.* (R. NiceTrans.). Chicago: University of Chicago Press.

Bourdieu, P. (2011). The forms of capital (1986). In I. Szeman and T. Kaposy (Eds.), *Cultural theory: An anthology*, (81–93). West Sussex: Wiley-Blackwell.

Bourdieu, P. and Passeron, J.-C. (1970). *La Reproduction: Elements pour une théorie du système d'enseignement.* Paris: Editions de Minuit.

Bourdieu, P. and Saint Martin (de), M. (1978). Le patronat. *Actes de la Recherche en Sciences Sociales*, 20(1), 3–82.

Bourdieu, P., Boltanski, L. and Chamboredon, J.-C. (1963). *La Banque et sa clientèle. Éléments d'une sociologie du credit.* Etude réalisée sous la direction de Pierre Bourdieu par Luc Boltanski et Jean-Claude Chamboredon. Unpublished manuscript. Paris: Rapport du Centre de sociologie européenne.

Boussard, V. (2013). Qui crée la création de valeur? *La Nouvelle Revue du Travail*, 3. Retrieved from http://nrt.revues.org/1020.

Boussard, V. (2015). De l'espace hybride au monde social: La coordination dans le marché en abyme des transactions d'entreprise. *L'année Sociologique*, 65(2), 357–390.

Boussard, V. (2016). Des écologies enchevêtrées. Observation croisée des trajectoires institutionnelles et individuelles d'une profession. In D. Demazière and M. Jouvenet (Eds.), *Andrew Abbott et l'héritage de l'école de Chicago*, Paris: Éditions EHESS.

Boussard, V. (2017). A new model of professions? When transnational financial services challenge the sociology of the professions. Lyon: SASE Congress, 29–30 June.

Boussard, V. and Dujarier, M.-A. (2014). Les représentations professionnelles en question. Le cas des intermédiaires dans les fusions-acquisitions, *Sociologie du Travail*, 56(2), 182–203.

Boussard, V., Loriol, M. and Caroly, S. (2006). Catégorisation des usagers et rhétorique professionnelle. Le cas des policiers sur la voie publique. *Sociologie du Travail*, 48(2), 209–225.

Boyer, R. (2000). Is a finance-led growth regime a viable alternative to Fordism? A preliminary analysis. *Economy and Society*, 29(1), 111–145.

Brancato, C.K. (1989). *Leveraged buyouts and the pot of gold: 1989 update.* Report Prepared for the Subcommittee on Oversight and Investigations, Committee on Energy and Commerce, U.S. House of Representatives.

Breiger, R. L. (1974). The Duality of Persons and Groups. *Social Forces*, 53(2), 181–190.

Browne, I. and Misra, J. (2003). The intersection of gender and race in the labor market. *Annual Review of Sociology*, 29(1), 487–513.

Bucher, R. and Strauss, A. (1961). Professions in process. *American Journal of Sociology*, 66(4), 352–334.

Burch, D., and Geoffrey, L. (2012). Financialization in agri-food supply chains: Private equity and the transformation of the retail sector. *Agriculture and Human Values*, 30(2), 247–258.

Burt, R. (1992). *Structural holes: The social structure of competition.* Cambridge: Harvard University Press.

Cabré, A. and Módenes, J. (2004). Home ownership and social inequality in Spain. In K. Kurz and H.-P. Blossfeld (Eds.), *Home ownership and social inequality in comparative perspective.* Stanford: Stanford University Press.

Callon, M. (1998). Introduction: The embeddedness of economic markets in economics. *The Sociological Review*, 46(S1), 1–57.

References 241

Callon, M. and Muniesa, F. (2009). La performativité des sciences économiques. In P. Steiner and F. Vatin (Eds.), *Traité de sociologie économique*, Paris: PUF.

Camblain, B. (2008). *Family office et famille*. Paris: Gualino.

Cameron, M. (2011). G14 dealer group adds two members. Risk Magazine. Retrieved from www.risk.net/risk-magazine/news/2127940/g14-dealer-adds.

Campbell, J. (2011). *Investing and spending: The twin challenges of university endowment management*. Paper presented at the Forum for the Future of Higher Education, Boston.

Capron, M. (2005). *Les normes comptables internationales: Instruments du capitalisme financier*. Paris: La Découverte.

Carruthers, B. (2015). Financialization and the institutional foundations of the new capitalism. *Socio-Economic Review*, 13(2), 379–398.

Carruthers, B. and Stinchcombe, A. (1999). The social structure of liquidity: Flexibility, markets, and states. *Theory and Society*, 28(3), 353–382.

Carswell, H.-J. (1938). Business news coverage. *The Public Opinion Quarterly*, 2(4), 613–621.

Cartier, M., Courant, I., Masclet, O. and Siblot, Y. (2016). The France of the little-middles. A suburban housing development in greater Paris. Oxford, New York: Berghahn Books.

Carvajal Molina, P. (2001). *El proceso financiero de titulización de activos*. Madrid: Dykinson.

Cazenave, E. (1997). Les mutations de la presse économique et financière. *Matériaux pour l'Histoire de notre Temps*, 46(1), 40–43.

Cédiey, E. and Foroni, F. (2007). Les discriminations à raison de l'origine dans les embauches en France. Une enquête nationale par tests de discrimination selon la méthode du Bureau International du Travail. *Cahiers des Migrations Internationales*, 85F, Genève: Bureau International du Travail.

Cetina, K. K. and Bruegger, U. (2002). Global microstructures: The virtual societies of financial markets. *American Journal of Sociology*, 107(4), 905–950.

Champagne, P. (2002). *L'Héritage refusé: La crise de la reproduction sociale de la paysannerie française, 1950–2000*. Paris: Seuil.

Champagne, P. and Marchetti, D. (2005). The contaminated blood scandal: Reframing medical news, In R. Benson and E. Neveu (Eds.), *Bourdieu and the Journalistic Field*. Cambridge: Polity.

Chandler, H. (1977). *The visible hand: The managerial revolution in American business*. Cambridge, Massachusetts: Belknap Press.

Charron, J.-O. (2010). *La relation entre estimation publique de la valeur fondamentale des sociétés cotées et évolution de leur cours: Une contribution basée sur des études de cas*. (Doctoral dissertation). Paris: Conservatoire national des arts et metiers (CNAM).

Chatriot, A, and Lemercier, C. (2002). Les corps intermédiaires. In V. Duclert and C. Prochasson (Eds.), *Dictionnaire critique de la République*, (691–698). Paris: Flammarion.

Chazel, F. (1983). Pouvoir, structure et domination. *Revue Française de Sociologie*, 24(3), 369–393.

Chiapello, E. (2005). Transformations des conventions comptables, transformation de la représentation de l'entreprise. In M. Capron (Ed.), *Les normes comptables internationales. Instruments du capitalisme financier*, Paris: La Découverte.

Chiapello, E. (2014). *The role of calculative instruments in the financialisation process*. Numbers from the bottom up, Workshop, 6–7 March 2014, Wissenschaftskolleg, Berlin.

Chiapello, E. (2015). Financialisation of valuation. *Human Studies*, 38(1), 13–35.

242 References

Choo, H.-Y. and Ferree, M.-M. (2010). Practicing intersectionality in sociological research: A critical analysis of inclusions, interactions, and institutions in the study of inequalities. *Sociological Theory*, 28(2), 129–149.

Christophers, B. (2015). The limits to financialization. *Dialogues in Human Geography*, 5(2), 183–200.

Clark, I. (2009). The private equity business model and associated strategies for HRM: Evidence and implications? *The International Journal of Human Resource Management*, 20(10), 2030–2048.

Clark, N.L. (1994). *Manufacturing apartheid: State corporations in South Africa*. New Haven: Yale University Press.

Cochoy, F. and Dubuisson, S. (2000). Introduction. *Sociologie du Travail*, 42(3), 335–359.

Cogut, C.A. and Flanagan, P.A. (1989, August 7). Letter to J. Sheinkman. JS Records, Box 102, Folder 8.

Coleman, J. S. (1990). *Foundations of social theory*. Cambridge: Harvard University Press.

Collins, H. M. (1974). The TEA set: Tacit knowledge and scientific networks. *Science Studies*, 4(2), 165–85.

Collins, P.-H. (1999). *Black feminist thought: Knowledge, consciousness and the politics of empowerment* (2nd ed.) London: Harper Collins.

Colombi, D. and Paye, S. (2014). Synchronising sequences: An analytic approach to explore relationships between events and temporal patterns. In P. Blanchard, F. Bühlmann and J.-A. Gauthier (Eds.), *Sequence analysis: Theory, method, applications*, (249–264). London: Springer.

Comby, J.-B. (2009). Quand l'environnement devient "médiatique". *Réseaux*, 157–158(5), 157–190.

Comín, F. and Torres, E. (2005). La confederación española de cajas de ahorro y el desarrollo de la red de servicios financieros de las cajas en el siglo XX. *Papeles de Economía Española*, 105–106, 48–65.

Cook, K. and Emerson, R. (1978). Power, equity and commitment in exchange networks. *American Sociological Review*, 43(5), 721–739.

Cooke, L.P. (2011). *Gender-class equality in political economies*. New York: Routledge.

Coriat, B. (2008). L'installation de la finance en France. Genèse, forme spécifique et impacts sur l'industrie. *Revue de la Régulation*, 3/4, 1–34.

Coudroy de Lille, L., Vaz, C., and Vorms, C. (Eds.) (2013). *L'urbanisme espagnol depuis les années 1970. La ville, la démocratie et le marché*. Rennes: Presses universitaires de Rennes.

Crompton, R. (1989). Women in banking : Continuity and change since the second world war. *Work, Employment and Society*, 3(2), 141–156.

Crompton, R. (Ed.) (1999). *Restructuring gender relations and employement*. Oxford: Oxford University Press.

Cronon, W. (1991). *Nature's metropolis: Chicago and the great West*. New York: W.W. Norton.

Crotty, J., (2005). The neoliberal paradox: The impact of destructuve product market competition and "modern" financial market on nonfinancial corporation performance in the neoliberal era. In G. Epstein (Ed.), *Financialization and the world economy*, (77–110). Northampton, Massachusetts: Edward Elgar.

Dacin, M.T., Goodstein, J. and Scott, W.R. (2002). Institutional theory and institutional change: introduction to the special research forum. *Academy of Management Journal*, 45(1), 45–57.

Dalton, M. (1959). *Men who manage. Fusions of feeling and theory in administration*. New York: John Wiley and Sons.

References 243

Darcillon, T. (2015). How does finance affect labor market institutions? An empirical analysis in 16 OECD countries. *Socio-Economic Review*, 13(3), 477–504.

Daune-Richard, A.-M. and Devreux, A.-M. (1992). Rapports sociaux de sexe et conceptualization sociologique. *Recherches Féministes*, 5(2), 7–30.

David, T., Davoine, E., Ginalski, S. and Mach, A. (2012). Elites nationales ou globalisées? Les dirigeants des grandes entreprises suisses entre standardisation et spécificités helvétiques (1980-2000). *Revue Suisse de Sociologie*, 38(1), 57–76.

Davis, G.F. (2005). New directions in corporate governance. *Annual Review of Sociology*, 31, 143–162.

Davis, G.F. (2009a). *Managed by the markets: How finance re-shaped America*. New York: Oxford University Press.

Davis, G.F. (2009b). The rise and fall of finance and the end of the society of organizations, *Academy of Management Perspectives*, 23(3), 27–44.

Davis, G.F. and Stout, S.K. (1992). Organization theory and the market for corporate control: A dynamic analysis of the characteristics of large takeover targets, 1980-1990. *Administrative Science Quarterly*, 37(4), 605–633.

Davis, G.F. and Greve, H.R. (1997). Corporate elite networks and governance changes in the 1980s. *American Journal of Sociology*, 103(1), 1–37.

Davis, G.F. and Useem, M. (2002). Top management, company directors and corporate control. In A. Pettigrew, H. Thomas and R. Whittington (Eds.), *Handbook of strategy and management*, (233–259). London: Sage.

Davis, K. (2008). Intersectionality as buzzword: A sociology of science perspective on what makes a feminist theory successful, *Feminist Theory*, 9(1), 67–85.

Davis, S.J., Haltiwanger, J., Handley, K., Jarmin, R., Lerner, J. and Miranda, J. (2014). Private equity, jobs, and productivity. *American Economic Review*, 104(12), 3956–3990.

Davoine, E. and Ravasi, C. (2013). The relative stability of national career patterns in European top management careers in the age of globalisation: A comparative study in France/Germany/Great Britain and Switzerland. *European Management Journal*. 31(2), 152–163.

Depecker, T. and Joly, N. (2015). La terre et ses manufacturiers. L'introduction d'une raison gestionnaire dans les domaines agricoles (1800-1850). *Entreprises et Histoire*, 79(2), 12–23.

Desrosières, A. (2000). *La Politique des grands nombres: Histoire de la raison statistique*. Paris: La Découverte.

Devillard, V. and Rieffel, R. (2001). L'insertion professionnelle des nouveaux journalistes: Parcours 1990-1998. In V. Devillard, M. F. Lafosse, C. Leteinturier and R. Rieffel (Eds.), *Les journalistes français à l'aube de l'an 2000: Profils et parcours*, (123–158). Paris: Université Panthéon-Assas.

Dietz, J.S., Chompalov, I., Bozeman, B., Lane, E. and Park, J. (2000). Using the curriculum vitae to study the career paths of scientists and engineers: An exploratory assessment. *Scientometrics*, 49(3), 419–442.

DiMaggio, P.J. (1988). Interest and agency in institutional theory. In L. Zucker (Ed.), *Institutional patterns and organizations: Culture and environment*, (3–22). Cambridge: Ballinger Publishing Company.

DiMaggio, P.J. (2001). *The twenty-first-century firm: Changing economic organization in international perspective*. Princeton and Oxford: Princeton University Press.

DiMaggio, P.J., and Powell, W.W. (1983). The Iron cage revisited: Institutional isomorphism and collective rationality in organizational fields. *American Sociological Review*, 48(2), 147–160.

Dobbin, F. (2009). *Inventing equal opportunity*. Princeton: Princeton University Press.

244 *References*

Dobbin, F. and Jung, J. (2010). The misapplication of Mr Michael Jensen: How agency theory brought down the economy and why it might again. In M. Lounsbury P.M. Hirsch (Eds.), *Markets on trial: The economic sociology of the U.S. financial crisis*, (29–64). Bingley: Emerald Publishing.

Dougal, C., Engelberg, J., García, D. and Parsons, C.-A. (2012). Journalists and the stock market. *Review of Financial Studies*, 25(1), 133.

Doyle, G. (2006). Financial news journalism: A post-Enron analysis of approaches towards economic and financial news production in the UK. *Journalism*, 7(4), 433–452.

"Draft proposal Employee Partnership Fund." (1988, November 4). JS Records, Box 10, Folder 1.

"Draft for an Equity Partnership Fund." (1989, Feburary). JS Records, Box 10, Folder 1.

Drexel Burnham, L. (1989). Report on Employee Partnership Fund. JS Records, Box 10, Folder 1.

Drucker, P. (1976). *The unseen revolution. How pension fund socialism came to America.* New York: Harper and Row.

Ducastel, A. (2016). *Cultiver le capital. Une analyse de la financiarisation de l'agriculture en Afrique du sud par les filières agro-financières du private equity.* (Doctoral dissertation defended on 28th of June 2016). Paris: Saclay University.

Dudouet, F.-X. and Grémont, E. (2009). *Les grands patrons en France.* Paris: Editions Ligne de Repères.

Dufumier, M. (1996). *Les projets de développement agricole: Manuel d'expertise.* Paris: Khartala.

Dujarier, M.-A. (2015). *Le management désincarné. Enquête sur les nouveaux cadres du travail.* Paris: La Découverte.

Duménil, G. and Lévy, D. (2005). Costs and benefits of neoliberalism: A class analysis. In G. Epstein (Ed.), *Financialization and the world economy*, (17–46). Northampton (MA): Edward Elgar.

Duru-Bellat, M. (2004). *L'Ecole des filles : Quelle formation pour quels rôles sociaux?* Paris: L'Harmatan.

Duval, J. (2004). *Critique de la raison journalistique: Les transformations de la presse économique en France.* Paris: Seuil.

Eaton, C., Goldstein, A., Habinek, J., Kumar, M., Lee Stover, T. and Roehrkasse, A. (2013). *Bankers in the ivory tower: The financialization of governance at the University of California.* Retrieved from http://www.escholarship.org/uc/item/5qm6t5xn.

Eccles, R.G. and Crane, D.B. (1988). *Doing deals: Investment banks at work.* Boston, MA: Harvard Business School Press.

Elias, N. (1991). *The society of individuals.* (M. Schröter Ed.) (E. Jephcott Trans.). Oxford: Blackwell.

Emerson, R. (1962). Power-dependence relations. *American Sociological Review*, 27(1), 31–41.

"Employee Ownership through an "Equity Partnership"." (1989, February). JS Records, Box 10, Folder 1.

Engelen, E. (2006). Resocializing capital: Putting pension savings in the service of financial pluralism? *Politics and Society*, 34(2), 187–218.

Engelen, E. (2008). The case for financialization. *Competition and Change*, 12(2), 111–119.

Epstein, G. and Jayadev, A. (2005). The rise of rentier incomes in OECD countries: Financialization, centrak bank policy and labor solidarity. In G. Epstein (Ed.), *Financialization and the world economy*, (46–74). Northampton (MA): Edward Elgar.

References 245

Ernst & Young (2011). US GAAP versus IFRS – The basics. Retrieved from http://www.ey.com/Publication/vwLUAssets/US_GAAP_v_IFRS:_The_Basics/$FILE/US GAAP v IFRS Dec 2011.pdf.

Ertuk, I., Froud, J., Johal, S., Leaver, A. and Williams, K. (2007a). Against agency: a positional critique. *Economy and Society*, 36(1), 51–77.

Ertuk, I., Froud, J., Johal, S., Leaver, A. and Williams, K. (2007b). The democratization of finance? Promises, outcomes and conditions. *Review of International Political Economy*, 14(4), 553–575.

Ertuk, I., Froud, J., Johal, S., Leaver, A. and Williams, K. (2008). General introduction: Financialization, coupon pool and conjuncture. In I. Ertuk, J. Froud, S. Johal, A. Leaver and K. Williams (Eds.), *Financialization at work*, (1–43). London: Routledge.

Erturk, I., Froud, J., Johal, S., Leaver, A. and Williams, K. (2010). Ownership matters: Private equity and the political division of ownership. *Organization*, 17(5), 543–561.

Evangelista, R. (2010). *Le family office*. Gualino: Paris.

Fabozzi, F. and Modigliani, F. (1992). *Mortgage and mortgage-backed securities markets*. Harvard: Harvard Business School Press.

Falconi, A.M., Guenfoud, K., Lazega, E., Lemercier, C. and Mounier, L. (2005). Le contrôle social du monde des affaires: Une étude institutionnelle. *L'Année Sociologique*, 55(2), 451–483.

Fama, E. and Jensen, M. (1983). Separation of ownership and control. *Journal of Law and Economics*, 26(2), 301–325.

Farell, C. and Hoerr, J. (1989, May 15). ESOPs: Are they good for you? *Business Week*, 116–124.

Feld, S.L. (1981). The focused organization of social ties. *American Journal of Sociology*, 86(5), 1015–1035.

Felouzis, G. (2003). La ségrégation ethnique au collège et ses conséquences. *Revue Française de Sociologie*, 3(44), 413–447.

Ferguson, J. (2010). The uses of neoliberalism. *Antipode*, 41(s1), 166–84.

Fernandez Garcia, A. and Petithomme, M. (Eds.) (2015). *Contester en Espagne. Crise démocratique et mouvements sociaux*. Paris: Demopolis.

Financial Accounting Standards Board (2006). Statement of financial accounting standards No. 157: Fair Value Measurements. Norwalk: Financial Accounting Standards Boards.

Fine, B. and Rustomjee, Z. (1997). *The political economy of South Africa: From minerals-energy complex to industrialisation*. Boulder, CO: Westview Press.

Flaherty, E. (2015). Top incomes under finance-driven capitalism, 1990-2010: Power resources and regulatory orders. *Socio-Economic Review*, 13(3), 417–447.

Flemming, R. B. (1998). Contested terrains and regime politics: thinking about America's trial courts and institutional change. *Law & Social Inquiry*, 23, 941–965.

Fligstein, N. (1990). *The transformation of corporate control*. Cambridge: Harvard University Press.

Fligstein, N. (2001). *The architecture of markets: An economic sociology of twenty-first-century capitalist societies*. Princeton: Princeton University Press.

Fligstein, N. and Brantley, P. (1992). Bank control, owner control, or organizational dynamics: Who controls the large modern corporation? *American Journal of Sociology*, 98(2), 280–307.

Fligstein, N. and Shin, T. (2004). The shareholder value society: Changes in working conditions and inequality in the U.S., 1975-2000. In K. Neckerman (Ed.), *Social inequality*, (401–432). New York: Russel Sage Foudation.

246 *References*

Fligstein, N. and Shin, T. (2007). Shareholder value and the transformation of the U.S. economy, 1984-2001. *Sociological Forum*, 22(4), 399–424.

Fligstein, N. and McAdam, D. (2012). *A theory of fields*. New York: Oxford University Press.

Fligstein, N. and Goldstein, A. (2015). The emergence of a finance culture in American households, 1989-2007. *Socio-Economic Review*, 13(3), 575–601.

Fourcade, M. and Kuhrana, R. (2013). From social control to financial economics: The linked ecologies of economics and business in twentieth century America. *Theory and Society*, 42(2), 121–159.

Foureault, F. (2014). *Remodeler le capitalisme: le jeu profond du leveraged buy-out en France, 2001–2009*. Paris: Institut d'Etude Politiques de Paris.

François, P. (2008). *Sociologie des marchés*. Paris: Armand Colin.

François, P. and Lemercier, C. (2014). Ebbs and flows of french capitalism. In T. David and G. Westerhuis (Eds.), *The power of corporate networks*, (149–168). London: Routledge.

François, P. and Lemercier, C. (2016). Une financiarisation à la française (1979-2009). Mutation des grandes entreprises et conversion des élites. *Revue française de sociologie*, 57 (2), 269–320.

Freidson, E. (1986). *Professional powers: A study of institutionalization of formal knowledge*. Chicago: University of Chicago Press.

Freund, B. (2007). South Africa: The end of apartheid & the emergence of the "BEE Elite". *Review of African Political Economy*, 34(114), 661–678.

Friedberg, E. (1993). *Le pouvoir et la règle*. Paris: Seuil.

Froud, J., Haslam, C., Leaver, A. and Williams, K. (2000). Shareholder value and financialization: Consultancy promises and management moves. *Economy and Society*, 29(1), 80–110.

Fuertes, J. (2010). *Preparación y estallido de una crisis. De 2004 a 2010: Seis años de peregrinación de Casandra*. Madrid: Instituto de Estudios Economicos.

Gabadinho, A., Ritschard, G., Müller, N.S. and Studer, M. (2011). Analysing and visualising state sequences in R with TraMineR. *Journal of Statistical Software*, 40(4), 1–37.

Gentier, A. (2012). Spanish banks and the housing crisis: Worse than the subprime crisis? *International Journal of Business*, 17(4), 342–351.

Gieryn, T. (1983). Boundary-work and the demarcation of science from non-science: Strains and interests in professional ideologies of scientists. *American Sociological Review*, 48(6), 781–795.

Glaser, B. (1968). *Organizational careers. A sourcebook for theory*. Chicago: Aldine Publishing Company.

Godechot, O. (2001). *Les traders. Essai de sociologie des marchés financiers*. Paris: La Découverte.

Godechot, O. (2012). Is finance responsible for the rise in wage inequality in France?. *Socio-Economic Review*, 10(2), 1–24.

Godechot, O. (2013). Financiarisation et fractures socio-spatiales, *L'année Sociologique*, 63(1), 17–50.

Godechot, O. (2016). Ce que la finance fabrique. In I. Chambost, M. Lenglet and Y. Tadjeddine (Eds.), *La fabrique de la finance. Pour une approche interdisciplinaire*, (21–32). Villeneuve d'Ascq: Presses Universitaires du Septentrion.

Godechot, O. (2017). *Wages, bonuses and appropriation of profit in the financial industry*. London: Routledge.

References 247

Goffman, E. (1973). *La mise en scène de la vie quotidienne. Tome 1: La présentation de soi.* Paris: Éditions de Minuit.

Goldberg, R., Segel, A.I., Herrero, G. and Terris, A. (2012). Farmland investing: A technical note. *Harvard Business School Background Note*, 211–222.

Gonick, S. (2015). *At the margins of Europe: Homeownership, inclusion, and protest in contemporary Madrid.* (Doctoral dissertation). Berkeley, California: UC Berkeley.

Grabosky, P.N. and Braithwaite, J. (1986). *Of manners gentle: Enforcement strategies of Australian business regulatory agencies* (Vol. 1). Melbourne: Oxford University Press.

Graeber, D. (2012). *Debt: The first 5,000 years.* New York: Melville House.

Granovetter, M. (1974). *Getting a job: A study of contacts and careers.* Cambridge, Massachusettes: Harvard University.

Greenwald, J. (1990, February 26). Predator's Fall. *Time*, 46–52.

Greenwood, R. and Scharfstein, D. (2013). The growth of finance. *Journal of Economic Perspectives*, 27(2), 3–28.

Gueslin, A. (1984). *Histoire des crédits agricoles*, (Vols. 1–2). Paris: Economica.

Guilhot, N. (2004). *Financiers, philanthropes. Vocations éthiques et reproduction du capital à Wall Street depuis 1970.* Paris: Raisons d'Agir.

Gunnoe, A. (2014). The political economy of institutional landownership: Neorentier society and the financialization of land. *Rural Sociology*, 79(4), 478–504.

Hager, S.B. (2015). Corporate ownership of the public debt: mapping the new aristocracy of finance. *Socio-Economic Review*, 13(3), 505–523.

Hardy, C. and Maguire, S. (2008). Institutional entrepreneurship. In R. Greenwood, C. Oliver, R. Suddaby and K. Sahlin-Anderson (Eds.), *The Sage handbook of organizational institutionalism*, London: Sage.

Harrington, B. (2009). Trust and estate planning: The emergence of a profession and its contribution to socio-economic inequality. Max Planck Institute Discussion Paper, 9, 1–28.

Harrington, J.C. (2005). *The challenge to power: Money, investing and democracy.* White River Junction, Vermont: Chelsea Green Publishing.

Hart, O. and Moore, J. (1988). Incomplete contracts and renegotiation. *Econometrica*, 56(4), 755–785.

Hassoun, J.P. (2005). Emotions on the trading floors: Social and symbolic expressions. In K. Knorr Cettina and A. Preda (Eds.), *The sociology of financial markets*, (102–120). Oxford: Oxford University Press.

Healy, K. (2011). *The American Sociological Association has interest rate swap obligations?* Retrieved from http://crookedtimber.org/2011/03/02/the-american-sociological-association-has-interest-rate-swap-obligations/.

Heemskerk, E. (2007). *Decline of the corporate community. Network dynamics of the dutch business elite.* Amsterdam: Amsterdam University Press.

Heilbron, J., Verheul, J. and Quank, S. (2014). The origins and early diffusion of "shareholder value" in the United States. *Theory and Society*, 43(1), 1–22.

Henno, J. (1993). *La presse économique et financière.* Paris: Presses Universitaires de France.

Herlin-Giret, C. (2016). Les mondes de la richesse. Travailler et faire le capital. (Doctoral dissertation). Paris: Université Paris Dauphine.

Hilaire, J. (1989). La Révolution et les juridictions consulaires. In R. Badinter (Ed.), *Une autre justice: Contribution à l'histoire de la justice sous la Révolution*, (243–266). Paris: Fayard.

248 *References*

Hirsch, J.P. (1991). *Les deux rêves du commerce: Entreprise et institution dans la région lilloise (1780-1860)*. Paris: EHESS Editions.

Ho, K. (2009). *Liquidated: An ethnography of wall street*. Durham, North Carolina: Duke University Press.

Huault, I. and Richard, C. (Eds.) (2012). *Finance: The discreet regulator: How financial activities shape and transform the world*. London: Palgrave.

Huault, I., Lazega, E. and Richard, C. (2012). Introduction: The discreet regulator. In I. Huault, I and C. Richard (Eds.) (2012). *Finance: The discreet regulator: How financial activities shape and transform the world*, (1–16). London: Palgrave.

Hughes, E. (1945). Dilemmas and contradiction of status. *American Journal of Sociology*, 50(1), 353–359.

Hughes, E. (1958). *Men and their work*. Glencoe: The Free Press.

Hughes, E. (1962). Good people and dirty work. *Social Problems*, 10(1), 3–11.

Hughes, E. (1971). *The sociological eye. Selected papers*. New Brunswick: Transaction Books.

IFRS Foundation (2013). International financial reporting standard 13: Fair value measurement. London: IFRS Foundation.

Industrial Union Department Executive Committee on Pension and Benefit Fund Policy (1991, February 16). Internal Report. JS Records, Box 139, Folder 4.

Industrial Union Department Executive Committee on Pension and Benefit Fund Policy (1993, August 2). Internal Report. JS Records, Box 139, Folder 4.

"Issues of EPF Working their Way Towards Resolution." (1989, May 19). JS Records, Box 10, Folder 1.

Jensen, M. (1986). Agency cost of free cash flow, corporate finance, and takeovers. *American Economic Review*, 76(2), 323–329.

Jensen, M.C. (1989). Eclipse of the public corporation. *Harvard Business Review*, 67(5), 61–74.

Jobard, F. and Névanen, S. (2007). La couleur du jugement: Discriminations dans les décisions judiciaires en matière d'infractions à agents de la force publique (1965-2005). *Revue Française de Sociologie*, 2(48), 243–272.

Joly, H. (2007). Les études sur le recrutement du patronat: Une tentative de bilan critique. *Sociétés Contemporaines*, 68(4), 133–154.

Joly, N. (2011). Shaping records on the farm: Agricultural record-keeping in France from the nineteenth century to the liberation. *Agricultural History Review*, 59(1), 61–80.

Jones, J. (1998). *AmericanwWork: Four centuries of black and white labor*. New York: W.W. Norton.

Jung, J. and Dobbin, F. (2013). Finance and institutional investors. In K. Knorr-Cetina and A. Preda (Eds.), *The Oxford handbook of the sociology of finance*, (52–74). Oxford: Oxford University Press.

Kadushin, C. (1995). Friendship among the French financial elite. *American Sociological Review*, 60(2), 202–221.

Kanter Moss, R. (1977). *Men and women in the corporation*. New York: Basic Books.

Kaufman, A. and Englander, E. (1993). Kohlberg, Kravits Roberts & Co and the restructuring of American capitalism. *Business History Review*, 67(1), 52–97.

Kessler, A.D. (2007). *A revolution in commerce: The Parisian merchant court and the rise of commercial society in eighteenth-century France*. New Haven: Yale University Press.

Kirkland, L. (1989, January 26). Testimony before the U.S. Senate Finance Committee, Hearing on Leveraged Buyouts and Corporate Debt.

References 249

Knorr-Cetina, K., & Bruegger, U. (2002). Global Microstructures: The Virtual Societies of Financial Markets. *American Journal of Sociology*, 107(4), 905–950.

Knorr-Cetina, K. (2005). How are global markets global? The architecture of a flow world. In K. Knorr-Cetina and A. Preda (Eds.), *The sociology of financial markets*, (38–61). Oxford: Oxford University Press.

Knorr-Cetina, K. and Preda, A. (2005). *The sociology of financial markets*. Oxford: Oxford University Press.

Kolopp, S. (2013). De la modernisation à la raison économique. *Genèses*, 93(4), 53–75.

Kornrich, S. and Hicks, A. (2015). The rise of finance: Causes and consequences of financialization. *Socio-Economic Review*, 13(3), 411–415.

Krippner, G.R. (2005). The Financialization of the American Economy, *Socio-economic Review*, 3(2), 173–208.

Krippner, G.R. (2012). *Capitalizing on Crisis. The Political Origins of the Rise of Finance*. Cambridge, Massachusetts and London: Harvard University Press.

L'Italien, F., Hanin, F., Duhaime, E. and Pineault, E. (2011). La financiarisation du secteur forestier: Le cas de produits forestiers résolu. *Revue Interventions économiques*, 44. Retrieved from https://interventionseconomiques.revues.org/1594.

Laferté, G. (2013). *L'embourgeoisement agricole dans les formes localisées de la structure sociale. Revisite et ethnographie collective*. Mémoire d'Habilitation à Diriger des Recherches, Paris: Université de Paris 4.

Laferté, G. (2014). L'embourgeoisement agricole. Les céréaliers du Châtillonnais, de la modernisation agricole à nos jours. *Sociétés Contemporaines*, 96(4), 27–50.

L'AGEFI éditions Ed. (2011). *Le Guide des états-majors des grandes entreprises*. Paris: Etats-majors éditions.

Lagneau-Ymonet, P. (2008). The French stockbrokers between the market and the state: A Lost Profession. *AIS Conference*. Oslo: AIS.

Lagneau-Ymonet, P. and Riva, A. (2011). *Histoire de la Bourse*. Paris: La Découverte.

Lamard, P. and Stoskopf, N. (Eds.) (2015). *L'entreprise rhénane, mythe ou réalité?* Paris: Picard.

Lamont, M. and Molnar, V. (2002). The study of boundaries in the social sciences. *Annual Review of Sociology*, 28, 167–195.

Langley, P. (2008). Securitizing suburbia: The transformation of anglo-american mortgage finance. *Competition and Change*, 10(3), 283–299.

Larder, N., Sippel, S.R. and Lawrence, G. (2015). Finance capital, food security narratives and Australian agricultural land. *Journal of Agrarian Change*, 15(4), 592–603.

Lareau, A. and Conley, D. (2008). *Social class: How does it work?* New York: Russell Sage Fondation.

Lascoumes, P. and Le Galès, P. (2007). Understanding public policy through its instruments —From the nature of instruments to the sociology of public policy instrumentation. *Governance: An International Journal of Policy, Administration, and Institutions*, 20(1), 1–21.

Laumann, E.O., and Knoke, D. (1987). *The organizational state: Social choice in national policy domains*. Wisconsin: University of Wisconsin Press.

Lavigne, A. (1991). Cent soixante-quinze ans de bilans. Jalons pour une histoire financière de la Caisse des dépôts et consignations. *Revue d'Économie Financière*, HS, 287–317.

Lawrence, T.B. and Suddaby, R. (2006). Institutions and institutional work. In S.R. Clegg, C. Hardy, T.B. Lawrence and W.R. Nord (Eds.), *Handbook of organization studies*, (215–254). London: Sage.

250 *References*

Lazarus, J. (2012). *L'épreuve de l'argent. Banques, banquiers, clients.* Paris: Calmann-Lévy.

Lazega, E. (1992). *Micropolitics of knowledge. Communication and indirect control in workgroups.* Hawthorne: Aldine de Gruyter.

Lazega, E. (1994). Analyse de réseaux et sociologie des organisations. *Revue Française de Sociologie*, 35(2), 293–320.

Lazega, E. (2003). *Networks in legal organizations: On the protection of public interest in joint regulation of markets.* Wiarda Chair Oratie. Utrecht: Wiarda Institute Publications, Faculty of Law, Utrecht University.

Lazega, E. (2011). Four and half centuries of new law and economics: Legal pragmatism, discreet joint regulation and institutional capture at the Commercial Court of Paris. In U. de Vries and L. Francot-Timmermans (Eds.), *Law's environment: Critical legal perspectives*, (179–204). The Hague: Eleven International Publishing.

Lazega, E. and Favereau, O. (2002). Introduction. In O. Favereau and E. Lazega (Eds.), *Conventions and structures in economic organization: Markets, networks, and hierarchies*, (1–28). Cheltenham: Edward Elgar Publishing.

Lazega, E. and Mounier, L. (2002). Interdependent entrepreneurs and the social discipline of their cooperation: a research programme for structural economic sociology in a society of organizations. In O. Favereau and E. Lazega (Eds.), *Conventions and structures in economic organization: Markets, networks, and hierarchies*, (147–199). Cheltenham: Edward Elgar Publishing.

Lazega, E. and Mounier, L. (2003a). Interlocking judges: On joint (exogenous and self) governance of markets. *Research in the Sociology of Organizations*, 20, 267–95.

Lazega, E. and Mounier, L. (2003b). Lorsque l'État se retire du contrôle de l'économie, qui prend le relais?. In J. Crête (Ed.), *Hommage à Vincent Lemieux : La science politique au Québec*, (155–78). Laval: Presses de l'Université Laval.

Lazega, E. and Mounier, L. (2003c). La régulation conjointe du marché: Le cas du Tribunal de Commerce de Paris. In B. Convert (Ed.), *Repenser le marché. Cahiers Lillois d'Économie et de Sociologie*, n° 41–42.

Lazega, E. and Mounier, L. (2009). Polynormativité et contrôle social du monde des affaires: l'Exemple de l'interventionnisme et de la punitivité des juges du Tribunal de commerce de Paris. *Droit et Société*, 1(71), 103–132.

Lazega, E. and Mounier, L. (2012). Networks of institutional capture. In B. Vedres and M. Scotti (Eds.), *Networks in social policy problems*, (124–137). Cambridge: Cambridge University Press.

Lazega, E., Mounier, L. and Brandes, U. (2011). Entrepreneurs institutionnels et 'détachement organisationnel' dans l'auto-discipline du monde des affaires: Le cas des juges consulaires du Tribunal de Commerce de Paris. In C. Bessy, T. Delpeuch and J. Pélisse (Eds.), *Droit et régulations des activités économiques*, Paris: Editions L.G.D.J.

Lazonick, W. and O'Sullivan, M. (2000). Maximizing shareholder value: A new ideology for corporate gouvernance. *Economy and Society*, 29(1), 13–35.

Le Bris, D. (2011). *Les actions françaises depuis 1854: analyses et découvertes.* (Doctoral dissertation). Orléans : Université d'Orléans.

Le Roux, B. and Rouanet, H. (2004). *Geometric data analysis. From correspondence analysis to structured data analysis.* Dordrecht, Boston: Kluwer Academic Publishers.

Lebaron, F. (2000). *La croyance économique. Les économistes entre science et politique.* Paris: Le Seuil.

Lecerf, O. (1991). *Au risque de gagner. Le métier de dirigeant.* Paris: de Fallois.

Lemercier, C. (2003). *Un si discret pouvoir. Aux origines de la Chambre de commerce de Paris, 1803–1853.* Paris: La Découverte.

References 251

Lemercier, C. (2007). The judge, the expert and the arbitrator. The strange case of the Paris Court of Commerce (ca. 1800–ca. 1880). In C. Rabier (Ed.), *Fields of expertise. A comparative history of expert procedures in Paris and London, 1600 to present*, (115–145). Newcastle: Cambridge Scholars Publishing.

Lemoine, B. (2016). *L'ordre de la dette. Enquête sur les infortunes de l'État et la prospérité du marché*. Paris: La Découverte.

Lépinay, V.A. (2011). *Codes of finance. Engineering derivatives in a global bank.* Princeton: Princeton University Press.

Leteinturier, C. (2014). *Les journalistes français et leur environnement: 1990–2012.* Paris: Pantheon Assas Paris II.

Lévêque, S. (2000). *Les journalistes sociaux. Histoire et sociologie d'une spécialité journalistique.* Rennes: Presses Universitaires de Rennes.

Leyshon, A. and Thrift, N. (1996). Financial exclusion and the shifting boundaries of the financial system. *Environment and Planning A*, 28(7), 1150–1156.

Lin, K. and Tomaskovic-Devey, D. (2013). Financialization and U.S. income inequality, 1970–2008. *American Journal of Sociology*, 118(5), 1284–1329.

Lordon, F. (2000). La "création de valeur" comme rhétorique et comme pratique. Généalogie et sociologie de la "valeur actionnariale". *L'année de la Régulation*, 4, 117–165.

Lorrain, D. (2011). La main discrète. La finance globale dans la ville. *Revue Française de Science Politique*, 61(6), 1097–1122.

Madigan, P. (2013). Exemptions in the balance. *Risk Magazine*, 26(12), 22–25.

Manning, P. (2013). Financial journalism, news sources and the banking crisis. *Journalism* 14(2), 173–189.

Marchetti, D., Devillard V. and Lafosse, M.-F. (2001). Les marches du travail journalistique. In D. Marchetti and D. Ruellen (Eds.), *Devenir journalistes. Les conditions d'entrée sur le marché du travail*, Paris: Documentation française.

Marcus, G. (1983). The fiduciary role in American family dynasties and their institutional legacy. In G. Marcus (Ed.), *Elites:Ethnographic Issues*, (221–256). Albuquerque: University of New Mexico Press.

Marry, C. (2004). *Les femmes ingénieurs: Une révolution respectueuse.* Paris: Belin.

Marsden, D. (2007). Labour market segmentation in Britain: The decline of occupational labour markets and the spread of 'entry tournaments'. Économie et Sociétés, série AB, 41(28), 1027–1056.

Martín, M. (2014). Análisis de los fondos de titulizacion espanoles: Caracteristicas en el momento de su constitucion y comportamiento durante los anos de la crisis. Comisión Nacional del Mercado de Valores, Documento de trabajo, 57, January 2014.

Martin, R. (2002). *The financialization of daily life.* Philadelphia: Temple University Press.

Mauss, M. (2012). *Essai sur le don.* Paris: Presses Universitaires de France.

Mayer, M. (1997). *The Bankers, the next generation.* NewYork: Truman Talley Books.

McCall, L. (2005). The complexity of intersectionality. Signs. *Journal of Women in Culture and Society*, 30(3), 1771–1800.

McCarthy, M. (2014). Turning labor into capital: Pension funds and the corporate control of finance. *Politics & Society*, 42(2), 455–487.

McCarthy, M., V.-P. Sorsa and van der Zwan, N. (2016). Investment preferences and patient capital: Financing, governance, and regulation in pension fund capitalism. Socio-Economic Review, 14 (4), 751–769.

MacKenna, C. (2006). *The world's newest profession, management consulting in the twentieth century.* Cambridge: Cambridge University Press.

252 *References*

MacKenzie, D. (2004). The big, bad wolf and the rational market: Portfolio insurance, the 1987 crash and the performativity of economics. *Economy and Society*, 33(3), 303–334.

MacKenzie, D. (2005). Opening the black boxes of global finance, *Review of International Political Economy*, 12(4), 555–576.

MacKenzie, D. (2006). *An engine, not a camera: How financial models shape markets.* Cambridge: MIT Press.

MacKenzie, D. and Millo, Y. (2003). Constructing a market. Performing theory: The historical sociology of financial derivatives exchange. *American Journal of Sociology*, 109(1), 107–145.

MacKenzie, D. and Spears, T. (2014a). 'The formula that killed Wall Street': The Gaussian copula and modelling practices in investment banking. *Social Studies of Science*, 44(3), 393–417.

MacKenzie, D. and Spears, T. (2014b). 'A device for being able to book P&L': The organizational embedding of the Gaussian copula. *Social Studies of Science*, 44(3), 418–40.

McIntosh, W.V. and Cates, C.L. (1997). Judicial entrepreneurship: The role of the judge in the marketplace of ideas, 83. Westport, CT: Greenwood Publishing Group.

Mendras, H. (1971). *The vanishing peasant: Innovation and change in French agriculture.* (J. Lerner Trans.). Cambridge: MIT Press.

Meyer, J.W. and Rowan, B. (1977). Institutionalized organizations: Formal structure as myth and ceremony. *American Journal of Sociology*, 83(2), 340–363.

Mignot-Gérard, S. and Musselin, C. (2005). *Chacun cherche son LMD. L'adoption par les universités françaises du schéma européen des études supérieures en deux cycles.* Paris: Rapport d'enquête CSO/ESEN.

Mignot-Gérard, S., Perrin-Joly, C., Sarfati, F. (coord.) and Vézinat, N. (2014). *Entrer dans la banque. Le cas des étudiants en alternance de filières banque et finance d'un IAE.* Paris: Rapport APEC.

Mignot-Gérard, S., Perrin-Joly, C., Sarfati, F. and Vézinat, N. (2017). Early careers in portfolio & wealth management. The roles of class, race and gender in occupational segmentations. In V. Boussard (Ed.), *Finance at work*, London: Routledge.

Milberg, W. (2008). Shifting sources and uses of profits: Sustaining US financialization with global value chains. *Economy and Society*, 37(3), 420–451.

Ministère de l'Economie, Conseil d'orientation des retraites. (réunion du 12 sept 2002). *Retraite par répartition et complément de retraite.* Direction de la prévision. Paris: Ministère de l'Economie.

Mizruchi, M.S. (2013). *The fracturing of the american corporate elite.* Cambridge: Harvard University Press.

Mizruchi, M.S. and Brewster Stearns, L. (2001). Getting deals done: The use of social networks in bank decision-making. *American Sociological Review*, 66(5), 647–671.

Montagne, S. (2006). *Les fonds de pension. Entre protection sociale et spéculation financière.* Paris: Odile Jacob.

Montagne, S. (2009). Des évaluateurs indépendants? Un impératif de la théorie économique soumis à l'enquête sociologique. *Cahiers Internationaux de Sociologie*, 1(126), 131–148.

Montagne, S. (2014). Go-go managers contre futurs prix Nobel d'économie. *Sociétés Contemporaines*, 93(1), 9–37.

Montagne, S. (2016). Penser la finance comma rapport social: la gestion d'actifs, nouvelle arène du conflit capital-travail. In I. Chambost, M. Lenglet and Y. Tadjeddine (Eds.), *La fabrique de la finance. Pour une approche interdisciplinaire*, (183 –190).Villeneuve d'Ascq: Presses Universitaires du Septentrion.

References 253

Morin, F. (1998). La rupture du modèle français de détention et de gestion des capitaux, *Revue d'économie financière*, 50(6), 111–132.

Morin, F. and Dupuy, C. (1993). *Le cœur financier européen*. Paris: Economica.

Morini, M. (2011). *Understanding and managing model risk: A practical guide for quants, traders and validators*. Chichester: Wiley.

Moulévrier, P. (2002). *Le mutualisme bancaire. Le Crédit Mutuel de l'Église au marché*. Rennes: PUR.

Muniesa, F. (2005). Contenir le marché: La transition de la criée à la cotation électronique à la Bourse de Paris. *Sociologie du Travail*, 47, 485–501.

Muniesa, F. (2007). Market technologies and the pragmatics of prices. *Economy and Society*, 36(3), 377–395.

Muniesa, F. (2011). Is a stock exchange a computer solution? Explicitness, algorithms and the Arizona Stock Exchange. *International Journal of Actor–Network Theory and Technological Innovation*, 3(1), 1–15.

Muniesa, F. (2012). A flank movement in the understanding of valuation. *Sociological Review*, 59(2), 24–38.

Naredo, J. (1996). La burbuja inmobiliario-financiera en la coyuntura económica reciente (1985-1995). Madrid: Siglo XXI.

Nawalkha, S.K. and Rebonato, R. (2011). What interest rate models to use? Buy side versus sell side. Journal of Investment Management, 9(3), 5–18.

Neveu, A. (2007). Trente années au service du financement de l'agriculture. *Économie Rurale*, 300, 85–88.

Oberlechner, T., and Hocking, S. (2004). Information sources, news, and rumors in financial markets: Insights into the foreign exchange market. *Journal of Economic Psychology*, 25(3), 407–424.

O'Donnell, P., Zion, L. and Sherwood, M. (2016). Where do journalists go after newsroom job cuts? *Journalism Practice*, 10(1), 35–51.

O'Meara, D. (2009). *Volkskapitalisme: Class, capital and ideology in the development of Afrikaner nationalism*, 1934-1948. Cambridge: Cambridge University Press.

Orange, M. (2006). *Ces messieurs de Lazard*. Paris: Albin Michel.

Orléan, A. (1999). *Le Pouvoir de La Finance*. Paris: Odile Jacob.

Orléan, A. (2004). L'économie des conventions: Définition et résultats. In A. Orléan (Ed.), *Analyse économique des conventions* (2nd ed.), Paris: PUF.

Orléan, A. (2014). *The empire of value. A new foundation for economics*. Cambridge: MIT Press.

Ortiz, H. (2014a). The limits of financial imagination: Free investors, efficient markets, and crisis. *American Anthropologist*, 116(1), 38–50.

Ortiz, H. (2014b). *Valeur financière et vérité. Enquête d'anthropologie politique sur l'évaluation des entreprises cotées en bourse*. Paris: Presses de Science Po.

Oubenal, M. (2015). *La légitimation des produits financiers*. Paris: Éditions EMS.

Ouroussof, A. (2010). *Wall Street at war. The secret struggle for the global economy*. Cambridge: Polity Press.

Oyer, P. (2008). The making of an investment banker: Stock market shocks, career choice and lifetime income. *The Journal of Finance*, 63(6), 2601–2628.

Padgett, J. F. (2012). Matrimonio y estructura de la élite en la Florencia Renacentista, 1282-1500. *REDES-Revista hispana para el Análisis de redes sociales*, 21(0).

Palomera, J. (2014). How did finance capital infiltrate the world of the urban poor? Home ownership and social fragmentation in a spanish neighborhood. *International Journal of Urban and Regional Research*, 38(1), 218–35.

254 *References*

Parodi, M. (1999). Opportunités d'embauche et carrière, *Revue de l'OFCE*, 68(1), 241–254.

Patterson, B. (1989, December 19). Letter to J. Sheinkman. JS Records, Box 10, Folder 5.

Peralta I.A. (2015). Financialization, non-financial corporations and income inequality: The case of France. *Socio-Economic Review*, 13(3), 449–475.

Perrin-Heredia, A. (2013). La mise en ordre de l'économie domestique. *Gouvernement et Action Publique*, 2(2), 303–330.

Perry, J. and Nölke, A. (2006). The political economy of international accounting standards. *Review of International Political Economy*, 13(4), 559–586.

Pezet, A. and Morales, J. (2010). Les contrôleurs de gestion, 'médiateurs' de la financiarisation. *Comptabilité Contrôle Audit*, 16(1), 101–132.

Pfeffer, J. and Salancik, G. (1978). *The external control of organizations: A resource dependence perspective.* Stanford: Stanford University Press.

Philippon, T. (2015). Has the US finance industry become less efficient? On the theory and measurement of financial intermediation. *American Economic Review*, 105(4), 1408–38.

Pickering, A. (1993). The Mangle of practice: Agency and emergence in the sociology of science. *The American Journal of Sociology*, 99(3), 559–89.

Piketty, T. (2014). *Capital in the twenty first century.* (A. Goldhammer Trans.). Cambridge, Massechsettes: Harvard University Press.

Plot, S. (2013). Le consommateur au crible de la commission de surendettement. *Actes de la Recherche en Sciences Sociales*, (1994), 88–101.

Polanyi, K. (2001). *The great transformation: The political and economic origins of our time.* Boston: Beacon Press.

Poon, M. (2009). From new deal institution to capital markets: Commercial consumer risk scores and the making of subprime mortgage finance. *Accounting, Organizations and Society*, 34(5), 654–674.

Power, M. (2010). Fair value accounting, financial economics and the transformation of reliability. *Accounting and Business Research*, 40(3), 197–210.

Preda, A. (2001). Sense and sensibility: Or, how should social studies of finance be have? A manifesto. *Economic Sociology: European Electronic Newsletter*, 2(2), 15–18.

Preda, A. (2005). The investor as a cultural figure of global capitalism. In K. Knorr-Cetina and A. Preda (Eds.), *The Sociology of Financial Markets*, (141–162). Oxford: Oxford University Press.

Purseigle, F. and Hervieu, B. (2009). Pour une sociologie des mondes agricoles dans la globalisation. *Etudes Rurales*, 183, 177–200.

Ragas, M.W. and Tran, H. L. (2015). The financial news ecosystem: Journalists' perceptions of group hierarchy. *Journalism*, 16(6), 711–729.

Ramirez, C. (2003). Du commissaire aux comptes à l'auditeur: les "big 4" et la transformation de la profession comptable libérale française depuis 1970. *Actes de la Recherche en Sciences Sociales*, 146–147, 62–79.

Rappaport, A. (1986). *Creating shareholder value: The new standard for business performance.* New York: Free Press.

Ravelli, Q. (2015). Le charme du *Ladrillo*. Une histoire de briques au coeur de la crise espagnole. *Vacarme*, 63, 143–161.

Ravelli, Q. (2016). *Bricks: A documentary on the economic crisis in Spain.* Paris: Survivance.

Ravetz, J.R. (1971). Science as craftman's work. In J.R. Ravetz (Ed.), *Scientific knowledge and its social problems*, (75–108). Oxford: Clarendon Press.

Rebonato, R. (2004). Interest-rate term-structure pricing models: A review. *Proceedings of the Royal Society A: Mathematical, Physical and Engineering Sciences*, 460(2043), 667–728.

Rebonato, R. (2013). How derivatives and risk models really work: Sociological pricing and the role of co-ordination. SSRN. Retrieved from http://papers.ssrn.com/sol3/papers.cfm?abstract_id=2365294.

Reich, G. (1986). *Un financier de genie, André Meyer*. Paris: Belfond.

Reinardy, S. (2011). Newspaper journalism in crisis: Burnout on the rise, eroding young journalists' career commitment. *Journalism*, 12(1), 33–50.

Renard, V. (2008). La ville saisie par la finance. *Le Débat*, 148, 106–117.

"Request for Proposal: Employee Partnership Fund." (1989, June 16). JS Records, Box 10, Folder 4.

Reynaud, J.-D. (1989). *Les règles du jeu*. Paris: Armand Colin.

Riles, A. (2010). Collateral Expertise. *Current Anthropology*, 51(6), 795–818.

Riutort, P. (2000). Le journalisme au service de l'économie. *Actes de la Recherche en Sciences Sociales*, 131(1), 41–55.

Roibás, M.I. (2014, August 9). Securitization in Spain: Past development and estimated future trends. Economic Watch – BBVA Research.

Rosenbaum, J.E. (1979). Tournament mobility: Career patterns in a corporation. *Administrative Science Quarterly*, 24(2), 220–241.

Roth, L.M. (2003). Selling women short: A research note on gender differentiation in compensation on Wall Street. *Social Forces*, 82(2), 783–802.

Roth, L.M. (2006). *Selling women short. Gender and money on Wall Street*. Princeton: Princeton University Press.

Sadr, A. (2009). Interest rate swaps and their derivatives: A practitioner's guide. Hobokon: John Wiley & Sons.

Sarfati, F. (2007). Quand la passion s'en mêle. La mixité à l'épreuve des modes d'engagement au travail. *Sociologies Pratiques*,14, 59–73.

Sarfati, F. (2012). *Du côté des vainqueurs. Une sociologie de l'incertitude sur les marchés du travail*. Presses Universitaires du Septentrion, coll. "Sciences Sociales".

Sarfatti, L.M. (1977). *The Rise of Prefessionalism. A Sociological Analysis*. Berkeley: University of California Press.

Sauviat, C. (2003). Deux professions dans la tourmente. L'audit et l'analyse financière. *Actes de la Recherche en Sciences Sociales*, 146–147, 21–41.

SAVCA (South African Venture Capital and Private Equity Association) (2015). Three decades. An account of the rise and establishment of South Africa private equity. Johannesburg: SAVCA.

SAVCA (South African Venture Capital and Private Equity Association) and KPMG. (2015). Members' directory. Private equity and venture capital in Southern Africa. Johannesburg: SAVCA.

Scott, J. (1990). Corporate control and corporate rule: Britain in an international perspective. *British Journal of Sociology*, 41(3), 351–373.

Selznick, P. (1960). *The organizational weapon: a study of Bolshevik strategy and tactics*. New York: Free Press.

Sheinkman, J. (1979). The Union Role in the Boardroom. *The Employee Relations Law Journal* 5(1), 14–20.

Sheinkman, J. (1989, February 6). Letter to I. Millstein. JS Records, Box 10, Folder 1.

Shepard, D. (2012). Situating private equity capital in the land grab debate. *Journal of Peasant Studies*, 39(3/4), 703–729.

256   References

Sherman, R. (2007). Service and inequality in luxury hotels. Berkeley and Los Angeles: University of California Press.

Shleifer, A. and Summers, L.H. (1988). Breach of trust in hostile takeovers. In S. Sibanda and S. Turner (Eds.), *Corporate Takeovers: Causes and Consequences*. Chicago: The University of Chicago Press.

Shydlo, B. (2007). Profit and loss explained. Energy Risk, July, 76–79.

Sibanda, S. and Turner, S. (1999). Land tenure reform and rural livelihoods in southern Africa. *Overseas Development Institute: Natural Resource Perspectives*, 39, 1–15.

Silici, L. and Locke, A. (2014). *Private equity investments and agricultural development in Africa: Opportunities and challenges*. Paper presented at the Food, finance and farmland workshop, Institute of Social Studies, The Haye.

Stearns, L.B. and Allan, K.D. (1996). Economic behavior in institutional environments: The corporate merger wave of the 1980s. *American Sociological Review*, 61(4), 699.

Stinchcombe, B. and Carruthers, A. (1999). The social structure of liquidity: Flexibility, markets, and states. *Theory and Society*, 28(3), 353–382.

Stovel, K., Savage, M. and Bearman, P. (1996). Ascription into achievement: models of career systems at Lloyds Banks 1890-1970. *American Journal of Sociology*, 102, 358–399.

Studer, M. (2013). Weighted cluster library manual: A practical guide to creating typologies of trajectories in the social sciences with R. *Lives Working Papers*, 24. DOI: http://dx.doi.org/10.12682/lives.2296-1658.2013.24.

Styhre, A. (2013). The economic valuation and commensuration of cultural resources: Financing and monitoring the Swedish culture sector. *Valutation studies*, 1(1), 51–81.

Swedberg, R. (2003). The case for an economic sociology of law. *Theory and society*, 32(1), 1–37.

Swoboda, F. (1990, February 20). AFL-CIO unveals fund for employee buyout. *The Washington Post*.

Tambini, D. (2010). What are financial journalists for? *Journalism Studies*, 11(2), 158–174.

Thomas, L. (2012). *Study on private equity in agribusiness in Southern Africa*. Southern Africa: USAID.

Tilly, C. (1998). *Durable inequality*. Berkeley: University of California Press.

Tomaskovic-Devey, D., Lin, K.L. and Meyers, N. (2015). Did financialization reduce economic growth?. *Socio-Economic Review*, 13(3), 525–548.

Tortosa, E. (2015). *Fulgor y muerte de la cajas de ahorros*. Valencia: Publicacions de la Universitat de València.

Tunstall, J. (1971). *Journalists at work: specialist correspondents: their news organizations, news sources, and competitor-colleagues*. London: Constable.

Useem, M. (1996). *Investor capitalism, how money managers are changing the face of corporate america*. New York: Basic Books.

Uzzi, B. (1997). Social structure and competition in interfirm networks: The paradox of embeddedness. *Administrative Science Quaterly*, 42(1), 35–67.

Uzzi, B. (1999). Social relations and networks in the making of financial capital. *American Sociological Review*, 64(4), 481–505.

Vallée, O. (2011). L'économique africain saisie par la finance. *Politique Africaine*, 124(4), 67–86.

Vallery, G. (1992). *Travail et concertation sociale de la conduite d'un projet informatique: Le cas de la Caisse d'Epargne de Paris*. Paris: ANACT.

References 257

Van der Zwan, N. (2014). Making sense of financialization. *Socio-Economic Review*, 12(1), 99–129.

Van der Zwan, N. (2011). *Contentious capital. The politics of pension investment in the United States and Germany, 1974–2003*. (Doctoral dissertation). New York: New School for Social Research.

Van Zanten, A. (2010). "L'ouverture sociale des grandes écoles: diversification des élites ou renouveau des politiques d'éducation ?" *Sociétés contemporaines*, 3 (19), 69–95.

Vargha, Z. (2011). From long-term savings to instant mortgages: financial demonstration and the role of interaction in markets. *Organization*, 18(2), 215–235.

Vatin, F. (2013). Valuation as evaluating and valorizing. *Valuation Studies*, 1(1), 83–117.

Vezinat, N. (2012). *Les métamorphoses de la Poste. Professionnalisation des conseillers financiers (1953–2012)*. Paris: PUF.

Vorms, C. (2013). Madrid années 1950: La question des baraques. *Le Mouvement Social*, 245(4), 43–57.

Wall Street Journal (February 16, 1990). "Buy-out fund Planned to Help Workers Finance Takeovers of their Employers."

Wasserman, S., & Faust, K. (1994). *Social Network Analysis: Methods and Applications*. Cambridge: Cambridge University Press.

Weber, M. (2001). *The protestant ethic and the spirit of capitalism*. (T. Parsons Trans.). London and New York: Routledge.

Welles, C. (1973). The bleak wasteland of financial reporting. *Columbia Journalism Review*, 12(2), 40–49.

White, H.C. (1981). Where do markets come from? *American Journal of Sociology*, 87(3), 517–547.

Whitley, R. (1986). The transformation of business finance into financial economics: The roles of academic expansion and changes in U.S. capital markets. *Accounting, Organizations and Society*, 11(2), 171–192.

Widmer, F. (2011). Institutional investors, corporate elites and the building of a market for corporate control. *Socio-Economic Review*, 9(4), 671–697.

Williams, J.W. (2014). Feeding finance: A critical account of the shifting relationships between finance, food and farming. *Economy and Society*, 43(3), 401–431.

Williamson, O. (1985). *The Economic Institutions of Capitalism*. New York: Simon and Schuster.

Windolf, P. (1999). L'évolution du capitalisme moderne. La France dans une perspective comparative. *Revue française de sociologie*, 40(3), 501–529.

Wolf, M. (2008, October 1). Congress decides it is worth risking another depression. *Financial Times*, p. 17.

World Bank (n.d.). Financial Access Survey of the International Monetary Fund, Commercial Bank Branches. Retrieved from http://data.worldbank.org/indicator/FB.CBK.BRCH.P5?page=1.

Wrong, D.H. (1961). The oversocialized conception of man in modern sociology. *American Sociological Review*, 26(2), 183–193.

Zaloom, C. (2006). *Out of the pits, traders and technology from Chicago to London*. Chicago and London: The University of Chicago Press.

Zelizer, V. (1985). *Pricing the priceless child: The changing social value of children*. Princeton: Princeton University Press.

Zelizer, V. (1992). Repenser le marché. *Actes de la Recherche en Sciences Sociales*, 94(1), 3–26.

258 References

Zelizer, V. (1994). *The social meaning of money: Pin money, paychecks, poor relief and other currencies*. New York: Basic Books.

Zorn, D., Dobbin, F., Dierkes, J. and Kwok, M.-S. (2005). Managing investors: How financial markets reshaped the American firm. In K. Knorr-Cetina and A. Preda (Eds.), *The sociology of financial markets*, (269–289). Oxford: Oxford University Press.

Zorn, D.M. (2004). Here a chief, there a chief: The rise of the CFO in the American firm. *American Sociological Review*, 69(3), 345–364.

Zuckerman, E.W. (1999). The categorical imperative: Securities analysts and the illegitimacy discount. *American Journal of Sociology*, 104(5), 1398–1438.

Index

Abbott, A. 20, 177, 217
abusive clauses 118
'accumulation' studies 5
agency theory 58–9, 223
American Sociological Association (ASA) 42
Analistas Financieros Internacionales (AFI) 108
Anseeuw, W. 123
asset management 210; forms of 105; internal plans to develop 102; master's degrees graduates trained in 18; specialists 14; survey 93

bank counsellors 94, 103–5
bankruptcy *see* Commercial Court of Paris (TCP) (2000–2005), bankruptcy proceedings at
Barclays 51
Barth, F. 26
Becker, H. 41
Benoist, G. 152
Berges, A. 108
"black box" of finance 25
Black-Scholes options pricing model 46
Blackstone 229
blind pool 64
boundary issue 9–20; boundary work 26; conversion 15; crossing boundaries 15–17; diversity, segmentation, stratification within financial occupations 17–20; finance (social closure and exclusionary process) 9–12; financiers as intermediaries in conversion to financial logics 13–15; individual careers as vehicles for financialisation 15–17; internal boundaries 17–20; passing through 13–15
bourgeois ethos, socialisation to 15
Boussard, V. 1, 16, 26, 140, 156, 220
Brantley, P. 156

CalPERS (California Public Employees' Retirement System) 67
capital allocation mechanism 5
capitalism: industrial capitalism 157; large- and small-scale 227–32, 235; shareholder 223; *see also* financial capitalism; managerial capitalism
Carswell, H.J. 175
Cates, C.L. 74
Chiapello, E. 4, 141
Commercial Court of Paris (TCP) (2000–2005), bankruptcy proceedings at 70–85; collective pragmatism, customs, and judgments 75; consular court 83–4; consular (public/private) justice in France 73–5; "don't feed the zombies" controversy 77–81; financial collective pragmatism, politicizing the judiciary by promoting 75–7; joint regulation of 74; "judicial entrepreneurs" 74; saving the financial zombie 81–3; shadow regulators and discreet policymakers, banks as 84–5; sources 72
commodified finance, rise of 164–6
"concierge service" 210
conversion 15
Cooke ratio 213
corporate "double-bind" 114
corporate investors 31
crossing boundaries 15–17

Delors, J. 153
derivatives quants 49
Diallo, A. 92
DiMaggio, P.J. 226
"don't feed the zombies" controversy 77–81
Dougal, C. 176
Doyle, G. 175
Drexel Burnham Lambert 60

260 *Index*

Drucker, P. 61
Ducastel, A. 123
Dujarier, M.-A. 26, 29
Duru-Bellat, M. 199

early careers in portfolio and wealth
management 194–209; APOGEE
software 196; back or middle offices
versus trading 203–4; class, race and
gender 198; contrasted trajectories in
wealth management 205–8; counselling
versus sales 202–3; influence of
"class" on the vertical segmentation
at the edge of employment 201–8;
"intersectionality" theories 194;
marginalized populations 194; Master's
programmes 195, 197–201; portfolio
management and wealth management
197–8; social capital, influence of on
vertical differentiation 204; socially
diversified cohorts 198–9; social
studies of finance 194; sources 196; US
scholars 194; women and non-nationals
199–201
economic activities, financialising of
89–91
Economics and Business Administration
(EBA) 184, 186
Employee Partnership Fund (EPF) 57;
imagining of 61–4; selling of 64–8
employee stock ownership plans 62
Employment Retirement Income Security
Act 63
Engelberg, J. 176
Enron 175
executive positions, ways to access 169–70
'exotic' derivatives 47

fair value accounting 42, 46–7
farmers, private wealth of 92–107;
bank counsellors 103–5; bankers'
representations of their farming clientele
94–100; diversified asset class, farmers
as 96–100; financialising of farmers'
assets: 100–3; sources 93–4
farmland *see* South African farmland,
assetisation of
Filippi, C.-H. 152
finance: boundaries of 10–13; employees,
growing social diversity among 195
financial backlash *see* social protest, when
local bankers face
financial capitalism: capital allocation
mechanism 5; financiers 6; LBOs and

230; occupations 156; radical practices
within 236
financialisation, as boundary dynamics of
finance 20–22
financialisation, investigating 2–6;
outcome of a specific work 6; shifts
in capital allocation mechanism 3–5;
three-fold definition 2–3; unpacking
financialisation 5–6
financialization, interrogation of an
analytic 25–8; boundary work 26
financiers at work 7–9; conditions of
employment and the career design 7–8;
organisational structure, characteristics
of 8; professional norms 8–9; working
day composition of 7–8
Fligstein, N. 89, 143, 156, 172, 229
fortune and privacy management 210–22;
asset management 210; competitive
advantages of a wealth planning
rhetoric 216–17; "concierge service"
210; cultivation of plans and secrets
214; dialectic of sales and consulting
213–14; emotions 210; exclusionary
rhetoric 217–18; family governance
becoming a masculine skill 219–21;
fragile boundary between wealth and
asset management 212–14; French
Family Office Association 218–19;
importance of wealth planning 215–16;
sources 211
Foureault, F. 223
France, business school graduates in
156–74; commodified finance, rise of
164–6; economic elites 157; executive
positions, ways to access 169–70;
financial roles across cohorts 161–4;
hypotheses 158; industrial capitalism
157; sources 159–61; top executive
positions, financial roles as springboard
for 167–72; trajectories in finance 166–7
France, second financialisation in 142–55;
conversion of experienced elite 143;
elite educational institutions 146;
finance departments 150–2; financial
vs. non-financial careers 146–9; loci of
conversion 149–55 Ministry of Finance
152–3; multi-functional careers 147;
private careers 153–5; "providential
men" 147; "Rhineland model" 154;
sources 144–5
François, P. 142, 145
French Family Office Association (FFOA)
218–19

Index 261

French financial elite, transformation of 139–41

French financial journalists 175–88; boundary between journalism and finance 177; erosion of journalistic careers 180–3; French case and its historical specifics 176–9; historic trajectory 177; legitimacy 176; "market opinion" 176; press releases 182; role of stock market activity and training 183–5; sociology of finance 176; "Stepping Stone" class 184; sources 178–9; unstable commitment of financial journalists 180; "watchdogs" 175

front office quants 45–9; agreement with 52; governing of 51–3

García, D. 176

Gieryn, T. 20

Godechot, O. 191, 195, 204

Goldman Sachs 51, 229

hedging 46–9

Herlin-Giret, C. 210

Hermelin, P. 152

high-potential managers 147

'historical-cost' accounting practices 42

Ho, K. 25, 68

HSBC 216

industrial capitalism 157

"institutional entrepreneurs" 74

interest rate swap 42

intermediary organisations 1

internal boundaries 17–20

"Internet bubble" 183

investing managers 31

investors, definition of 225

Journalism *see* French financial journalists

J.P. Stevens 61

"judicial entrepreneurs" 74

Kirkland, L. 61

KKR (Kohlberg, Kravis and Roberts) 61, 229

Laferté, G. 92

Lagayette, P. 152

Lazega, E. 26, 70

Lebègue, D. 153

Lecerf, O. 147

Lemaire, S. 26, 70

Lemercier, C. 142, 145

Lemoine, B. 152

leveraged buy-out (LBO) field, duality of 223–36; agency theory 223; agents of change 223; career paths 232–5; definition of LBO 223; formalizing the field 226–7; French model 236; generation of LBO field 224–7; investors, definition of 225; large- and small-scale capitalism 227–32, 235; multi-dimensional scaling 227; segmentation 230–2; sources 226–7; stratification 227–30; three-way game 225–6

"Livret A" passbook products 99

Locke, A. 126

logic: bankers' institutional entrepreneurship and *see* Commercial Court of Paris (2000–2005), bankruptcy proceedings at; changeover from wealth maximization to wealth planning 216; example of 89

Machut, A. 16, 175

MacKenzie, D. 43, 47, 89

managerial capitalism: LBO and 225; notion of 'manager' in 6; shareholder position and 59; shift to shareholder capitalism 223

markets: "consensus" 176; exogenous regulation of 71; -implied calibration 49; joint regulation of 74; "opinion" 176

Marry, C. 220

Mauroy, P. 153

McAdam, D. 229

McIntosh, W.V. 74

Mendras, H. 92

mergers and acquisitions (M&A) firms, professional representations in 29–41; abstract representation 35–6; company (commodity to trade) 36–40; corporate investors 31; division of work 31–3; figures and abstractions 34–6; financial modelling 32; gaming 37; hierarchical organization 32; investing managers 31; leveraged buy-outs 31; M&A services firms (division of work and career process) 31–4; promotion and recruitment 33–4; quantitative representation 35; sources 30–1; standardised data

Merrill Lynch 229

Mignot-Gérard, S. 194, 219

Milken, Michael 60

monetary quantifications 4

262   Index

Montagne, S. 139
Mora, A. G. 108
Morgan Stanley 229
mortgage: fixed-rate 42; liberalization of markets 118; secondary market 111; securitization of 108; subprime 89, 108; underwriters 109; victims 120
Mortgage Victims Platform 115
Mounier, L. 26, 70
multi-dimensional scaling (MDS) 227

New York Stock Exchange index 175

occupational segmentations *see* early careers in portfolio and wealth management
OPCVMs (Organizations for Collective Investment in Transferable Securities) 99
"open breaches" 115
organisational structure, characteristics of 8
ownership of cash flows 215

Parsons, C.-A. 176
Paye, S. 16, 140, 156
Perrin-Joly, C. 194, 219
Philippon, T. 90
Pickering, A. 54
P&L attribution report 49
portfolio management: counsellors specializing in 102; Master's programme in 195; *see also* early careers in portfolio and wealth management
Powell, W.W. 226
pragmatic judgments 75
privacy *see* fortune and privacy management
"private banking departments" 197
private equity (PE) 223
professional norms: accuracy 8; closed network 12; commodification and 30, 36; lack of challenge about 41; moral hierarchies produced by 22
professional representations 30
profit and loss (P&L) attribution report 49
"providential men" 147

quants, calibration and 42–56; Black-Scholes options pricing model 46; calibration and model building 49–51; contemporary financialisation, microcosm of 42; derivatives quants 48; 'exotic' derivatives 47; fair value accounting 42,

46–7; front office quants 45–9; 'Greeks' 48; hedging 46–9; interest rate swap 42; model validators 51–3; P&L attribution report 49; social studies of finance 54; sources 44–5; 'supermanagers' 45

Ravelli, Q. 108
RBS (Royal Bank of Scotland) 51
Reynaud, J.-D. 71
"Rhineland model" 154
RJR Nabisco, buyout of 60
Royal Bank of Scotland 228

Sarfati, F. 194, 219
savings banks managers, metamorphosis of 113–16
Service Employees Industrial Union 61
shareholders: activism 61; agreement 128; ascendancy studies 4; capitalism 223; foreign 150; knowledge of 36; number of, privatisation and 177; relationships with 151
shareholder value 3, 36; change in orientation towards 143; control 29, 41, 89; ideology 139; logic of 21, 157; model of 16
Sheinkman, J. 61
Sherman, R. 216
Silici, L. 126
social capital, influence of on vertical differentiation 204
social closure and exclusionary process 9–12
socialisation, financialisation through 57–69; agency theory 58–9; blind pool 64; colonisation, financialisation as 68–9; Employee Partnership Fund 57, 61–8; employee stock ownership plans 62; "imaginary community of market actors" 58; leveraged buyouts and the market for corporate control 59–61
social protest, when local bankers face 108–22; abusive clauses 118; firewalls against social movements, branch managers as 119–20; increasing pressure and increasing autonomy 114–16; liberalization of banking practices 111–12; low-income immigrants, targeting of 116–18; methodology 109–10; savings banks managers, metamorphosis of 113–16; social movements, political role of bank managers facing 118–20; social networks 112–13; Spanish subprime loans, history of 110–13; subprime

invasion 113; tense situations 118
social studies of finance (SSF) 54, 194
sociology of finance 176, 191–3
South African farmland, assetisation of
123–36; asset management industry in
South Africa 125–6; depoliticisation of
the asset 133–4; farmland's coalitions
126–9; leveraging South African
farms 129–31; long-term investors
127; methodology 124–5; production
of the asset 129–34; standardised and
benchmarked, farms as 131–3
Spanish banks *see* social protest, when
local bankers face
Spanish subprime loans, history of 110–13
Spears, T. 27, 42–3, 47
specialised occupations 1
stockholders: minority 77; union rights as
61; *see also* shareholders
subprime invasion 113
subprime mortgages 89, 108
Sweeney, J. 61

"tombstones" 37
TPG 229

UBS 51
"up or out" policy 33

value, worker-oriented notion of 68
van der Zwan, N. 3, 5, 57
Vegara, D. 108
Vézinat, N. 194–5, 219

wealth management: analysis 103;
counsellors, branch-level advising
by 102; Master's programme in 195;
see also early careers in portfolio and
wealth management; fortune and privacy
management
Welles, C. 175, 183
Widmer, F. 156
work: analysis, dimensions of 2; boundary
26; capital allocation and 2–3; division
of (M&A) 31–3; finance and 1
working day composition of 7–8

Zelizer, V. 215
"zombies" debate *see* Commercial Court
of Paris (2000–2005), bankruptcy
proceedings at
Zorn, D.M. 143, 155

Taylor & Francis eBooks

Helping you to choose the right eBooks for your Library

Add Routledge titles to your library's digital collection today. Taylor and Francis ebooks contains over 50,000 titles in the Humanities, Social Sciences, Behavioural Sciences, Built Environment and Law.

Choose from a range of subject packages or create your own!

Benefits for you
- Free MARC records
- COUNTER-compliant usage statistics
- Flexible purchase and pricing options
- All titles DRM-free.

Benefits for your user
- Off-site, anytime access via Athens or referring URL
- Print or copy pages or chapters
- Full content search
- Bookmark, highlight and annotate text
- Access to thousands of pages of quality research at the click of a button.

REQUEST YOUR FREE INSTITUTIONAL TRIAL TODAY

Free Trials Available
We offer free trials to qualifying academic, corporate and government customers.

eCollections – Choose from over 30 subject eCollections, including:

Archaeology	Language Learning
Architecture	Law
Asian Studies	Literature
Business & Management	Media & Communication
Classical Studies	Middle East Studies
Construction	Music
Creative & Media Arts	Philosophy
Criminology & Criminal Justice	Planning
Economics	Politics
Education	Psychology & Mental Health
Energy	Religion
Engineering	Security
English Language & Linguistics	Social Work
Environment & Sustainability	Sociology
Geography	Sport
Health Studies	Theatre & Performance
History	Tourism, Hospitality & Events

For more information, pricing enquiries or to order a free trial, please contact your local sales team:
www.tandfebooks.com/page/sales

Routledge
Taylor & Francis Group

The home of Routledge books

www.tandfebooks.com